The Problem of Pure Consciousness

The Problem
of Pure Consciousness

Mysticism and Philosophy

Edited by

Robert K. C. Forman

OXFORD UNIVERSITY PRESS
New York   Oxford

Oxford University Press

Oxford   New York
Athens   Auckland   Bangkok   Bogota   Bombay   Buenos Aires
Calcutta   Cape Town   Dar es Salaam   Dehli   Florence   Hong Kong
Istanbul   Karachi   Kuala Lumpur   Madras   Madrid   Melbourne
Mexico City   Nairobi   Paris   Singapore   Taipei   Tokyo   Toronto

and associated companies in
Berlin   Ibadan

Copyright © 1990 by Robert K. C. Forman

First published in 1990 by Oxford University Press, Inc.
198 Madison Avenue, New York, New York 10016

First issued as an Oxford University Press paperback, 1997

Oxford is a registered trademark of Oxford University Press, Inc.

Library of Congress Cataloging-in-Publication Data
The Problem of pure consciousness : mysticism and philosophy
edited by Robert K. C. Forman.
p.   cm.   Includes index.
ISBN 0-19-505980-8; ISBN 0-19-510976-7 (pbk.)
1. Mysticism.   2. Consciousness—Religious aspects.   I. Forman, Robert K. C.
BL625.P76 1990   291.4'22—dc20   89-3403   CIP

1 3 5 7 9 8 6 4 2
Printed in the United States of America
on acid-free paper

dedicated to the memory of
Stephen Bernhardt

Preface

Like so many things, the idea for this book was first scribbled down on a paper napkin at a lunch. The lunch was with Anthony Perovich, whom I am honored to count among my friends. We discussed the need for a volume like this, which draws together, from a variety of vantage points and subjects, some of the objections to the "received view" on mysticism. That view states that mysticism is primarily caused by the mystic's expectations and beliefs, especially his or her religious beliefs and expectations. Although this view has an initial plausibility, we agreed, on closer analysis it misrepresents and systematically misconstrues mysticism as we understand it. Furthermore, it is a profoundly ill-established thesis, argued more by rhetoric than philosophy. To bring out its problems, and to begin the task of building a more plausible theory, this book was born. Thus this volume owes much to Professor Perovich, and I thank him.

We naively supposed that getting others to write chapters for such a project would be an easy way to write a book and state the arguments. Were we ever wrong! Getting this volume from paper napkin to printed paper has been a long and arduous process, eased only by the help of many hard working people.

I am especially grateful to the contributors, each of whom has put up with my editorial suggestions with admirable good humor. It is due largely to their thoughtfulness and efforts that this volume makes, I believe, a substantial contribution to the field.

I thank the staff at Oxford University Press for its sometimes thankless labors putting a volume like this one together. To Bansie Vasvani and to Henry Krawitz, who each kept doggedly after an often recalcitrant editor, my thanks.

Preface

My heartfelt gratitude goes especially to Cynthia Read, who guided us through this maze-like process with warmth, skill, and an invaluable sense of humor.

Finally, for her advice, support, and unflagging encouragement which has kept me going through the years of the gestation of this volume, I wish to thank my wife Yvonne.

Contents

Contents

The Problem of Pure Consciousness

Introduction:
Mysticism, Constructivism,
and Forgetting

ROBERT K. C. FORMAN

From where—or Whom—does mysticism come? What causes it? What gives mysticism its peculiar but fascinating shape? Is mystical experience a source of reliable knowledge? Is mysticism the same around the world, or nearly so? Or does mysticism differ among various traditions, cultures, and ages?

The twelve authors of this book are responding to the recent "received view" on such questions, which may collectively be called "constructivism," the view that mystical experience is significantly shaped and formed by the subject's beliefs, concepts, and expectations. This view, in turn, emerged as a response to the so-called perennial philosophy school. Perennialists—notably William James,[1] Evelyn Underhill,[2] Joseph Maréchal,[3] William Johnston,[4] James Pratt,[5] Mircea Eliade,[6] and W. T. Stace[7]—maintained that mystical experience represented an immediate, direct contact with a (variously defined) absolute principle. Only after that immediate contact with the "something more," according to this school, is such a direct contact *interpreted* according to the tradition's language and beliefs. Since interpretive categories (e.g., concepts, beliefs, the background set) do not enter the transcendental experience, mysticism is by and large transculturally homogeneous, having a small number of "core characteristics" that could, indeed, should be analyzed indepen-

3

dently of any specific, culturally bound mystical philosophies.[8] Several perennialist philosophers—notably Frithjof Schuon,[9] Rudolf Otto,[10] W. T. Stace,[11] Aldous Huxley,[12] and, more recently, Huston Smith[13]—went further, arguing that a transcultural perennial philosophy can be grounded in this experiential base. Indeed, this view supported an argument for the existence of a (variously defined) divinity on the basis of experience.

During the last twenty-five years students of religious experience have severely criticized this position. First, they charged that the perennialist case was made through a naive and methodologically unsound use of primary texts. Passages from primary sources were mistranslated, quoted misleadingly out of context, misinterpreted, and altogether mishandled. Second, the perennialist's claim that mystical experiences are the same for all mystics (e.g., a Dogen's mystical experiences were the same as a Saint John's) was *assumed* to be true but never proven. Based only on assumptions, similar-sounding passages were searched out and offered as "evidence" for homogeneity. A methodologically sound, careful investigation of the similarities *and* differences between two or more portraits was never successfully undertaken.[14] Thus, the case came to be seen as a form of circular reasoning. Third, insofar as they claimed that experiences were identical despite interpretive differences, the perennialists maintained that they could "divine" the experiences "behind" the texts. Yet no one was ever able to philosophically or methodologically justify the leap from the text to the experiences behind them. As a result, perennialism was accused of being hermeneutically naive.

These criticisms were well taken. But as Philip Almond points out in the present volume, the real reason perennialism came into disfavor was greater than any individual arguments: the underlying cause was the broad paradigm shift in the humanities and social sciences toward constructivism. According to this constructivist paradigm, all experiences— prosaic, religious, artistic, mystical—are in significant ways formed, shaped, mediated, and constructed by the terms, categories, beliefs, and linguistic backgrounds which the subject brings to them. This notion has become so dominant that it has taken on the status of a self-evident truism. Although I cannot here explore the full range of this model's importance, let me suggest a few of its more obvious ramifications. The sociology of knowledge and anthropology have both detailed how a culture's worldview structures and controls perception and beliefs.[15] Psychologists since Freud have argued that past experiences—especially those of childhood—control, shape, and determine adult emotions, behavior patterns, and perceptions.[16] Constructivism may be viewed as the controlling model in linguistic analysis; in other words, that a person's language constrains, determines, and informs the judgments one makes about oneself and others. As Iris Murdoch has stated, "Man is a creature who makes pictures of himself and then comes to resemble the picture."[17] Historians of culture, ideas, and religion all base their work explicitly on this model. Even the study of modern art[18] and art criticism[19] may be viewed as grappling with the implications of this constructivist picture.

This was the underlying conceptual paradigm at the heart of the complaint about perennialism. Insofar as it seemed to deny that the linguistic background played a role in the shaping and perception of the mystical experience (during, not after), perennialism seemed to deny this "self-evident" truth. In other words, the dissatisfaction with perennialism is grounded in the astonishing degree of general agreement on this broad constructivist model.

One question, then, that this book poses: Is this broad constructivist picture of things plausibly and convincingly applied to mysticism? Has it been conclusively established that mysticism, indeed, is like most other experiences in the sense that it results from a process of introducing, imposing, or entertaining one's beliefs, expectations, judgments, and categories? These questions have broader implications that can only begin to be explored in the present volume. For example: Are there limits to the general constructivist theory of human experience and, if so, what are they? How can we recognize them? Are there some experiences, or some specifiable aspects of human experience, that are not "constructed" by our language and belief?

MYSTICISM DEFINED

Before introducing the constructivist model of mysticism in detail, I want to define mysticism as I will use the term. Part of the problem in this field is that "mysticism" is defined so variously. It may be applied to the unintelligible statements of an illogical speaker, the strained visions of a schizophrenic, hallucinations or drug-induced visions, the spiritual visions of a Julian of Norwich or a Mechthild of Magdeburg, and the quiet experiences of a divine "darkness" or emptiness as described by a Meister Eckhart or a Zen *roshi*. Clearly, for our epistemological and philosophical inquiries, the field must be narrowed.

Roland Fischer (see figure) has put forward a "cartography" of conscious states—states of arousal that include all of the so-called mystical states.[20] Hallucinations, visions, and the auditions of a Julian of Norwich,

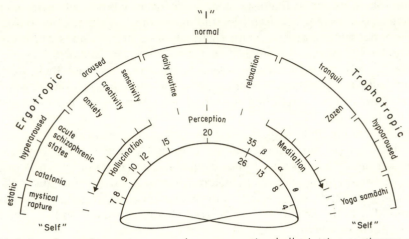

Varieties of conscious states mapped on a perception-hallucination continuum of
increasing ergotropic arousal (left) and a perception-meditation continuum of
increasing trophotropic arousal (right). These levels of hyper- and hypoarousal are
interpreted by man as normal, creative, psychotic, and ecstatic states (left) and
Zazen and samādhi (right). The loop connecting ecstasy and samādhi represents
the rebound from ecstasy to samādhi, which is observed in response to intense
ergotropic excitation. The numbers 35 to 7 on the perception-hallucination continuum are Goldstein's coefficient of variation [see L. Goldstein, H. Murphree, A.
Sugarman, C. Pfeiffer, and E. Jenney, *Clin. Pharmacol. Ther.* 4 (1963), 10],
specifying the decrease in variability of the EEG amplitude with increasing ergotropic arousal. The numbers 26 to 4 on the perception-meditation continuum, on the
other hand, refer to those beta, alpha, and theta EEG waves (measured in hertz)
that predominate during, but are not specific to, these states. Reprinted from R.
Fischer, "A Cartography of Understanding Mysticism," *Science,* vol. 174, November 26, 1971, pp. 897–904. Copyright 1971 by the AAAS.

according to Fischer, would fall on the ergotropic scale, which is characterized by increasing work. They are states of hyperarousal: cognitive and
physiological activity are at high levels. On the other hand, *samādhi,*
mushinjo in *zazen,* or the restful state associated with the divine "darkness" as described by Eckhart or *The Cloud of Unknowing* would fall on
to the trophotropic scale. These are states of hypoarousal, marked by low
levels of cognitive and physiological activity.

The trophotropic and ergotropic phenomena have sharply divergent—
even opposite—levels of metabolic excitation, emotional arousal, and
mental activity. Physiological parameters such as heart rate, skin temperature, spontaneous galvanic skin responses (GSRs), and electroencephalogram (EEG) patterns all differ markedly. Given the differences,

these two sets of states are unlikely to have identical psychological characteristics, causes, and etiologies. If so, we must be careful not to apply (without further justification) models developed to explain phenomena on the trophotropic scale to ergotropic phenomena and vice versa.

To avoid committing such an error I propose reserving the term "mysticism" only for trophotropic states. Let us call ergotropic phenomena such as hallucinatory visions and auditions, "visionary experiences." Thus, in the *Bhagavad Gītā* Arjuna describes a visionary experience in chapter 11:

> With many arms, bellies, mouths and eyes,
> I see Thee [Kṛṣṇa], infinite in form on all sides;
> No end nor middle nor yet beginning of Thee
> Do I see, O All-God, all Armed!
>
> With diadem, club, and disc,
> A mass of radiance, glowing on all sides,
> I see Thee, hard to look at, on every side
> With the glory of flaming fire and sun, immeasurable.[21]

When, on the other hand, Kṛṣṇa describes a contemplative experience, he describes a trophotropic, mystical state:

> But with desire-and-loathing-severed
> Senses acting on the objects of sense,
> With (senses) self-controlled, he, governing his self,
> Goes unto tranquillity.
>
> In tranquillity, of all griefs
> Riddance is engendered for him;
> For of the tranquil-minded quickly
> The mentality becomes stable[22]

Thus, we might employ Ninian Smart's as our working definition of mysticism: "[m]ysticism describes a set of experiences or more precisely, conscious events, which are not described in terms of sensory experience or mental images."[23] Such authors as Eckhart, Dogen, al-Hallaj, Shankara, and Saint Teresa of Avila (when she describes nonsensory union)[24] exemplify "mysticism" as I intend it. Schizophrenics, St. Teresa (when she speaks of her visions and auditions), Mechthild of Magdeburg, Muhammad, Isaiah, and Nichiren, for example, are "visionaries" as I will use the term. In restricting the term "mysticism" to experience not described with sensory language, I believe I am in accord with its original meaning of "to close" and to the overtones of the term as it was employed by Pseudo-Dionysius, that is, separate from the sensory ("rapt out of himself").[25]

In this book we have further focused the field of inquiry. As the title suggests, we will be dealing predominantly with the phenomenon we might call the Pure Consciousness Event (PCE), defined as a wakeful though contentless (nonintentional) consciousness. This is a form of what W. T. Stace called "introvertive mysticism," which he distinguished from "extrovertive mysticism." In extrovertive mysticism one preceives a new relationship—one of unity, blessedness, reality, or what have you—between the external world and the self. In introvertive mysticism there is no awareness of the external world per se; the experience is of the self itself. Although Stace does provide several core characteristics of each type, he overlooks what seems to me to be a central distinguishing mark. It can be seen most readily in a distinction made by Ramana Maharshi, the twentieth-century Hindu guru, between *samādhi* and *sahaja sa-mādhi*.[26] *Samādhi* is a contemplative mystical state and is "introvertive" as Stace employs the term. *Sahaja samādhi* is a state in which a silent level within the subject is maintained along with (simultaneously with) the full use of the human faculties. It is, hence, continuous through part or all of the twenty-four-hour cycle of (meditative and nonmeditative) activity and sleep. This distinction seems to be key: introvertive mysticism denotes a transient state (after all, no one who eats and sleeps can remain entranced forever), whereas extrovertive mysticism denotes a more permanent state, one that lasts even while one is engaged in activity.

Because it involves several aspects of life—that is, external activity and some sort of internal and quiet aspect—and their relationship(s), *sahaja samādhi* seems inherently more complex than *samādhi*. While this is a claim which would require another book to establish, I believe that such a permanent mystical state is typically a more advanced stage in the mystical journey.[27] It seems to me that much misunderstanding has arisen because people have looked at the most advanced, sophisticated, and (perhaps) interesting form of experience—*sahaja samādhi*, extrovertive—prematurely, that is, without first understanding the more rudimentary form of experience. Accordingly, I have asked the contributors to focus their remarks on this more rudimentary stage and thus to begin at the beginning. I hope that someday we can extend the discussion to include the more advanced and interesting extrovertive states.

I must emphasize one point: while we will be looking at the PCE—one important form of introvertive mysticism that is, as we will show, rela-tively common—no one of us claims that this form of mysticism is the only important phenomenon in mysticism. Like *sahaja samādhi*, there are many other interesting and important mystical events. We have empha-sized the PCE primarily because it is: relatively common; rudimentary, and may thereby indicate certain features of other more complex (perhaps more advanced) mystical phenomena; and philosophically quite interesting. But I do not claim that it is everywhere, nor necessarily claimed to be, ultimate or salvific. Indeed, I do not regard it as salvific in and of itself, although the discussions by Griffiths and the editor suggest that it may play an important (perhaps preparatory) role in some forms of the advanced spiritual life.[28]

KATZ'S MYSTICAL CONSTRUCTIVISM

The constructivist model for mysticism—that mystical experience does not escape the formative influence of culture and belief—was argued in the sixties and seventies by Bruce Garside,[29] R. C. Zaehner,[30] H. P. Owen,[31] John Hick,[32] and others. This had its forebears in such thinkers as Dean Inge[33] and Rufus Jones[34]. But the most forceful and influential statement of this view undoubtedly came in 1978 with the publication of *Mysticism and Philosophical Analysis* (ed. Steven Katz) and especially Katz's own, "Language, Epistemology and Mysticism."[35] Katz's article is backed up by other contributions to that book, notably those by Robert Gimello, Peter Moore, Frederick Streng, and Ninian Smart as well as supporters like Jerry Gill. But Katz's essay has so forcefully stated this position that it has become virtually the received view of the eighties on mysticism.[36] Because it is so seminal and forceful, many of the contributors to this work have focused on Katz's piece, though similar reasoning stands at the heart of many of the above-mentioned constructivist articles.

Steven Katz maintains two interconnected theses which are linked by an unstated presupposition. He offers a negative version of the first thesis when he opens his essay with a renowned summation of his "single epistemological assumption":

> There are NO pure (i.e., unmediated) experiences. Neither mystical experience nor more ordinary forms of experience give any indication, or any grounds for believing, that they are unmediated. . . . The notion of unmediated experience seems, if not self-contradictory, at best empty. This epistemological fact seems to me to be true, because of the sorts of beings we are, even with regard to the experiences of those ultimate objects of concern with which mystics have had intercourse, e.g., God, Being, nirvana, etc.[37]

Katz unfortunately does not define "mediate." The term "mediate" (from the Latin *mediatus*, to be in the middle) means to transmit or carry as an intermediate mechanism or agent. As Anthony N. Perovich, Jr., points out in his contribution, this suggests a neo-Kantian picture whereby our concepts and set serve as a filter or conduit between the object of experience and the subject. Katz sometimes suggests such a filtering process, as when he states that "all experience is processed through, organized by, and makes itself available to us in extremely complex epistemological ways."[38] Thus, he seems to be assuming that no experience can avoid being processed through and thereby shaped by these conceptual filters. His assumption that there are no nonmediated experiences is thus a double-negative version of the first thesis, the **constructivist thesis or model,** which is the essay's controlling model. According to this view, "The [mystical] experience itself as well as the form in which it is reported is shaped by concepts which the mystic brings to, and which shape, his experience."[39] This is the general constructivist thesis applied to mysticism.

The second thesis is **an unstated presupposition,** but it is indispensible for understanding this article. I believe no right-thinking person would disagree with it. It is that different religious traditions provide their members with different concepts and beliefs—different sets. Subjects will come to their respective religious or mystical experiences with different values, conceptual backgrounds, patterns of behavior, and so on. Even within a single tradition, different schools, different periods, or even different teachers within the same school will provide their adherents with different sets. As the adept matures she or he will acquire new concepts and beliefs—hence, even one person will come to different experiences with different concepts and beliefs.[40]

The third axiom of the essay is the logical product of the first two theses. This we may call the **pluralism thesis.** Since all mystical experiences are, in part, shaped and formed by the concepts and beliefs of their religious tradition and since different traditions and schools supply individuals with different concepts and beliefs, subjects of experiences from different religious traditions will have experiences which are conditioned and shaped differently. Katz writes:

> Thus, for example, the nature of the Christian mystic's pre-mystical consciousness informs the mystical consciousness such that he experiences the mystic reality[41] in terms of Jesus, the Trinity, or a personal God, etc., rather than in terms of the non-personal, non-everything, to be precise, Buddhist doctrine of nirvana. Care must also be taken to note that even the plurality of experience found in Hindu, Christian, Muslim, Jewish, Buddhist mystical traditions, etc., have to be broken down into smaller units.[42]

Katz, Gill, Hick, Penner, and many (if not most) other constructivists argue explicitly for a pluralism thesis.[43]

The pluralism thesis is important to these authors inasmuch as it is their response to the perennial philosophers' arguments that mysticism is by and large the same across time and tradition. Unlike perennialists, Katz and his colleagues claim that constructivism can do justice to the full diversity of mystical traditions. The constructivists pride themselves, with some justification, on the success of their "plea for the recognition of differences".[44]

These two theses, constructivism and pluralism, are the twin theses of this essay and of the camp as a whole. Since the logical foundation of pluralism is constructivism, I will now turn to it.

Capitalizing on perceptual psychology, Katz provides us with a single "non-controversial example" of how an experience might, in part, be constructed, shaped, or determined by someone's set. This is a very important passage, since it offers the only familiar model for how an experience might be shaped by concepts and beliefs:

> [B]eliefs shape experience, just as experience shapes belief. To take, for the moment, a non-controversial example of this, consider Manet's paintings of Notre Dame. Manet "knew" Notre Dame was a Gothic cathedral, and so "saw" it as a Gothic cathedral as testified to by his paintings which present Notre Dame with Gothic archways. Yet close examination will reveal that certain of the archways of Notre Dame which Manet painted as Gothic are in fact Romanesque. As Coleridge reminded us: "the mind half-sees and half-creates."[45]

(With all due respect, I believe it was Monet, not Manet.) This is a good example, for it is clear how Monet's experience might have been shaped by what he expected to see. The visual information before him was of Romanesque (i.e., rounded) archways. Owing to his *expectation* that he would see a Gothic (i.e., pointed) archway, he *altered* the visual information before him and instead "saw" pointed archways. He overlooked what was there and *substituted* for it something that was not there.

When the perceptual psychologist E. H. Gombrich (to whom Katz refers in a gloss) provides parallel examples of this phenomenon, he generalizes the kind of process involved in such a perceptual error, "The individual visual information . . . [is] entered, as it were, upon a pre-existing blank or formulary. And as often happens with blanks, if they have no provisions for certain kinds of information we consider essential, it is just too bad for the information.[46] In this often-studied process, we *replace* one segment of visual data with another based on what are called perceptual "automatizations," habits.[47] Katz is, thus, suggesting that by a shaped or colored experience he has in mind a process in which we impose our blanks or formularies onto the manifold of experience and encounter things in the terms those formularies define for us. It is easy to see why Katz uses the term "mediate," for here the formulary or concept stands between (*mediatus*) the visual information and our perception of it. Mystical experiences are created by a process similar to this one. They differ from ordinary experiences only because they result from the super-imposition of a *new* set of beliefs and expectations—new blanks and formularies—which are applied to the objects of experience. The yogi, for example, imposes a new set of automatizations onto his experience, that is, yogic. According to Katz, "Properly understood, yoga, for exam-ple, is not an unconditioning or deconditioning of consciousness, but rather it is a reconditioning of consciousness, i.e., a substituting of one form of conditioned and/or contextual consciousness for another, albeit a new, unusual, and perhaps altogether more interesting form of condi-tioned-contextual consciousness."[48] The mystic's acculturation, or rather re-culturation, might be analogous to, say, a Chinese painter who moves to Paris and learns to see with a new set of formularies (i.e., Gothic). If this painter comes to impose these onto Notre Dame, he is doing something quite close to what the mystic is.

Now, like his fellow constructivists, Katz is making an epistemologi-cally heavy claim here. He is not asserting that previously held beliefs and concepts will come into play only in the postexperiential shaping of the descriptions and the texts, but rather that they will play their role in the shaping of the actual mystical experience(s) themselves:

> The experience itself as well as the form in which it is reported is shaped by concepts which the mystic brings to, and which shape, his experience.[49]

> [A]s a result of his process of intellectual acculturation in its broadest sense, the mystic brings to his experience a world of concepts, images, symbols, and values which shape as well as colour the experience he eventually and actually has.[50]

Just as Monet's expectations led him to "see" Gothic arches (not just paint them) so, too, the mystic purportedly sees in the terms with which his tradition provides him. Katz repeatedly emphasizes that not only will the circumstances surrounding the mystical experience be formed by the tradition, but the actual character of the experience itself will be shaped and determined by the subject's expectations:

> This process of differentiation of mystical experience into the patterns and symbols of established religious communities is experiential . . . it is at work before, during and after the experience.[51]

> The creative role of the self in his experience is not analogous to the passive role of the tape-recorder or camera. Even in mystical experience there seems to be epistemological activity of the sort we know as discrimination and integration and, in certain cases at least, of further mental activities such as

relating the present experience to past and future experience, as well as traditional theological claims and metaphysics.[52]

The subjects undergo this experience using terms provided by their backgrounds. Another and more precise way of stating this point is that a complete phenomenological description of the experience itself will reveal traces of the subject's conceptual background.

So far, we have an explanatory (or descriptive) model: the mystic is undergoing something like an imposition, or superimposition, of his or her formularies (or blanks) onto this experience; hence, the subject "experiences the mystic reality in terms of Jesus Christ, the Trinity, or a personal God, etc."[53] That is, he or she will have an experience under a description; he or she will "experience as." When the Hindu has an experience, he experiences it "as" of Brahman, imposing the term "Brahman" more or less consciously onto the manifold of experience. The associations of that term are thereby called in and with them its full range of significance.

There are two or three possible interpretations of the constructivist model. When Robert Gimello writes that mysticism is "simply the psychosomatic enhancement" of one's beliefs, he suggests that there is a **complete constructivism** at work, that is, the experience is one hundred percent shaped, determined, and provided by the set: "[M]ystical experience is simply the psychosomatic enhancement of religious beliefs and values or of the beliefs and values of other kinds which are held 'religiously.'" [54] A hallucination may be one such example, for no sensory input is involved. It may be that only the subject's set, scrambled by whatever idiosyncratic psychophysiological processes, is playing a constitutive role.

There may also be an **incomplete constructivism** at work: some of the shape of the experience is provided by the set, although some is provided by something else—sensory input or whatever. Monet's misperception, in part, was set-provided and, in part, was a result of his response to the gray mass before him. Most "shaped" sensory experiences seem thus.

While incomplete constructivism is, on its face, the more plausible, it cannot do the work required by the pluralism thesis. This is clearest in the case in which the role of the set is minimal, for if so, then experiences from different cultures would be distinguishable in only minimal ways. Under such a circumstance the perennialist might say, as Ninian Smart does, that mysticism is largely the same but for the "different flavors" that accrue to those experiences as a result of the constructive activities of the subject.[55] If there are only different flavors to a common experience type, then the perennialists can base their arguments on the underlying parallelism; Katz's plea for the recognition of differences would go unheard. Thus—and this is key—the best way (perhaps the only way) to protect the pluralist hypothesis is through a complete constructivism.

There is a third possible interpretation of the kind of construction which is at work. We might call it **catalytic constructivism.** It is that the adept's generating problems leads him or her to hold to beliefs and perform practices which themselves act as catalysts for mystical experiences. The following passages may be read in this light:

> The respective "generating" problems at the heart of each tradition suggest their respective alternative answers. . . . The mind can be seen to contribute both the problem and the means of its overcoming: it defines the origin, the way, and the goal, shaping experience accordingly. . . . These constructive conditions of consciousness produce the grounds on which mystical experience is possible at all.[56]

> The Buddhist experience of *nirvāṇa*, the Jewish of *devekuth,* and the Christian of *unio mystica,* the Sufi of *fana,* the Taoist of *Tao* are the result, at least in part, of specific conceptual influences, i.e., the "starting problems" of each doctrinal, theological system.[57]

> [O]ntological structures inherent in language and judgement pre-create the contours of experience . . . this structural matrix works to locate both experience and the experiencer (the mystic) in a given socio-historic conceptual field whose problems and problematic he or she adopts and aims to solve.[58]

The idea here seems to be that it is only by holding to certain beliefs and by having certain problems that someone will take up spiritual practices and thereby come to experience, for example, *samādhi.* This, however, is not the epistemologically heavy version of the thesis Katz requires. After all, someone may very well come to a mystical experience by having certain "starting problems" and performing certain practices, yet that experience may not be epistemologically shaped by those problems or practices (i.e., a complete phenomenological description of that experience might not reveal traces of the set). The generative problems and meditative techniques may serve as a catalyst for the experience but not play an epistemologically heavy role in shaping its actual character. Unless we can see on other grounds an epistemologically heavy connection between set and experience, the connection here is insufficient to make the constructivist's case.

Occasionally Katz also seems to argue for a causal model, "What I wish to show is only that there is a *clear causal connection* between the religious and social structure one brings to experience and the nature of one's actual religious experience."[59] Emphasizing the role of specifically spiritual models (gurus, saints, etc.), Katz notes that "our deconstruction and re-conceptualization suggests that models play an important role in providing our map of reality and of what is real and, thus, contribute heavily to the creation of experience—I repeat to the creation of experience."[60] That is, one's models and expectations actually generate and cause the mystical experience. Gimello's thesis, (quoted earlier) that mysticism results from a psychosomatic enhancement of one's beliefs, is making a similar causal claim.

Unfortunately, it is hard to say just what Katz's "clear causal connection" means. Just how does it "cause" an experience? How complete is this cause? Everybody has models, and thus everyone has similar "causes." Why do so few have mystical experiences? What are the mechanics of causation? Which are primary and which secondary "causes"? How do we distinguish a necessary cause from a merely contingent connection? Thus the causal thesis is, at best, vague.

Katz's Account Considered

This constructivist model has several not inconsiderable virtues. First, considering the plausibility and, for most phenomena, widespread acceptance of this picture of experience as, in part, shaped and constructed, it is certainly credible. It seems to make sense. Second, with reference to mysticism, the account cannot help but make the distinctions between mystics found in different traditions stand in relief. Katz and his colleagues are to be congratulated for drawing attention to the differences great and small between mystics in different traditions and within the same tradition. The approach has generated a great deal of very interesting and useful work. His "plea for the recognition of differences" has been heard.

Despite its virtues, this position has several major failings (some of which I touched on before) which militate against its acceptance. First, I will discuss those failings which are specific to Katz's articles. Then I will move to the broader problems with the constructivist position in general.

Structure of the Article
As I noted earlier, Katz opens with an assumption concerning the character of all experience, in particular mystical experience. But his essay claims to provide "evidence and argumentation" which will *establish* such a constructed character.[61] This commits the fallacy of *petitio principii*, assuming what is to be proved. It is ironic that Katz claims that this is an improvement on other approaches because, unlike these other

approaches, his makes no "a priori assumption" and proves its case by "convincing logical argument."[62] For just the opposite is true of his article: once he has assumed that language enters and, in part, shapes and constructs all experiences, the remaining thirty-nine pages of the article provides virtually no further argumentation but only instances of this assumption. Here are two examples: after describing the pre-experiential set of the Jewish mystic, he writes, "that this complex pre-experiential pattern affects the actual experience of the Jewish mystic is an unavoidable conclusion."[63] After noting the differences in the pre-experiential set between the Jewish and Buddhist mystic, he says, "[J]ust setting this Buddhist understanding of the nature of things over against the Jewish should, in itself, already be strong evidence for the thesis that what the Buddhist experiences as *nirvāna* is different from what the Jew experiences as *devekuth*."[64] However, merely describing the background set of the Jewish mystic or distinguishing it from the Buddhist's set could serve as "evidence and documentation" that the set effects the experience if, and only if, the connection between set and experience is *assumed* to hold. As it stands, Katz has provided evidence only that the belief systems differ—evidence, in other words, for the second and undisputed thesis that different religions provide different sets. In neither case does Katz show just how a constructive process may take place or how one experience actually had different phenomenological characteristics than another. All he offers are summaries of religious doctrines and restatements of the original assumption. These are *instances* of an assumed claim, not arguments.

Systematically Incomplete

I noted that one of the twin theses of Katz's articles and those of the constructivists in general is the pluralism thesis (which is their answer to the perennial philosophical claim that mysticism is everywhere the same). The implied argument here is that any difference in religious concepts *ipso facto* means a difference in mystical experiences. If so, then differences in any single concept held by two mystics implies differences in their experiences.

It may be that a certain concept held by a subject will play a role in forming some experience(s), but as Anthony Perovich has shown, it is an overstatement to claim that *each and every* concept held by a subject will necessarily play a role shaping *each and every* experience.[65] If I change any concept at all, do *all* my experiences necessarily undergo modifications? If this is so, all of my experiences would change with every new notion learned. This is clearly absurd, for what would it then mean to learn something? I can only learn within a coherent set of experiences which are part of a single consistent background for any experience.

Katz does not specify just which concepts enter into just which experiences. He implies that it is largely *religious* concepts which play the significant role. Papers by Moore, Gimello, and others may be viewed as elucidating some of the relevant concepts which play the constructivistic role.[66] But the problem here is an embarrassment of riches. Not only is it suggested that notions of God effect experiences, but so too do the following effect mystical experiences (according to various constructivists): religious architecture; religious music and dance forms; epistemological and rhetorical teachings; principles of dogma and traditional beliefs; religious institutions; religious practices; one's concepts, expectations, and intentions; and even the mystic's wider cultural background.[67] We are again very near to a claim that "every concept affects every experience." Clearly, we are in need of a plausible delimitation of the relevant concepts.[68]

But this the Katzian will probably be unwilling to do, for to do so would be to undercut the logical foundation of the antiperennialist pluralism thesis. If differences in some concepts do not imply changes in mystical experiences, then the perennialist might argue that concepts like *shunyata* and *samādhi* are "close enough" to claim a parallelism of experience. In his essay, for example, Phillip Almond argues that despite minor differences, parallels can be found in the doctrines of medieval Jewish, Christian, and Sufi mystics inasmuch as they were all deeply indebted to neo-Platonism.[69] And these parallels, according to the constructivist's thesis, must create a similarity of experience. A similar set of mutual influences could probably be argued for mystics of Hinduism, Buddhism, and perhaps Taoism.[70] Hence, if the constructivists clearly delimit their contextualistic claims, they are in danger of threatening the very foundation of their pluralism.

The incompleteness of the constructivist case may be intended as a protective device. It allows Katz to say that, as quoted earlier, "just setting this Buddhist understanding of the nature of things over against the Jewish should, in itself, already be strong evidence for the thesis that what the Buddhist experiences as *nirvāṇa* is different from what the Jew experiences as *devekuth*"—without showing in detail how this is so.[71] Were he to show precisely which concepts differed and how they created actually different experiences, someone else could point to parallels in concepts and argue similarly for parallels in experiences. Thus, as used, vagueness serves to protect the case for pluralism.

Sense and References

Katz implicitly assumes a one-to-one relationship between concept and experience. This leads to absurdities, I have argued. Let us grant Katz a lesser but more defensible claim of a one-to-one relationship between the concept of the mystical "object" and the mystical experience. There must be a difference between the Hindu's experience of the "object" [sic] he encounters as samādhi (or its equivalents) and the Buddhist's experience of the "object" [sic] he encounters as shunyata (or its equivalents).

However, even this lesser claim is fallacious. It implicitly denies the possibility that there may be two terms with different senses which have the same referent. As Friedrich Frege pointed out, like the North Star and the Pole Star, two terms with different senses can have the same referent. So, too, it may be that a single *experience* can plausibly be referred to with two different terms.

This is no mere logical nicety. Certainly, there have been people who have participated in one tradition, were later converted, and may therefore have used two different terms to think or speak of one experience. "I used to think of that experience as samādhi, but now I think of it as sunyáta," *makes sense*. Yet on Katz's account of the incomparability between experiences in different traditions, this sentence should be utter nonsense since the experience of samādhi must be so different from the experience of shunyata.

Extending this, given care in communication, I see no reason that different people could not refer to a single experience differently. Were a Hindu guru and a Buddhist roshi to simultaneously hear someone report an experience, it would make sense that the guru might say, "that's an instance of samādhi," whereas the roshi might say, "Oh, you've experienced shunyata." There is no problem in using different terms with different senses to refer to the same experience. Whether this is, in fact, what they would say is not a matter for a philosopher to decide in advance, strictly on the basis of an (assumed) theory. It is an empirical matter. A roshi or a guru, not Steven Katz, should decide whether someone's experience qualifies as an instance of samādhi or sunyata.

While this is impressionistic, it is my sense that at some interreligious conferences, mystics from various traditions have been able to identify common experiences or, at least, commonalities within experiences.[72] However difficult in practice, certainly the possibility of one mystic saying to another, "yes, I experienced something just like that" *makes sense*.

It is true that there have undoubtedly been instances of disagreement—Shankara's renowned disputes with Buddhist thinkers seems an obvious case in point. But in an example like this, it is not at all clear whether the argument was over experiential differences or over interpretive differences and differences in emphasis.[73] Even if one decides that Shankara was disagreeing with a Buddhist about experiences or that any two aver to different experiences, counterevidence would still be more persuasive: if one could find two humans who speak of a similar, or identical, experience-type differently, this would show that the pluralist claim is not universal.

Post Hoc or Propter Hoc?

As Almond (chap. 6), Bernhardt (chap. 7), and others have pointed out in their essays, even if we grant Katz that every mystical experience does match the subject's tradition (which I do not grant), nonetheless, in making his causal claim, Katz may still be accused of committing the fallacy of *post hoc, ergo propter hoc*. Wainwright offers the example of a Frenchman and an Eskimo's gastrointestinal experiences.[74] Their cultures differ; probably, their gastrointestinal experiences will differ. Probably, too, their expectations about those feelings and sensations will be highly correlatable with their cultures. But that does not mean that either their culture or their expectations *caused* those experiences. The relationship between experience and expectation may be contingent, not necessary.

CONSTRUCTIVISM CONSIDERED GENERALLY

These are some of the problems with this particular keynote constructivist article. There are also problems with mystical constructivism in general that will apply to any constructivist position. The first problem has to do with novelty, the second with the PCE, the subject of this book.

Novelty

Whether constructivism is asserted to be complete or incomplete, there can be no doubt that the purportedly formative and shaping concepts, expectations, and models must have been acquired before—indeed, long before—any mystical experiences. Otherwise, how could they contribute to the "creation" or "formation" of such experiences? It should be clear that this is a fundamentally conservative hypothesis, that mystical experiences are created or shaped by long-held knowledge and beliefs, for example. But I do not think that such a conservative hypothesis can stand up to the data of mysticism. The history of mysticism is rife with cases in which expectations, models, previously acquired concepts, and so on, were deeply and radically *dis*confirmed.

There are two types of such cases: the neophyte and the adept. Concerning these cases, we have only scanty information; further research is called for. But in a preliminary way, we can observe that it is not unusual to hear of an untrained and uninitiated neophyte who has a mystical experience without any deep preconditioning. For example, Richard Maurice Bucke—author of the early twentieth-century book *Cosmic Consciousness*—and Bernadette Roberts—author of the recent *The Experience of No Self*—both came to their mystical experiences without the hypothesized preconditioning.[75] Bucke describes himself as a student of poetry and of "speculative books" (such as those by Darwin), but he mentions no specifically religious background. Roberts says that her contemplative experiences began "at an early age" before her indoctrination into the Christian contemplative tradition.[76] When her specifically mystical experiences commenced, she was "surprised and bewildered" by them. "I was left without a way to account for this experience. . . . Clearly, I had fallen outside my own, as well as the traditional, frame of reference when I came upon a path that seemed to begin where the writers on the contemplative life had left off."[77] In fact, it was just the lack of relevant models, she notes, which led her to write her account.[78] I recently interviewed D.A., a twenty-eight-year-old American man whose first mystical experience, at fifteen, was utterly unanticipated and led him into Buddhism.[79] In each case, the subjects assert that they had experiences which qualify as mystical and that they were led *to* religious texts, doctrines, and living exponents by their experiences—not the other way around. Religious and mystical interpretations of their experiences did come, but only months and years after the experiences. What were the deeply assimilated and automatized "mystical" categories that may have played the constructive role that "created" their respective experiences?

Perhaps it will be argued that a Bucke or a Roberts, simply by virtue of a life lived in the United States, which is so deeply informed by the Judeo-Christian *weltanschauung*, acquired the appropriate mystical identificatory terms.[80] There is some plausibility to this argument—let us call it the prefigurement by osmosis argument—though not, it will be granted, as much plausibility as has the theory on its home, that is, conservative turf. Or D.A., it may be argued, was unconsciously persuaded by the non-Western *weltanschauung*. Again, there is some plausibility to this: let us call this the "argument by reverse prefigurement."

But, at best, such arguments lessen the rhetorical impact of constructivism: the theory starts to sound *ad hoc* and lacking in the kind of elegance we expect from a good hypothesis. A conservative theory like constructivism has difficulty accounting for creative novelty.

A second type of divergence between expectation and experience occurs to the initiated and intellectually assimilated. When Teresa of Avila reports that until she underwent her experiences, "[I] did not know what I was doing"; she alludes to the irrelevance of her expectations.[81] Before a thirty-six-year-old woman practitioner of transcendental meditation I interviewed gained a higher state of consciousness (my term, not hers), she experienced some fingerlike sensations atop her head, and her cranium seemed to open up like flower petals.[82] The key feature here is novelty—not just any novelty, but one that seems to stand at the very nub of the alteration. The mode of transformation is utterly unexpected, un-understood, and surprising.[83] Something besides expectations and beliefs seems to be playing the decisive formative role in such events. Further-more, it is rare that mystics do not report *surprise* over their experiences.[84] That itself suggests that there is a disconfirmation of some expectations.

Though it is logically possible that one could be merely superficially acquainted with a formative concept or model, for the hypothesis to continue to seem plausible in these mystical events, as in the Monet *mis*painting, we would expect to see signs of a deep and thoroughgoing acquaintance with that concept or model before constructing a mystical experience in its terms. Monet would have been very unlikely to mistake a round archway for a pointed one had he not a thoroughgoing acquain-tance with things Gothic. Yet here we have cases in which there is no thoroughgoing acquaintance, and apparently little or no previous ac-quaintance, with the peculiarities of one's experiences. Does it not seem that Monet's visual automatisms and mystical transformations are *not* analogous—the data just do not match the framework. Does it not seem that some causal factor besides the imposition of an automatization is at work here.

Constructivism and the Pure Consciousness Event (PCE)

The four essays that comprise Part I of this volume establish beyond a reasonable doubt, I believe, the existence of reports of PCEs, defined as wakeful contentless consciousness. In Part II Norman Prigge and Mark Kessler's as well as Mark Woodhouse's contributions argue powerfully that despite common philosophical presuppositions to the contrary, claims that one can be conscious, or awake—though without content—make sense and are plausible. If we grant the existence of PCEs as a mystical phenomenon, then constructivism must plausibly account for it. This I believe it cannot do.

As I see it, the arguments which most directly demonstrate that constructivism cannot persuasively handle the PCE are as follows. (I direct the reader especially to the articles by Staphen Bernhardt, Phillip Almond, B. L. Franklin, and Anthony Perovich, Jr., of which the following is in large part a condensation.)

Bernhardt and Almond observe that despite the constructivists claims of being able to handle "all the evidence," there is a striking absence of clear and convincing accounts of just how a PCE actually is shaped or constructed by one's language and belief system. Intuitively, the problem is that the flat, contentless PCE does not show signs of being so shaped or formed. Bernhardt writes:

> [I]t is hard to see how one could say that the pure consciousness event is mediated, if by that it is meant that *during the event* the mystic is employing concepts, differentiating his awareness according to religious patterns and symbols, drawing upon memory, apprehension, expectation, language or accumulation of prior experience, or discriminating and integrating. Without the encounter with any object, intention or thing, it just does not seem that there is sufficient complexity during the pure consciousness event to say that any such conceptually constructive elements are involved.[85]

Drawing out this intuition that there is not sufficient complexity in the PCE to militate for its constructed character, Perovich has pointed out that in general an experience may show signs of being shaped or constructed in two senses: the content or the form may be supplied by one's background or context. To these two I would add a third: in the connecting links, the process of experiencing something may show evidence of being context-supplied. With reference to the PCE, however, none show signs of being implicated.

FORM. By using such terms as "shape," "form," and so on, Katz, Gimello, and others suggest that they have formal shaping pictures in mind. A concept (or set of concepts) may be thought to produce an objective unity out of the formless flux which is presented to our senses by *imposing a form* on it. This imposition of form may be thought to operate in one of two directions. In the Kantian picture, the operations of the mind bring a unity to (or impose it on) the complexity of the manifold. By imposing our categories onto them, we bring the many bits of sensory stimulation to a unity "as" an object. For Kant the unity was provided by the categories; but in more modern parlance, each belief or language system is thought to impose its own kind or categories of unity onto the formless flux of experience.

The other direction through which form may be imposed on the flux of experience is from the one to the many. The given may be regarded as a formless or seamless whole, and it becomes the task of concepts to introduce divisions into this whole. As Benjamin Lee Whorf states it, the result of imposing concepts is an "artificial chopping up of the continuous spread and flow of existence."[86] As already stated, the pluralism thesis grows naturally out of this picture: the categories in whose terms we introduce distinctions will differ; hence, experiences will differ.

However virtuous these approaches may be in unpacking the exigencies of ordinary experience, they cannot plausibly explain a PCE. The reason is that any combining of a manifold will to some extent result in an experience which is *complex* in some way. The shaping of a pluriform manifold will add connections and divisions to such a manifold; it would not erase complexity entirely. But complexity is just what is lacking in PCEs.

On the other hand, the notion that concepts lend complexity to a seamless whole is similarly incapable of accounting for the PCE. If this process is occurring during a PCE, then a uniformity (the seamless whole) becomes divided up into a complexity in such a way that a new contentless uniformity results. But by Occam's razor we should eliminate the intervening step. Concepts which distinguish cannot be thought to be playing a role in a conscious event devoid of distinctions. Hence, it is implausible that concepts lend form in either sense to the PCE.

CONTENT. In Monet's Notre Dame experience, expectations and beliefs lead him to introduce certain elements (which are not present in the flow of sense perception) into experience. Through the automatization process, he provided himself with experiential content. Gimello's suggestion that the mystical experience results from a "pychosomatic enhancement" of his beliefs and expectations is of a piece with this notion. The suggestion here is that expectations somehow provide the content as well as the form of the experience. The pluralism thesis grows out of this notion: different expectations produce different experienced content.

Visionary experiences may be quite nicely explained by this picture of a mind providing its own content. The Hindu's context and background does seem to play a significant role, for example, in the etiology of Arjuna's vision of Kṛṣṇa. Furthermore, it is significant that, to my knowledge, we have no records of a Christian seeing Kṛṣṇa or a medieval Vaiṣṇavite seeing Christ.

However, it is not clear that expectations are providing content in specifically mystical experiences. My reasons are three: (1) In the PCE there is no experienced content for consciousness. Hence, no content is being supplied. (2) As I argued earlier, in mysticism expectations are frequently confounded. The neophyte is the clearest example; the advanced adept also frequently encounters phenomena for which she or he was ill prepared. If expectations are playing the critical role in providing content in the PCE, it is hard to see how someone can possibly have a counterexpectational experience. (3) Finally, if the mystic's "set" provides his or her content, the different "sets" from the various traditions should provide sharply different experiences. But, as is demonstrated in Part I, there are experiences from many traditions and ages which are not sharply different. How could experiences with identical definitions (wakeful objectless consciousness) arise from such divergent sources if different contents are being provided?

In sum, PCE are plausibly explained neither as the product of a formal shaping of the flux of experience nor as the result of a providing of content.

SHAPING PROCESS. Not only is the constructivist position ill-suited to make sense of the experience as it is reported, it is also ill-suited to account for the process which, from all we can tell, goes on during the experience. In ordinary experiences it is possible (at least in phenomenological theory) to trace out the succession of epistemological processes involved during any period of time. Through introspection one should be able to specify just which connections led from this thought to that one, from this sensation to that perception, and so on. Although a complete list of shaping processes would be virtually impossible to draw up, the kind of processes which seem to be involved are well stated by Katz, "[T]he kind of beings that we are requires that experience be not only instantaneous and discontinuous, but that it also involves memory, apprehension, expectation, language, accumulation of prior experience, concepts, and expectations, with each experience being built on the back of all these elements and being shaped anew by each fresh experience."[87] It would not be difficult to imagine a succession of thoughts and perceptions which involved all of these. And the epistemological processes, if involved at all, can be seen to be always involved in, and through, each successive step in experience. Each fresh experience is relatively discontinuous from each previous experience; yet it stands on the back of, and moves forward from, each previous moment in a more or less clearly specifiable way. And the processes and connections involved in making the transition from one thought to the next may be analyzed as context-related.

However, it is difficult to see how any such processes may be occurring during the PCE. For here we have a phenomenon, two successive moments of which are, for all intents and purposes, identical. No report states, for example, "I had a rough few moments during the PCE and then it grew quieter," or "It was a happy PCE but got more somber." The reports we have are of a period of time in which, once it begins, no subjectively observed changes occur. It is utterly homogeneous. Under such circumstances it is difficult to see how someone may be actively differentiating their awareness, remembering this or that, building on the back of the previous moments, shaping the new experience through a process of comparison or imposition of concepts, and so on.

The PCE is a conscious event which has been measured to last as long as forty-four seconds and yet may be described adequately with a single noncompound sentence.[88] Think how complex a sentence would have to be to describe a forty-four-second continuum of thoughts! Or how many sensations and perceptions must be processed, organized, and sifted through while driving a car in city traffic for forty-four seconds! It is hard to see how such ordinary events result from identical mental processes as those "involved" in the PCE. One involves comparison, computation, elimination, and incorporation of sensory imput, determination of direction, etcetera, etcetera. The other is more like, if you will, just being present. The two cases are just not similar: the processes necessary to one are irrelevent to the other.

In conclusion, PCEs show signs of being neither constructed nor shaped in either form, content, or process. Without further argumentation the claim that PCEs are significantly shaped, constructed and formed by epistemological processes like those that are responsible for ordinary constructed experiences fails.

STRUCTURE OF THE PRESENT VOLUME

What follows is an outline of the structure of this work and summaries of the basic arguments of each of the contributions and, where appropriate, my own reflections on individual issues.

Professor Katz asserted that "there is no substantive evidence to suggest that there is any pure consciousness per se achieved by these various, common mystical practices, for example, fasting, yoga, and the like."[89] In Part I evidence is offered demonstrating that this is a mistaken claim: PCEs do, indeed, occur. Authors in this section were asked to respond to the following "Call for Papers on the Reports of Experience":

1. Does your tradition(s) report or describe one or several cases of the experience of pure (nonintentional, objectless) consciousness?
2. If so, what is the significance of such experiences for that tradition or for one particular figure in that tradition? If they (or she or he) interpret the pure consciousness experience, how do they do so?
3. What does your tradition(s) say about the role of language, belief, expectation, concepts, feelings, and so on, in either the experience itself (in its phenomenological characteristics) or in its cause or shaping?

4. (Optional) What do you make of said experience reports?
5. (If applicable) What are the externally measurable correlates (physiological, psychological, etc.) of pure consciousness. Are there good reasons to
associate these correlates with the experience of pure consciousness per se?

Christopher Chapple opens Part I with an admirable summary of
Sāṃkhya (Hindu) thought. He shows that the *Sāṃkhya Kārikā* analyzes
how the mind, senses, and the notion of the self become associated
(wrongly) with consciousness. Reversing that analysis, the text asserts that
the mind, senses, and so forth, can be *dis*associated from consciousness
in liberation—one aspect of which is yogic *samādhi*, a state without
mental content. This state is described in the *Yoga Sūtras* as one in which
the "fluctuations of the mind are stilled"—that is, a state in which the
wandering mind is brought to quietude. Chapple concludes by arguing
that recent accounts of Sāṃkhya are in error when they overlook the
grounding of Sāṃkhya thought in such experiences as these.

Paul J. Griffiths's shining article on Yogācāra (Buddhist) thought opens
up with a clearly articulated set of distinctions among several theses
concerning the claim of pure consciousness that nicely clarify some of the
issues involved. In his presentation of Yogācāra texts, he argues that,
though there are problems in describing a PCE with the term "consciousness" or the term "mental" (both of which carry intentional overtones), he
does find support for the existence of PCEs in Yogācāric accounts of the
experience of *nirodhasamāpatti* (cessation), in which no mental content is
entertained. Griffiths then shows how current philosophical issues may be
usefully elucidated by turning to primary texts. In this vein he concludes
about constructivism that "it seems unlikely that [Yogācāra Buddhists]
would wish to allow that any element of any conceptual scheme could be
present in the phenomenology of [cessation]."

In my own contribution on Meister Eckhart (late-thirteenth, early-
fourteenth-century German Dominican mystic), I note that contrary to
some scholarly opinion, Eckhart does describe introvertive mystical
events. He calls them *gezucket*, the state of being enraptured. How
Eckhart understands these events and the nature of the language he uses
to speak of them becomes the focus of the remainder of my article. I have
tried to show how Eckhart uses intentional language to speak of a nonintentional event.

Daniel C. Matt's contribution about Jewish mysticism is a wide-ranging
and thorough look at the background and history of the Jewish notion of
ayin, nothingness. Jewish mystical writings cannot be understood, Matt
nicely shows, without seeing their profoundly experiential foundations.
He goes on to describe some of those experiences, among which are

descriptions of PCEs. The history of *ayin* and its experiential grounding should do much to begin a rethinking of Jewish mysticism.

To this strong evidence for the existence of the PCE, I want to add the following three reports. Recently I ran across the first two, which both describe experiences resulting from the practice of transcendental meditation; the third is an autobiographical account.

The first describes an experience that occurred during the very first meditation of this subject.

> I distinctly recall the first day of instruction [in the transcendental meditation technique], my first clear experience of transcending. Following the instruction of the teacher, without knowing what to expect, I began to drift down into deeper and deeper levels of relaxation, as if I were sinking into my chair. Then for some time, perhaps for a minute or a few minutes, I experienced a silent inner state of no thoughts; just pure awareness and nothing else; then again I became aware of my surroundings. It left me with a sense of deep ease, inner renewal, and happiness.[90]

It is striking that the subject notes that he did not "know what to expect," for this tends to support the claim that one may have a PCE even without the purportedly shaping expectations.

The second report describes how, if they are undergone regularly, someone's experiences of PCEs can mature over time. It is one of the most detailed and precise descriptions I have ever run across.

> After about two years, my experience of the transcendent started to become clearer. At that time, I would settle down, it would be very quiet . . . and then I would transcend, and there would just be a sort of complete silence void of content. The whole awareness would turn in, and there would be no thought, no activity, and no perception, yet it was somehow comforting. It was just there and I could know when I was in it. There wasn't a great "Oh, I am experiencing this." It was very natural and innocent. But I did not yet identify myself with this silent, content-free inner space. It was a self-contained entity that I transcended to and experienced.
>
> Then, with increased familiarity and contingent on the amount of rest I had, the process of transcending became more and more natural. The whole physiology was now accustomed to just slipping within, and at some point it would literally "click," and with that, the breath would almost cease, the spine would become straight, and the lungs would cease to move. There would be no weight anywhere in the body, the whole physiology was at rest. At this point I began to appreciate that this inner space was not an emptiness but simply silent consciousness without content or activity, and I began to recognize in it the essence of my own self as pure consciousness. Eventually, even the thin boundary that had previously separated individuality from

unbounded pure consciousness began to dissolve. The "I" as a separate entity just started to have no meaning. The boundaries that I put on myself became like a mesh, a net; it became porous and then dissolved; only unbroken pure consciousness or existence remains. Once I let go of the veil of individuality, there is no longer "I perceiving" or "I aware." There is only that, there is nothing else there. In this state the experiencer is not experiencing as it normally does. It is there ready to experience, but the function has ceased. There is no thought, there is no activity, there is no experiencer, but the physiology after that state is incredible. It is like a power surge of complete purity.[91]

Lest anyone still deny that there is good evidence for reports of PCEs, I want to add the following modest autobiographical report to Part I's increasingly redundant evidence for them. I, too, have undergone a PCE. In 1972 I was several months into a nine-month meditation retreat on a neo-Advaitan *sādhana* (path). I had been meditating alone in my room all morning when someone knocked on my door. I heard the knock perfectly clearly, and upon hearing it I knew that, although there was no "waking up" before hearing the knock, for some indeterminate length of time prior to the knocking I had not been aware of anything in particular. I had been awake but with no content for my consciousness. Had no one knocked I doubt that I would ever have become aware that I had not been thinking or perceiving. The experience was so unremarkable, as it was utterly without content, that I simply would have begun at some point to recommence thinking and probably would never have taken note of my conscious persistence devoid of mental content.

I have argued elsewhere that this report should be viewed as proof that there is substantial evidence for PCEs.[92]

Part II presents a philosophical investigation. Based on the data of Part I, philosophers were asked to consider the plausibility and applicability of the received constructivist view on mysticism and in particular on the PCE. Contributors were asked to respond to the following "Call for Papers on Philosophical Problems Concerning PCEs":

> This section will comprise the second half of the book. In the first half evidence will be offered which demonstrates that there are reports of the experience of pure (nonintentional, objectless) consciousness found in a variety of traditions. Given this fact: What philosophical implications do these experiences (as reported) have? Does such an experience require a novel form of analysis? Are the extant forms of analysis and the current models adequate to account for these experiences?
>
> Principally, the book will be addressed to the positions taken in the two

Katz volumes; other positions of which you are critical may also be described and then criticized. Are there compelling reasons to believe that the
reports of PCEs are necessarily mistaken, that there are "intentions" when
their reports deny them? Or, conversely, are there compelling reasons for
believing those reports? Finally, does the existence of PCEs have implications
for the pluralism question that (mystical) experiences do or do not differ from
culture to culture? Is there any reason to believe that this experience is
universal?

Donald Rothberg opens Part II by describing the philosophical context
out of which the constructivist thesis developed. First, he shows how
mystical constructivists are merely applying the broad constructivist
model as it has developed over the past half-century. Then he shows—on
strictly a priori epsitemological grounds—how, as it has been applied to
mysticism, constructivism has systematically excluded any possible validity of either PCEs or interpretive traditions that give credence to these
events. Despite their claims to neutrality, Rothberg argues, the modern
constructivists must argue against certain religious traditions. Filling in the
theoretical blanks in the theory as we have it, Rothberg powerfully demonstrates the limitations of the principal constructivist approaches. Finally, he offers several suggestions for a more adequate epistemological
account.

Anthony N. Perovich, Jr., Steven Bernhardt, and Philip Almond all take
issue with the methodological, hermeneutical, and logical presuppositions of Katz's article and book. Each argues that mysticism is not
adequately understood by this approach; and all frame conditions for a
more adequate account. Bernhardt submits that Katz's position and those
like it are epistemologically fuzzy and argue about the PCE in a circle.
Almond notes that according to the constructivists, mystical texts are
deeply influenced by historical antecedents and are thus all incomparable
and different. Yet, he argues, insofar as different texts—from Jewish,
Christian, or Moslem mystics—are all influenced by the same antecedents (i.e., Neo-Platonism), they must have some features in common
and, hence, must be comparable. In one of the most sophisticated contributions to the volume, Perovich argues that the Kantian background of
constructivism does not support the weight being placed on it. Kant
himself and the arguments of the *Critique of Pure Reason* would not
support the arguments of mystical constructivists.

Mark Woodhouse as well as coauthors Norman Prigge and Gary Kessler argue in a more positive vein. Both articles begin by noting that many
philosophical traditions have conceived of consciousness in ways that
disallow the possibility of PCEs; they then discuss the notion of conscious-

ness to see if it need necessarily commit this error. Their questions then become: Does it make sense to say that consciousness may be experienced as contentless?

I see these as complimentary arguments. Woodhouse takes a more or less kataphatic direction, arguing that the notion of pure consciousness makes good sense even with reference to ordinary (i.e., nonmystical) experience. Prigge and Kessler, taking a more apophatic approach, argue that our notion of being conscious is consistent with the absense of mental content. Woodhouse, Prigge, and Kessler all assert that there are no logical blocks to the claim of PCEs. Prigge and Kessler draw out the relationships of their insights vis-a-vis the question of pluralism and diversity.

R. L. Franklin, the author of the concluding article, comments on the significance of the PCE and the philosophical debate thereon as well as the future of the discussion on mysticism. As befits a concluding essay in a volume of this nature, his very helpful and insightful comments are irenic.

A NEW MODEL FOR MYSTICISM

The authors of Part I (myself included) claim that PCEs actually occur. In Part II the argument is that constructivism has not, and cannot, plausibly account for these experiences. If we are correct, then the question becomes: What does cause or account for mysticism? A somewhat less ambitious question is: What *is* the relationship between the language system and mystical experiences? How is it possible that someone might practice a spiritual technique and hold to certain beliefs, yet not construct an experience in their terms?

Rather than beginning with a *priori* epistemological or ontological assumptions, I propose looking at mystical texts. For example, Eckhart writes, "[T]he more completely you are able to draw in your [intellectual and sensory] powers to a unity and *forget* all those things and their [mental] images which you have absorbed . . . the nearer you are to [this experience]."[93] "Forgetting" (*vergezzen*) and the state of having forgotten or being oblivious (*Vergezzenlicheit*) is one of Eckhart's more common themes.[94] Most typically, this term describes a "forgetting of all creatures," in the sense of forgetting the exclusive concern with those people who previously had occupied one's principal attentions. It also denotes a forgetting of all desires and compulsions, if you will, as in the following, "The soul takes four steps into God. The first is that fear, hope and desire [for God] grow in her. Again she steps on, and then fear and hope and desire are quite cut off. At the third stage she comes to a forgetfulness of all temporal things."[95]

Vergezzen also is used to signify a contemplative's forgetting of the images and forms in whose terms she or he normally thinks. As the mystic attempts to gain union with God, she or he must forget just such images and forms, "To achieve an interior act, a man must collect all his powers as if into a corner of his soul . . . *hiding away* from all images and forms. . . . Here, he must come to a *forgetting* and an *unknowing*."[96] The key technique by means of which Eckhart here (and elsewhere) instructs his listeners to bring about the experience he advocates is a turning away from ideas and conceptual forms, a *gelazen*—letting them go. It denotes a retreat from thought; a coming to forget all things in what Pseudo-Dionysius called an "unknowing."

Eckhart is not well known for his employment of this term.[97] Probably, the most renowned Christian mystic who wrote in terms of a comtemplative "forgetting" was the the fourteenth-century English mystical author of *The Cloud of Unknowing*. He emphasizes that some form of forgetting is critical in the development of the contemplative. "The cloud of forgetting" is intimately related to the goal he seeks, entry into "the cloud of unknowing."[98]

The expression, "the Cloud of forgetting," appears nine times in *The Cloud of Unknowing*, mostly in its first third.[99] It is used with nuances similar to the two we saw in Eckhart. The first is affective: the contemplative is instructed to put a "cloud of forgetting beneath thee, between thee and all the creatures that have ever been made."[100] Here one is to "forget," in the sense of ceasing to allow the affections to be drawn toward one's fellow men or "any condition or works," like wealth or power, that one may associate with them.[101] The objects of one's affections are to be, in this sense, ignored or forgotten.

In its other and more frequent usage, "the cloud of forgetting" describes an event in which thought ceases, by which I understand a PCE. The author teaches a mantramlike meditation technique, that is, a mental repetition of a one-syllable word. With it "thou shall smite down all manner of thought under the cloud of forgetting," that is, cease all thinking.[102] The thoughts specifically mentioned are thoughts of God's sweetness, grace, and mercy;[103] of one's own past sinful deeds;[104] and of Jesus.[105] However, any thoughts whatsoever should be understood by "all manner of thoughts." Thus, both emotional attachments and all thoughts, feelings, and sensations are to be "forgotten."

Such an empty consciousness is provided with its most extensive treatment in this anonymous author's *Deonise Hid Divinity,* a somewhat free

rendering of Pseudo-Dionysius's *Mystical Theology,* with which our author is in complete accord, he states.[106] In this work the presence of one
form of cognitive content after another is ruled out from the contemplative
experience he advocates: sensation, understanding, external and internal
imagery, future and past imaginings, and so on. Although this passage
employs the term "forsake" instead of "forget," I take the two as having
a similar intent:

> [L]ook thou forsake, with a strong and a sly [subtle] and a listy contrition,
> both thy bodily wits (as hearing, seeing, smelling, tasting, and touching), and
> also thy ghostly wits, the which be called thine understandable workings,
> and all those things the which may be known with any of thy five bodily wits
> without-forth; and all those things the which may be known by thy ghostly
> wits within-forth; and all those things that be now, or yet have been, though
> they be not now; and all those things that be not now, or yet may in time for
> to come, though they be not now. . . . [T]hrough the overpassing of thyself
> and all other things, and thus making thyself clean from all worldly, fleshly,
> and natural liking in thine affection, and from all things that may be known
> by the proper form in thy knowing, thou shalt be drawn up above mind in
> affection to the sovereign-substantial beam of the godly darkness, all things
> thus done away.[107]

This draws out the nature of the quiet moment denoted by "the cloud of
forgetting." All affections and all thoughts are to be "overpassed" and
"forsaken." One is to become "clean" of them. All things are to be "thus
done away." Both cognitive and affective content is to be forgotten. The
entire manifold of consciousness, in other words, is to be put behind a
"cloud of forgetting."

Turning to Buddhism, we see passages in which a similar notion of
forgetting or of leaving thoughts and emotions "behind" is put forward.
The Zen Buddhist Rosen Takashina speaks, for example, of being "without thoughts". We are to stop the workings of the thinking mind, he
writes: "[This] means to cut off at the root and source *all our discriminating fancies.* . . . 'In Zen the important thing is to stop the course of the
heart.' It means to stop the workings of our empirical consciousness, the
mass of thoughts, ideas and perceptions.[108] All such workings of the mind
are to be cut off or forgotten for the duration of the meditation.

Takashina is hearkening back to ancient Hinayana thought. A similar
picture is seen, for example, in Buddhaghosa's fivefold progression that
leads to *nirodhasamāpatti* (meditation without conceptualization or cessation) as well as to the Yogācārin Paramārtha's description of the process
that leads to the same state.[109]

In Buddhaghosa's encapsulation of the standard Theravādin fivefold series that leads to the attainment of cessation, he describes a hierarchical series of stages in which the meditator progressively rids himself (or "forgets") the structures of each previous stage:

1. By the transcendence of all conceptualizations of form, by the disappearance of conceptualizations based upon sense-data, by paying no attention to conceptualizations of manifoldness, having attained to the sphere of infinite space, [the practitoner] remains therein, thinking "space is unending."

2. By entirely transcending the sphere of infinite space, having attained to the sphere of infinite consciousness, [the practitioner] remains therein, thinking "consciousness is infinite."

3. By entirely transcending the sphere of infinite consciousness, having attained to the sphere of nothing at all, [the practitioner] remains therein, thinking "there is nothing."

4. By entirely transcending the sphere of nothing at all, having entered the sphere of neither conceptualization nor non-conceptualization, [the practitioner] remains therein.

5. By entirely transcending the sphere of neither conceptualization nor non-conceptualization, having attained the cessation of sensation and conceptualization, [the practitioner] remains therein.[110]

Here, spelled out in formulaic detail, we have how the practitioner is to successively eliminate, or "forget," the defining features of each preceding stage. Each stage denotes an ascending state of consciousness,[111] with its own phenomenological flavor in which one has removed the key features, of each of the previous stages. As a result of this process of removal of content, each marks a consciousness that is progressively more abstracted from content.

Now, what might an Eckhart or a Takashina mean when they counsel their listeners to forget something? *Webster's* suggests the following definitions (which I paraphrase) of "forget," which may be what these writers have in mind.

1. To *permanently* lose the remembrance of, to cease permanently to retain in one's memory, be unable to think of or recall, as in "I once knew it, but I have forgotten the year of Kant's birth." Though I once knew it, I no longer can recall the data, even if I try, without further lookup. Generally, this is a *countervolitional* phenomenon, though there are some painful things we are glad to have forgotten or some trivial things we donot care enough to remember. This cannot be the usage Eckhart or Buddhaghosa had in mind, however, when they spoke of forgetting all ideas and forms, for certainly their disciples were each still able to recall at will and use ideas, thoughts, and forms.

2. To unintentionally omit or disregard, neglect, overlook—as in, "I forgot to bring my keys" or "Oh, I forgot to tell you about this call." This is again countervolitional and is often behavioral. One is capable of remembering or doing something, but often, for some time neglects to perform an act or to bring some idea or thought to mind.

However, this cannot be the sense in which these mystics intend "forget," for each is inviting the hearer to forget something, go beyond some notion, or cease thinking *intentionally*. Thus, we are drawn to the third meaning.

3. To disregard *intentionally*, to purposely ignore, as in "forget about it" or "disregard what you heard about ghosts." One may understand and be capable of thinking of something; but for some reason, one purposely lays aside this knowledge or capacity.

This intentional holding in abeyance seems to be nearest to the kind of forgetting of which Eckhart and Takashina spoke, for both are advocating a ceasing to think intentionally.

If someone said to Monet, "[F]orget what you know of Gothic arches and look over there," the painter would intentionally lay aside his "Gothic" blanks or formularies and look at the visual information before him. He would not be forgetting (in sense 1), for he could recall the nature of a Gothic arch anytime he had a reason to. Nonetheless, if he was good at this, his notions of Gothic arches would play no substantial part in determining the characteristics of his painting. For the moment, he will have forgotten Gothicness utterly, we might say. He will temporarily hold those conceptual formularies in abeyance such that they will play no role in determining the shape of his thought, perception, and so on. This seems to be the nearest to the kind of forgetting which the *roshi*, Buddhaghosa, or Eckhart had in mind. When these mystical authors council their readers to forget creatures or go beyond conceptualizing, clearly they are not advocating becoming incapable of using such concepts correctly. They are not advocating becoming morons! Rather, they are counseling people to intentionally set these notions aside, at least, for the moment. On emerging from contemplation—or *satori* or *zazen*—one will, of course, be able to recommense the thinking process. But for the duration of the meditation process, thoughts and conceptual systems are to be set aside and put on hold.

In other words, if I understand the instructions provided by Eckhart and Takashina aright, then Katz has the Monet example backwards. The mystic's technique seems more akin to Manet's forgetting Gothicness than remembering and superimposing it.

But the reader is perhaps thinking, not much is gained so far. It may be true that on being told to "forget Gothicness and look" Monet might come to cease applying his Gothic formulary; but certainly, he would not do without *all* formulas or constructions whatsoever. Probably, he will simply replace one formula with another—say Romanesque—or, if that does not suit, adapt and modify that one still further until the fit is pretty close. Gombrich describes just this process of schema trial and correction, which one might adopt when trying to copy what is called a nonsense figure, say an inkblot or an irregular patch:

> By and large, it appears, the procedure is always the same. The draftsman tries first to classify the blot and fit it into some sort of familiar schema—he will say, for instance, that it is triangular or that it looks like a fish. Having selected such a schema to fit the form approximately, he will proceed to adjust it, noticing for instance that the triangle is rounded at the top, or that the fish ends in a pigtail. Copying, we learn from these experiments, proceeds through the rhythms of schema and correction. The schema is not the product of a process of abstraction, of a tendency to simplify; it represents the first approximate, loose category which is gradually tightened to fit the forms it is to reproduce.[112]

Such a process of replacing one schema with another and altering it is perfectly in accord with the constructivist picture—that we move as if horizontally from one conditioned and constructed form of consciousness to another.

Here, however, is one of the places where my analogy between Monet's dropping his Gothic formula and mystical experience falls short. Rosen Takashina did not say substitute one form of discrimination for another, but rather "cut off . . . *all* our discriminating fancies." The *Cloud* author said that one must be rid of:

> *All* those things the which may be kown with any of thy five bodily wits without-forth; and *all* those things the which may be known by thy goostly wits within-forth; and *all* those things that be now, or yet have been, though they be not now; and *all* those things that be not now, or yet may be in time for to come, though they be not now. . . . [T]hrough the overpassing of thyself and *all* other things, and thus making thyself clean from *all* worldly, fleshly, and natural liking in thine affection, and from *all* things that may be known by the proper form in thy knowing.[113]

Eckhart said that the more you can forget your ideas the nearer you will come to the experience he advocates—implying that the experience comes by dropping "ideas and forms" *altogether*. Monet would trade schemata. Incredible as it sounds, these men counsel dropping them altogether.

How might a mystic bring himself or herself to forget on a massive scale? Tell Monet to "forget what you know of Gothic," and he may put aside something of what he knows about cathedrals. This will be a limited kind of forgetting. However, there are other subtler and more effective techniques which might bring about a more massive forgetting. The most well documented and striking is occular. Newton was the first to note that when a retinal image is stabilized it tends to disappear. In his *Opticks* he wrote, "When a Man in the dark presses either corner of his eye with his finger, and turns his eye away from his Finger, he will see a Circle of Colours like those in the Feather of a Peacock's Tail. If the Eye and the Finger remain quiet these Colors vanish in a second Minute of Time, but if the Finger be moved with a quavering Motion they appear again."[114] And Troxler noticed that if one steadily fixates on patches of color, they tend to fade. This, which has been verified by many experiments, is called the "Troxler effect."[115]

A more reliable way of maintaining a steady visual image on the retina was developed by a group of physiological psychologists who mounted a tiny projector on a contact lens. As the eyeball moved around, the projected image remained in a constant position on the retina. The effect on awareness of this unchanging image was similar to the Troxler effect in which colors faded. Here, the image itself tended to disappear or, if you will, be forgotten.[116] The fading of the image, which generally takes between five to ten seconds, is called the Ditchburn–Riggs effect.

The effect with the closest parallel to mystical "forgetting" may be the one that is produced when an observer is placed in a so-called *Ganzfeld*, a completely patternless visual field. A whitewashed surface or a blizzard can serve as a *Ganzfeld*, as can two halves of a Ping-Pong ball taped over the eyes.[112] At first, observers may see the whiteness as a fog or cloud; within several minutes, things seemed to go black. Some experimental *Ganzfeld* subjects even thought that someone turned the lights off. After a while (ten to twenty minutes), observers frequently reported what they called "blackout", "This was not merely the experience of seeing nothing but that of not seeing, a complete disappearance of the sense of vision for short periods. . . . During blackout, the observers did not know, for instance, whether their eyes were open or not, and they could not even control their eye movements. . . . [C]ontinuous uniform stimulation resulted in the failure of any kind of image to be produced in consciousness."[118] The point here is that under conditions of unchanging visual stimulation, one comes to lose or "forget" the projected image or, in a *Ganzfeld*, the sense of vision altogether. These, then, may be viewed as techniques that bring about something like a complete forgetting of occular imput and function. Unlike the kind of forgetting Monet would do as he forgot "Gothic" and shifted to "Romanesque," these seem to represent moves from constructed visual experiences to nonvisual experiences—and, hence, not epistemologically constructed visual experiences at all.

"Forgetting" of other forms of steady or unchanging sensory imput is so common as to hardly need comment: we soon cease hearing the ticking of a clock, the whine of an engine, or the calling of birds outside our window. We stop feeling the pressure of the seat under our buttocks or the sensation of our shirt cuffs. People who live near oil refineries are renowned to cease smelling the odor that is so offensive to those who drive by. They, like most of us, even come sometimes to "forget" their olfactory sense altogether. Under conditions of steady or regular sensory imput, in other words, senses and sensations are commonly forgotten.

Turning to mystical techniques, Ornstein and Naranjo[119] and Piggins and Morgan[120] have suggested that the common meditative practices of restricting awareness to a single unchanging process may be analogous, since both involve a great deal of repetition. They point out that the object of one's attention may be in any sense modality: verbal-like mantras, dervish calls, or short prayers; visual (a *yantra* candle or guru's picture); or the concentration may be on a regular bodily process like the heartbeat or the breath. What seems critical is that the procedure typically incorporates repetition of a "mental subroutine:"

> This process might be considered in psychological terms as an attempt to recycle the same subroutine over and over again in the nervous system. The instructions for meditation are consistent with this; one is instructed always to rid awareness of any thought save the object of meditation, to shut oneself off from the main flow of ongoing external activity and attend only to the object or process of meditation. Almost any process or object seems usable and has probably been used. The specific object of meditation (for this analysis) is much less important than maintaining the object as the single focus of awareness over a long period of time.[121]

Just as the processes are parallel, the effect of such a recycling of a single subroutine is parallel with those of the *Ganzfeld* or the constant auditory stimulus. Not merely does the recycled stimulus itself ultimately fade, but there is a complete disappearance of any sense of thinking, perceiving, and so on. All perception and mental activity come to be forgotten. A vacuous state of emptiness, a nonresponsiveness to the external world, is evoked in the central nervous system by the catalytic action of the continuous subroutine. Such an emptiness, it should be clear, is not like remembering something and applying it to form or reform visual information, rather it is more akin to a massive forgetting.

This is the model that I propose for the epistemological structure of the spiritual transformative process which culminates in the PCE and which is, I believe, more adequate than is the constructivist's model of "remembering and superimposing." Meditators or mystics practice a technique in which they recycle a constant mental subroutine. This technique serves as a catalyst to enable the mind to come to "forget" all thought and sensation. Gradually or suddenly, just as one comes to forget the sense of vision during the *Ganzfeld* experience, the mind comes to forget all of its usual processes during the PCE.

A state thus produced is not epistemologically "constructed." When a person undergoing a *Ganzfeld* first thinks that someone has turned the lights out, he or she may be thought to be having a "constructed" experience of seeing blackness. But as time progresses and that person comes to full blackout, in which the sense of sight has disappeared altogether, he or she simply stops employing the sense of vision. That person has stopped building or constructing visual images. All the usual visual patterns, memories, images, and so on, are simply, for the duration, forgotten. Rather than constructing, we should say that the subject has *ceased* constructing visual images. To stop seeing at all is to stop "seeing anything as," that is, to stop visually constructing. The PCE, which emerges after recycling a single subroutine during meditation, is the result of a similar, though more massive, forgetting. As subjects cease thinking and sensing, they have not only ceased constructing sensually, they have ceased constructing anything at all. If to think is to construct thoughts, and to construct is to think, to cease thinking is to cease constructing.

It is important to note that what is forgotten altogether in the PCE is expressly stated by many mystics to include the very concepts and teachings of the mystical traditions themselves. When Eckhart talks for example about *gelazen* (letting go), he expressly includes all notions of God—and his own belief system—as part of that which must be given up; "He must be so lacking in all knowledge that he neither knows nor recognizes nor feels that God lives in him: more still, he must be free of all the understanding that lives in him . . . a man should be as free from his own knowledge as he was when he was not . . . a man must be poor of all his own knowledge: not knowing any thing, not God, nor creature nor himself."[122] Or, similarly, in the summit in the soul, the "place" to which one goes in *gezücken*, "I stand free of my own will, of God's will, of all His works, and of God himself, then I am above all creatures. . . ."[123]

I have argued elsewhere that in Yogācāra and Zen Buddhist thought, that which is "forgotten" in the PCE is expressly understood to include the Buddhist categories.[124] This is, in part, how I understand the famous Zen aphorism, "If you see Buddha on the road, kill him." It states a similar requirement: all beliefs and emotional attachments to one's own Buddhist interpretive categories, including all images or notions of Buddha himself, must be "killed"—that is, intentionally forgotten—before the final "goal" can be achieved. One must become empty of such.

It is a strange, paradoxical claim that these mystical writers are making, if I understand them correctly. In claiming that all concepts are to be passed beyond in the fifth *jhana* or that in the end one must go beyond all concepts of God, these authors allude to a self-immolation of their own conceptual systems. One is to be so devoid of concepts, at least during the PCE, that even the very conceptual system which has lead one to it is itself to be forgotten. The famous Buddhist image of the raft captures this nicely. The Buddhist doctrine is like a raft, this very old metaphor states, which carries one across the realm of ignorance. Once one has gained that "other" (*nirvāṇic*) side, the raft serves no further function. It is to be henceforward forgotten (except as a teaching tool). Like that, religious doctrines, images, words, thoughts, or what have you, serve no function in the PCE and must be forgotten, transcended utterly. In short, to temporarily forget everything includes forgetting even the very belief system which may have led to that forgetting.

This model for understanding the pure consciousness event has an interesting result for the pluralism question, that of the similarity of experience between two traditions. If Monet forgot Gothicness and Picasso forgot Gothicness, we would still expect them to paint the archways differently, for there are so many other formularies and constructs involved in perception that they would still not see alike. However, the story changes drastically if two or more people were able to forget *everything* for awhile. Strange to say, but a *Ganzfeld* would produce an indistinguishable visual experience for Picasso or Monet. Both are without content, image formation, and so on. Similarly, if a Buddhist, Hindu, or African was able to forget every thought, sensation, emotion, and so on, for some time, then no historically conditioned idea, form, category, or even sensory information would remain conscious to differentiate the resultant events from one another. In general if a concept is for a moment truly forgotten—be it Monet's concept of Gothic or his mother's maiden name—then it plays no role in an experience. If something is utterly forgotten, it does not form or cause or mediate or construct an experience.[125] Hence, a formless trance in Buddhism may be experientially indistinguishable from one in Hinduism or Christianity.

While I hope it does so with greater epistemological plausibility and sophistication, this model swings the pendulum back toward the perennial philosophy camp, that mysticism is alike from one culture to another.

I am not arguing for *universality*, however. It is not clear to me that *all* traditions harness a forgetting technique or that all techniques *are* equally effective. This can only be determined case by case. Rather than making a universalistic philosophical argument, I am making a more modest claim: when a tradition uses techniques which effectively bring about a forgetting, then concepts do not play the "heavy" formative role the constructivist gives them. If in objectless consciousness, all concepts are indeed forgotten, as I have argued throughout, then they will play *no* constructive role during the event.

With this forgetting model, it is not difficult to find a place for the physiological data as we have it. In a famous set of experiments Stanley Schachter hypothesized that emotions arise to account for visceral *arousals*—one mark of which is a rise in heart rate, oxygen consumption, and spontaneous GSRs, and so on.[126] Wayne Proudfoot has argued that mystical emotions arise similarly (i.e., that the subject undergoes an arousal similar to those artifically created by Schachter) and are, in turn, labeled with religious as opposed to emotional terms.[127] One problem with this thesis is that physiological studies of meditators point in the opposite direction: successful meditation is characterized by a *decrease* in heart rate, oxygen consumption, breath rate, GSRs, and so on. Studies by J. T. Farrow and J. R. Hebert even have found a *stoppage* of breathing for prolonged periods.[128] Given the fact that two fundamentally similar mental processes are purportedly at work, the proponent of the Schachterian thesis, to be convincing, must explain why we see arousals in one set of experiences and de-arousals in the other.

The model I am putting forward can account for the psychophysiological data of mysticism more elegantly than can the Proudfoot–Schachter one. It is a psychological truism that if all else remains constant, the magnitude of physiological activity may be correlated with the magnitude of cognitive or emotional arousal. On just such a connection, Schachter made the hypothesis which led to his studies: he expected that an experimentally induced increase in physiological arousal would lead to an increase in emotional arousal, which would, in turn, lead to the emotion-labeling process.

If meditative procedures decrease cognitive activity, as this model has it, then given this connection between the mind and physiological arousal levels during meditation we should expect to see physiological activity decrease. And this is precisely what is found. Schachter could increase emotional activity by injecting a physiological stimulant, adrenaline; conversely, we have here a decrease in cognitive or emotional activity which should result in a corresponding decrease in physiological activity. Were the mental activity level to drop to nil, we would expect the physiological arousal level to decrease sharply. And so we do if we can believe the absence of breath findings reported by Russell and Hebert. Contrary to the constructivist's thinking, such a restful physiology will require not "mystical" emotion labels to be constructively applied, but rather it will require the application of fewer or no emotion labels. The lessening of physiological arousal may be thought to buttress the case that less mental activity is found here and that thoughts and emotions will not be "constructed" or "reconstructed" but will approach a being forgotten altogether.

This model also accounts nicely for the well-known ineffability of mystical experiences. In general: What makes me able to speak of something without feeling that "words are inadequate"? When I look at the shiny, brass, cylindrical object near the edge of the door in front of me, the word "doorknob" comes readily to mind. It is not a later addition to my wordless experience of the cylindrical object, it is part and parcel of my experience. To see a doorknob is to think—consciously or very nearly so—the word "doorknob." Were I to report on that experience, I would say that I saw or turned a doorknob. The language I use to express the experience would include the very term I had employed in the original experience (or something very near to it). This is why my report seems to "fit" my experience. The language of the experience is the *same* as the report. Logically, there is a necessary connection between descriptive language and the language of the primary experience. Change the language of the experience—"Oh that's not a doorknob, it's a cardboard model!"—and the language of the report must change.

Similarly, when I tell my friend of an insight I had, I do so using just the language—or something very near to—the very words which I originally thought. Again the language of the secondary report may be (and probably is) just the same or very similar to the language used in the primary experience.

According to the forgetting model, however, during the PCE, language, *all* language, is forgotten. Therefore, any language used to describe or report on that experience is *not* language which was employed in the primary event. There *can* be no identity of language between the primary experience and the report: there *must* be a disjunction. Logically, there is only a *contingent* connection between descriptive language and the primary experience. It is to this intuition of a linguistic disjunction that the mystic correctly avers with the term "ineffable."

What then does the mystic's language signify? Because with reference to PCEs linguistic systems are afloat—not pinned down to the terms in which the mystic undergoes the event—many language systems or belief systems may be used equally well to depict a PCE. Thus, it is plausible that someone may assert, "I used to think of that event as *samādhi*, but now I call it *nirodhasamāpatti*." It is also plausible that a guru and a *roshi* may hear a single experience report of an empty but awake consciousness and provide it with two different names with very different backgrounds of meaning. For given the peculiar nonlinguistic nature of the PCE, they would be doing something intrinsically correct: applying descriptive terms which did not enter into the original experience. There can be as many terms for such a nonlinguistic event as there can be terms for, say, the North Star, for the relationship between language and that to which it refers is contingent. Thus, logically, it is plausible that there can be many different terms, significances, and so on, offered for a single mystical experience or experience type. The term "Pure Consciousness Event" is one way—but only that—of denoting such an event. Given alternative cognitive contexts, other terms would be equally appropriate.

It is on this basis that I can write the present analysis using the vocabulary I do. I am not, obviously, using just the language that an Eckhart or a Buddhaghosa used to describe şuch experiences. But since I maintain that language here is only contingently related to the experience, then I am justified in using nonprimary language to speak of these events.

In sum, the inherently conservative linguistic constructivist model is ill-suited to account for the radically novel, radically nonlinguistic data of mysticism, especially the PCE. There is no causal prefiguration at work which shapes and constructs these quiet moments. Nor does language determine the form or content of these formless, contentless events. Rather, the only way it can be engendered is through a process of ceasing to think—ceasing, in other words, to use language. It is not brought on by imposing old, habituated categories but by *forgetting* them.

In conclusion, this discovery suggests that there are real limits to the range of the constructivist thesis. For not all experiences are constructed.

I will leave the reader with some of the broader philosophical questions which this book raises: Are there any other limits to the range of constructivism? How might we think about an experience which is not shaped or constructed by an experience? What are the marks of an unconstructed experience? Can you have an experience with some constructed and some unconstructed aspects? The question I hope to address in the next book I am editing is: If mystical phenomena are not caused by the imposition of language, then to what may we attribute them? Is there some sort of capacity within the human being to which we can point as the source? If so, what sort of capacity might it be? Can we approach these experiences gradually by working with the ordinary world and language or do we suddenly and simply "turn on" this capacity? And finally, what is the relationship between these pure consciousness events and other— perhaps more advanced—mystical phenomena?

NOTES

I am grateful to Donald Rothberg and the anonymous reader of this volume for their helpful comments and suggestions for improving this chapter.

1. William James, *The Varieties of Religious Experience* (New York: Longmans, Green and Co.; 1902 rept. Penguin, 1982).

2. Evelyn Underhill, *Mysticism* (New York: Dutton, 1911).

3. Joseph Maréchal, S. J., *Studies in the Psychology of the Mystics,* trans. Algar Thorold (London: Burns Oakes & Washburne 1927).

4. William Johnston, *The Still Point* (New York: Harper & Row, 1970).

5. James Pratt, *The Religious Consciousness* (New York: Macmillan, 1923).

6. While not discussing mystical experience per se, Mircea Eliade (*The Sacred and the Profane,* trans. Willard R. Trask [New York: Harcourt Brace Jovanovich, 1959]) takes a fundamentally perennialist view.

7. W. T. Stace, *Mysticism and Philosophy* (London: Macmillan, 1960; repr. Atlantic Highlands, N.J.: Humanities Press, 1978).

8. "Core characteristics" was, of course, Stace's term in *Mysticism and Philosophy*. Ninian Smart, "Interpretation and Mystical Experience," *Religious Studies* 1 (1965), 75–87, suggested that there are commonalites to which "different flavors" accrue.

9. Frithjof Schuon, *The Transcendental Unity of Religions,* trans. Peter Townsend (New York: Harper & Row, Torchbooks, 1975).

10. Rudolf Otto, *Mysticism East and West,* trans. Bertha Bracey and Richenda Payne (New York: Macmillan, 1960).

11. W. T. Stace, *Mysticism and Philosophy.*

12. Aldous, Huxley, *The Perennial Philosophy* (New York: Harper & Row, Colophon, 1944; repr. 1970).

13. Huston Smith, *Forgotten Truth: The Primordial Tradition* (New York: Harper & Row, Colophon, 1976). A similar view is found in his more recent *Beyond the Post Modern Mind* (New York: Crossroads Press, 1982).

14. Otto's unfortunate and deeply flawed *Mysticism East and West* was an attempt to compare Shankara and Meister Eckhart. It was never well received, however.

15. I first discovered its significance through Clifford Geertz's *Islam Observed* (Chicago: University of Chicago Press, 1968) and *The Interpretation of Cultures* (New York: Harper & Row, Colophon, 1975). On the sociology of knowledge see: Peter Berger, *The Social Construction of Reality: A Treatise in the Sociology of Knowledge* (Garden City, N.Y.: Doubleday, 1967); Robin Horton, ed., *Modes of Thought: Essays on Thinking in Western and Non-Western Societies* (London:

Faber & Faber, 1973); Peter Hamilton, *Knowledge and Social Structure: An Introduction to the Classical Argument in the Sociology of Knowledge* (London: Routledge & Kegan Paul, 1974).

16. A good general introduction is Walter Bromberg, *The Mind of Man: A History of Psychotherapy and Psychoanalysis* (New York: Harper & Row, Colophon, 1959). Two recent schools of psychology emphasize the formative role of early experiences: on the personal construct theory see Robert Neimeyer, *The Development of Personal Construct Theory* (Lincoln: University of Nebraska Press, 1985); on object relations theory see both H. Guntrip, *Personality Structure and Human Interaction*, (New York: International Universities Press, 1961); and J. Greenberg and S. Mitchell, *Object Relations in Psychoanalytic Theory* (Cambridge: Harvard University Press, 1983).

17. Iris Murdoch in D. F. Pears, *Nature of Metaphysics* (London: Macmillan, 1956), p. 122.

18. Ever since Duchamp, much modern art has been preoccupied with the role of the viewer's concepts in the experience of art. Dadaism, pop art, superrealism, and other twentieth-century movements have focused much of their writings and written defenses here. See Douglas Davis, *Art Culture: Essays on the Post Modern*, (New York: Harper & Row, 1977), esp. pp. 1–28; Herschel Chipp, ed., *Theories of Modern Art: A Source Book by Artists and Critics*, (Berkeley: University of California Press, 1968), esp. Vincent van Gogh, "Paint Your Garden as It Is," pp. 44–45; Dada and surrealism, pp. 366–96.

19. E. H. Gombrich, *Art and Illusion: a Study in the Psychology of Pictorial Representation* (Princeton, N.J.: Princeton University Press, 1960).

20. Roland Fischer, "A Cartography of the Ecstatic and Meditative States," in Richard Woods, O.P., ed., *Understanding Mysticism* (Garden City, N.Y.: Doubleday, Image Books, 1980), pp. 270–85.

21. *Bhagavad Gītā*, 11:16–17, trans. Franklin Edgerton (New York: Harper, 1944), p. 56.

22. Ibid., 2:64–65.

23. Cf. Smart, "Interpretation and Mystical Experience," p. 75.

24. Saint Teresa of Avila, *Complete Works of St. Teresa*, vol. 1, trans. E. Allison Peers, (London: Sheed & Ward, 1957), p. 119.

25. Louis Bouyer, "Mysticism: An Essay on the History of the Word," in Woods, *Understanding Mysticism*, pp. 42–55.

26. See, for example, in Arthur Osborne, *Ramana Maharshi and the Path of Self-Knowledge*, (New York: Samuel Weiser, 1973), p. 204, also Arthur Osborne, ed., *The Collected Works of Ramana Maharshi* (London: Rider, 1959), p. 47. The term *sahaja* is an ancient one (according to Monier-Williams, it was seen as early as the *Harivamsa* [4238]) that means having a quality as a disposition or constant feature.

27. For John Farrow's suggestion that what he terms "transcendental consciousness" is preliminary to a more advanced and permanent state, see "Physiological Changes Associated with Transcendental Consciousness, the State of Least Excitation of Consciousness," in David Orme Johnson, ed., *Scientific Re-

search on the Transcendental Meditation Program (Livingston Manor, N.Y.: MERU Press, 1977), p. 132. This is congruent with the suggestion made in Osborne, *Ramana Maharshi,* pp. 17–19, where the first experience of *samādhi* preceded *sahaja samādhi* by several years.

28. See preceding note.

29. Bruce Garside, "Language and the Interpretation of Mystical Experiences," *International Journal for Philosophy of Religion* 3 (Summer 1972), 91–94.

30. R. C. Zaehner, *Hindu and Muslim Mysticism* (New York: Schocken Books, 1969); idem, *Mysticism Sacred and Profane* (New York: Schocken Books, 1961).

31. H. P. Owen, "Experience and Dogma in the English Mystics," in Steven T. Katz, ed., *Mysticism and Religious Traditions* (New York: Oxford University Press, 1983), pp. 148–62.

32. John Hick, "Mystical Experience as Cognition," in Woods, *Understanding Mysticism,* pp. 415–21.

33. W. R. Inge, "Ecstasy," in James Hastings, ed., *Encyclopedia of Religion and Ethics* (Edinburgh: T. & T. Clark, 1912), p. 157.

34. Rufus M. Jones, *Studies in Mystical Religion* (New York: Russell & Russell, 1909; repr. 1970), p. xxxiv.

35. Steven T. Katz, "Language, Epistemology, and Mysticism," in Katz, *Mysticism and Philsophical Analysis,* pp. 22–74.

36. Robert Gimello, "Mysticism and Meditation," pp. 170–99; Peter Moore, "Mystical Experience, Mystical Doctrine, Mystical Technique," pp. 101–31; Frederick Streng, "Language and Mystical Awareness," pp. 141–69; and Ninian Smart, "Understanding Religious Experience," pp. 10–21—all in Katz, *Mysticism and Philosophical Analysis;* Jerry Gill, "Mysticism and Mediation," *Faith and Philosophy* 1 (1984), 111–21.

37. Katz, "Language, Epistemology and Mysticism," p. 26. [Emphasis in original.]

38. Ibid., p. 26.

39. Ibid. I point out that the truth and applicability of this model is thus assumed from the outset, not proven or even argued for. It is, therefore, on a very soft philosophical foundation. Its rhetorical and logical force rests entirely on the fact that the model is taken over en bloc, as an assumption, from the body of material which has argued for its application to other, that is, *ordinary* experience. Neither Katz (nor anyone else for that matter) ever argues that it is appropriate to apply the constructivist model (developed to account for ordinary, nonmystical experiences) to mystical phenomena. Ordinary experiences may be so different from mystical ones that it would be misleading to apply this model to the latter.

40. Ibid., pp. 27, 59.

41. With this phrase, Katz seems to present mystical experiences from a variety of traditions as having a single ontological object, a single reality, which are then encountered or experienced differently. One wonders what he means by this notion.

42. Katz, "Language, Epistemology and Mysticism," p. 27.

43. Gill, "Mysticism and Mediation"; Hick, "Mystical Experience as Cognition"; Hans H. Penner, "The Mystical Allusion," in Steven Katz, ed., *Mysticism and Religious Traditions* (New York: Oxford University Press, 1983), pp. 89–116; Robert Gimello, "Mysticism in Its Contexts," in Katz, *Mysticism and Religious Traditions*, pp. 61–88.

44. Katz, "Language, Epistemology and Mysticism," p. 25.

45. Ibid., p. 30.

46. Gombrich, *Art and Illusion*, p. 73.

47. For an early study to this effect see Jerome Bruner and Leo Postman, "On Perception of Incongruities: A Paradigm," *Journal of Personality* 18 (1949), 213.

48. Katz, "Language, Epistemology and Mysticism," p. 57.

49. Ibid., p. 26.

50. Ibid., p. 46.

51. Ibid., p. 27.

52. Ibid., p. 60.

53. Ibid., p. 27.

54. Gimello, "Mysticism in Its Contexts," p. 85.

55. Smart, "Interpretation and Mystical Experience," pp. 75–87.

56. Katz, "Language, Epistemology and Mysticism," pp. 62–63.

57. Katz, "Language, Epistemology and Mysticism," p. 62.

58. Steven Katz, "The 'Conservative' Character of Mystical Experience," in Katz, *Mysticism and Religious Traditions*, p. 41.

59. Katz, "Language, Epistemology and Mysticism," p. 40. [Emphasis added.]

60. Katz, " 'Conservative' Character," p. 51.

61. Katz, "Language, Epistemology and Mysticism," p. 27.

62. Ibid., p. 65.

63. Ibid., p. 34.

64. Ibid., p. 38.

65. Anthony Perovich, "Mysticism and the Philosophy of Science," *Journal of Religion* 65 (1985), 63–82.

66. Moore, "Mystical Experience, Mystical Doctrine, Mystical Technique"; Gimello, "Mysticism and Meditation"; Streng, "Language and Mystical Awareness"; Gimello, "Mysticism in Its Contexts"; Katz, " 'Conservative' Character." And Ninian Smart, "The Purification of Consciousness and the Negative Path," in Katz, *Mysticism and Religious Traditions*, pp. 117–30.

67. Moore, "Mystical Experience, Mystical Doctrine, Mystical Technique," pp. 114, 116.

68. Cf. Perovich, "Mysticism and the Philosophy of Science."

69. Phillip Almond, "Mysticism and Its Contexts." (In the present volume.)

70. For example, Ninian Smart, *Doctrine and Argument in Indian Philosophy* (Atlantic Highlands, N.J.: Humanities Press, 1976), pp. 104–5, argues for parallels between Hindu Advaitan and Buddhist accounts of such events.

71. See n. 64.

72. At the 1985 Conference on World Religions, sponsored by the Unification Church, this seemed to be the case.

73. On this point, see Smart, *Indian Philosophy*, pp. 104–5.

74. William Wainwright, *Mysticism: a Study of Its Nature, Cognitive Value, and Moral Implications* (Madison: University of Wisconsin Press, 1981), p. 20.

75. Richard Maurice Bucke, *Cosmic Consciousness*, (New York: A & W Publishers, Causeway Books, repr. 1974 [originally published, 1900]), p. 8.

76. Bernadette Roberts, *The Experience of No Self*, (Boulder' Colo: Shambhala Publications, 1984), p. 9.

77. Ibid., p. 10.

78. Ibid., pp. 13–14.

79. Interview with D.A., November 21, 1985.

80. This idea was suggested to me by Wayne Proudfoot in a private conversation, November 1983.

81. Teresa of Avila, *The Life of St. Teresa*, trans. E. Allison Peers (London: Sheed & Ward, 1944), p. 210.

82. Interview with M.M., August 10, 1985.

83. The woman I interviewed told me she was unacquainted with the so-called *chakras* at the time of her transformation.

84. Although this is with reference to a vision, Francis of Assisi's response is common: "[He] wondered exceedingly at the sight of so unfathomable a vision," according to Bonaventure. II:171.

85. Stephen Bernhardt, "Are Pure Consciousness Events Unmediated?" (In the present volume.)

86. Benjamin Lee Whorf, *Language, Thought and Reality*, ed. John B. Carroll (Cambridge: MIT Press, 1956), p. 253. Quoted by Perovich in the present volume, p. 226.

87. Katz, "Language, Epistemology and Mysticism," p. 59.

88. This period is the longest duration noted in K. Badawi, R. K. Wallace, D. W. Orme-Johnson and A. M. Rouzere, "Electrophysiological Characteristics of Respiratory Suspension Periods Occurring During the Practice of the Transcendental Meditation Program," *Psychosomatic Medicine* 46 (1984), 267–76. I have read reports of people being in samādhi for as long as a week.

89. Katz, "Language, Epistemology and Mysticism," p. 57.

90. Charles N. Alexander, Ken Chandler, and Robert W. Boyer, "Experience and Understanding of Pure Consciousness in the Vedic Science of Maharishi Mahesh Yogi," unpublished paper, pp. 5–6.

91. Ibid., p. 6.

92. Robert K. C. Forman, "Pure Consciousness Events and Mysticism," *Sophia* 25, no. 1 (1986), 49–58.

93. *Meister Eckhart: German Sermons and Treatises*, vol. 1, trans. M. O'C Walshe, (London: Watkins, 1979), p. 7. Hereafter cited as Walshe.

94. Not counting the extra sermons found as of now only in the Pfeiffer edition, there are twenty-four uses of the terms *"vergezzen," "Vergezzenlich-*

keit," and so forth, in the *Sermons and Treatises.* See the indexes of Josef Quint, *Die Deutsche Werke herausgegeben in Auftrage der Deutschen Forschungsgemeinschaft* (Stuttgart and Berlin: W. Kohlhammer Verlag, 1936). See also Robert K. C. Forman, "A Psychological Account of Meister Eckhart's Mystical Transformation," *Journal of Christianity and Psychology* 6, no. 1 (Spring 1987), 21–33; and "Eckhart's Stages of Mystical Progression," *Downside Review* (April 1987), 132–42.92.

    95. Walshe, vol. 2, p. 259.

    96. Ibid., vol. 1, pp. 20–21.

    97. I know of no other scholar who has commented on this.

    98. See Robert K. C. Forman, "Mystical Experience in the Cloud Literature," in Marion Glasscoe, ed., *The Medieval Mystical Tradition in England: Exeter Symposium IV* (Cambridge: D. S. Brewer, 1987), pp. 177–95.

    99. Phyllis Hodson, ed., *The Cloud of Unknowing and the Book of Privy Counselling,* Early English Text Society (London: Oxford University Press, 1944; repr. 1958), pp. 24, 27–28, 29, 31, 33, 61, 66, 82. Except where noted, all translations are mine.

    100. Ibid., p 24.

    101. Ibid., Cf. p. 61.

    102. Ibid., p. 28.

    103. Ibid., p. 27.

    104. Ibid., p. 66.

    105. Ibid., p 46.

    106. Ibid., p. 125.

    107. Phyllis Hodson, ed., *Deonise Hid Diuinite,* Early English Text Society, (London: Oxford University Press, 1955), p. 3. *The Cloud of Unknowing and Other Treatises,* trans. Justin McCann (Westminister, MD.: Newman Press, 1952), pp. 140–41.

    108. Edward Conze, ed., *Buddhist Scriptures* (Baltimore, Md.: Penguin, 1959), p. 139. [Emphasis added.]

    109. See Robert K. C. Forman, "Paramārtha and Modern Constructivists on Mysticism: Epistemological Monomorphism vs. Duomorphism," *Philosophy East and West,* forthcoming 1989. See also, idem, "Constructivism in Zen Buddhism, Paramārtha and in Eckhart" Ph.D. diss., Columbia University, 1988, chap. 4.

    110. Such a fivefold set of stages is found frequently in the four *Nikāya.* This is from the *Mahasīhanādasutta* of the *Dīghanikāya,* 2.71.2–17. Translation in Paul J. Griffiths, *On Being Mindless: Buddhist Meditation and the Mind-Body Problem* (La Salle, Ill.: Open Court Press, 1986), p. 17.

    111. Griffiths calls them "altered states of consciousness."

    112. H. Gombrich, *Art and Illusion,* pp. 73–74.

    113. Hodson, *Deonise Hid Diuinite,* p. 3. [Emphasis added.]

    114. Isaac Newton, *Opticks,* 4th ed. (London: Innys, 1730). Quoted in Douglas Piggins and Douglas Morgan, "Perceptual Phenomena Resulting from Steady Visual Fixation and Repeated Auditory Input Under Experimental Condi-

tions and in Meditation," *Journal of Altered States of Consciousness* 3 (1977–1978), 199.

115. D. Troxler, *Opthalm Bibliotek,* vol. 2, ed. (Jena: von Himly and Schmidt, 1804); reference in F. J. J. Clarke, "A Study of Troxler's Effect," *Optica Acta* 7 (1960), 219–36. See also F. J. J. Clarke, "Rapid Light Adaptation of Localized Areas of the Extro-Foveal Retina," *Optica Acta* 4 (1957), pp. 69–77; J. E. Hochberg, W. Triebel, and G. Seaman, "Color Adaptation Under Conditions of Homogeneous Visual Stimulation (*Ganzfeld*)," *Journal of Expermental Psychology* 41 (1951), pp. 153–59.

116. R. M. Pritchard, "Stabilized Images on the Retina," *Scientific American,* 204 (June 1961), 72–78. R. W. Ditchburn and B. L. Ginsburg, "Vision with a Stabilised Image," *Nature* 170 (1952), pp. 36–37; L. A. Riggs, F. A. Ratcliff, J. C. Cornsweet, and T. N. Cornsweet, "The Disappearance of Steadily Fixated Visual Test Objects," *Journal of the Optical Society of America,* 43 (1953), 495–501.

117. W. Cohen, "Spatial and Textural Characteristics of the *Ganzfeld*," *American Journal of Psychology,* 70 (1957), pp. 403–10. W. Cohen and T. C. Caldwallader, "Cessation of Visual Experience" Under Prolonged Uniform Visual Stimulation," *American Psychologist* 13 (1958), 410 (abstract).

118. Claudio Naranjo and Robert Ornstein, *On the Psychology of Meditation,* (London: Penguin 1977), p. 166. It is interesting that the alpha EEG pattern, one common mark of meditative states, is found during this experience, indicating a physiological similarity between these two phenomena.

119. Ibid., pp. 142–69.

120. Piggins and Morgan, "Perceptual Phenomena Resulting from Steady Visual Fixation," pp. 197–203.

121. Naranjo and Ornstein, p. 161. They are here describing concentration meditation.

122. Walshe, vol. 2, pp. 272–73.

123. Ibid., vol. 2, p. 275.

124. Forman, "Constructivism in Zen Buddhism," chap. 4.

125. R. L. Franklin, "Experience and Interpretation in Mysticism" makes a similar point. (In the present volume.)

126. Stanley Schachter, *Emotion, Obesity and Crime* (New York: Academic Press, 1971). Stanley Schachter and Jerome Singer, "Cognitive, Social and Physiological Determinants of Emotional State," *Psychological Review* 69 (1962), 379–99.

127. Wayne Proudfoot, *Religious Experience* (Berkeley: University of California Press, 1985).

128. J. T. Farrow and J. R. Hebert, "Breath Suspension During the Transcendental Meditation Technique," *Psycholomatic Medicine* 44 (1982), 133–153.

Part I

THE EMPIRICAL INVESTIGATION

The Unseen Seer and the Field: Consciousness in Sāṃkhya and Yoga

CHRISTOPHER CHAPPLE

Two birds, fast-bound companions,
find the same tree for their perch.
the one eats sweet berry;
the other just looks on, not eating.
(*RG VEDA* I:164:20)

From the earliest text of Indian philosophy, the *Ṛg Veda*, comes an image that has profoundly influenced the Upanisads, the formal schools of Sāṃkhya and Yoga as well as epic and purāṇic literature. This image is a simple one: two birds in the same tree, one active, the other looking on. The identical passage quoted in the epigraph is repeated in the *Muṇḍaka Upaniṣad* (III:1:1) and the *Śvetāśvatara Upaniṣad* (4:6). At first glance, this verse might appear to be a direct reference to dualism: two diametrically opposed birds are portrayed; one bird eats, the other does nothing. However, the tree, the universal symbol of life, brings the two together, linking them for as long as the one bird looks on or for as long as the other bird is not satisfied. At any moment, either could fly away. Yet, in this tableau, both are present in proximity to one another. Does the eating bird know it is being watched? Probably not; no one likes to eat while another stares on. Is the onlooker truly interested in what transpires? Again, probably not; if so, then he himself would eat. Of the pair, the less familiar is the onlooker. It is easy for the reader of the text to identify with the eater of sweet berry; we all have done the same. But what does it mean to be a mere onlooker?

Herein is the departure for one major thread of Indian philosophical and religious thought, a thread that can be traced through the various texts and traditions just mentioned. In each of these there looms the presence of an anonymous witness who, by his or her mere silence and noninvolvement, is said to ultimately vivify and allow shape to be given to that which is human. The active bird represents a self involved and identified with the world; the inactive bird is that other mode of being human that neither claims nor rejects the world, remaining ever aloof and, hence, always free. In the *Bṛhadāraṇyaka Upaniṣad,* Uddālaka Āruṇi refers to what may be equated with the onlooking bird as "the unseen Seer, the unheard Hearer, the unthought Thinker, the un-understood Understander . . . the Self (*ātman*)," the Inner Controller (*antaryāmin*), the Immortal (*amṛta*)" (III:7:23). In contrast to this is the realm of activity, the bird that eats and enjoys, typologized in the *Bhagavad Gītā* as the field, spanning the "gross elements, the sense of I, the intellect, the unmanifest, the ten senses and one (mind), and the five sensory realms" (XIII:5). In the Sāṃkhya and Yoga schools of thought, both of these are seen as integral to being human, interacting and complementing one another until true knowledge of the seer is gained.

THE *SĀṂKHYA KĀRIKĀ*

The unseen seer and the field are the basis for the way of philosophy or seeing (*darśan*) known as Sāṃkhya, which, in turn, is the basis for the many practices outlined in the *Yoga Sūtra* of Patañjali. Although Sāṃkhya terminology pervades the *Śvetāśvatara* and *Maitri Upaniṣads* and is used extensively in the *Mahābhārata* and the Purāṇas, its formal expression is found in a different genre of literature, the *Sāṃkhya Kārikā* (*SK*) of Īśvarakṛṣṇa, probably written in the third century c.e. Unlike the picturesque Vedic and Upaniṣadic texts, the *Sāṃkhya Kārikā* is terse and precise—in the classical tradition of stringing together epigrammatic philosophical statements. The entire system is laid out in seventy-two short verses; in the analysis that follows, I will investigate the Sāṃkhyan position on consciousness, the nonconscious, and the relationship between the two, focusing on the key *tattvas* of *puruṣa, prakṛti,* and *buddhi.*

The first usage of a term equivalent to the English word conscious is found in negative form, when *prakṛti* (the realm of manifestation, the "seen") is said to be nonconscious (*acetana*). In this and other aspects, *puruṣa* (the seer) is said to be the opposite: other than the three constituents (*guṇas*) of *prakṛti* (i.e., not light, passionate, or dull), distinct, specific, conscious, and nonproductive (*SK* XI). Furthermore, the *puruṣa* is also said to be uncaused, infinite, all-pervasive, inactive, single, unsupported, nonemergent, not made of parts, and independent (*SK* X), which are qualities also used to describe *prakṛti* in her unmanifest form. A few passages later, Īśvarakṛṣṇa positively describes *puruṣa* as "witness, isolated, indifferent, spectator, inactive" (*SK* XIX), which may be translated more poetically as a "free, nonaligned witnessing, a state of nonreactive looking on." Owing to this characterization, *puruṣa* will be henceforth regarded as analogous with the English words "pure consciousness": it has been made clear that this is a consciousness that remains unattached to that which it is conscious of. Although *puruṣa* in other contexts refers to man or cosmic man (cf. the *Puruṣa Sūkta, Ṛg Veda* X:90), because of the inclusion of the terms "witness" ("*sākṣitva*") and "spectator" ("*draṣṭṛtva*") in the epigraph verse and the use of the word "*cetana*" (derived from the verbal root *cit*, meaning "to be conscious") in other verses (*SK* XX, XI, LV), it consistently is seen to signify a specialized mode of consciousness, a free, actionless witnessing.

Five proofs are given for the existence of *puruṣa*, listed by Īśvarakṛṣṇa as follows:

1. because aggregations exist for another
2. because this other must be different from the *guṇas*
3. because there must be an organizing power
4. because there does exist an enjoyer
5. because there is activity for the sake of (eventually leading to) liberation.

(*SK* XVIII)

The first four proofs are various ways of stating that in order for something to be perceived, there must be a seer; the last proof, as we will see, says that all activity takes place for the ultimate purpose of letting one know that one's true self is in no way linked to activity. It should also be noted that the text asserts the existence of multiple *puruṣas*, thus distinguishing Sāmkhya from the monistic thought of Vedānta. It is stated that plural *puruṣas* exist because of the multiplicity of births and deaths; each life requires its own organizing consciousness. Furthermore, each person operates in his or her own sphere of action and each exhibits different combinations of the three *guṇas* (see *SK* XVIII).

In its pure state, consciousness or *puruṣa* is unable to create anything of its own accord. It is only when *puruṣa* comes into association with the nonconscious *prakṛti* that the world is generated and consciousness becomes aware of things. This process is described in *Sāmkhya Kārikā* XXI, which likens the association (*saṃyoga*) of *puruṣa* and *prakṛti* to the teaming up of a blind man with a lame man. The blind man is like *prakṛti*, who can move but cannot see because she is nonconscious; the lame man is like *puruṣa*, who can see but cannot move. The joining of these two forces is to their mutual benefit; *puruṣa* is given something to see and *prakṛti* gains the perspective of consciousness that illumines all her wares.

After *saṃyoga*, the emergence of the manifest world takes place through the unfoldment of twenty-three other *tattvas* (literally, thatnesses), each of which is composed of varying degrees of three constituents or strands (*guṇas*): heaviness (*tamas*), passion (*rajas*), and lightness (*sattva*). The first *tattva* to emerge is intellect (*buddhi*), closely followed by sense-of-self (*ahaṃkāra*) and the perceptive vehicle, or mind (*manas*). These three are collectively referred to as the inner organ (*antaḥkaraṇa*); predominated by *sattva*, they determine how the rest of the world will be perceived.

Through the combined qualities of *sattva* and *rajas*, the five sense organs and the five organs of action are generated. These ten (eye, ear, nose, tongue, skin, voice, hands, feet, and the respective organs of reproduction and excretion) constitute the conditions necessary for human corporeality. Concurrently, *rajas* combines with *tamas* to bring out of *prakṛti* the five subtle elements (sound, touch, form, taste, smell), which are said to generate the five gross elements (space, wind, fire, water, earth). These twenty-three, like *prakṛti* herself, are nonconscious; the aggregate of them provides the subjectivity and objectivity essential for experience to be presented to consciousness. In an inversion of the Western Cartesian model, the "physical world" appears only after the basic constituents of mind and the sense and action organs have been formed.

The attainment of liberation in the Sāṃkhya system requires that one thoroughly comprehend the process of manifesting the world and gain the ability to reverse the process. The project of world production is the basic human condition—the three *guṇas* pervade all things and all personalities—but all of this is fundamentally nonconscious. Although everyone is conscious according to Sāṃkhya, few people know their own pure consciousness as distinct from the manifest and unmanifest forms of *prakṛti*. To achieve this goal Sāṃkhya examines how perception works, thereby giving clues as to how the world-generating process can be reversed and arrested, allowing pure consciousness to shine unimpaired.

The key to this liberating investigation is the *buddhi* (intellect), the first product to issue from *prakṛti* when she associates with *puruṣa*. According to the *Sāṃkhya Kārikā*, *buddhi* serves two functions, both as the conduit that allows the data collected by *prakṛti* to be presented to *puruṣa* (v.36) and as the vehicle for liberation (v.37). But let us examine its function as conduit first. Because of its elevated status, the *buddhi*, although a product of *prakṛti* and, hence, nonconscious, appears to be conscious: "From the association [of *puruṣa* and *prakṛti*], the nonconscious [bears] the mark of consciousness. Thus, in the movement of the *guṇas*, the indifferent one is as if active" (v.20). The *buddhi* is the venue for this confusion: being mistaken for *puruṣa*, it causes action to be attributed to the consciousness that in reality is forever inactive. When this happens, the world-spinning process begins. The sense-of-self (*ahaṃkāra*) mistakenly claims responsibility for, and authority over, all actions of consciousness, thus ignoring the fact that the person who says "I know" is merely a product of *prakṛti* and is incapable of knowing anything without consciousness. It becomes impossible to distinguish the pure, undefiled, neutral witness (*puruṣa*) from the "I-maker" (*ahaṃkāra*), the temporally bound aspect of *prakṛti* that laid claim to the manifest and mistakenly attributed consciousness to itself. Access to the world subsequently generated is limited to, and defined by, this all-pervasive, I-centered interpretation, which is subject to change and continually vascillating between experiences of, and identification with, pleasure and pain. Life thus lived—nonconsciously— is an unending repetition of bitter and sweet as long as the *buddhi* remains confused as to its authentic nature as nonconscious. Furthermore, the undisciplined *buddhi*, in addition to its fundamental confusion, is laden with the impressions of past action. These embedded inclinations determine the outlook and orientation of the sense-of-self (*ahaṃkāra*); this, in turn, influences the constitution of one's corporeality and thence the perception of the world. As long as the *buddhi* remain confused and sullied by the influence of previous *karma*, the world as generated leads to repeated pain and delusion. It is this automatic reponse conditioned by latent impressions that must be slowly dropped. Cognition rather than being reflexive and reflective of the past must enter into a nonreactive mode.

We have seen that *buddhi* is where things first go awry; it is also the locus wherein liberation may be brought about. *Buddhi* has the possibility of learning what it is not and thereby the capability of releasing *prakṛti* from her ignorance (v.37). Several verses in the *Sāṃkhya Kārikā* discuss *buddhi*, dividing this *tattva* into *bhāvas*, states of being that illustrate specific modes of action. Two grouping *bhāvas* are cited by Īśvarakṛṣṇa. The first, an eightfold analysis, outlines the means by which the intellect may be elevated to the point of being able to discriminate between the changes of *prakṛti* and the unchanging witness of *puruṣa;* this analysis will be examined in detail. The second grouping details fifty forms of delusion, including five types of ignorance, twenty-eight varieties of incapacity, nine illusory complacencies, and eight false perfections (see *SK* XLVII–LI).

The eight *bhāvas* fall into two syzygetic groups, one termed "sattvic," the other "tamasic." Virtue (*dharma*), knowledge (*jñāna*), nonattachment (*virāga*), and power (*aiśvarya*) constitute its sattvic aspect; the tamasic aspect is composed of four *bhāvas* opposite to those listed above: nonvirtue (*adharma*), ignorance (*ajñāna*), attachment (*rāga*), and weakness (*anaiśvarya*). These states of being pervade and shape the body—the lower consciousness—that is then generated, including one's sense-of-self, its corresponding effect on one's perception of the world, and the path of action pursued as a result. If the *buddhi* finds its predominant expression in inability to succeed (*anaiśvarya*), that person is said to be lazy and his or her attitude is most likely to be, "The world is against me"; thus, his or her actions would prove ineffectual. On the other hand, when vigor and positive thinking prevail, as would be the case for someone established in the power (*aiśvarya*) *bhāva,* success in action undoubtedly follows, even though such action would remain nonconscious action. Similarly, fixity in the attachment *bhāva* results in the constant pursuit of desire and inevitable periodic disappointment; nonattachment brings a state of contentment. Ignorance leads to continued bondage. Virtue allows one to ascend to happier states; nonvirtue results in descent into activities associated with lower states of existence (v.44). Each of these *bhāvas* further bind one to inauthentic consciousness, with one notable exception.

Now the *Sāṃkhya Kārikā* reverses its analysis to show how liberation may result. The formative impressions found in the seven *bhāvas* listed earlier are set aside by the predominance of discriminative knowledge (*jñāna*). Of the intellect's eight forms, knowledge holds the most elevated position, the key to liberation through which the distinctiveness of *puruṣa* from *prakṛti* is discerned. *Sāṃkhya Kārikā* states:

> It is by seven forms (of *bhāvas*)
> that *prakṛti* binds herself for herself.
> And indeed, for the sake of *puruṣa,*
> she frees herself by means of one (knowledge).
> (v.63)

Through the application of knowledge, cultivated and nurtured by contemplation on the process by which *prakṛti* creates the world and then mistakes an aspect of herself to be consciousness, the *puruṣa* is seen to have always been free of identity with the world of action. This state, which may be correlated with the descriptions of yogic *samādhi* (discussed later) is the culmination of Sāṃkhya. Hence, the experience of liberation is described by Īśvarakrṣṇa:

> Thus, from the analysis of the *tattvas*,
> arises the knowledge "I am not, nothing is mine,
> I do not exist." [This knowledge] is all-encompassing,
> free from error, pure, and final.
>
> (v.67)

The *buddhi* awakens to its mistake; the cultivation of knowledge results in the cessation of the conception of self which sets itself up as the candidate for suffering. All such action is seen to be merely a manifestation, a play of false consciousness and self-consciousness, taking place while *puruṣa*, one's authentic identity, remains eternally unaffected, unattached. At this juncture, consciousness has been purified. Rather than being mediated and adulterated by the flaw of self-reference, the world stands before one with the sediment of expectation and attachment having been removed. A pure state of awareness emerges, not in the sense that a self is aware of something pure, but in the sense that one is purely aware.

At this moment of release, *prakṛti* desists, no longer compelled to continue her dance. However, this experience does not necessarily cancel the possibility that *puruṣa* will ever again experience her; the hiatus from the dance will only be temporary, as indicated in *Sāṃkhya Kārikā:*

> The body, due to the force of past impressions,
> continues, like a potter's wheel.
>
> (v.68)

Not until death is an eternal and absolute isolation *(kaivalyam)* from *prakṛti* attained. However, action which previously had been claimed by the sense-of-self is now performed selflessly, without concern for doership or results.

The image of the potter's wheel, in addition to showing how life continues after knowledge is gained, also provides an excellent simile for understanding Sāṃkhya's philosophy of freedom through detachment in action, a way to be conscious in the midst of the nonconscious. A potter creates dishes, bowls, and other utensils for use in everyday life. The first task for the potter is to center all the elements and confine the clay on the rotating wheel. In order for this to take place, the mind has to be stilled. The hands do the work; if a thought enters such as, "I am going to make a perfect pot," the process is ruined and the pot is knocked off center. A steady detachment must be maintained: the action is performed but the doer does not claim its fruits. Sitting above the spinning wheel, distanced and yet intimately involved, the witness silently watches the pot grow and take shape. There is reciprocity between the stillness—the authentic consciousness—and the activity, the realm of manifestation, the unconscious pot that is being created. The two modes work together for the creation of a new order.

This skill in action, taken beyond the metaphor of the potter's wheel, liberates a person to move through life using what is needed but avoiding the pitfalls and broken dreams inherent in inauthentic consciousness. When the mind fills up with thoughts preoccupied with the sense-of-self, it becomes impossible to move unencumbered; when the mind is pacified it no longer inserts the artificial "I" barrier between the pure witness and the task at hand. Consciousness becomes authentic when I, me, or mine no longer intrudes. Self-conscious identity, the locus of ignorance, doubt, and discomfort, must be transcended in order for the silent, unseen witness to be realized.

We have briefly surveyed what in Sāṃkhya constitutes consciousness, the nonconscious, and the link between the two. Consciousness is *puruṣa*, the unmanifest witness, not *prakṛti* or any fabrication of her *guṇas*. The association of the two results in the emergence of *buddhi*, often translated as intellect. From *buddhi* then arises the *ahaṃkāra*, the sense of personal identity, which serves as the focal point for all data regarding the "outside" world. However, the ego only appears to be conscious because of ignorance. *Ahaṃkāra* claims to be conscious but, in fact, never is.

The question may be posed, is consciousness continuous with the cosmos? By "realizing" *puruṣa*, are all things known? Both ideas—cosmos and all things—denote structure, the universe, "reality." *Puruṣa* can take part in no such constructs: it has been defined as without parts, noncreative, inactive, and independent. Descriptions of *puruṣa* in Sāṃkhya, though not elsewhere (cf. *Ṛg Veda* X:90), are indisputably antistructure, acosmic. Only *prakṛti* is associated with creation or cosmos and at best she would be dubbed inauthentic consciousness. However, it is asserted that by gaining knowledge, by discriminating the difference between the seer and the seen, the highest human modality is attained, a way of seeing that cannot be paralleled or surpassed.

Modern scholarship has raised this question: Should the so-called Sāṃkhya evolutionary scheme be interpreted as a cosmogonic myth or is it illustrative of processes taking place within each individual? Dasgupta, as noted by Frank R. Podgorski and Erich Frauwallner, interpreting Sāṃkhya in light of the Purāṇas, have both seen the "*tattvas* as primarily the constitutive cosmological substructure underlying our universe; their interpretation resembles in some ways our modern scientific theories of subatomic particles" (Podgorski, p. 88). To the contrary, Podgorski agrees with Gerald J. Larson, who writes that in Sāṃkhya "the world is not understood in itself apart from the fact of human existence. In a sense, then, the world is uniquely human" (Larson, p. 135). I would like to add that cosmological explanations are simply irrelevant to the Sāṃkhyan thrust: questions about the origins of things can only be asked or answered by a limited sense of self (*ahaṃkāra*) and, hence, are outside the domain of what Sāṃkhya considers to be true knowledge.

A further question might be raised: Can consciousness be utilized for liberation? By definition, consciousness cannot *do* anything and hence cannot advance one to liberation. Discriminative knowledge is said to be the only vehicle by which liberations are attained, but it is a knowledge that paradoxically reveals the fact that consciousness can never be bound. "No one is bound, no one is released . . . only *prakṛti* in its various forms is bound, and released" (*SK* LXII). It is only the nonconscious that strives for release, and this release comes about only when all effort, all show, all dance cease, as articulated in this verse, "Just as a dancer stops dancing after having been seen by the audience, so does *prakṛti* cease after having exhibited herself to *puruṣa*" (*SK* LIX). It is when one becomes aware of the bondage that keeps one active that one can begin the process of reversal. The *Maitri Upaniṣad* articulates this dilemma, dialectically implying the solution:

> Now, because of being overcome,
> he goes to confusedness,
> he sees not the blessed Lord,
> the causer of action
> who stands within oneself.
> Borne along and defiled by the stream of *guṇas*,
> unsteady, wavering, bewildered, full of desire,
> distracted, this one goes to the state of self-conceit.
> In thinking "This is I" and "That is mine,"
> he binds himself with his self,
> as a bird does with a snare.
>
> (3:2)

The telos of Sāṃkhya is found in the opposite, when the liberated one proclaims, "I am not, nothing is mine, I do not exist." All confusion, unsteadiness, desire, and self-conceit have been dissolved, resulting in purification and liberation.

THE *YOGA SŪTRA*

The Sāṃkhya system as articulated by Īśvarakṛṣṇa is closely linked to the yoga philosophy of Patañjali, as given in the *Yoga Sūtra* (45) (ca. 200 C.E.) Both speak of the seer and the seen; both stress suffering as the reason to seek release from bondage. However, whereas the former focuses exclusively on the cultivation of knowledge as the means to liberation, yoga, while not denying the efficacy of knowledge, advances several ancillary techniques to help bring about what it, like Sāṃkhya, describes as isolation, (*kaivalyam*), the nonmistaking of the seen for the seer. The practices of yoga are myriad and, as Frauwallner has remarked, "The *Yoga Sūtra* of Patañjali is composed of different constituents or elements which in no way give a uniform, homogeneous picture" (Frauwallner, p. 335). However, despite the variegated array of paths described in the text, the references to pure consciousness (*draṣṭṛ* [seer]) are consistent both within the *sūtras* and with the Sāṃkhya system.

In the second of Patañjali's *sūtras*, we find what may be considered the definition of yoga: yoga is the suppression of fluctuations in the mind (*yogaścitta–vṛtti–nirodhaḥ,* YS I:2). In order to understand this epigrammatic rendering of yoga, it is necessary to first explicate the nature of that which yoga is not: the fluctuations (*vṛtti*) of the mind (*citta*), the process of grasping and appropriating the world of objects.

The term "*citta,*" variously translated as mind, mind-complex, consciousness, or thinking principle, is central to the yoga system. Like the Sāṃkhyan term "*cetana,*" it is derived from the verbal root *cit,* but whereas *cetana* implied a purified form of consciousness, the *citta* is assumed within yoga to initially be impure. The *citta* is regarded as the vehicle for perception wherein the contents of experience take form for presentation to the seer. It is also the receptacle for the effects of *karma,* the residue (*saṃskāra or vāsanā*) left by past activity that conditions future actions. The function of the *citta* is instrumental; in a sense, it is like a computer ready to be programmed. It takes coloration with the arising of each fluctuation (*vṛtti*), a wave that pervades the *citta* in the form of various perceptions, thoughts, emotions, and so forth.

Five fluctuations are listed and described in the first section of the *Yoga Sūtra* (I:5–11). In valid cognition (*pramāṇa*), objects are perceived: such cognition is any experience wherein *prakṛti* finds full manifestation in one or more of the gross elements. Such experience is verified by means of three avenues: perception, inference, or a credible verbal account (*pratyakṣa, anumāna, āgama*). Any perception of plants, animals, automobiles, buildings, clothing, oceans, and so on, or any inference or testimony of any such object is typologized as belonging to the first class of fluctuation. Such "things" are, metaphorically speaking, no more than a ripple (*vṛtti*) in the field that allows for the perception of objectivity (*citta*). The second class or fluctuation is error (*viparyaya*), considered to be a misguided ripple, one that does not correspond to reality. The third, imagination (*vikalpa*), involves a notion, not necessarily an error, that does not correspond to an object but may, in fact, serve a useful function. Examples would be metaphor and simile in poetry. In states of meditation, the engagement of imagination is considered important to strengthen the mind. In the fourth fluctuation, sleep (*nidrā*), one thought predominates to the exclusion of all others, perhaps analogous to a brain scan wherein sleep is registered as a distinct, uniform wave pattern. Memory (*smṛti*), the fifth fluctuation listed, operates exclusively on the level of the inner organ (intellect, sense-of-self, and mind) when the contents of a previous experience are returned to consciousness through thought, although there is no longer any corresponding structure on the gross level. The five fluctuations of valid cognition, error, imagination, sleep, and memory represent five discrete moments, five aspects of reality that account for nearly all human experience. Each, as listed in the system, is a mechanical operation. This analysis, which explains the scope of awareness-with-content, is not unlike the account of states of consciousness that might be given in psychology. However, modern psychology (with the notable exception of the transpersonal movement) limits itself to seeing that the operations of these five modes are socially acceptable. For the yogi, the goal is to transcend all five by entering the state of *citta–vṛtti–nirodha*. Hence, by definition, the practitioner of meditation is entering into a state of being that cannot be described in the same way one would describe conventional sensory or mental experience.

The *citta–vṛtti* analysis summarizes the normal range of human functioning, encompassing three modes of conventional transactions: things (as registered in *pramāṇa*), thoughts (in *pramāṇa*, *viparyaya*, *vikalpa*, and *smṛti*), and sleep (*nidrā*). Each of these states is linked directly to a subjective appropriator, an "I" that claims experience. In *Yoga Sūtra* IV:4, it is stated that "states of awareness (in particularized form) arise from the sense-of-I (*asmitā*) exclusively." That is, the perceptions of discrete objects or thoughts as described in the *citta–vṛtti* complex arise from the sense-of-self (*ahaṃkāra*). In such a state the "higher" self, the noncreative witness (*draṣṭṛ*), is forgotten; the *ahaṃkāra* grabs the experience, thinking it to be its own. The unseen seer is blended into the seen; the impure is taken for the pure, the nonself is taken for the self (*YS* II:5–6). The result is evolution, the emergence of the *that*, the reification and solidification of the world in the form of fluctuations. This movement, the perception of things, thoughts, or sleep as appropriated by the sense-of-self and, therefore, separate from it, constitutes conventional experience. If one's world is limited to consciousness of things, life is spent in the unending generation of essentially the same patterns, like the bar in a ripple tank, continuously emanating a surface of interfering waves, with the still water, the bearer of other possibilities, forgotten.

Citta–vṛtti is by nature fraught with the causes of affliction (kleśa), rooted in ignorance (avidyā), and characterized as impermanent, impure, and painful (anitya, aśuci, duḥkha) (YS II:5). The text states, "To the one who possesses discrimination, all is pain" (YS II:15).

However, yoga does not stop with existential despair; we are not condemned to eternally generate the same painful wave patterns. As with Sāṃkhya and Buddhism, the purpose of yoga is the cessation of pain effected by states of suppression (nirodha) of the wave-generated habituations. This suppression, which is defined as yoga, takes many forms. The wide range of methods indicates an emphasis on the ongoing application of yogic techniques, not a deadening of the mental faculties that merely leaves one in a stupor. But it is important that yoga not be construed as therapy in the psychological sense of the word. Rather than being a method of behavior modification, it is way of undoing the inclination to do any compulsive behavior whatsoever. The radical nature of suppression (nirodha) cannot be overemphasized.

The first method mentioned by Patañjali is composed of practice and dispassion (abhyāsa and vairāgya YS I:12–16), which transform randomly held vṛttis into responsible intentions (pratyaya), thus inducing a "working state" of nirodha. Another method is to apply faith, energy, mindfulness, concentration, and wisdom (śraddhā, vīrya, smṛti, samādhi, prajñā, YS I:12–16), a practice parallel to the Brahma Vihara in Buddhism. Yet another is to dedicate one's meditation to the primal teacher, īśvara, who remains untainted by the ravages of change inflicted by association with prakṛti (I:23–32; II:1, 32, 45). Appropriate behavior in interpersonal relationships is seen to be another tool for achieving yoga: Yoga Sūtra I:33 states, "One should cultivate friendship with the joyful, compassion for the sorrowful, gladness for those who are virtuous, and equanimity in regard to the nonvirtuous; through this, the mind is pacified." In gaining control over the breath, the yogin masters the senses, including the thinking process (YS I:34; II:49–53). Other practices in the first section of the text include directing one's consciousness to one who has conquered attachment, or meditating on an auspicious dream experience, or centering the mind in activity, or cultivating thoughts that are sorrowless and illuminating, or by any other means, as desired (YS I:35–39). Each of these practices serve to help quiet the fluctuations of conditioned consciousness.

The second section (*pāda*) of the *Yoga Sūtra* outlines two main forms of practice, each designed to achieve the same goal, each containing multiple aspects. The first, *Kriyā Yoga*, involves austerity, self-study, and dedication, with the express purpose of uprooting the influence of impurity (*kleśa*) (*YS* II:1–27). The second, *Aṣṭaṅga Yoga*, contains the well-known eight limbs of yoga, each of which may be considered a distinct form of practice: abstinences (*yama*), observances (*niyama*), postures (*āsana*), breath control (*prāṇāyāma*), nonattachment (*pratyahara*), concentration (*dhāraṇā*), meditation (*dhyāna*), and unitive attention, or absorption (*samādhi*) (*YS* II:28–III:3). The last three stages constitute "inner yoga" and are referred to collectively as *saṃyama* (*YS* III:4), a process that dissolves the separation between the seer and the field that arises owing to the mistaken notions of the *ahaṃkāra*. The most intriguing of the three is *samādhi*, said to involve "the shining forth of the intended object alone, as if empty of own form" (*YS* III:3). In this state the interpretive obscurations that dictate sedimented experience are dissolved, thus rendering the experience ineffable, "empty of own-form" (*svarūpa-śūnya*), an experience described as shining or luminous (*nirbhāṣa*).

In the first section of the *Yoga Sūtra*, appropriately titled the *Samādhi Pāda*, Patañjali outlines a progression of levels of *samādhi*. In the beginning stages, one uses thought (*vitarka*) and reflections (*vicāra*) to enhance the concentration process. Then one leaves these behind, entering into states free of thought and reflection. When the higher forms of concentration are achieved, the world of manifestation is called back to its source through a process known as *pratiprasava*. The configuration of the gross elements are seen to rely on one's perceptions of them; one's perceptions are seen to be determined by one's thoughts and attitudes, which, in turn, are seen to be activities due to impurities in the intellect (*buddhi*). When discriminative knowledge (*jñāna*) arises, the fluctuations of the mind (*citta vrtti*) cease and *prakṛti* is held in abeyance. The practitioner is ready for the state of pure consciousness:

> The accomplished one of diminished fluctuations,
> like a clear jewel assuming the color of a
> near object, has unity among the grasper,
> the grasping, and the grasped.
>
> (*YS* I:41)

Through the application of states of *samādhi*, the effects of past action are obstructed (*YS* I:50). The yogin arrests the tendency to generate and be captivated by the manifest world that is seen as separate from himself or herself. Ultimately, the state of seedless (*nirbīja*) or objectless (*asampraj-ñatā*) *samādhi* is achieved, which burns out all afflicted influences from the past and brings about the total suppression of mind's fluctuations.

To better understand this culminating phase of yoga we need to examine its descriptions in the later sections of the *Yoga Sūtra*. The third *pāda* describes how the practice of inner yoga allows one to gain control over the way in which the world is construed. Through *samyama,* the subtle body experiences various abilities, from learning the history of one's past actions to obtainment of a beautiful and robust body (see *YS* III:18–48). These are seen as merely preparatory to the cultivation of discriminative discernment, the type of knowledge that secures liberation:

> Of the one who has the pure discernment between *sattva*
>   (the most subtle aspect of the world of emergence)
>   and *puruṣa* (the nonemergent pure seer)
>   there is sovereignty over all and
>   knowledge of all.
>
> (YS III:49)

However, even this falls short of the goal because it, too, can be a coveted experience. Hence, the final phase is described as being disinterested even in knowledge:

> From dispassion even toward this,
> and from the destruction of the seed
> of this impediment, arises *kaivalyam*.
> (YS III:50)

This final attainment, referred to as *kaivalyam* (pure aloneness), is of special interest for the present study. Its correlate in the first book is seedless absorption (*nirbīja samādhi*). In this state all is said to be halted (*sarva nirodha*): the world generating process of *citta–vṛtti* stops (*YS* I:51). The second book refers explicitly to *kaivalaym*. It restates the goal of liberation as it is given in the *Sāmkhya Kārikā:* the reason for the seen is the seer (*YS* II:22). One misperceives oneself as the owner of experience owing to ignorance (*YS* II:22–23); when this mistaken notion ends, liberation takes place, defined as "isolation from the seen" (*tad-drseh kaival-yam, YS* II:25). When one transcends objectifying consciousness, *kaival-yam,* a moment of pure freedom ensues.

Three terms appear in the final *pāda,* aptly named *kaivalyam,* which characterize the attainment of yoga: *kaivalyam, dharma-megha,* and *citi-śakti.* The first has been used in the two earlier sections of this discussion, and it is clearly referring to the state wherein the seer shines forth, convinced of his or her independence, not subject in any way to the seductive wiles of *prakṛti*. *Kaivalyam,* often translated as isolation, can also be seen as singleness, oneness, aloneness. This carries a sense of fulfillment, an absence of the need to look outward to confirm one's position in the world of circumstance. As such, this term can be seen as describing a moment of mystical fulfillment.

The term *dharma-megha* appears only once, but the image it projects is powerful. In this state all debts have been paid (*prasaṃkhyāne*); there is no concern for gain (*akusīdasya*). It is said to proceed from discriminative discernment (*viveka khyāti*), a reference to the power of seeing the difference between the one who sees and the one who is mistaken for the seer. And it is referred to as a *samādhi* (*YS* IV:29). Furthermore, it is said in this *sūtra* that action of a special nature ensues from it: "From that, there is the cessation of afflicted action" (*YS* IV:30). The usage and implications of the term "*dharma-megha*" indicate that the yogin, having penetrated and obliterated his former, limited *dharma,* now takes on a *dharma* as unlimited as the clouds, what then proceeds is a cloud of righteousness.

Citi-śakti, the third word used in the fourth section to denote the status of the yogin, emphasizes the purity and power of the mystical experience. The word "*citi*" appears twice, the first time in explanation of how higher awareness (*citi*) at times does not become dissolved into *prakṛti*. This occurs in *samādhi* when the intellect (*buddhi*) takes the form of the perceived object (*YS* IV:22). The implication here is that a purified state has been entered into; no "lower self" or *ahaṃkāra* is claiming the experience. This ability is then more fully amplified in the final passage of the *Yoga Sūtra:*

> *Kaivalyam* is the calling back of the *guṇas,*
> which have been emptied of their purpose
> (of performing) for *puruṣa.*
> Then there is steadfastness
> in the own-form (of the seer):
> the power of pure consciousness (*citi-śakti*).
> (*YS* IV:34)

Thus defined, *kaivalyam* is not isolation in the sense of a shuttered retreat from the world. Rather, it is a way of being in the world without falling into the trap of considering oneself different from what is seen: a moment of pure consciousness takes place wherein the seer does not become enmeshed in *prakṛti*.

In states of conventional consciousness, the "I" (*ahaṃkāra*) thinks it is the seer. When it is revealed that "I am not the seer" (cf. *SK* LXIV, "I do not exist, nothing is mine, I am not") a perception of the distinction of seer from seen arises (*viveka khyāti*). This breaks down the theoretical self (ahaṃkāra) that stood apart from the object. In samādhi, when the "I" no longer appropriates experience, there arises the consubstantiation of seer, seeing, and seen, a purified, clarified form of consciousness, a state of unitive attention. In the thirteenth chapter of the Bhagavad Gītā (BG), the one who sees the field (prakṛti: citta–vṛtti, ahaṃkāra) as distinct from the knower of the field (puruṣa) is called wise. Krishna advises Arjuna, "He who sees himself not to be the doer, he sees indeed" (BG XIII:29). When the seer is perceived as distinct from the "I" that claims, the yogin then loses interest in the generation of compulsive citta–vṛttis; in a sense there is no longer anyone home to collect the interest (cf. SK LXVI). Nothing is claimed by the "I." With this movement, the sediment of prior conditioning (saṃskāra) is cleared away; objects "shine forth; devoid of inherent, defined form (svarūpa-śūnya); the consciousness-of or "I versus that" consciousness has retreated; pure witnessing takes place. In this state of pure consciousness, attention cannot be separated from the intended: awareness is both subject-free (anahaṃvādi) and object-free (nirvastuka). Yoga may thus be defined not as a union of an appropriating self with objects—even religious objects—nor as a Cartesian separation of the thinker from the thought, but rather as a moment in which there is the nonseparation of knower, knowing, and known. The point of yoga is to have direct access to the intended world without the interference of impure residues; the world, hence, becomes the occasion for mystical experience. Yoga seeks to sever projects (present from a time without beginning) that obscure the direct perception of the seer. The technique is almost shamanistic: the yogi excises a part of his corpus of being—citta–vṛtti—so that the unseen seer, the witness, the power of citi-śakti, may be known.

In summary, the Sāṃkhya and Yoga schools advance as their telos the cultivation of a specialized state of consciousness that implicitly presupposes the ability of human consciousness to transcend its defiled limitations. In the process of collapsing the distinctions among seer, seeing, and seen, a mystical, undetermined, unconditioned moment of consciousness takes place, free of content. This consciousness, in which the seer is unseen and, hence, both unspeaking and unutterable, is a pure state of witnessing, referred to in some Hindu literature as sākṣin. The Sāṃkhya Kārikā, as stated earlier, describes this consciousness as a "free, non-aligned witnessing, a state of nonreactive looking on." This mode of being is brought about in Sāṃkhya through the cultivation of knowledge (jñāna) of one's essential noninvolvement with the world of change. In yoga it is brought about by numerous means (sādhana) that still the mind. These states of restraint (nirodha) culminate in a state known as *asamprajñatā samādhi,* a moment wherein there is no distinction between subject and object and, hence, no attachment to the subtle sense of sense (*ahaṃkāra*) or to the gross realm of manifestation.

POSTSCRIPT

Through the meditation techniques of Buddhism and various practices of Jainism, Yoga has shown itself to be a pan-Asian phenomenon not necessarily limited to the limitations of the Sāṃkhyan metaphysic. More recently, yogic techniques have been used to enhance Christian meditation. The work of Mircea Eliade, Dasgupta, and others has shown that Yoga is not bound to a fixed theology or a fixed body of images; it is used ultimately to empty one of all images. Yoga, as a system of applied mysticism, is a kenotic tool for undoing dualistic consciousness. Rather than being bound to one particular cultural form, it demonstrates how all cultural forms and expectations, including that of the limited self, can be transcended. The result is the quiet emergence of the unseen seer, the one one who looks on, the presence of unspeaking, unspeakable consciousness. For the yogin, the Sāṃkhyan, the Buddhist, and even the Jaina, it is this unspeaking mode that is held to be sacred, a mode that is beyond even the conditioning from when it was born.

To define these decidedly orthopractic traditions in light of their stated theologies without giving due attention to the methods without which the theology would be inoperative is to commit a grave hermeneutical error. In looking at the evidence from Buddhism, we see that the no-self teaching, which is an experience embodied by the five hundred arhants who gained enlightenment during the lifetime of the Buddha, involves the same practical assertion that is found in Sāṃkhya; "I am not this, this is not the self of me." Such a statement can only be uttered by one who has uprooted notions of self, as we have seen in both Sāṃkhya and Yoga. In all three instances, no positive theological statement is proffered. Likewise, in Jainism any possible theological position is relativized and, hence, circumvented with the careful sevenfold dismantling of the possibility of holding any statement as factual. The goal of perfect, detached isolation (*kevala*), the telos of Jainism, where one observes all reality from the highest of mountaintops, again underscores the pan-Indian emphasis on the supremacy of purified consciousness.

Metaphysical or theological descriptions are explicitly exposed as inherently flawed in each of the traditions mentioned here, Yoga and Sāṃkhya in detail, Buddhism and Jainism in passing. To arrive at the characterizations of these traditions based on terms such as *ātman* and *anātman* is misleading without closely examing how these terms function in the context of practice. A Buddhist or yogi practices meditation to purify his or her consciousness, not in pursuit of an object-oriented attainment that can be conveyed in terms of either self or no-self. It is made clear from the onset in each of these traditions that the knowledge to be gained is not analagous to any sort of conventional knowledge. What is attempted here is to attain a purified consciousness that is beyond characterization. In the literal sense, the descriptions of *samādhi* in Yoga and of *kaivalyam* in Sāṃkhya ultimately allow for the substantial existence of neither the objective, sensorial world nor for a locus of self-reference. In this place beyond words, there is no content to speak of, no consciousness that stands apart, no seer to be seen, but only pure seeing. The witnessing that results is beyond form; it is a truly sacred form of consciousness that has been purified of any bifurcating tendencies.

REFERENCES

The translations are those of the author, with the exception of passages cited from the Upaniṣads, which were taken from *The Thirteen Principal Upanishads* by Robert Ernest Hume.

Frauwallner, Erich. *History of Indian Philosophy*, vol. 1. Translated by V. M. Bedekar. Delhi: Motilal Banarsidass, 1973.

Hume, Robert Ernest. *The Thirteen Principal Upanishads*. London: Oxford University Press, 1931.

Larson, Gerald J. *Classical Sāṃkhya*. Delhi: Motilal Banarsidass, 1979.

Podgorski, Frank R. *Ego: Revealer/Concealer, a Key to Yoga*. Lanham, Md. University Press of America, 1984.

Pure Consciousness
and Indian Buddhism

PAUL J. GRIFFITHS

§1 THEORETICAL CONSIDERATIONS

There has been a good deal of discussion in the philosophical journals recently about the possibility of a special type of consciousness.[1] This special kind of consciousness is called, variously, pure consciousness, unmediated consciousness, contentless consciousness, and so forth. Much of the debate has taken place in response to Steven Katz's attempt to show that such consciousness—which he calls pure unmediated experience (1978:26)—neither logically can nor as a matter of fact does occur. The debate has been concerned mostly with two questions: (1) Is such consciousness logically possible? In other words, Is the concept self-contradictory or can it easily be shown to issue in a contradiction? (2) Do reports of such consciousness occur, and, if they do, can such reports properly be taken as evidence for the occurrence of the type of consciousness in question?

The participants in these debates have considered such questions important because their answers are taken to be intimately linked with the issue of the nature and transcultural similarities, or lack of such, among

I am grateful to Robert Forman for stimulating editorial comments on an earlier version of this paper.

instances of (what is often called) mystical experience. Briefly, the question is often seen to be important for something like the following reasons. If pure consciousness is both (logically) possible and (actually) instanced, then we (may) have access to examples of consciousness events which are unconditioned by any contingent local factors (cultural, conceptual, linguistic, or other) and which are also (as a matter of fact) recommended by religious virtuosi from all cultures. And if this is true, then the idea that there is a *philosophia perennis,* a set of propositions assented to by religious virtuosi from all cultures, may be grounded experientially. If, on the other hand, there occur only historically and socially conditioned experiences, experiences irredeemably shaped by their conceptual and psychological setting, then the idea that there is a *philosophia perennis* seems to be conceptually on all fours with such intellectual pacifiers as the Hegelian dialectical principle or the Buddhist concept of *upāyakauśalya:* pleasant to suck on but not very nourishing.

I do not intend to enter into the byways to this theoretical discussion here, partly because I consider much of it to be confused; partly because my purpose in this essay is primarily to set forth some of the more important Indian Buddhist perspectives on the nature of consciousness and its potentials. But it seems impossible to avoid offering some theoretical comments to begin with, for without them the enterprise of interpreting the Indian texts from which I shall draw my material would prove difficult if not impossible.

First, then, terminology: the terminology I shall use is designed to reflect (some of) the concepts used by Indian Buddhist intellectuals. I shall speak of mental events and shall intend by that usage any event which is not physical. I shall not attempt to state what differentiates mental events from physical ones; thus, this definition is merely formal. In speaking of mental events, I have in mind the Sanskrit compound *cittacaittāḥ* (often translated, mind and mental concomitants). I shall also speak of the *phenomenological attributes* of mental events, by which I shall mean simply those attributes (or properties, or qualities) which are accessible to phenomenological analysis and which make it possible to classify any particular mental event as being of a particular *kind.* Finally, I shall speak of the 'content' of any particular mental event, by which I shall mean that which individuates it from other members of its class (perhaps the closest Sanskrit analogue here is *ākāra,* best translated as 'mode of appearance' and semantically very close to what I mean by "content"). Consider an instance of ordinary visual sense-perception, say seeing a tree. This is a mental event. Its chief phenomenological attribute is that it belongs to the class of visual presentations (I have in mind here both Franz Brentano's

Vorstellung and the Sanskrit *vijñapti*). This is a descriptive statement that could, of course, be elaborated by stating in detail what the phenomenological attributes of visual presentations are and what distinguishes them from, say, olfactory presentations or conative presentations, but for the moment this brief statement will suffice. The *content* of the mental event in question, then, will be "tree-presentation": this, together with appropriate temporal and causal specifications (i.e., occurring at time *T* in continuum *C*) will serve to individuate the mental event in question from other members of its class. Of course, a much richer description of its content could be given: one could include "brown-trunk-presentation," "green-leaf-presentation," and the like.

It should be clear that the division between phenomenological attributes and content is of heuristic value only. The dividing line between the two concepts cannot be sharply drawn, but the division will prove useful in what follows.

To talk of the phenomenological attributes of mental events in this manner, describing them solely in terms of complex presentations belonging to certain kinds or classes, is intended to leave open the possibility that mental events may have both phenomenological attributes and content without necessarily having a subject–object structure. The need to preserve this distinction (between the phenomenological attributes and content of a mental event, on the one hand, and its structure, on the other) also explains why I prefer not to use the intentionality language that has been so important in Western theorizing about the mental since Brentano. Brentano claims that every mental event is intentional in the following sense:

> Every mental phenomenon is characterized by . . . reference to a content, direction upon an object . . . every mental phenomenon includes something as an object within itself, although they do not all do so in the same way. In presentation something is presented, in judgement something is affirmed or denied, in love loved, in hate hated, in desire desired and so on . . . we can, therefore, define mental phenomena by saying that they are those phenomena which contain an object intentionally within themselves.
> (1973:88–89)

Brentano goes on to argue this position, a position which differentiates any mental event from that which it intends, even for such apparently nonintentional experiences as pain. It sounds (linguistically) odd to ask what the intentional object of a pain-experience is; we don't ask what we are having a pain *of* in the same way that we ask what we are thinking *of* or what is the object *of* our lust. But Brentano makes the argument by suggesting that even in the case of pain-experience the intentional object of the experience is a "presentation of a definite spatial location which we usually characterize in relation to some visible and touchable part of our body" (1973:82–83). The idea seems to be that the intentional object of a pain-experience must necessarily be a spatiotemporally located presentation; thus, even here the object-directed structure of the mental event in question is preserved.

This thesis is objectionable, at least on some readings of it, from a Buddhist viewpoint (and from many others), largely because the way in which Brentano states it seems to separate mental events too sharply from their intentional objects (as he puts it)—or from their phenomenological attributes and content (as I would rather put it). Brentano's formulation raises the question of what ontological status the intentional objects of mental events have (and with it the specter of psychologism) and seems to prejudge the (purely phenomenological) question of whether, in fact, mental events always do have a dualistic subject–object structure. He also does not seem to allow for the possibility that mental events may be exhaustively described by describing their phenomenological attributes and content. Brentano's language is not well adapted to a discussion of the Buddhist event-based ontology of discrete processes.

Brentano's intentionality thesis has, since Chisholm's (1957) work on perceiving, been given new life by restating it in linguistic form and by applying it as a criterion to distinguish sentences that are about the physical from those that are about the mental. This is a complex subject and not one that I can enter into here; the point to notice is that intentional *sentences* (as distinct from Brentano's intentional *mental events*) typically have the form *S Fs Y*, where *S* represents some subject, *Y* some object, and *F* some predicate, of which verbs such as thinks, hopes, believes, and perceives are paradigmatic examples. So, *"The Buddha assents to the proposition that all things are impermanent"* would be an instance of a complex intentional sentence. To recast such intentional sentences so that they represent the phenomenological attributes of a mental event without assuming that such attributes necessarily include the subject-predicate-object structure expressed in *S Fs Y* requires some thought, but in the example given something like the following would result: *"There occurs, in a particular mental continuum, an event whose attribute is assent and whose content is the proposition that all things are impermanent."* The subject drops out, and the abstract form of the resultant sentence is, "There occurs a mental event with attribute *F* and content *C*." In the case of a straightforward intentional sentence expressing sense-perception (say, *Amy sees the black cat"*), the rendering *there occurs in the mental continuum conventionally labeled "Amy," a mental event whose attribute is visual presentation and whose content is black cat* seems appropriate (if clumsy). The important distinctions in this rendering are not those among subject, predicate, and object but rather those among event, (phenomenological) attribute(s), and content. The claim is, as I shall try to show when I come to discuss the (largely Yogācāra Buddhist) idea of *nirvikalpajñāna* (unconstructed awareness) that the latter rendering is more adequate to certain possible kinds of experience and, moreover, that it reflects a different phenomenology. That is, the kind of experience adequately represented by a standard subject-predicate-object intentional sentence is, it is claimed, phenomenologically different from the kind adequately represented by an event-attribute-content sentence.

Bearing these theoretical and terminological considerations in mind, I shall now try to make some distinctions between various forms of the thesis that was briefly discussed at the beginning of this essay, the thesis that pure consciousness and the like is a genuine possibility. I shall distinguish three different theses: the *pure consciousness thesis* (PCT), the *unmediated consciousness thesis,* and the *nondualistic consciousness thesis.* First, the PCT. A proponent of this view will adhere to (at least) the following proposition:

(1) It is logically possible that there occur a mental event with no phenomenological attributes and no content

Further, a proponent of PCT will usually hold that such mental events occur as a matter of fact, that they occur in all cultures, and that they are identical with some form of mystical experience. To illustrate that some persons do hold this thesis I shall cite a recent description of it:

I had been meditating alone in my room all morning when someone knocked on my door. I heard the knock perfectly clearly, and upon hearing it I knew that, although there was no "waking up" before hearing the knock, for some indeterminate length of time prior to the knocking I had not been aware of anything in particular. I had been awake but with no content for my consciousness . . . the experience was . . . utterly without content.
(Forman 1986:55)

There seems to be certain logical problems with such an account. If the pure consciousness event in question really has no content and no phenomenological attributes, it is hard to see how its subject can, at a later time, know that it was different from the unconsciousness of dreamless sleep. Presumably, a postulated pure consciousness event cannot be phenomenologically distinct from dreamless sleep, for, if it is, it has at least the phenomenological attribute of being differentiable from dreamless sleep and is, thus, not strictly a pure consciousness event. Perhaps this problem may be avoided by differentiating a pure consciousness event from dreamless sleep (or other unconscious states) not in terms of phenomenological attributes or content, but rather in terms of causal powers.[2] It may also be the case that (at least) some proponents of PCT wish to assert only that pure consciousness has no *content,* not that it has no phenomenological attributes. This way of putting the matter (although it would need a good deal of fine-tuning which I do not propose to give it) might possibly allow pure consciousness events to be phenomenologically distinguished from other mental events which are characterized by insensibility (trance, dreamless sleep, etc.). However, whatever the merits of PCT (and it is my purpose at this stage only to state it, not to support or refute it), it has many supporters and is one of the theses for which I shall try to find support in Indian Buddhist material.

The second thesis to be defined is the *unmediated consciousness thesis.* This also has many forms, the one I expound will be based largely on what Steven Katz (1978; 1983) and Anthony Perovich, Jr. (1985a; 1985b) have said about it. Katz opposes the idea that there can be any unmediated experience. By this he seems to mean two quite different things. The first has to do with the necessary conditions for the occurrence of any (so-called) mystical experience (and perhaps, though this is somewhat less clear, for any experience at all). Katz suggests that the occurrence of any (mystical) experience to any subject at any time requires the possession by that subject at that time of a specifiable conceptual scheme. Crudely put, you just cannot have certain experiences unless you have the appropriate equipment (conceptual, religious, sociocultural, and the like) to make them possible. This thesis seems, though not obviously universally true, at least intuitively plausible. But it is often combined with a second thesis (and may be so combined by Katz, though he is not entirely clear on this) which has rather less initial plausibility. This second thesis states that the phenomenological attributes and content of any (mystical) experience occurring to any subject at any time are constituted by, and inevitably reflect the content of, the conceptual scheme possessed by that subject— a conceptual scheme which, remember, is a necessary condition for the occurrence of that experience in the first place. The adherent of the unmediated consciousness thesis will, of course, reject (at least) this second thesis, even if he or she accepts the former and will thus assert:

(2) For any experience (E), subject (S), time (T), and conceptual scheme (CS), it is possible that S's possession of CS at T-minus 1 be a necessary condition

for the occurrence to *S* of *E* at *T* without *E*'s phenomenological attributes or content reflecting any element of *CS*.

I take it that Perovich (1985b:181ff.) would assent to (2), as also probably would Forman. I find myself inclined to do so as well. It seems not hard to find examples of experience which fulfill the requirements of (2). Let us imagine a believer in voodoo whose conceptual scheme includes the belief that a voodoo practitioner's sticking of red-hot needles into the abdomen of a wax image of the believer will cause that believer intense abdominal pain and eventual death. Given the appropriate circumstances—circumstances in which a practitioner of voodoo actually does stick red-hot needles into the abdomen of an appropriate wax image and the believer knows that she or he does—it seems not unreasonable to think that our believer will experience intense abdominal pains and (perhaps) eventual death. It also seems not unreasonable to think that the believer's conceptual scheme is a necessary condition for the occurrence of this experience; this, if true, would entail that I, as a nonbeliever in the efficacy of voodoo, would not have a similar experience in otherwise identical circumstances. However, it also seems reasonable to think that the thesis expressed as (2) is correct here: as our voodoo believer writhes on the ground in intense agony, approaching death, why should we think that the phenomenology of his or her experience is significantly different from that of (say) an individual in the extreme abdominal agony caused by a burst appendix or by advanced peritonitis. That is, there seems no reason to think that the phenomenological attributes of our voodoo believer's experience reflect in any significant way the structure of the conceptual scheme which gave rise to that experience.[3] And so (perhaps) *mutatis mutandis* for mystical experience. Once again, much more could be said on the merits of the unmediated consciousness thesis; my aim in what follows will be to see whether there is any support for it in the Indian Buddhist material.

Third, there is the *nondualistic consciousness thesis*. A proponent of this position will assert the following:

(3) For any experience (*E*) it is possible that *E*'s phenomenological attributes and content not include any structural opposition between subject and object, apprehender and apprehended.

There seems no logical absurdity involved here; by structured opposition between subject and object, I mean simply that phenomenological attribute of any experience which irresistibly leads the ostensible subject of an experience to separate herself or himself from the content of that experience. Such a separation is most naturally expressed in standard subject-predicate-object sentences. This is an attribute common to most experiences of most mature adults. However, it is probable that it is not an attribute constitutive of *any* experiences belonging to babies of less than three months. It is also not present in some drug-induced experiences; in many aesthetic and some sexual experiences; and (perhaps most important for the purposes of this study) in many experiences produced by specifiable kinds of meditational techniques. What, then, would nondualistic consciousness of this kind be like? It would consist in a series of presentations (*Vorstellungen, Vijñaptayaḥ*) without there being any sense of separation between the presentation in question and the subject "having" it. There would be a series of pictures without any viewer. It is important to note that the "pictures" in question could possess any degree of complexity (i.e., have as much content as required); the nondualistic consciousness thesis is, thus, very different from the PCT.

Bearing these conceptual distinctions in mind, I shall now turn to an analysis of some Indian Buddhist material to see how it bears on these questions. I shall treat, necessarily too briefly, two significant kinds of altered states of consciousness described and recommended by Indian Buddhist thinkers, and I shall try to offer some comments on their significance for the three theses distinguished earlier. In no case shall I offer a comprehensive discussion of the material available on these altered states. The Indian Buddhist intellectual tradition produced a vast corpus of literature, which means that on any given topic there is an *embarras du choix;* my comments will, therefore, be preliminary in the extreme.

§2 THE ATTAINMENT OF CESSATION

The intellectuals of the Indian Buddhist traditions describe and recommend a condition, produced by specified meditational techniques, in which there occur no mental events of any kind. They call this condition the attainment of cessation (*nirodhasamāpatti*) or the cessation of sensation and conceptualization (*saṃjñāvedayitanirodha*). I have devoted a good deal of space to discussing this condition elsewhere (1983b; 1986); there are many complexities contained in the Buddhist discussions of it that will have to be passed over in this synopsis (see my other studies for a full picture).

The attainment of cessation is defined as "the non-occurrence of mind and mental concomitants,"[4] and is described as being mindless (*acittaka*). If indeed, there is such a condition—and the Buddhist traditions are almost unanimous in agreeing that there is, even if they disagree as to its

proper definition and soteriological significance—some obvious problems arise. The first has to do with (what we might call) the phenomenology of such a condition: How is it different from other standard examples
of insensibility such as straightforward unconsciousness, dreamless sleep,
or, for that matter, death itself? In an attempt to differentiate the attainment of cessation from death, we find the following passage:

> What is the difference, revered one, between a dead person who has passed
> away and a monk who has attained the cessation of conceptualization and
> sensation? Revered one, the physical, verbal, and mental functions of the
> dead person who has passed away have ceased and subsided; his vitality is
> destroyed, his heat is extinguished, and his sense-organs are scattered. But
> although the physical, verbal, and mental functions of the monk who has
> attained the cessation of conceptualization and sensation have ceased and
> subsided, his vitality is not destroyed, his heat is not extinguished, and his
> sense-organs are purified. This, revered one, is the difference between a
> dead person who has passed away and a monk who has attained the cessa-
> tion of conceptualization and sensation.
>
> (*Majjhimanikāya*, Trenckner, Chalmers,
> and C.A.F. Rhys-Davids, eds. 1888–1925:I.296.11–23)

It seems that both a dead man and one in the attainment of cessation lack
"physical, verbal, and mental functions," which is to say that such persons cannot perform any bodily action, cannot speak, and cannot think.
A commentarial discussion of this passage[5] notes that there is some
question as to what it means to say that "mental functions" have ceased.
Some Buddhist scholastics apparently thought that the term in this context
refers only to the cessation of mental *activity* and not to the complete
cessation of everything mental; on this view it might still be proper to say
that the attainment of cessation possesses mind (is *sacittaka*), or, in my
terminology, consists in mental events. But the orthodox view is that the
phrase intends to reject the existence of anything mental in the attainment
of cessation, to designate it as mindless (*acittaka*). The only difference
between death and the attainment of cessation, then, is that in the former
condition "vitality" and "heat" are gone and the "sense-organs are scattered," whereas in the latter condition "vitality" and "heat" are still
present and the "sense-organs are purified." The terms "vitality" and
"heat" refer (approximately) to what in Western physiology are thought of
as the autonomic processes of the central nervous system (heartbeat,
basic metabolic functions, and [perhaps] a low level of respiration). The
presence of these autonomic functions in the attainment of cessation is
likened by the tradition to the glowing embers of a fire covered with ash:
such embers are capable of being rekindled into a blazing fire, given the

appropriate conditions, but they are not visible to the casual observer. Finally, the idea that the "sense-organs are purified" in the attainment of cessation is usually explained through another analogy: the mirror wrapped in a bag and placed in a box.[6] Such a mirror, even though not actually reflecting anything, shines with unpolluted radiance inside its wrappings. One contrast is with a mirror set up at a busy public cross-roads (i.e., the sense-organs of a normally conscious person) that is always more or less polluted and dimmed by accumulated dust and dirt; another is with the sense-organs of a dead person that are "scattered" in the obvious sense that they are decayed and incapable of reflecting anything.

The following picture of the attainment of cessation thus emerges: *physically*, it is a condition much like that of some mammals in deep hibernation. Respiration has either ceased or is at a very low level; heart rate has dropped almost to zero; body temperature is low. *Mentally*, the ordinary functions of sense-perception, concept-formation, and ratiocination have completely ceased. The closest analogy in Western psychology might be to a person in a deep cataleptic trance. No reaction to stimuli is observable and no initiation of action occurs. The Budhdist depiction of the attainment of cessation perhaps goes further, in that any internal mental life (image-formation, dreaming, and the like) is ruled out. The attainment of cessation is, in brief, a condition in which no mental events of any kind occur, a condition distinguishable from death only by a certain residual warmth and vitality in the unconscious practitioner's body.

The methods used to bring about this condition are almost entirely enstatic, that is, they are aimed first at withdrawing the practitioner from every kind of interaction (perceptual, conative, and affective) with the outside world and, then, at reducing the content of her or his consciousness to zero. There is a standardized description of the ascending series of altered states of consciousness through which the practitioner passes on the way to the attainment of cessation that makes this very clear:

> By the transcendence of all conceptualizations of form, by the disappearance of conceptualizations based upon sense-data, by paying no attention to conceptualizations of manifoldness, having attained to the sphere of infinite space [the practitioner] remains therein, thinking space is unending. By entirely transcending the sphere of infinite space, having attained to the sphere of infinite consciousness [the practitioner] remains therein, thinking 'consciousness is infinite'. By entirely transcending the sphere of infinite consciousness, having attained to the sphere of nothing at all [the practitioner] remains therein, thinking 'there is nothing'. By entirely transcending the

sphere of nothing at all, having entered the sphere of neither conceptualization nor non-conceptualization, [the practitioner] remains therein. By entirely transcending the sphere of neither conceptualization nor non-conceptualization, having attained the cessation of sensation and conceptualization, [the practitioner] remains therein.

(*Dīgha-nikāya*, T. W. Rhys-Davids, Carpenter,
and Estlin. 1890–1911:II.71.2–17)

This description portrays the practitioner ascending through a series of
spheres (*āyatana*), beginning with that of infinite space, progressing from
there to that of infinite consciousness (*vijñāna*), then to that of nothing at
all, then to that of neither conceptualization nor its absence, and finally to
the attainment of cessation proper. These spheres are thought of as both
cosmic realms, locatable in space, and also as psychological conditions,
what I have been calling altered states of consciousness. As the practitioner ascends through them, his mental functions become increasingly
attenuated, until finally they cease altogether. The description cited does
not explain in detail exactly how to ascend through this hierarchy of
altered states. But it is significant that as the practitioner passes from the
sphere of infinite space to that of infinite consciousness, he thinks consciously that space is unending. This active contemplation of the unend-
ingness of space is instrumental in enabling the practitioner to attain the
next stage, that of infinite consciousness: nothing other than space's
endlessness is present to the awareness of the practitioner as he or she
makes this transition—similarly, for the succeeding stages. The practitioner contemplates successively more tenuous spheres until at last he or she
enters the attainment of cessation where no further contemplation is
possible because all mental life has ceased. There can be no doubt that
the use of such methods is ideally suited to the result produced by them.

There are a large number of interesting philosophical and hermeneutical problems created for Buddhist scholastics by the prominent witness in
the texts of their tradition to the possibility and desirability of such a
condition. Prominent among these is the question of emergence from the
attainment of cessation: if it is really the case that there are no mental
events of any kind in the attainment of cessation and that such absence of
mental events endures for at least a while (often for as long as seven days),
then it is difficult to explain how mental events can begin again in a
continuum that has been altogether without them. Important also (for
Buddhists) is the question of the soteriological significance of the attainment of cessation: How, if at all, does this condition relate to *nirvāṇa*?
What are the proper reasons for wanting to attain it? And so forth. These

questions lie outside the purview of this study; I am concerned here only to see whether, and in what ways, the Buddhist descriptions of the attainment of cessation provide support for any of the three theses stated at the beginning of this paper. And to this I now turn.

It seems at first sight that Buddhist descriptions of the attainment of cessation support the PCT. Since this condition contains no mental events of any kind, it certainly follows that it has no phenomenological attributes or content. However, it is not so clear that, as my formulation of the pure consciousness thesis requires, it is proper to call the attainment of cessation a mental event. As I have shown, the standard definitions of it explicitly avoid predicating any of the standard terms for mental phenomena ("citta," "manas," "vijñāna," terms that are said by some texts to be synonymous but which are not strictly so)[7] for the attainment of cessation. Instead, it is called acittaka (mindless).

There are, however, some Buddhist thinkers who attempt to show that there must be some kind of consciousness (vijñāna) present within the attainment of cessation. Their motivations for making this assertion—which appears to go against the canonical definitions of the attainment of cessation—mostly have to do with the need to provide some causal account of the re-emergence of the mental from the attainment of cessation. The postulation of some inactive or unmanifest consciousness will allow them to say that when the practitioner's mental life starts up again, when one exits from the attainment of cessation, one does so in virtue of that unmanifest or inactive vijñāna which persists even while one is in the attainment. This move, however, raised some problems for Buddhists, largely because the standard model for consciousness used by the traditions is an intentional one. Thus we find vijñāna defined as a specific presentation (prativijñapti), an act of apprehension (upalabdhi) relating to some particular object (viṣaya).[8] The paradigm case in mind here is that of sensory perception, a mental event which is a presentation (vijñapti) of a specific kind, that is to say, it has specifiable phenomenological attributes (e.g., that it belongs to the class of visual perceptions) and specifiable content (e.g., that the presentation in question is blue). Given that this is the standard Buddhist definition of consciousness, applying the term to a condition wherein there is a complete lack of both phenomenological attributes and content is not without its problems. That the Buddhist traditions were aware of this can be seen by a brief glance at the debates that such an application generated.

One attempt to deal with the problem postulated the existence of an unmanifest mental consciousness (aparisphuṭamanovijñāna), a consciousness without manifest phenomenological attributes or experience-able content. This view is attributed, in Vasubandhu's *Abhidharmakośab-hāṣya*, an important fifth-century scholastic treatise, to one Vasumitra; Vasubandhu also preserves a critique of this position by another Buddhist thinker, Ghoṣaka. Ghoṣaka's position, in essence, is that it makes no sense to speak of consciousness (*vijñāna*) existing in an unmanifest condition. For Ghoṣaka, the occurrence of any instance of consciousness entails the occurrence of (some kind of) experience: consciousness without phenomenological attributes is, for him, a meaningless concept. The occurrence of any consciousness event is, as he puts it, a sufficient condition for the occurrence of (various kinds of) sensation (*vedanā*) and conceptualization (*saṃjñā*).[9]

Vasumitra's position is left relatively undeveloped in the brief exposition given to it in the *Abhidharmakośabhāṣya*. A fuller statement of what is essentially the same position—that an individual in the attainment of cessation, though entirely without experience and, thus, apparently without any mental events, is actually still conscious in some sense—can be found by looking at what Yogācāra Buddhist theorists have to say about the store-consciousness (*ālayavijñāna*). This consciousness, like Vasumitra's unmanifest mental consciousness, is said to persist even in the apparently mindless attainment of cessation. And since the Yogācāra theorists do not suggest that anything in the phenomenology of the attainment of cessation changes (i.e., it is still apparently without phenomenological attributes or content), it seems clear that they wish to postulate some form of contentless and attributeless consciousness and, thus, to argue (perhaps) for some version of the PCT.

A full exposition of Buddhist ideas about the store-consciousness cannot be given here. Very briefly, and somewhat too simply, the store-consciousness is seen as a receptacle for the seeds (*bīja*) planted in it by the volitional actions that occur within a particular continuum of events (a continuum that is conventionally referred to as a person), seeds that will have specifiable effects upon what occurs in that same continuum at some future time. The store-consciousness is often described by the epithet, "holder of all seeds" ("*sarvabījaka*"). These seeds are not objects of experience; they are not available to introspection. Apart from perpetuating their own existence, they remain causally inactive until the proper time comes for them to mature and have their effects.[10] There are many philosophical puzzles connected with the store consciousness, only one of which is of primary importance for the purposes of this discussion; Is the store-consciousness, which is conceived as a stream (*srotas*), or continuum (*saṃtāna*), of consciousness events (i.e., seeds) an example of contentless and attributeless consciousness? If it is, we shall have found an instance of Buddhist support for the PCT (and also, incidentally, and somewhat trivially, for the nondualistic consciousness thesis—though since this is less problematic—I shall not argue this aspect of the case here).

Unfortunately, the question is not easy to answer. Even the most enthusiastic Buddhist supporters of the store-consciousness are somewhat unwilling to say that it is objectless (*nirālambana*) or without any content (*nirākāra*). To do so would be to deny that the store-consciousness is, in any meaningful sense, an instance of consciousness,[11] and no Buddhist thinker wished to take that step. However, the objects and content of the store-consciousness have a special status. They are indistinct or imprecisely delineated (*aparichinna*) and extremely subtle (*atisūkṣma*), and this means that they are not experienced (*asaṃvidita*): the possessor of the store-consciousness has no awareness of the objects and content of that consciousness, even though it has them.[12] To put this another way: the store-consciousness consists in a series of presentations (*vijñapti*) that are sufficiently indistinct and sufficiently subtle for it to be impossible that they come to awareness. When defenders of this position are pressed to explain in what sense this kind of thing can properly be called consciousness (*vijñāna*), the standard response is by appeal to the very attainment of cessation, which the store-consciousness was, in part, invoked to explain. Sthiramati, for example, makes this move in the *Triṃśikābhāṣya* and goes on to say that both scripture and reason require the existence of some sort of consciousness in the attainment of cessation (a conclusion which other Buddhist intellectuals did not feel called upon by either scripture or reason to assert!) and that the store-consciousness is the only reasonable candidate.[13]

Bearing in mind the terms of this debate, it remains to ask whether the attainment of cessation can properly be seen as an instance of pure (attributeless) consciousness. For those Buddhists who deny the existence of anything mental in this condition, the answer is clearly negative: the attainment of cessation is not for them an instance of consciousness at all. For those who assert that consciousness does persist in the attainment of cessation (either the unmanifest mental consciousness or the store-consciousness), the answer would also at first sight seem to be negative since these kinds of consciousness are said to have some content. However, this point may be no more than verbal since proponents of this thesis also argue that this postulated content is not accessible to experience and that nothing whatever comes to awareness when only the store-consciousness exists. This would seem to mean that (as already suggested), a phenomenological description of the store-consciousness would reveal exactly nothing. And this is what is wanted by the proponent of the PCT.

There does seem, then, to be some support, albeit not unambiguous, for those who argue that (at least some) religious traditions preserve reports and recommendations of pure consciousness. The attainment of cessation, for those who assert the persistence of the store-consciousness therein, may be such a case. There is certainly no better candidate in the history of Indian Buddhist discussion of altered states of consciousness. Even if we accept (some) Buddhist descriptions of the attainment of cessation as descriptions of a pure consciousness event, however, it is important to note the uneasiness that Buddhist scholastics seem to have felt in applying mentalistic terms to such a condition. It seems to have sounded as odd to them as it does to us, to label such a condition as an instance of consciousness: What is left of consciousness when all phenomenological attributes and content are removed?

Further, it seems that the reasons why the proponents of the store-consciousness felt it necessary to postulate the persistence of some kind of consciousness in the attainment of cessation had to do not with any desire to embrace the PCT (*pace* many of its Western defenders), but only with the need to provide some causal account of the re-emergence of mental life from such an apparently mindless condition. It would not (perhaps) be misleading to think of the existence of that consciousness which persists in the attainment of cessation as being reducible to its causal powers: it exists only insofar as it is capable of causing the emergence of new (proper) consciousness events in a continuum where such have temporarily ceased. And perhaps this is also what Western proponents of the PCT have in mind when they use pure consciousness language. If so, it is difficult to see what soteriological value (or even practical interest) such consciousness can have. But that opens up axiological questions too deep to enter into here.

§3 UNCONSTRUCTED AWARENESS

The Indian Buddhist traditions also have a good deal to say about the possibility and desirability of a kind of awareness (*jñāna*) which is said to be free from *vikalpa* or conceptual construction. In discussing this kind of awareness, we move close to the heart of the tradition, for unconstructed awareness is given very high soteriological status by Buddhist intellectuals, especially by those belonging to the Yogācāra school.

Vikalpa is an important term which deserves some discussion: it is derived from the verbal root *klrp-*, whose semantic range runs from the functions of ordering, arranging, and adapting to those of ornamenting and embellishing. A derived nominal form—*kalpanā*—is often associated with literary creation: *kavikalpanā* means the literary creation of a poet. Adding the prefix *ví-* to produce the nominal form *vikalpa* gives a distributive sense to the term: it can often mean to create or contrive options, to set up antitheses, to ornament by opposing, and so forth.[14] The term *"vikalpa"* as used by Indian Buddhist intellectuals preserves many of these semantic connotations, but it has to do more precisely with the constructive, conceptual, classificatory activities of the mind—activities that are like those of the poet or *kavi*, in that they create a fictional universe, one that does not exist as it appears. In some contexts "imagination" is a good translation; but in the more strictly philosophical and soteriological contexts that I shall be concerned with, "construction" or (adjectivally) "constructive" seem preferable.

An interesting analysis of the technical concept *vikalpa* is found in the fourth chapter of the first book of the *Bodhisattvabhūmi*.[15] There, the constructive activity of the mind is divided into eight categories. The first three are: "construction of essences" (*svabhāvavikalpa*); "construction of distinctions" (*viśeṣavikalpa*); and "construction of the apprehension of material forms" (*piṇḍagrahavikalpa*). These are connected with (what Buddhists take to be) the mind's construction of a world of distinct material objects, of substances with properties both theoretically and practically separable one from another—the material universe, that is, of everyday experience. The construction of such a world is, according to Asaṅga (the probable author of the *Bodhisattvabhūmi*), both itself a function of *vikalpa* and allows the proliferation of further *vikalpa*: *vikalpa* consisting this time in language, the separation and designation of those existents which *vikalpa* has itself created. The fourth and fifth kinds of *vikalpa* are "construction concerning 'I' " (*aham iti vikalpa*) and "construction concerning 'mine' " (*mameti vikalpa*). These have to do with the construction of a sense of personal identity, "the root-error" as our text puts it "of the conceit 'I am' " (*asmimānamūla*) and of the (false) philosophical view that persons exist. The final three kinds of *vikalpa* are "construction of what is pleasant" (*priyavikalpa*), "construction of what is unpleasant" (*apriyavikalpa*), and "construction of what is contrary to both" (*tadubhayaviparītavikalpa*). Dividing and classifying our percepts into things we like, things we don't like, and things we are indifferent to is, thus, also a function of *vikalpa*: these kinds of *vikalpa* "generate greed, hatred, and delusion" and are, thus, productive of all the wrong kinds of affect.

This eightfold classification of *vikalpa* (about which much more could be said) is intended as a complete account of the various ways in which we construct for ourselves the world of everyday experience, a world of existent subjects experiencing existent objects and reacting to such experiences in various ways. The removal of all these constructive operations of the mind is one of the primary soteriological goals of Indian (especially Yogācāra) Buddhism. As the *Mahāyānasūtrālaṃkāra* puts it: "Bodhisattvas who are free from constructive activity see this entire [cosmos], just as it has been described, as nothing but construction: they attain enlightenment" (IX 81; Lévi 1907:49.3–4). What, then, is unconstructed awareness phenomenologically like? What support do the descriptions given of it provide for any of the three theses about consciousness which are the concern of this essay?

A detailed exposition of unconstructed awareness is given in the eighth chapter of Asaṅga's *Mahāyānasaṃgraha*. What follows is largely based on that text, though very many of the details found therein cannot be touched on in the brief discussion given here.[16] Asaṅga begins by defining the essence (*svabhāva*) of unconstructed awareness, and he does so solely by using negation. This, one of his commentators explains, is because speaking of unconstructed awareness affirmatively—predicating anything of it—would be like speaking of visible forms to a man blind from birth.[17] This apophatic method is not used because unconstructed awareness is without phenomenological attributes or content; rather, it seems, the apophatic method is used for the more pragmatic reason that those who have not experienced unconstructed awareness will not be able to understand it. Indeed, the idea that unconstructed awareness might be in any way like the attainment of cessation or other examples of insensibility is explicitly rejected by Asaṅga. Two of the negations that he uses to describe its essence indicate this. They are the negation of the idea that unconstructed awareness is without mental activity and the negation of the idea that unconstructed awareness is identical with the attainment of cessation. The point of these negations, as the commentators indicate, is to dispose of the idea that unconstructed awareness might simply be identified with such states as dreamless sleep or the insensibility produced by drunkenness.[18]

The difference between unconstructed awareness and such states is that unconstructed awareness has both an object (*dmigs/ālambana*) and some content (*rnam pa/ākāra*). The object of unconstructed awareness is given precise definition by Asaṅga: it is the "indescribability of things" (*chos rnams brjod du med/dharmanirabhilāpyatā*) which is, in turn, identified with the "Thusness of absence of self" (*bdag med de bzhin nyid/nairātmyatathatā*). This definition introduces important technical terminology which cannot be fully explored here. Suffice it to say that the

expression "indescribability of things" is used to indicate that all the ways
we have of describing things, of dividing the world into subjects and
predicates, are the product of the constructive activity of the mind. Such
divisions reflect, it is said, no external reality; in reality, the world is not
such that it can adequately be described by language. The way the world
actually is is pointed to by the *terminus technicus* "Thusness" (*tathatā*);
this, too, is unpacked negatively. It consists in the fact that (what we take
to be) independently subsisting entities, in fact, have no self, no enduring
essence which gives them identity and marks them off from other things.[19]
What this amounts to is that the object of unconstructed awareness is the
totality of things as they really are. While the text under consideration
here tells us about this only negatively, it is important to note that the
awareness in question is not, strictly speaking, objectless and, thus, that
the descriptions of it do not seem to provide support for the pure consciousness thesis.

Neither is unconstructed awareness contentless since, according to
Buddhist theory, possession of an object entails possession of some content.[20] The content in question here, though, is somewhat attenuated. It
consists in the absence of "defining marks" (*mtshan ma/nimitta*) since
"defining marks" are those things which our constructive intellect develops in order to divide and classify objects in the world of experience.[21]
But this is not very illuminating: it still is not clear what an awareness
whose content is simply the absence of separate substances might be *like*.
The *Mahāyānasaṃgraha* does provide us with similes that are of some
help. We are told that unconstructed awareness is like a dumb man who,
seeking some object, finds it but is (being dumb) unable to state what he
has found; or it is like an idiot who, seeking some object, finds it but is
unable (being idiotic) to state what he has found. And so forth. The similes
do not, perhaps, sound all that complimentary to Western ears, especially
when it is realized that they are being applied to a kind of awareness
which is given an extremely high soteriological value. But dumbness and
idiocy here are not intended negatively; they have to be understood in the
context of the Yogācāra (and basic Buddhist) negative evaluation (for
soteriological purposes) of their antonyms, 'speech' and 'intelligence',
since these faculties (as I have tried to show) are those involved above all
others in the construction of a world which does not exist in the way it
appears to exist.

Further help in understanding what unconstructed awareness is awareness *of* may be had from a consideration of one of its synonyms, mirrorlike awareness (*ādarsajñāna*). Another important Yogācāra text called the
Mahāyānasūtrālaṃkāra, somewhat earlier that Asaṅga's *Mahāyāna-*

saṃgraha, gives an important definition and analysis of mirrorlike awareness: it is free from possessiveness (*amama*, literally without mine), and it
does not confront (*āmukha*) objects of awareness (i.e., actual or potential
things that one might be aware of). The commentators make these characteristics of mirrorlike awareness somewhat clearer: mirrorlike awareness
is without possessiveness because it creates neither of the constructed
ideas 'I' and 'mine,' and because (as would seem to follow) there is in it
no division between subject and object.[22] Further, it never confronts
objects of awareness, in that it does not function in accordance with the
usual divisions of objects of awareness into such things as physical form;
this, in turn, is because in mirrorlike knowledge there is no difference
between apprehension and that which is to be apprehended.[23]

The key points here are that mirrorlike awareness (which, remember, is
the same thing as unconstructed awareness) occurs without the usual
divisions between subject (apprehender) and object (thing apprehended).
This, bearing in mind what has already been said about unconstructed
awareness, makes it an instance of that kind of consciousness whose
existence was postulated by the nondualistic consciousness thesis stated
in §1. Further, the statement that mirrorlike awareness does not confront
objects of awareness in the same way that ordinary consciousness does
(i.e., by constructing rigid divisions among them, attributing defining
characteristics to them, etc., although a clear rejection of awareness with
the usual phenomenological atttributes and content is not meant as a
rejection of *all* content. Mirrors, after all, reflect something, even if they
do not conceptualize what they reflect, have no stake in classifying the
something, and are emphatically not interested in constructing an identity
for themselves over against what they are aware of. So also for Buddhist
practitioners who reach the exalted stage of unconstructed awareness: for
them, accurate cognition of the way things really are (of "Thusness")
occurs spontaneously, and can only be expressed apophatically.

A word might be said at this point about the way in which this unconstructed awareness is arrived at. One important part of the Buddhist
soteriological path is that known as the path of vision (*darśanamārga*). It
is here that practitioners internalize the categories of Buddhist metaphysics and transforms their perceptions and cognitions to accord with them.
In several Yogācāra texts, this path of vision is divided into a set of three
successive cognitive insights, each produced by self-consciously deconstructing the categories through which normal (dualistic) consciousness
occurs.[24] The first of these cognitive insights involves learning to see one's
own person as without "self" or enduring substantive existence (*pudgala-
nairātmya*); the second extends this insight to the absence of enduring

substantive existence even in the events, mental and physical, which seem to comprise one's person (*dharmanairātmya*); and the third involves learning to see *all* existents as without "self," without anything that definitively and eternally marks them off from other things. These three cognitive insights are summarized in the phrase; "an awareness in which what is cognized and that which cognizes are identical" (*samasamālam-byālambakajñana*).[25] This, of course, is simply another way of referring to unconstructed awareness; cognized and cognizer are seen to be identical when this kind of awareness is reached not in the Vedāntin monistic sense (in which the two are identical because of the view that there is only one unique undifferentiated substance in the world), but rather in the sense that both (cognizer and cognized) are concepts (and terms) without a referent. They are constructed concepts, and the practice of the path of vision is devoted exclusively to deconstructing them, to changing the practitioner's perceptions and cognitions, so that he or she no longer either conceives that these terms have any referent and (more important) is no longer able to perceive the world through the distorting filter of such ideas.

In sum, when describing and recommending unconstructed awareness Buddhist philosophers seem to have in mind (what Western philosophers and psychologists might think of as) a kind of preverbal, preconceptual awareness—an awareness that is thought to provide those who possess it with direct unmediated contact with reality. That this is what is in play is shown by the systematic epistemological tradition (*pramāṇavāda*) which developed both within and outside the Buddhist schools in India not long after the Yogācāra texts that I have been considering were composed. The major thinkers within this tradition—principally Dignāga and Dhar-makīrti—spent a great deal of philosophical energy in trying to show that all sensory perception, when properly understood, is actually unconstructed awareness of momentary bare particulars (*svalakṣaṇa*) and that the later application of the mind's constructive activity to this unconstructed awareness is necessarily distortive of it.

§4 CONCLUSIONS

In §1, I tried to distinguish three different theses, theses which are often confused in current Western discussions of pure consciousness and the like. These theses I labeled the PCT, the unmediated consciousness thesis, and the nondualistic consciousness thesis. I also offered very brief comments on these theses. In §2, I gave a brief presentation of what Indian Buddhist thinkers have said about one altered state of consciousness, a state they call the attainment of cessation. I concluded that while some analyses of this state sound as though they might support the PCT, those that do so most strongly are unwilling to call the state in question an instance of consciousness at all; thus, there is no clear support for the PCT to be drawn from Buddhist analyses of the attainment of cessation. It does seem to follow, though somewhat trivially, from (some) Buddhist descriptions of this condition that it is an instance of nondualistic consciousness: for any *X*, if *X* contains no consciousness events, then *X* contains no nondualistic consciousness events. It may also (and more interestingly) be the case that the Buddhist concept of store-consciousness—a concept constructed in part to explain the re-emergence of consciousness from the attainment of cessation—provides some support for the nondualistic consciousness thesis. But here, too, the evidence is not unambiguous.

In §3, I presented some elements of what classical Indian Yogācāra Buddhist thinkers have said about unconstructed awareness, my conclusions there were that, while Buddhist analyses of this kind of awareness provide no support for the PCT, they do provide interesting and powerful support for the nondualistic consciousness thesis. I do not mean to argue either for or against the coherence and usefulness of the nondualistic consciousness thesis, I merely wish to suggest that many Indian Buddhist thinkers would have given it their full support.

It remains to offer some comments on the unmediated consciousness thesis as it pertains to both the attainment of cessation and unconstructed awareness. Indian Buddhist thinkers tend not to discuss this question directly. Their presentations of both the attainment of cessation and unconstructed awareness tend to stress the fact that arriving at such exalted states depends on the lengthy practice of specifiable and precisely described meditational practices. This suggests, at least, that the possession of certain conceptual schemes might be a necessary condition for the attainment of the states in question. But this does not entail that any element of the schemes in question need be reflected in the phenomenology of the altered state. And in the case of the attainment of cessation, which effectively has no phenomenological attributes, it is hard to see how any element of any conceptual scheme *could* be so reflected. The attainment of cessation might well be taken, then, as supporting evidence for the unmediated consciousness thesis. It is probable that our Indian Buddhist scholastics would also have wished their descriptions of unconstructed awareness to be taken as supportive of the unmediated consciousness thesis. Since (as I have shown) they present unconstructed awareness as the result of removing all strictly conceptual activity, it is unlikely that they would wish to allow that any element of any conceptual scheme could be present in the phenomenology of this condition. It might be wondered why, if the possession of some conceptual scheme is among the necessary conditions for the attainment of unconstructed awareness (even if only in the sense that one needs to have something to get rid of) and, second, if the conceptual scheme in question includes propositions such as *nondualistic consciousness is both possible and desirable* and *unconstructed awareness, when I get it, will dispose of my tendency to differentiate myself from the objects of my awareness,* unconstructed awareness does not reflect *these* elements of the conceptual scheme in question. But since my main purpose in this study has been to pursue what Buddhists have said (or would be likely to say in a given situation) about these matters, such normative questions need not be pursued here.

NOTES

1. Notably Kessler and Prigge (1982); Griffths and Lewis (1984); Gill (1984; 1985); Perovich (1985a; 1985b); Forman (1986).

2. This seems to be the point of Forman's suggestion (in a letter to me) that the only difference one needs to postulate between a pure consciousness event and dreamless sleep is that one needs to wake up from the latter but not from the former.

3. Cf. Wainwright's (1981:20–21) discussion of the gastrointestinal experience of an Eskimo.

4. *Cittacetasikānāṃ dhammānām appavatti/Visuddhimagga* 23.18 (Rewatadhamma 1969–1972:1665).

5. *Papañcasūdanī,* Woods, Kosambi, and Horner (1922–1938:II.351.14–352.4).

6. Ibid., II.352.1–4.

7. In Sanskrit, as in English, terms for mental phenomena are many and complex; they overlap with one another in interesting ways and are not always systematically differentiated in use by even the most careful of Indian Buddhist philosophers. Some of the key terms—*"citta," "manas,"* and *"vijñāna"* as well as the important term *"vijñapti,"* on which see Hall (1986)—are said by Vasubandhu to be synonyms (*"cittaṃ mano vijñānaṃ vijñaptis ceti paryayāh" Viṃsatikāvṛtti.* [Lévi 1925:3]) and to have the same referent (*"cittaṃ mano 'tha vijñānam ekārtham" Abhidharmakośakārikā* II.34 [Gokhale 1946:79]). I have discussed these matters elsewhere (Griffiths 1986:55.95–96.169.182); all that can be said here is that this claim does not entail that it is possible to replace any occurrence of any of these terms with any of the others in Buddhist philosophical texts without thereby altering their meaning.

8. *Abhidharmakośabhāṣya*—(Pradhan 1975:11.6–8).

9. The details of the debate between Vasumitra and Ghoṣaka are discussed fully in my monograph on the *nirodhasamāpatti* (Griffiths 1986:67–70, 127–28).

10. Jaini (1959) has discussed the image of seed and growth in the Sautrāntika. Cf. La Vallée Poussin (1934:151–52; 1928–1929:100ff.) for discussion of the same image. On the store-consciousness as *sarvabījaka* see *Mahāyānasaṃgraha* I.2–3 (Lamotte 1934:175–76; Nagao 1982:10,111–16) and I.14 with commentaries thereto (Lamotte 1934:221–25; Nagao 1982:22–23, 133–35). Compare *Karmasiddhiprakaraṇa* §33 (Lamotte 1935:198–99,247–49) and *Triṃśikābhāṣya* on *Triṃśikā* 2ed (Lévi 1925:18.22–19.2).

11. In the *Triṃśikābhāṣya* Sthiramati's opponent asks what the object and content of the postulated store-consciousness are meant to be since, as he puts it, "consciousness without object of content is impossible" ("*na hi nirālambanaṃ nirākāraṃ vā vijñānaṃ yujyate.*" [Lévi 1925:19.3–4]). Sthiramati agrees: "*naiva tat* (i.e., ālayavijñāna) *nirālambanaṃ nirākāram veṣyate.*"

12. I base the account given here largely upon Sthiramati's *Triṃśikābhāṣya* (Lévi 1925:18.21–19.8). Compare *Karmasiddhiorakaraṇa* §36 (Lamotte 1935:250–51) and the *Vijñaptimātratāsiddhi* (La Vallée Poussin 1928–1929:142).

13. There is a standard eightfold proof of the existence of the store-consciousness, perhaps originally developed by Asaṅga (Hakamaya 1978) and cited by Sthiramati in the *Abhidharmasamuccayabhāṣya* (Tatia 1976:11.18–13.20). I have discussed this proof in detail elsewhere (1986:129–38). One of the elements in this proof is the fact of entry into and exit from the attainment of cessation. Thus, the attainment of cessation is used to demonstrate the existence of the store-consciousness, a kind of consciousness that is (almost) attributeless and contentless when, in fact, the concept of the store-consciousness was developed, in part to explain just that phenomenon.

14. Matilal (1986:Chap. 10) gives a useful discussion of *vikalpa* and associated technical terms.

15. This is the *tattvārthapatala*. The text is found in Dutt (1978:34.32ff.), and a translation with comments is given by Willis (1978:127ff.). The *Bodhisattvabhūmi* is one of the earliest Yogācāra texts available to us; it may date from the fourth century CE.

16. The *Mahāyānasaṃgraha*, although originally written in Sanskrit, does not survive in that language. What follows is based in part on Etienne Lamotte's (1973) French translation of Asaṅga's text. It is also based, in part, on the commentaries of Vasubandhu (*Mahāyānasaṃgrahabhāṣya*) and Asvabhāva (*Mahāyāna-saṃgrahopanibandhana*). These works also are lost in their original Sanskrit: I have consulted the Tibetan translations.

17. "*Bzlog pai sgo nas mtshan nyid ston te/ dmus long la gzugs bsnyad pa bznin du bsgrub pa'i sgo nas brjod par mi nus pa'i phyir ro*"/ *Mahāyāna-saṃgrahopanibandhana* (Derge Tanjur, sems-tsam RI 266a7–266bi).

18. *Mahāyānasaṃgraha* (Peking Tanjur, sems-tsam LI 39b5–6); *Mahāyāna-saṃgrahabhāṣya* (Peking Tanjur, sems-tsam LI 212b4ff.); *Mahāyāna-saṃgrahopanibandhana* (Derge Tanjur, sems-tsam RI 266b2ff.).

19. Both Vasubandhu (*Mahāyānasaṃgrahabhāṣya* [Peking Tanjur, sems-tsam LI 213b3–6]) and Asvabhāva (*Mahāyānasaṃgrahopanibandhana* [Derge Tanjur,

sems-tsam RI 267a7–267b2]) comment on this passage, as might be expected, by using standard *trisvabhāva* terminology.

20. *"Dmigs pa dang bcas pa'i chos rnams ni rnam pa dang bcas pa'i phyir dmigs pa dang 'dzin par byed do"*/ Mahāyānasaṃgrahopanibandhana (Derge Tanjur, sems-tsam RI 267b2). It is interesting to note that the Mahāyānasūtrā-laṃkārabhāṣya, a text that may be by Vasubandhu seems to explicitly deny that *ādarsajñāna* (a synonym of *nirvikalpajñāna*) has content, saying of it that it is *anākāratva* or "contentless" (Mahāyānasūtrālaṃkārabhāṣya [Lévi 1907:46.22–23]). But the standard Yogācāra view, I think, is that *nirvikalpajñāna* possesses *ākāra*. On the idea and symbol of the mirror, see especially Demiéville 1947.

21. The term *"nimitta"* is usually used in connection with the term *"saṃjñā,"* ("conceptualization"). Nimittas (defining marks) are precisely those things which are grasped or conceptualized by the mind. Yasomitra, for example, in his Abhidharmakośavyākhyā, defines *nimitta* as those things, such as the condition of being blue, which are specific states of something" (nimittaṃ vastuno`avasthā-viśeṣo nīlatvādi/ Abhidharmakośavyākhyā [Sāstrī 1981:48.18]).

22. *"Me long ye shes nga yi med/ yongs su ma chad ces bya ba ni ngar 'dzin pa dang/ nga yir 'dzin pa dang/ gzung ba dang 'dzin pa med pa'i phyir nga yi ba med pa yin no"*/ * Asvabhāva, Mahāyānasūtrālaṃkāratīkā (Derge Tanjur, sems-tsam BI 74a4–5).

23. *"De* [i.e., me long lta bu ye shes] *ni shes bya dag la gzugs la sogs pa la dmigs pa bzhin du dmigs pa'i bye brag gam/ sngon po la sogs pa'i rnam pa'i bye brag gis 'jug pa ma yin pa'o/ de ni dmigs par bya ba dang/ dmigs par byed pa mnyam pas mnyam pa rnam par mi rtog pa de bzhin nyid la dmigs pa'i ngo bo nyid de/* * Asvabhāva, Mahāyānasūtrālaṃkāratīkā (Derge Tanjur, sems-tsam BI 74a6–7).

24. What follows is based largely on the definition and discussion given to the *darśanamārga* in the Abhidharmasamuccaya (Derge Tanjur, sems-tsam RI 92b7–94al: [Pradhan, 1950:66.3–68.2]) and in the Abhidharmasamuccayabhāṣya (Tatia 1976:76.19–78.22]). See also my own translation and analysis of this text (1983a:chap. 4) and Schmithausen's (1983) excellent study of it. A similar passage is found in the Yogācārabhūmi (Peking Tanjur, sems-tsam ZI 72b3ff.); on this see Schmithausen (1983:263ff.).

25. The Tibetan reads, *"dmigs par bya ba dang dmigs par byed pa mnyam pas mnyam par shes par."* Tatia reads *samasamālambyālambanajñāna* (1976:76.20). Schmithausen's emendation (1983:262) is to be preferred; cf. Mahāyānasūtrā-laṃkāratīkā (Derge Tanjur, sems-tsam BI 74a6–7).

WORKS CITED

Brentano, Franz. 1973. *Psychology from An Empirical Standpoint*. Trans. Antos C. Rancurello, D. B. Terrell, and Linda McAlister. Ed. Linda McAlister. Atlantic Highlands, N.J. Humanities Press.

Chisholm, Roderick. 1957. *Perceiving: a philosophical study.* Ithaca, N.Y.: Cornel University Press.

Demiéville, Paul. 1947. Le miroir spirituel. *Sinologica* I/2:112–37. Reprinted in Demiéville 1973:131–56.

Dutt, Nalinaksha, ed. 1978. *Bodhisattvabhūmiḥ.* Tibetan-Sanskrit Works Series No. 7. 2d ed. Patna:Kashi Prasad Jayaswal Research Institute.

Forman, Robert K. C. 1986. Pure consciousness events and mysticism. *Sophia* 25/1:49–58.

Gill, Jerry H. 1984. Mysticism and mediation. *Faith and Philosophy* 1/1:111–21.

Gill, Jerry H. 1985. Response to Perovich. *Faith and Philosophy* 2/2:189–90. (See herein, Perovich 1985b.)

Gokhale, V. V., ed. 1946. The text of the *Abhidharmakośakārikā* of Vasubandhu. *Journal of the Bombay Branch of the Royal Asiatic Society* New Series 22:73–102.

Griffiths, Paul J. 1983a. "*Indian Buddhist meditation-theory: history, development, and systematization,*" Ph.D. diss., University of Wisconsin, Madison.

Griffiths, Paul J. 1983b. On being mindless: the debate on the re-emergence of consciousness from the attainment of cessation in the *Abhidharmakośabhāṣyam* and its commentaries. *Philosophy East and West* 33:379–94.

Griffiths, Paul J. 1986. *On being mindless: Buddhist meditation and the mind-body problem.* La Salle, Ill.: Open Court Press.

Griffiths, Paul J., and Lewis, Delmas. 1984. Wainwright on mysticism. *Religious Studies* 20:293–304.

Hakamaya Noriaki. 1978. Āraya-shiki sonzai no hachi ronsho ni kansuru shōbunken. *Komazawa Daigaku Bukkyōgakubu Kenkyū Kiyō* 36:1–26.

Hall, Bruce. 1986. The meaning of *vijñapti* in Vasubandhu's concept of mind. *Journal of the International Association of Buddhist Studies* 9/1:7–23.

Jaini, Padmanabh S. 1959. The Sautrāntika theory of bīja. *Bulletin of the School of Oriental and African Studies* (University of London) 22:236–49.

Katz, Steven T., ed. 1978. *Mysticism and philosophical analysis.* Oxford: Oxford University Press.

Katz, Steven T., ed. 1983. *Mysticism and religious traditions.* Oxford: Oxford University Press.

Kessler, Gary E., and Prigge, Norman. 1982. Is mystical experience everywhere the same? *Sophia* 21/1:39–55.

La Vallée Poussin, Louis de, trans. 1928–1929. *Vijñaptimātratāsiddhi: la Siddhi de Hiuan Tsang.* Buddhica, documents et travaux pour l'étude du Bouddhisme, 1st series, vol. 1 and 5. Eight fascicles, continuous pagination. Paris: Geuthner.

La Vallée Poussin, Louis de. 1934. Note sur l'ālayavijñāna. *Mélanges chinois et bouddhiques* 3:145–68.

Lamotte, Etienne, trans. 1934. L'Ālayavijñāna (Le receptacle) dans le Mahāyānasaṃgraha (Chapitre II). *Mélanges chinois et bouddhiques* 3:169–255.

Lamotte, Etienne, ed. and trans. 1935. Le Traité de l'acte de Vasubandhu. *Mélanges chinois et bouddhiques* 4:151–263.

Lamotte, Etienne, ed. and trans. 1973. *La Somme du grand véhicule d'Asaṅga*

(Mahāyānasaṃgraha). 2 vols. Publications de l'Institut Orientaliste de Louvain No. 8. Louvain-la-Neuve: Institut Orientaliste de Louvain.

Lévi, Sylvain, ed. 1907. *Mahāyāna-Sūtrālaṃkāra: Exposé de la doctrine du Grand Véhicule selon la systeme Yogācāra*. Tome 1: Texte. Bibliothèque de l'Ecole des Hautes Etudes, sciences historiques et philologiques, fascicule 159. Paris: Librairie Honoré Champion.

Lévi, Sylvain, ed. 1925. *Vijñaptimātratāsiddhi. Deux traités de Vasubandhu: Viṃsatikā (La Vingtaine) accompagnée d'une explication en prose, et Triṃśikā (La Trentaine), avec le commentaire de Sthiramati*. Bibliothèque de l'Ecole des Hautes Etudes, sciences historiques et philologiques, fascicule 25. Paris: Librairie Ancienne Honoré Champion.

Matilal, Bimal Krishna. 1986. *Perception: an essay on classical Indian theories of knowledge*. Oxford: Clarendon Press.

Nagao Gadjin, ed. and trans. 1982. *Shodaijōron: wayaku to chūkai*. Tokyo: Kodansha.

Perovich, Anthony, Jr. 1985a. Mysticism and the philosophy of science. *Journal of Religion* (Chicago) 65:63–82.

Perovich, Anthony, Jr. 1985b. Mysticism or mediation: a response to Gill. *Faith and Philosophy* 2/2:179–87. (See herein, Gill 1985.)

Pradhan, Pralhad, ed. 1950. *Abhidharmasamuccaya of Asaṅga*. Santiniketan: Visvabharati.

Pradhan, Pralhad, ed. 1975. *Abhidharmakośabhāṣyam of Vasubandhu*. Tibetan-Sanskrit Works Series No. 8, 2d ed. Patna: Kashi Prasad Jayaswal Research Institute.

Rewatadhamma, ed. 1969–1972. *Buddhaghosācariya's Visuddhimagga with Paramatthamañjūsātīkā of Bhadantācariya Dhammapāla*. 3 vols., continuous pagination. Varanasi: Vārānaseya Saṃskṛta Viśvavidyālaya.

Rhys-Davids, T. W., and Carpenter, J. Estlin, eds. 1890–1911. *Dīgha-Nikāya* 3 vols. London: Pali Text Society.

Sāstrī, Dwārikādās, ed. 1981. *Abhidharmakośa and Bhāṣya of ācārya Vasubandhu with Sphutārtha commentary of ācārya Yasomitra*. Bauddha Bharati Series Nos. 5–8. 2 vols., continuous pagination. Varanasi: Bauddha Bharati.

Schmithausen, Lambert, 1983. The *Darśanamārga* section of the *Abhidharmasamuccaya* and its interpretation by Tibetan commentators (with special reference to Bu Ston Rin Chen Grub). In *Contributions on Tibetan and Buddhist Religion and Philosophy*, ed. Ernst Steinkellner and Helmut Tauscher, 259–74. Wiener Studien zur Tibetologie und Buddhismuskunde, Heft 11. Proceedings of the Csoma de Körös Symposium held at Velm–Vienna, Austria, 13–19 September 1981, vol. 2. Vienna: Arbeitskreis für Tibetische und Buddhistische Studien.

Tatia, Nathmial, ed. 1976. *Abhidharmasamuccayabhāṣyam*, Tibetan-Sanskrit Works Series No. 17. Patna: Kashi Prasad Jayaswal Research Institute.

Trenckner, V., Chalmers, Robert, and Rhys-Davids, C.A.F., eds. 1888–1925. *Majjhimanikāya*. 4 vols. (including index vol.). London: Pali Text Society.

Wainwright, William J. 1981. *Mysticism: a study of its nature, cognitive value and moral implications*. Madison: University of Wisconsin Press.

Warren, Henry Clarke, and Kosambi, Dharmānanda, eds. 1950. *Visuddhimagga of Buddhaghosācariya*. Harvard Oriental Series No. 41. Cambridge: Harvard University Press.

Willis, Janice Dean, trans. 1978. *On knowing reality: the Tattvārtha chapter of Asaṅga's Bodhisattvabhūmi*. New York: Columbia University Press.

Woods, J. H., Kosambi, Dharmānanda, and Horner, I. B., eds. 1922–1938. *Papañcasūdanī*. 5 vols. London: Pali Text Society.

Eckhart, *Gezücken,*
and the Ground of the Soul

ROBERT K. C. FORMAN

In his presentation of the thesis that all experience is, in part, constructed or mediated by the subject's conceptual system, Jerry Gill points to the purported intentionality of all experience as a fundamental truth. According to him, all human experience is vectorial in nature. That is to say, "[o]ur consciousness is always consciousness *of* some concrete aspect of the world, of some particular aspect whose reality for us is constituted by our intentional activity in relation to it. This intentionality is clearly a mediational factor which undercuts the possibility of unmediated experience."[1] Gill clarified what he means by vectorial character of experience in his "Religious Experience as Mediated."[2] He notes that the basic character of mediated experience is what he calls its basic "from-to" structure: "Mediational awareness is always *of* something, *through* something else, or the prehender can be said to attend *from* certain factors *to* other factors."[3] Because he maintains this is so, he can assert that the system of belief plays a critical role in either constructing or mediating the experience. We "construct" experience inasmuch as we attend toward some factor(s) which we determine on the basis of our categories and set. All experience is "mediated," we may continue somewhat oversimply, in part because we label or understand that discriminated factor in the terms and context which that set provides.

Many scholars of mysticism have also argued for a constructivistic theory of mysticism that is, in part, based on the claim that all experience is intentional. Steven Katz,[4] John Hick,[5] Terence Penelhum,[6] and others all argue to this effect. However, I have argued elsewhere that this claim is philosophically suspect and empirically false. First, no one has ever argued that the claim that all experience is intentional is necessarily true for all possible forms of consciousness; nor is it obvious that this is so nor how one might argue to this effect.[7] In fact, there is very strong evidence that some people have reported events in which they were awake and also devoid of content for consciousness.[8] In addition, the essays in the present volume, taken together, show that the claim that all forms of possible experience is everywhere and always relational can no longer be maintained without further argument.

Despite its questionable foundations, this belief has been extremely influential. The belief that all experience is vectorial and relational is at the heart of what we may call the "constructivistic" account of mysticism, the position that all experience is, in part, shaped, determined, and constructed by the subject's beliefs and concepts.[9] I do not have space here to argue that this position dominates present theoretical and textual work on mysticism.[10] In mystical scholarship today it has led to a wide-spread tendency to eliminate or write off evidence of experiences which are nonrelational because they do not "fit" with this purported vectorial character of all experience. Gill is most explicit on this point:

> I am in agreement that the Hebrew way of thinking is vastly superior to that of Greek dualism, *because it fits better* with the general character of religious experience and because it makes better Biblical theology. A mediational view of religious experience—and thus a relational understanding of en-counter with the divine—*does negate the sort of absorption or unity motif* that is properly associated with the influence of Neoplatonism.[11]

Katz, too, claims that "there is no substantive evidence that there is any pure consciousness per se achieved."[12]—by which he seems to mean both that there is no good evidence of reports[13] and also that any good reports of such are philosophically mistaken.[14] Gill and Katz, however, are not alone: rather, they are giving voice to a common tendency among scholars to eliminate out of hand any possibility of nonintentional or nonrelational experiences. This, too, requires considerably more justification than heretofore provided.

This constructivistic approach also has given rise to the tendency to read primary mystical sources in its terms. Thus, any mention of an encounter with something which is expressed in intentional grammatical form (Jones sees, hears, thinks . . . *P;* or Jones *M's* that *P*) is taken to necessarily and always signify an intentional or relational experience. However valid this leap from grammer to experience may be for ordinary experiences—experiences out of which the grammer was developed, I may add—it may not be valid when it comes to nonrelational experiences. Steven Bernhardt has argued that even though a mystic uses intentional language, sometimes there may be no intentional object or content for consciousness encountered during the event. Speaking of Plotinus's description of God, he explains that "the experience spoken of as "of X" . . . *just is* the state of pure consciousness, consciousness without any object or content of consciousness. In the case of Plotinus . . . the undifferentiated state of the soul *just is* the experience of the One. This is what Plotinus means when he says that 'we are ever present to Him as soon as we contain no more difference.' "[15] If a mystic attempts to describe a nonrelational experience, he or she may very well (from linguistic habit, conscious choice, or what have you) employ relational or intentional language to describe it. If so, he or she would be employing the grammar in an odd or askew—though not unintelligible or meaningless—sense. We must remain alive to such a possibility in any textual analysis.

In this article, I will argue that the fourteenth-century Christian mystic, Meister Eckhart, does describe certain experiences which are nonrelational. Second, I will argue that, while he generally avoids intentional language, the occasional utterances which employ the intentional terms "God" or "Godhead" as experiential "objects" do not necessarily imply the presence of intentional or relational experiential structures. Finally, I will suggest Eckhart's attitude toward these events and briefly outline the place Eckhart provides them in his mystical itinerary.

ECKHART ON *GEZÜCKEN*

Some Eckhart scholars have denied that Eckhart discusses or advocates temporary or rapturous mystical experiences. In the early 1960s Heribert Fischer denied any interest in mysticism at all in the Meister.[16] In English, Carl Kelley denies mysticism of Eckhart because, he claims, the Meister does not advocate rapturous states.[17] These views, however, represent a generally discredited scholarly opinion.[18] While agreeing that Eckhart should be viewed as a mystic, John Caputo and Richard Kieckhefer find virtually no interest on the Meister's part in any transient mystical states. Instead, they both argue for an interest in "habitual" states.[19] Reinier Schurmann, while finding an interest in a mystical "itinerary," denies any interest in transient phenomena.[20] Bernard McGinn states that Eckhart "shows no real interest in rapture,"[21] and claims that "a careful search [of the Eckhart corpus] reveals that there are only three treatments of *raptus* or what one might call mystical ecstasy in his voluminous writings."[22]

Caputo, McGinn, Kieckhefer, and others, are correct in claiming that Eckhart emphasizes a Union with God that he calls the Birth (*geburt*) of the Son in the Soul and the Breakthrough (*durchbruch*) of the Soul to the Godhead. They are incorrect, however, that he shows no real interest in transient episodes. He calls them *gezucken*, rapture.

Gezucket, which is the past participial adjective form of the root *zücken* and the related terms *verzücken* and *entzücken*, have never, to my knowledge, been explicated in the secondary literature.[23] Eckhart translates the Latin *raptus* as *gezucket* (it is usually translated as rapture, enraptured or sometimes borne up).[24] Paul was *gezucket* to the third heaven, says Eckhart's version of 2 Cor. 12:2.[25] Peter was *entzucket . . . unwizzende,* (transported . . . unknowingly).[26] The claims of McGinn and others notwithstanding, I have found nine passages in the German works which discuss an experience using "*gezucket*" and the other above-mentioned words, as well as two discussions of rapture in the Latin works.[27] In other passages Eckhart does not use *gezucket sin* but is unquestionably speaking of rapture.[28]

One of the clearest characterizations of *gezucket* is found in the sermon *Dum medium silentium*,[29] a sermon which will be a focus of this article. Eckhart introduces the medieval notion of the powers of the soul in that sermon:

> Whatever the soul effects, she effects with her powers. What she understands, she understands with the intellect. What she remembers, she does with the memory; if she would love, she does that with the will, and thus she works with her powers and not with her essence. Every external act is linked with some means. The power of sight works only through the eyes; otherwise it can neither employ nor bestow vision, and so it is with all the other senses. The soul's every external act is effected by some means.[30]

In addition to the five senses there are six powers: three lower (lower intellect, desire, and anger) and three higher (memory, higher intellect and will). It is by their activity that the soul enters into, and interacts with, the external world.[31] We look at objects with our eyes, hear sounds with our ears, and so on.[32] The activity of the six higher powers generates thought and desire, that is, willing and cognitive or mental activity. So far, pretty standard scholastic psychology.

This picture of the powers in the soul describes our "fallen" state only, that is, our present state. Before the fall, all minds were hierarchically oriented to God, like filings to a magnet, " 'This was,' and is, 'man's correct condition,' when the sensitive faculty obeys, looks to and is ordered to the inferior reason, and the inferior reason cleaves and adheres to the superior reason as it in turns does to God. . . . [T]his was and is the state of nature that was set up before sin, 'the state of innocence.' "[33] But having lost that divine "center" in the fall, the powers have lost their one-pointed orientation, "When the bond and order of the height of the soul to God was dissolved through the injury of sundering sin ('Your iniquities have divided you from your God,' Is a. 59:2), it followed that all the powers of the soul, inferior reason and the sensitive faculty as well, were separated from contact with the rule of the superior reason."[34] Replacing the orientation toward the one, the soul and the powers have become preoccupied with the world. Each of the powers now is turned to its respective domain—seeing to visible objects, hearing to sounds, and so on. This multiplicity of concern has ramifications for the quality of our attention: because the soul is "so firmly attached to the powers," she "has to flow with them wherever they flow, because in every task they perform the soul must be present and attentive, or they could not work at all."[35] As a result the mind attends now to this visible object, now to that sound, and then to some thought. The mind is drawn hither and thither towards various thoughts, sensations, or what have you. At one point, Eckhart calls this phenomenon the "storm of inward thoughts."[36]

Despite the overlay of the theological interpretation through the doctrine of the fall, unmistakable here is a very commonplace pattern of mental activity. It is that we attend now to seeing this, hearing the other, or thinking one thought after another. Such activities, especially thoughts themselves, are in constant flux, a "storm." In a word, our minds *wander*. With this common fact each and every one of my readers is, no doubt, all too familiar. (I believe that such a pattern may be seen cross-culturally, but I cannot discuss the point or its implications here.)

Perhaps because Eckhart's listeners, like my readers, were no doubt familiar with this utterly prosaic fact of life—the wandering mind— Eckhart need not have dwelt on it in great detail. This is very much his style, for he focuses almost exclusively on the "goal" to be attained rather than the starting point.[37] Thus, I will have to rely on other, more explicit sources here. One of the clearest descriptions of this ordinary (i.e., "stormy") pattern of mental activity in the Christian mystical literature is found in the immensely popular and seminal fifth-century volume, *The Conferences of Cassian*.[38] Cassian's Abba Moses describes the ordinary mind as "fluttering." It "flutters hither and thither," he says, "according to the whim of the passing moment and follows what ever immediate and external impression is presented to it."[39] Abba Isaac describes thoughts similarly as "career[ing] about the soul" and like bubbling, effervescent "boiling water."[40] In a more extended description of these mental "flutterings," Abba Isaac states:

> When the mind has begun to take the meaning of a psalm, it passes on unawares and unintentionally to some other text of Scripture. When it has just begun to meditate upon that text and has half considered it, its attention is caught by another passage and it forgets all about the earlier matter for meditation. And so it goes on, hopping from text to text, from psalm to psalm, from Gospel to Epistle and thence to a prophetic book and thence to a narrative in the historical books of the Old Testament, meandering vaguely. . . . At the time of the office it totters about like a drunkard, its worship very inadequate. During the prayers it is thinking about a psalm or lesson. During the singing of the psalter, it is thinking about something quite outside the text of the psalm. During the lesson, it is thinking about something that has to be done, or remembering something that has been done. So it receives or rejects nothing in a disciplined and orderly manner, but seems to be knocked about by haphazard assaults, powerless to keep or to linger over the text which pleases it.[41]

This Cassian's Isaac calls (as I did) the "wandering mind."[42] Cassian and Eckhart are obviously referring to the same fact of life. The mind wanders, weaving from hither to thither, and flits about from fantasy to thought to sensation to concern, to. . . . This pattern of mental activity may be roughly characterized in terms of two primary characteristics: first, there is some *content of consciousness,* be it thought, sensation, emotion, or what have you.[43] Through the agency of the powers, the soul attends to some "outward" content.[44] This is of a piece with the constructivist's claim of "relational" experience. Second, that content is in a *constant state of flux or mutability.* It "wanders," "flutters," or "meanders," as Cassian put it. As Eckhart puts this, we "turn from one thing to another."[45]

Returning to our sermon, *Dum medium silentium,* after having introduced the powers and alluding thereby to this phenomenon of the wandering mind, Eckhart writes of the *gezucket* of Saint Paul, the archetype of "a man" (i.e., anyone) having this experience:

> [T]he more completely you are able to draw in your powers to a unity and forget all those things and their images which you have absorbed, and the further you can get from creatures and their images, the nearer you are to this and the readier to receive it. If only you could suddenly be unaware of all things, then you could pass into an oblivion of your own body as St. Paul did. . . . In this case . . . memory no longer functioned, nor understanding, nor the senses, nor the powers that should function so as to govern and grace the body. . . . In this way a man should flee his senses, turn his powers inward and sink into an oblivion of all things and himself.[46]

Here, Eckhart specifically asserts the absence of sensory content ("nor the senses") as well as mental objects ("devoid of" memory, understanding, senses, etc.). One has become oblivious of "[one's] own body" and "all things." One even loses the awareness of oneself. In short, in this phenomenon of *gezucket,* one is "unaware of all things."

In another passage Eckhart specifically notes that the contemplative "withdrawal" from cognitive activity includes both "internal" and "external" powers: "If a person wanted to withdraw into himself with all his powers internal and external." The "external" powers are (as I mentioned) the senses, the lower intellect (common sense), anger, and desire—the powers by which we notice and respond in rudimentary ways to the external world. The "internal" powers are intellect, will, and desire, the "higher" powers with which we generate thought and desire. Hence, withdrawal of both implies that neither the powers of thought nor of sensation "flow out" into their usual activities. In other words, both the sensing and the thinking aspects of the mind are inactive. Responding to his conditional, Eckhart continues, "[T]hen he will find himself in a state in which there are no images and no desires in him and he will therefore stand without any activity, internal or external."[47] With both internal and external powers withdrawn one experiences neither thought, affective feeling, sensation, nor vision.

In *gezucket* one is, therefore, aware of (according to Eckhart) neither thought, word, speech, or even vague daydreams. Even oblivious of "himself," such a man becomes completely silent and at rest, without cognitive content: he is blank yet open and alert. Restated, according to this passage, in *gezucket* the subject is merely awake, simply present. No manifold for awareness, either sensory or mental, is encountered.

In terms of the primary characteristics of the ordinary waking pattern of mental activity described earlier, *gezucket* is without both. First, there is no sensory or mental *content for consciousness* since it is devoid of the operation or products of the mental or sensory powers. Second, without content there can be no flutter or *mutability* since it is only the sensations and thoughts which draw our awareness this way and that. When a few lines later Eckhart exhorts his listeners, he describes the process as one of withdrawing from the "turmoil of inward thoughts", "Withdraw from the unrest of external activities, then flee away and hide from the turmoil of inward thoughts (*gesturme . . . inwendiger gedanken*)."[48] In short, the turmoil and unrest of both external sensations and responses as well as internal thoughts and desires are denied of this quiet state.

In the oft-quoted *Intravit Jesus,*[49] Eckhart characterizes the three ways into "the circle of eternity." The first is seeking God "in all creatures with manifold activity and ardent longing." The second way involves rapture, *gezucket.* Peter is the archetype here. Eckhart says:

> The second way is a wayless way, free and yet bound, raised, rapt away (*gezucket*) well-nigh past self and all things, without will and without images, even though not yet in essential being. . . . St. Peter did not see God unveiled, though indeed he was caught up by the heavenly Father's power past all created understanding to the circle of eternity. I say he was grasped by the heavenly Father in a loving embrace, and borne up unknowingly (*unwizzende*) with tempestuous power, in an aspiring spirit transported (*entzücket*) beyond all conceiving by the might of the heavenly Father.[50]

Peter was borne up "beyond all conceiving," past all "created understanding." His rapture was beyond the use of the rational powers; he was borne up "unknowingly" (*unwizzende*).

This term, "*unwizzen*" (sometimes "*nihtwizzen*"), literally to "unknow," marks a feature of the experience which results when one stops the activity of those external and internal powers. To bring on *unwizzen*, one must "collect" all of one's powers away from such outward activity and thought and bring them to a quiet still silence, "Accordingly a master says: 'To achieve an interior act, a man must collect all his powers as if into a corner of his soul where, hiding away from all images and forms, he can get to work.' Here he must come to a forgetting (*vergezzen*) and an unknowing (*nihtwizzen*). There must be a stillness and a silence."[51] Hence, when Eckhart speaks of the "unknowing," which Peter underwent in his rapture to the circle of eternity, he alludes to such a stillness and silence.[52]

The silence gained in this experience results from a forgetting (*vergezzen*) of the ordinary sensory and ratiocinative powers. Obviously, Eckhart means that one forgets in the sense of ceasing for the moment to employ and use those powers, not in the sense that one forgets things permanently or ceases being able to use one's powers forever.[53] The point is that in his *gezücken* Saint Peter ceased thinking.

A similar portrait comes in the treatise *On Detachment.* The truly detached man is sometimes "enraptured (*gezucket*) into eternity in such a way that no transient thing can move him and he experiences nothing at all that is physical. He is said to be dead to the world, for he savors nothing worldly."[54]

I noted that sometimes such a thoughtless moment is depicted without using the term "*gezucket.*" This passage, in which Eckhart quotes Pseudo-Dionysius, may be read as one such. It says that one must have an "untroubled mind," by which I understand that the anxious mental "storm" has been "stilled." One must "soar above" the powers of thought and activity, arriving at a place of stillness and darkness, "Dear son Timothy, do you with untroubled mind soar above yourself *and all your powers, above* ratiocination *and reasoning,* above works, *above all modes and existence,* into the secret still darkness."[55] By such a "soaring into a darkness" I understand the contemplative quiet of *gezucket.* One soars above the operations of the powers, above ratiocination and reason. One achieves a state of darkness (without content) and stillness.

In sum, I characterize the pattern of mental functioning denoted by Eckhart's term *"gezucket"* as a pure consciousness event, *a mind which is simultaneously wakeful and devoid of content for consciousness.* Eckhart does not expressely state that one is awake (i.e., not unconscious or asleep) in *gezucket.* It seems obvious, however, that this is so since it would be absurd to suppose that Eckhart would spill such ink over a mere sleeping or blackout. In one discussion of Saint Paul's rapture, Eckhart comes close to saying that one is wakeful during *gezucket:* Had anyone touched Saint Paul with a needle during his rapture, "[W]ould he have felt it? I say, 'Yes.' . . . [I]f anyone had then touched him with the point of a needle, he would have been aware of it . . . he would have known it."[56] In *gezucket* Paul could have responded had a need arose, only he had no such need. Had he been utterly blacked out he could not have felt anything. This capacity to respond to sensory input implies that the mind was not unconscious.[57]

However paradoxical and strange this contentless but alert mind may sound, it may not be idiosyncratic to Eckhart. Similar events may be found in writers from a wide array of traditions. The other essays in Part I also argue to this effect. The character of such events is suggested by W. T. Stace's summary of his forty pages of cross-cultural evidence for such events, which he calls "introvertive mystical experiences":

> Suppose that, after having got rid of all sensations, one should go on to exclude from consciousness all sensuous images, and then all abstract thoughts, reasoning processes, volitions, and other particular mental contents; what would there then be left of consciousness? There would be no mental content whatever but rather a complete emptiness, vacuum, void. One would suppose *a priori* that consciousness would then entirely lapse and one would fall asleep or become unconscious. But the introvertive mystics—thousands of them all over the world—unanimously assert that they have attained to this complete vacuum of particular mental contents, but that what then happens is quite different from a lapse into unconsciousness. On the contrary, what emerges is a state of *pure* consciousness—

"pure" in the sense that it is not the consciousness of any empirical content. It has no content except itself.[58]

If Stace's and our research is correct, such an experience may be common in many traditions.

GOD AND *GEZUCKET*

The constructivist, who has a philosophical need to see relationality in all mystical experiences, may at this point object, "Is not God encountered in *gezucket*? After all, Eckhart says, '"Paul rose from the ground and with open eyes saw nothing."' He saw nothing, that is: God.[59] Does this not clearly imply a relational experience of seeing God?

The question is: What does it mean to have an experience of God in *gezucket*? Does it necessarily imply a relational or intentional experience? How God is encountered can be best understood through a consideration of the "faculty" involved. I noted earlier that in scholastic thought the "powers" are those "agents" within the soul which lead one into the external world. They are the machinery as it were of the outward "dissipation" experienced by "fallen" humanity. But they are distinguished from man's "essence." Eckhart states in a passage from *Dum medium silentium* (quoted before); "Whatever the soul effects, she effects with her powers. What she understands, she understands with the intellect. What she remembers, she does with the memory; if she would love, she does that with the will and thus she works with her powers and not with her essence."[60] The soul works with her powers and not with her essence. Conversely, when she eliminates the activities of her powers she arrives at her "essence," also called her "ground" (*grunt*).

The "ground" of the soul is a central concept in Eckhart. Over this "innermost" man to which the powers have no access, Eckhart devotes his most enthralling language.[61] Within the soul there is a nameless place,[62] an "inmost part,"[63] a "silent middle." It is one's "being" or one's "essence." It is *in dem hôchsten der sele,* the highest in the soul; *der sele geist,* the spirit of the soul; *das innigeist,* the inward spirit; *der grunt,* the ground; *das burgelin,* the little castle; and so on. It is the *scintilla animae,* or *das funkelin der sele,* the spark of the soul.[64]

Most important, this "ground" within is "akin to the nature of the deity":[65]

There is something [the ground] that transcends the created being of the soul, not in contact with created things, which are nothing; not even a angel has it, though he has a clear being that is pure and extensive: even that does not touch it. It is akin to the nature of the deity, it is one in itself, and has naught in common with anything. It is a stumbling-block to many a learned cleric.[66]

It is here, to this "essence" or "place" within, that man retires when he drops all external and internal works in *gezucket*. When Eckhart continues this passage, he describes this transcendent "place":

> . . .It is a strange and desert place, and is rather nameless than possessed of a name, and is more unknown than it is known. If you could naught yourself for an instant, indeed I say less than an instant, you would possess all that this is in itself. But as long as you mind yourself or anything at all, you know no more of God than my mouth knows of color or my eye of taste.[67]

The key fact to be remembered about this "place" within the soul is its utterly *apophatic* status. One arrives "there" by "naughting" oneself for an instant. There, no "minding" of anything at all occurs. No activity enters there nor does one entertain any images there. It is no-thing, utterly silent and restful, ". . .in the soul's ground and innermost recess, into which no image ever shone or (soul) power peeped."[68] In *Dum medium silentium* he describes this "ground":

> In the summit of the soul (*hôchsten der sele*) . . . where time never entered, where no image ever shone in. . . .[69]

> In the soul's essence there is no activity, for the powers she works with emanate from the ground of being. Yet in that ground is the silent "middle": here [in the ground is] nothing but rest and celebration.[70]

In the same sermon Eckhart calls this "place" silent:

> There is the silent "middle," for no creature ever entered there and no image, nor has the soul there either activity or understanding, therefore she is not aware there of any image, whether of herself or of any other creature.[71]

This "place," in other words, is the "place" to which one retires when one has dropped all of the activity of the powers of the soul, that is, all cognitive activity. It is the "place" to which one "comes" when utterly still within, "When the soul comes to the nameless place, she takes her rest. There . . . she rests."[72]

In short, "the ground," or "essence," is that which is entered in the experience of *gezucket*.[73] Because this is so, the "ground's" relationship with the deity becomes important for understanding the way God is encountered in this experience. Critical here is that the "ground" for Eckhart is the locale in man in which God has always remained:

> Here [the essence] God's ground is my ground and my ground is God's ground.[74]

There is something in the soul [namely, "the ground"] in which God is bare and the masters say this is nameless, and has no name of its own . . . God is always present and within it. I say that God has always been in it, eternally and uninterruptedly. . . .[75]

. . . God is nowhere so truly as in the soul, and . . . in the inmost soul, in the summit of the soul.[76]

God shares a "ground" with the soul's "ground," and He has so shared it since man's preexistence. But this is "obscured" in "ordinary" experience, in which man is drawn through the incessant bubbling of thoughts and the turmoil of sensations to various "creaturely" concerns. By looking in the wrong direction, outwards instead of inwards, the religious "overlooks" this "place" within himself, "The soul has something in her, a spark of intellect, that never dies. . . . But there is also in our souls a knowing directed towards externals, the sensible and rational perception which operates in images and words to obscure this from us."[77] Creaturely activities cover over this nameless place like a "cloud or mist" hiding the sun.[78] Yet encountering this "locale" always remains possible.

If God is in contact with the "ground" of the soul and if the "ground" is that which is realized during the moments in which the powers are brought to stillness, then, according the Eckhart, the "place" of God within the soul is revealed during these moments of emptiness. Self-abnegation and the silencing of the powers is equated with the discovery of God within. In and through the nothing, God is present. Here is the complete passage describing Paul's encounter with God in *gezucket:*

"Paul rose from the ground and with open eyes saw nothing." I cannot see what is one. He saw nothing, that is: God. . . . When the soul is unified and there enters into total self-abnegation, *then she finds God* as in Nothing. It appeared to a man as in a dream—it was a waking dream—that he became pregnant with Nothing like a woman with child, and *in* that nothing God was born. He was the fruit of nothing. God was born *in* the Nothing. Therefore he says: "he arose from the ground with open eyes, seeing nothing."[79]

God is that which is encountered during the nothing. He is "in" the nothing. God is "born" when one is "pregnant" with nothing. The act of silencing the cognitive mechanism and the senses is none other than the encounter with God. "Where creature stops God begins to be."[80]

Summarizing, it is *God* who is met in the silence, and He has been "there" all along. We were usually so preoccupied, we did not notice. If we are able to slough off the activity of the powers which have preoccupied us, there He will be. *Gezucket* is a mode of access to the divine (though not, I must reaffirm, its final perfection).

I noted at the outset that Bernhardt has argued his essay herein that it is possible that a pure consciousness event "just is" the encounter which is described as an encounter with God. The question is: Is this encounter with the deity at the "ground" one of these instances or is it like an intentional encounter with some object? I have three reasons for thinking that Eckhart is not referring to an encounter with God which is experienced as intentional but rather as contentless—the pure consciousness event.

First Eckhart's phraseology that describes the experienced relationship between God and the soul in *gezucket* suggests a nonintentional experience. Eckhart is linguistically very careful. As a rule, Paul does not "see something," he is "locked in the embrace of the Godhead."[81] Peter does not stare wondrously at a God "over there," as it were, but is "caught up by the heavenly Father's power," and is "grasped by the heavenly Father in loving embrace."[82] Such expressions, reminiscent of the mystical marriage motif of many Rhineland mystics (the so-called *Brautmystik* [bride mysticism]), pointedly *avoid* asserting the presence of an intentional object. When Eckhart says that Timothy soared above himself "into the secret still darkness," he connotes again the absence of any intentional object. It is striking that the preacher typically avoids the most natural phraseologies like "one sees God there" or "one thinks of God."

The second reason concerns the nature of the purported "object" of *gezucket*. Paul was locked in the embrace of the *Godhead*. While this grammatically sounds like an object, what kind of an object might it be? The Godhead, you will recall, is the God beyond God, utterly without numeration or distinguishing marks.[83] If I were to encounter something absolutely without phenomenal distinctions, then there could be no distinguishing marks by means of which I could distinguish myself as subject from something over against me as an intentional object.[84] There could be no sensed "borders" between It and some "other," that is, me. Similarly, when Eckhart says one is "grasped by the heavenly Father in loving embrace," he is asserting both by syntax and also by theological implications that Peter experienced no intentional object.[85]

My final reason for believing that God is not encountered as an intentional object concerns the "place" where God is encountered. In that "highest place" within my soul, it will be recalled, "God's ground and the soul's ground are one ground."[86] I share, at the deepest level within my own self, a "ground" with God. Thus, when I "turn off" my powers and drop all mental content I do not "go" someplace else; rather, I "arrive" at none other than *my own "ground"* within myself. The "place" to which I go is none other than the summit of *my* soul. The soul cannot know something in an intentional sense here. Rather, it comes to simply persist "in" its own being or, in what amounts to the same thing, it comes to be immersed "in" God, "For the first thing on which blessedness depends is that the soul should contemplate God unveiled. In this experience the soul receives all her being and her life, and draws all that she is from the ground of God, and knows nothing of knowledge, or of love, or of anything at all. She becomes entirely and absolutely passive in the being of God."[87] When I drop all content, I rest quietly within myself. There is no other thing there. I am passive—that is, inactive—merely resting in what is at heart within my own soul. I simply am what I have always been in the ground itself.

While this being ourselves and nothing else sounds peculiar to us who are so accustomed to thinking that all experiences are intentional, it may not be idiosyncratic to Eckhart. I am reminded here again of Stace's description of introvertive mystical experiences, "Suppose then that we obliterate from consciousness all objects physical or mental. When the self is not engaged in apprehending objects it becomes aware of itself. The self itself emerges. The self, however, when stripped of all psychological contents or objects, is not another thing, or substance, distinct from its contents. It is the bare unity of the manifold of consciousness from which the manifold itself has been obliterated."[88]

In conclusion, when Eckhart says that in *gezucket* one comes to the highest within the self, and that God is "there," I do not believe that he means that the self "goes" anywhere or "sees" anything intentionally. Rather, he simply describes a state in which the self simply rests within itself. This encounter with the self within is *analytically* understood to "share a ground" with God. The *phenomenology* of the experience is that one simply ceases to pay attention to or to use the powers. One ceases to think or feel anything and has an experience without seams or borders. But the self—or rather its "ground"—Eckhart *analyzes* to be associated with God or the Godhead.[89] By forgetting the powers one "arrives at" this locale which is so associated. To be without intentional content (phenomenological description) just is the same thing as being "locked in the embrace of the Godhead" (analysis).

If this is the case, then the ordinary (intentional) phenomenological relations which normally can be read off intentional language cannot be assumed to hold. Rather, as Stephen Bernhardt and Franklin Merrill-Wolff have both noted, the subject comes into relation with its "object" through a relation of identity.[90] Eckhart encounters God not by "seeing" Him but by being identified with Him. While one always retains this contact with God within oneself, one comes to persist in *gezucket* only so identified.

When Eckhart asserts that one is "locked in the embrace of the God-

head" in *gezucket,* he is providing a term, "the Godhead," for the "some-thing" encountered within the self itself in this "nothing" experience. He may be understood to be providing an *analytical,* theological "content" for a phenomenological contentlessness. This is why we should not say that one achieves God through the employment of some sort of "powers."
Rather, it is more in harmony with Eckhart's thinking and language to say that one simply discovers one's contact with God by living it and nothing else.

THE PLACE OF *GEZÜCKEN* IN THE MYSTICAL LIFE

I want to address an objection which has been raised against my claims of Eckhart's sympathy toward *gezucket* by certain Eckhart scholars.[91] As I noted early on, many have argued that the Meister did not emphasize or advocate rapture. Rather, he advocated something closer to what Richard Kieckhefer called *habitual* mysticism—that is, a permanent or semiper-manent lived experience of union with God. Kieckhefer writes, "Eckhart did not view ecstatic or abstractive union with God as integral to the life of the soul, or even as a goal to be sought or particularly treasured. The state to which he invites his reader is that of habitual and nonabstractive union; he nowhere says that other forms are necessary or even helpful in the attainment of that goal."[92] I agree that rapture is not the *summum bonum* for Eckhart. I have shown in chapters 6 and 7 of my *Meister Eckhart* that he advocates a more permanent transformation.[93]

However, it would be false to claim, as some scholars have, that Eckhart denigrates rapture in itself.[94] Authors who believe that Eckhart denigrates rapture have appealed to passages like the following:[95]

> But now some complain that they have no inwardness nor devotion nor rapture nor any special consolation from God. Such people are still not on the right way: one can bear with them but it is second-best. . . . [These] people want to see God with their own eyes as they see a cow, and they want to love God as they love a cow. You love a cow for her milk and her cheese and your own profit. That is what all those men do who love God for outward wealth or inward consolation—and they do not truly love God, they love their own profit. I truly assert that *anything* you put in the forefront of your mind, if it is not God in Himself, is—however good it may be—a hindrance to your gaining the highest truth.[96]

One can hardly be blamed for reading an antagonism toward rapture in this. The desire for rapture is the "wrong way." People desirous of rapture want to "see God with the eyes one sees a cow." This passage certainly sounds antiecstatic!

Yet, on closer scrutiny, what Eckhart disparages is not precisely rapture. What he preaches against here and elsewhere is the *desire* for it. People who crave such consolations are on the wrong track not because they seek something evil in itself but because they have a craving at all. The desire for inwardness or rapture functions as nothing more than a substitute for some other desire. Such people still seek their own profit: instead of something material, the profit is now the ecstatic "flash," as it were.[97] It is desire against which he rails.

Not only does he not devalue rapture, but he twice herein covertly affirms it: "good as [inwardness, devotion, or rapture] may be" and "however good it may be." He does not deny its value. He allows that rapture is a taste of something worthwhile, indeed a taste, albeit momentary, of the *summum bonum*. Addressing himself to those who sought the ecstatic flash (presumably the Beguines and "Dominicanized" Beguines, who were so conspicuous in his day), what he disparages is either seeking or being attached to such moments.

Here is another popular passage among those who claim an antiecstasy of Eckhart:

> I say truly, as long as you do works for the sake of heaven or God or eternal bliss, from without, you are at fault. It may pass muster, but it is not the best. Indeed, if a man thinks he will get more of God by meditation, by devotion, by ecstasies or by special infusion of grace than by the fireside or in the stable—that is nothing but taking God, wrapping a cloak round His head and shoving Him under a bench. For whoever seeks God in a special way gets the way and misses God, who lies hidden in it.[98]

Note again the overt debunking and the covert affirmation. Seeking God by some special way represents an attachment to the process rather than to the goal. Yet experiences in meditation, devotion, or ecstasy are indeed experiences of God: it is *His* head around which the cloak gets wrapped. Eckhart's point is that to desire Him via these special ways and consolations is to *have a desire at all*. Desire implies a self-will and the whole syndrome of *eigenschaften* (attachments).[99] In this case, the attachment is to the way, the contemplative routine: "all those who are bound with attachment [*Miteigenschaft gebunden*] to prayer, fasting, vigils and all kinds of outward discipline and mortification."[100] Whatever its object, for Eckhart attachment remains attachment.

Rather than discrediting it utterly (as we have seen), Eckhart presents *gezucket* as one form of real contact with God. Yet in itself it is not worth pursuing. One key factor marring it is that Eckhart seeks transformations which are permanent and *gezucket* is temporary. Eckhart mentions its transiency frequently. Paul's archetypical rapture into the third heaven lasted but a short while.[101] Even the residual effects lasted but three days.[102] Peter, tempestuously borne aloft, soon returned.[103] No one in the world can be withdrawn for very long: perhaps an instant,[104] perhaps an hour, perhaps even as long as Moses, forty days.[105] But even Moses' forty days were but a brief interlude in his long years. Temporary experiences, no matter how wonderful, are wonderful only as long as they last. One is left with but a memory.

Eckhart advocates not an ephemeral flash, but a permanent and more far-reaching change in the entire constitution of the religious. He is not interested in a life of light, as it were, which is prey to intervening "spells of darkness."[106] He advocates no "gifts of the Holy Spirit," that is, visions, auditions, or other consolations. Nor does he seek His "likeness" in transient transcendental moments, for these also do not "abide with you." Rather, he seeks to establish a relationship with God which is constant, "It is true that you may receive the gifts of the Holy Ghost, or the likeness of the Holy Ghost, but it does not abide with you—it is impermanent. In the same way a man may blush for shame or blench, but that is accidental and it passes. But a man who is by nature ruddy and fair, remains so always. So it is with a man who is the only begotten Son, the Holy Ghost *remains* in his being."[107] Eckhart advocates a habitual union with God, in which the Holy Ghost "remains" in his being.[108]

He does not advocate pursuing such experiences, but as I have shown above, he does in fact sympathetically discuss them. Let me reiterate, however, that I have chosen to discuss *gezucket* not because it is Eckhart's primary focus, but because it is mine.

One of Eckhart's purposes in discussing *gezucket* is to stress that the contemplative life is only complete when brought into action. For example, immediately following the passage describing "a state in which there are no images and no desires in him and . . . without any activity, internal or external," Eckhart instructs his hearers that "one should learn to act in such a way that one breaks up the inwardness (*innicheit*) into reality and leads reality into inwardness, and that one should thus become accustomed to work without compulsion."[109] "Inwardness" or the "inward man" is what is discovered in that moment when one is "without any activity, internal or external." The listener is enjoined to drag the inwardness outwards, as it were, bringing it into activity. One is to learn to act in such a way that reality (*würklicheit*)—here activity, thought, perception, and so on—is perceived and undergone *while not losing* the interior silence encountered in contemplation. Simultaneously, one is to lead "reality into the inwardness," that is, make the silent inwardness, if you will, dynamic. In other words, the advanced adept is to learn to think, speak, walk, and work without losing the profoundest quietness inside.

This is Eckhart's advocated goal: the dynamic, habitual goal of a life in which the divine silence is never lost. The pure consciousness event is a milepost—an interesting one, but only a milepost—along the path to that goal.

NOTES

1. Jerry H. Gill, "Mysticism and Mediation," *Faith and Philosophy* 1 (1984), 113.

2. Jerry Gill, "Religious Experience as Mediated." Paper delivered to the American Academy of Religion, November 1980.

3. Ibid., p. 7.

4. Steven T. Katz, "Language, Epistemology and Mysticism," in *Mysticism and Philosophical Analysis* ed. Steven T. Katz (New York: Oxford University Press, 1978), p. 63.

5. John Hick, "Mystical Experience as Cognition," in *Understanding Mysticism*, ed. Richard Woods, O. P. (Garden City, N.Y.: Doubleday, Image Books, 1980), p. 425.

6. Terence Penelhum, "Unity and Diversity in the Interpretation of Mysticism," in *Understanding Mysticism*, Woods, p. 120.

7. Robert K. C. Forman, "Constructivism in Zen Buddhism, Paramārtha, and in Eckhart," Ph.D. diss., Columbia University, 1988, chap. 2.

8. See my article "Mysticism and Pure Consciousness Events," *Sophia* 25, no. 1 (1986), 49–58; see also "Constructivism in Zen Buddhism, Paramārtha and in Eckhart," chaps. 4–6.

9. Forman, "Constructivism in Zen Buddhism, Paramārtha, and in Eckhart," chap. 1.

10. See Donald Rothberg, "Contemporary Epistemology and the Study of Mysticism," in the present volume.

11. Gill, *"Mysticism and Mediation,"* 118–19. [Emphasis added.]

12. Katz, "Language, Epistemology and Mysticism," p. 56.

13. This is the position he took in 1985 at the American Academy of Religion's philosophy of religion discussion section.

14. While the point is never clearly argued, this seems to be the tenor of the claim made in 1978 Katz's essay (see n. 4). Taken together these two claims are incoherent.

15. See Stephen Bernhardt, "Is Pure Consciousness Unmediated?: A Response to Katz," pp. 12–13. Paper delivered to the American Academy of Religion, November 1985. [Emphasis in original.] A revised version ("Are Pure Consciousness Events Unmediated?") is in the present volume.

16. Heribert Fischer, "Zur Frage nach der Mystik in den Werken Meister Eckharts," in *La Mystique Rhénane: Colloque de Strassbourg* (Paris: Presses Universitaires de France, 1963).

17. C. F. Kelley argues that Eckhart is no mystic but a "pure metaphysician." see *Meister Eckhart on Divine Knowledge* (New Haven, Conn.: Yale University Press, 1977).

18. In German, see Josef Quint, "Introduction," in *Meister Eckehart: Deutsche Predigen und Traktate* (Munich: Carl Hanser, 1955); and Alois Haas, "Das Verhältnis von Sprache und Erfahrung in der deutschen Mystik," in *Deutsche Literatur des späten Mittelalters,* ed. W. Harms and L. P. Johnson (Berlin: E. Schmidt, 1975), pp. 240–64.

19. John Caputo, "Fundamental Themes in Meister Eckhart's Mysticism," *Thomist* 42 (1978), 197–225; Richard Kieckhefer "Meister Eckhart's Conception of Union with God," *Harvard Theological Review* 71 (1978), 203–25.

20. Reiscier Schurmann, *Meister Eckhart: Mystic and Philosopher,* (Bloomington: Indiana University Press, 1978), pp. 15, 84.

21. Bernard McGinn, "Meister Eckhart," in *An Introduction to Medieval Mystics of Europe,* ed. Paul Szarmach (Albany: SUNY Press, 1984), p. 248.

22. Idem, "The God Beyond God: Theology and Mysticism in the Thought of Meister Eckhart," *Journal of Religion* 61 (1981) 16.

23. The following abbreviations have been used throughout this essay: DW = Josef Quint, ed., *Meister Eckhart: Die deutsche Werke herausgegeben im Auftrage der Deutschen Forschungsgemeinschaft* (Stuttgart and Berlin: W. Kohlhammer Verlag, 1936–). LW = Josef Koch, ed., *Meister Echhart: Die latinische Werke herausgegeben im Auftrage der Deutschen Forschungsgemeinschaft* (Stuttgart and Berlin: W. Kohlhammer Verlag, 1936–). PF = Franz Pfeiffer, ed. *Meister Eckhart* (Göttingen: Vandenhoeck & Ruprecht, 1924). W = M. O'C. Walshe, ed. and trans., *Meister Eckhart: German Sermons and Treatises,* 3 vols. (London: Watkins, 1979, 1981, 1987). Clark and Skinner = James Clark and John Skinner, eds. and trans., *Meister Eckhart: Selected Treatises and Sermons* (London: Faber & Faber, 1958). I have considered all sermons in DW authentic, with the following standard proviso: because one volume is yet to appear, I will count the sermons in Quint's German translation as equally authentic; if a sermon is not in DW, I will refer to PF as source material. In addition, I regard this as one way of counteracting any biases inadvertently produced by Quint's manner of authenticating sermons. He used as his sine qua non for authenticity the papal bull and related documents. While a systematic procedure, it may be skewed as it is less likely to include sermons which focus on the most obviously mystical material. Finally, because we have several excellent translations, there is no need for a new one; I will use W's translations of the complete sermons and Clark and Skinner's translations of the tractates, retranslating where noted.

24. *Zücken,* the infinitive, means to draw quickly and forcefully, to seize or tear away from. It indicates a force beyond the individual which grabs one, as when a sword is drawn from its sheath. As used by Eckhart in its mystical sense, especially in the passive voice, it indicates that the mystic is, as it were, pulled up

or out of himself or herself by something (or some One) beyond his or her control. *Gezücket werden,* the passive voice, becomes the participial adjective *gezucket* on occasion (e.g., DW 3:486:13). Since this form is closest to English phraseology, I will generally use it. For help on these terms I am grateful to Eckhard Kuhn-Osius.

25. DW 3:381:3 = W 2:321.

26. DW 3:487:2 = W 1:84.

27. The passages I have identified using the term *gezücken* are: DW 1:403:1 = W 2:72; DW 3:36:6 = W 2:213; DW 3:38:2 = W 2:214; DW 3:381:3 = W 2:321; DW 3:487:2–487:10 = W 1:84; DW 3:483:4–9 = W 1:83; DW 5:411:6 = Clark and Skinner, p. 163; DW 420:10 = Clark and Skinner, p. 166; PF 273:30 = W 2:280; LW 4:202; LW 5:93–95 (discussing *ecstasis mentis*).

28. For example, PF 7 = W 1:7; DW 5:290:5–8 = Clark and Skinner 101; DW 5:116:20–29 = Clark and Skinner, p. 156.

29. Number 57 in Quint's translation = Number 1 in Walshe's.

30. PF 4:29–36 = W 1:3.

31. PF 5:8–18 = W 1:4.

32. PF 5:18–23 = W 1:4.

33. *Parables of Gen.* 143. Trans. Edmund College and Bernard McGinn, *Meister Eckhart* (New York: Paulist Press, 1978), p. 112.

34. *Para ables of Gen.* 144, College and McGinn, p. 112.

35. PF 14:13–17 = W 1:20.

36. DW 3:18:3 = W 2:14.

37. Kelley, throughout *Eckhart on Divine Knowledge,* observes the same thing, though he phrases it in terms of principal knowledge.

38. *The Conferences of Cassian in Western Asceticism,* trans. and ed. Owen Chadwick (Philadelphia: Westminster Press, 1958). Eckhart demonstrates his acquaintance by paraphrasing Cassian in DW 3:481:2ff. and 5:279ff.

39. *Conferences of Cassian,* p. 198.

40. Ibid., p. 241.

41. Ibid, p. 244–45.

42. Ibid, p. 245.

43. See Norman Prigge and Gary Kessler's essay in this volume, "Is Mystical Experience Everywhere the Same?"

44. PF 14:17–18 = W 1:20.

45. PF 14: 13–15 = W 1:20.

46. PF 7:8–25 = W 1:7. This is one of the mentioned cases in which rapture is being described without use of the term *gezucket.* Since Saint Paul is so often the archetype of *gezucket* and since the experience being described is clearly rapturous, I believe that *gezucket* is being spoken of here.

47. DW 5:290:5–8 = Clark and Skinner, p. 101.

48. PF 7:27 = W 1:7.

49. DW Sermon 86 = W Sermon 9

50. DW 3:486–87 = W 1:83–84.

51. PF 14:31–36 = W 1:20.

52. Indeed, Eckhart associates the heavenly eternity with unchanging stillness. Letters traced there in the sand will remain unchanged forever. DW 3:41:4–
5 = W 2:215.

53. See My "Introduction" to the present volume.

54. DW 5:411:6–9, translation mine. Cf. Clark and Skinner, p. 163.

55. PF 8:1–4 = W 1:8; Quoting *De mystica theologia* (W 1:13, n.13).
[Emphasis added.]

56. DW 1:404:2–405:6 = W 2:72–73.

57. As is the case in ordinary usage, I equate "awake" with not being unconscious or not being asleep. See n. 42.

58. W. T. Stace, *Mysticism and Philosophy* (London: Macmillan, 1960; rpt.
Atlantic Highlands, N.J.: Humanities Press, 1978), pp. 85–86.

59. DW 3:222:11–223:1 = W 1:157.

60. PF 4:29–33 = W 1:3.

61. James Clark says, "many are the passages in which [Eckhart] speaks of the
"ground" of the soul or the spark of the soul." *Meister Eckhart: An Introduction to
the Study of His Works with an Anthology of His Sermons* (Edinburgh: Thomas
Nelson, 1957), p. 61.

62. DW 2:192:2 = W 1:275.

63. DW 2:95:3 = W 1:147

64. The "spark" was Peter Lombard's expression who, it is said, borrowed it
from Saint Jerome. The concept itself has had an illustrious history among Christian mystics. To Hugh of Saint Victor, it was *acumen mentis,* a high and elevated,
subtle element. For Richard of Saint Victor it was *summum mentis,* a deep and
hidden element. To Teresa it was the center of the soul, the spirit of the soul. It was
Eckhart however who made the concept and expression "spark of the soul"
famous.

65. DW 2:66:4 = W 1:144.

66. DW 2:66:2–6 = W 1:144.

67. DW 2:66:6–11 = W 1:144.

68. PF 11:25–26 = W 1:16.

69. DW 2:95:3–2:96:1 = W 1:147.

70. PF 4:36–40 = W 1:3.

71. PF 4:26–29 = W 1:3.

72. DW 2:189:2–3 = W 1:274.

73. PF 9 = W 1:10–11.

74. DW 1:90:8 = W 1:117.

75. DW 1:417–19:2 = W 2:312–13.

76. DW 2:95:1–3 = W 1:147.

77. DW 3:315:6–316:2 = W 1:64.

78. DW 5:113:14–16 = Clark and Skinner, p. 153. Cf. DW 2:401:7–402:2
= W 1:183.

79. DW 3:222:11–223:1, 224:4–225:1 = W 1:157–158. [Emphasis
added.] Walshe suggests that this passage is probably a record of a personal
experience in which Eckhart uses the third person just as Saint Paul does in 2 Cor.
12:2ff.

80. DW 1:92:7 = W 1:118.
81. DW 1:404:3–4 = W 2:72.
82. DW 3:486:19–487:1 = W 1:83–84.
83. Cf. McGinn, "The God Beyond God."
84. This need not imply pantheism, by the way. There can be analytical distinctions without phenomenolgical ones.
85. DW 3:486:19:–487:1 = W 1:84. "Father" is here equivalent to the distinctionless aspect of God. Thus, in this passage, the same lack of distinguishing marks holds true of the Father.
86. DW 1:253:5–6 = W 2:53.
87. DW 5:116:27–117:2 = Clark and Skinner, pp. 156–57.
88. Stace, *Mysticisn and Philosophy*, p. 86.
89. The "ground" may have analytical distinctions without implying phenomenal ones. For example, God is omnipotent, creator, and so on, whereas, the "ground" is not. Thus, the identity with God may analytically have implications far beyond the specific phenomenology of the experience.
90. Franklin Merrill-Wolff, *Pathways Through to Space* (New York: Warner Books, 1973), pp. 93–96; and Bernhardt's essay, "Are Pure Consciousness Events Unmediated?" in the present volume. See also my introduction to the present volume.
91. Bernard McGinn, Richard Kieckhefer and others raised such at a talk I delivered in 1986 at Kalamazoo, Michigan.
92. Kieckhefer, "Eckhart's Conception of Union with God," p. 224. See also McGinn "Master Eckhart."
93. Robert K. C. Forman, *Meister Eckhart: Mystic as Theologian* (Amity, N.Y.: Amity House Press, forthcoming).
94. Kelley, *Eckhart on Divine Knowledge*, argues throughout that Eckhart does not advocate passing states. Schurmann, "Mystic and Philosopher," p. 15, denies that Eckhart was interested in an "instantaneous 'raptus' or a mystique of vision' " (p. 23; cf. p. 84). I noted that McGinn, "The God Beyond God," found "only three" references to it, p. 16. Elsewhere he writes that Eckhart "shows no real interest in rapture" p. 248).
95. This passage is used to buttress this claim in College and McGinn, (see "Meister Eckhart," *Meister Eckhart*, p. 57, and Kieckhefer, "Eckhart's Conception of Union with God," p. 223.
96. DW 1:272:6–274:8 = W 1:126–27. [Emphasis added.]
97. Cf. DW 1:8:5–7 = W 1:56.
98. DW 1:90:12–91:8 = W 1:117–18.
99. See Frank Tobin, "Eckhart's Mystical Use of Language: The Contexts of *eigenschaft*," *Seminar* 8 (1972), 160–68. See also my "Eckhart and Psychological Transformation," *Journal of Christianity and Psychology* 6 (1987), 21–33.
100. DW 1:28:8–10 = W 1:72, another popular passage among the antimystics.
101. PF 8:31–40 = W 1:9.
102. PF 7:20–21 = W 1:7.
103. DW 3:486:17–487:5 = W 1:84.

104. DW 2:66:8 = W 1:144.
105. PF 7:21 = W 1:7.
106. DW 3:485:18 = W 1:83.
107. DW 2:85:1–86:1 = W 1:138–39. [Emphasis added.]
108. Cf. Kieckhefer, "Eckhart's Conception of Union with God," p. 224.
109. DW 5:291 = Clark and Skinner, p. 102.

Ayin: The Concept of Nothingness in Jewish Mysticism

DANIEL C. MATT

There is allure and terror in mystical portrayals of nothingness: Eckhart's *Nichts*, John of the Cross's *nada*, the Taoist *wu*, the Buddhist *sunyata*. Despite appearances, these terms do not express an identical meaning since each mystic names the nameless from within a realm of discourse shaped by his own training, outlook, and language.[1] My *aim* here is *to* trace the development of the concept of *ayin* (nothingness) in Jewish mysticism. In medieval Kabbalah *ayin* functions as a theosophical symbol, part of the elaborate system of the *sefirot*, the stages of divine manifestation. Everything emerges from the depths of *ayin* and eventually returns there. As we proceed from Kabbalah to Hasidism, the focus changes. Now the psychological significance of *ayin* is emphasized and it becomes a medium for self-transformation. The mystic experiences *ayin* directly and emerges anew.

The word "nothingness," of course, connotes negativity and nonbeing, but what the mystic means by divine nothingness is that God is greater than any *thing* one can imagine, like *no thing*. Since God's being is incomprehensible and ineffable, the least offensive and most accurate description one can offer is, paradoxically, *nothing*. David ben Abraham ha-Lavan, a fourteenth-century kabbalist, corrects any misapprehension, "Nothingness [*ayin*] is more existent than all the being of the world. But since it is simple, and all simple things are complex compared with its simplicity, it is called *ayin*." David's mystical Christian contemporaries concur. The Byzantine theologian Gregory Palamas writes, "He is not being, if that which is not God is being." Meister Eckhart says, "God's *Nichts* fills the entire world; His something though is nowhere."[2]

PHILO AND THE GNOSTICS

Mystics contemplate the void but not in a vacuum. The kabbalists were influenced not only by Jewish philosophers, but also, directly or indirectly, by pagan and Christian Neoplatonic thinkers: Plotinus, Pseudo-Dionysius, and John Scotus Erigena. Philo, the mystical philosopher who straddled the first centuries B.C.E. and C.E. was unknown to the kabbalists, but it was he who introduced the concept of the unknowability and indescribability of God. Philo paved the way for negative theology, emphasizing the unlikeness of God to things in the world. "God alone has veritable being. . . . Things posterior to him have no real being but are believed to exist in imagination only."[3] The goal of religious life is to see through the apparent reality of the world and to shed the consciousness of a separate self, "This is the natural course: one who comprehends himself fully, lets go totally of the nothingness that he discovers in all creation, and one who lets go of himself comes to know the Existent."[4] One of the great mysteries is the contrast between the power "of the Uncreated and the exceeding nothingness of the created."[5]

Philo's nothingness (*oudeneia*) refers to the unreality of creation in the face of the only true reality, the divine. Here, nothingness has a purely negative quality; it describes a fundamental lack. In the overwhelming discovery that everything is an expression of the divine, creation as an independent entity collapses and is reduced to nothing. By contemplating this basic fact, one is transported into the presence of God, "For then is the time for the creature to encounter the Creator, when it has recognized its own nothingness." The ideal is "to learn to measure one's own nothingness."[6]

God is immeasurable, nameless and ineffable. In this Philo foreshadows the Gnostics, some of whom surpass him in applying negative language to God. The Gnostic God, as distinct from the creative demiurge, is totally different, the other, unknown. He is "the incomprehensible, inconceivable one who is superior to every thought," "ineffable, inexpressible, nameable by silence."[7] Trying to outdo his predecessors in negative theology, Basilides, the second-century Alexandrian Gnostic, opposes even the term "ineffable" as a predicate of God. His words are preserved by Hippolytus of Rome, who cites him in his attack against various prevalent heresies: "That which is named [ineffable] is not absolutely ineffable, since we call one thing ineffable and another not even ineffable. For that which is not even ineffable is not named ineffable, but is above every name that is named."[8]

God transcends the capacity of human language and the category of being. Basilides speaks of the "nameless nonexistent God." This negation is clarified in another Gnostic treatise, *Allogenes,* "Nor is he something that exists, that one could know. But he is something else . . . that is better, whom one cannot know. . . . He has nonbeing existence."[9]

Nonbeing best describes God's incomprehensible otherness. For Basilides a distinct but related nonbeing is also the source of creation:

> The nonexistent God made the cosmos out of the nonexistent, casting down and planting a single seed containing within itself the whole seed-mass of the cosmos. . . . The nonexistent seed of the cosmos cast down by the nonexistent God contained a seed-mass at once multiform and the source of many beings. . . . The seed of the cosmos came into being from nonexistent things [and this seed is] the word that was spoken: "Let there be light!"[10]

CREATION FROM NOTHING AND FROM DIVINE NOTHINGNESS

Basilides, thus, offers an extreme formulation of creation ex *nihilo,* a theory whose mystical career entwines with negative theology. In the Hellenistic Age it was widely held that the stuff of which the world is made is amorphous *hyle* (formless matter). Thales and Parmenides had taught that nothing can arise from what does not exist, and Aristotle writes, "That nothing comes to be out of that which is not, but everything out of that which is, is a doctrine common to nearly all the natural philosophers." Until the rise of Christianity, there was apparently no Greek, Roman, or Jewish Hellenistic thinker who asserted creation from nothing.[11]

The theory of creation ex *nihilo* first appears in second-century Christian literature, evoked by the confrontation with Gnostic heresy and Greek philosophy. It represents a denial of the prevailing Platonic notion that creation was out of eternal primordial matter, a notion that compromises the sovereignty of God. As Augustine writes, "Nor had you any material in your hand when You were making heaven and earth." Theophilus, bishop of Antioch, points out that if God made the world from uncreated matter, He would be no greater than a human being who makes something out of existing materials.[12] The formula *creatio ex ni-*

hilo, in fact, may have been coined in opposition to the philosophical principle that nothing is made from nothing, *ex nihilo nihil fit.* Christian thinkers also felt challenged to refute the Gnostics, who had set up other powers alongside God and asserted that one of these created the world. (Basilides' apparent attribution of creation to the hidden God is unusual for a Gnostic.) Creation *ex nihilo* provided a defense for the belief in one free and transcendent Creator not dependent on anything. It became the paradigm for God's miraculous powers and served as the chief underpinning for the supernatural conception of deity. Its denial was tantamount to the undermining of revealed religion. In the words of Moses Maimonides, "If the philosophers would succeed in demonstrating eternity as Aristotle understands it, the Law as a whole would become void."[13]

There is little if any evidence that the normative rabbinic view was of creation *ex nihilo.*[14] The passage from *Sefer Yezirah (The Book of Creation)* later exploited as an expression of *ex nihilo* is ambiguous, "He formed something actual out of chaos and made what is not [*eino*] into what is [*yeshno*]. He hewed enormous pillars out of the ether that cannot be grasped."[15] *Sefer Yezirah* was composed sometime between the third and sixth centuries. Here is the first time in Hebrew literature that we find mention of creation from *ayin* or, rather, the circumlocutional *eino.* The noun *ayin* appears in an ontological sense only much later. "What is not" may refer to *hyle* (primordial matter), which the Platonists called the nonexistent (*to me on*).[16] The intent would then be not absolute nothingness but rather that which is not yet formed or endowed with qualities.

Though the doctrine of *creatio ex nihilo* was not indigenously Jewish, under the influence of Christian and Moslem thinkers, it penetrated Jewish philosophical and religious circles. The phrase *yesh me-ayin* (something out of nothing) came to describe the process of Creation, though the theory was less venerated and theologically crucial than in Christian thought. Creation from nothing was accepted by Maimonides; yet he suggests that various obscure passages in the Torah seem to prove the validity of the Platonic theory. The philosopher Joseph Albo admits that one may understand the biblical account of creation without the aid of *yesh me-ayin.*[17]

The theory of *ex nihilo* inevitably collided with the theory of emanation taught by Plotinus, a master of negative theology whose God creates without will. Plotinus denies the biblical story of creation by design. Everything that exists emerges from the One in a gradated yet eternal process of emanation and everything aspires to return to the One.

Plotinus established negation as a type of divine attribute, which he included in a formal classification. He employs the technique of *aphaire-*

sis (removing, abstraction) to negate predicates of God, which means not that the opposite can be predicated but that God is excluded from that realm of discourse. The One is "something higher than what we call 'being.' " "Even being cannot be there."[18]

The mystic experiences the One not as some transcendent substance, but in an objectless vision, "The vision floods the eyes with light, but it is not a light showing some other object; the light itself is the vision. . . . With this, one becomes identical with that radiance."[19] As the spiritual explorer discovers that the One is beyond images, his own image of a separate self also dissolves, "One formed by this mingling with the Supreme . . . becomes the Unity, nothing within him or without inducing any diversity. . . . Reasoning is in abeyance and all intellection and even, to dare the word, the very self: caught away, filled with God. . . . He is like one who, having penetrated the inner sanctuary, leaves the temple images behind him."[20]

Plotinus's conception of simplicity (*haplosis*) requires the abolition of all difference between oneself and the One. In the ultimate bliss of the "flight of the alone to the alone," the One is no longer other. "How can one describe as other than oneself that which, when one discerned it, seemed not other but one with oneself?"[21] The mystic shares the sublimity of nonexistence, "The essential person outgrows being, becomes identical with the transcendent of being."

Medieval Christian, Moslem, and Jewish philosophers were deeply influenced by Plotinus's negative theology and his theory of emanation. The contradiction between creation *ex nihilo* and the eternal emanation of the world from God was unmistakably clear. Augustine, defending the traditional Christian position, writes, "They were made from nothing by Thee, not of Thee."[22] Though *ex nihilo* was widely espoused, certain Christian thinkers more enamored of Neoplatonism attempted to resolve the contradiction between emanation and creation from nothing. They reinterpreted *ex nihilo* as implying the temporal generation of the world from the essence of God. The troublesome Plotinian element of eternity was eliminated, and "creation from nothing" was transformed into a mystical formula for emanation from the divine.

The apophatic theology of Dionysius the Areopagite contributed to this transformation. The fifth-century Syrian monophysite who wrote under this pseudonym calls God *hyperousion* (beyond being). God is the "cause of being for all, but is itself nonbeing, for it is beyond all being."[23] Ecstatic experience matches this theological insight. "By going out of yourself and everything . . . you will raise yourself to the ray of divine darkness beyond being."[24]

From the ninth century on, both Islamic and Christian sources offer a Neoplatonized, mystical version of ex *nihilo*. The Irish theologian redundantly known as John Scotus Erigena was the first Christian to teach such a theory and the first Latin thinker to focus on negative theology. His thinking was deeply influenced by Dionysius, whom he translated from Greek into Latin, though John's pantheistic tendencies go far beyond his Dionysian sources. He applies the name *nihil* to God, intending by this not the privation but the transcendence of being. Because of "the ineffable, incomprehensible and inaccessible brilliance of the divine goodness. . . . [I]t is not improperly called 'nothing.' " It "is called 'nothing' on account of its excellence."[25]

John takes the expression ex *nihilo* to mean ex *Deo;* the nothing from which the world was created is God. In bold imagery, he interprets the entire first chapter of Genesis according to this new sense of ex *nihilo*. Creation is the procession of the transcendent *nihil* into differentiated being, into the division of nature. In its essence, the divine is said not to be, but as it proceeds through the primordial causes, it becomes all that is, "Every visible creature can be called a theophany, that is, a divine appearance" and "God is created in creation in a remarkable and ineffable way."[26] The *nihil* is the ground for this divine self-creation. God descends into His own depths, out of which all proceeds and to which all eventually returns. Unknowable in itself, the divine nature becomes knowable in its manifestations.

Medieval Christian mystics who speak of divine nothingness (e.g., Meister Eckhart, the Franciscan Petrus Olivi, the anonymous author of *Theologia deutsch,* and Jacob Boehme) are indebted to John Scotus and Dionysius. John's impact would have been even greater if the exploitation of his work by Albigensian heretics and philosophical pantheists had not resulted in its condemnation by Pope Honorius III in 1225.

Meanwhile, in the world of Islam, Neoplatonic emanation theory engendered a similar reinterpretation of ex *nihilo*. Plotinus's doctrine became widely known under the guise of *The Theology of Aristotle,* an Arabic synopsis of Neoplatonism based on the *Enneads* and the teachings of Porphyry, Plotinus's disciple. In the long version of the *Theology,* the divine word (*kalima*) is said to transcend the conflict of the categories, to be beyond motion and rest. It is called nothing (*laysa*), a nothing from which creation stems. A similar view is found among the Shiite Isma'iliya: God and the Nothing-with-him are one unity. This nothing is not outside of God but rather a manifestation of His hidden essence from which all proceeds.[27]

MAIMONIDES' NEGATIVE THEOLOGY AND THE *AYIN* OF KABBALAH

Maimonides did not endorse a mystical interpretation of "nothing," but his negative theology, inspired by the Moslem philosophers Alfarabi and Avicenna, was an important ingredient in the kabbalistic theory of *ayin*. All three thinkers claimed that existence is predicated of God and of other beings—not in the same sense but ambiguously and equivocally. God has nothing in common with any other being. His existence is totally unlike anything we conceive: God "exists but not through existence."[28]

Avicenna made negative theology philosophically respectable; Maimonides extended and radicalized it, developing a system of negative attributes. He was the first to state explicitly that all positive terms affirmed of God are to be taken both negatively and equivocally. Thomas Aquinas cites and disputes Maimonides' view, as does the Jewish philosopher Gersonides.[29] For his part, Maimonides openly promotes the controversial method and encourages his reader to progress in discovering what God is not, "Know that the description of God . . . by means of negations is the correct description, a description that is not affected by an indulgence in facile language and does not imply any deficiency with respect to God. . . . You come nearer to the apprehension of Him, may He be exalted, with every increase in the negations regarding Him."[30] Even negation, though, cannot capture the infinite. Maimonides concludes that "apprehension of Him consists in the inability to attain the ultimate term in apprehending Him. . . . The most apt phrase concerning this subject is the dictum in the Psalms [65:2]: 'To You silence is praise,' which means: Silence with regard to You is praise."[31]

The medieval Jewish mystics adopted Maimonides' negative theology, at least as it pertains to the infinite nature of God. The thirteenth-century kabbalist Azriel of Gerona, who was deeply influenced by Neoplatonism, notes the similarity between the mystical and philosophical approaches, "The scholars of inquiry [philosophers] agree with the statement that our comprehension is solely by means of 'no.'"[32] Shem Tov ibn Gaon grants that "the words of the philosophers and the wise are correct . . . [in that] they have instructed us to negate from Him all negations. . . . Since the root of all is endless and incomprehensible, it is impossible to call Him by any name."[33]

Yet, paradoxically, the very strategy of negation provides a means of indicating the ineffable. Negative attributes carve away all that is false and culminate in a positive sense of nothingness. The mystics now claim

to surpass the philosophers, "How hard they toiled and exerted themselves—those who intended to speak of negation; yet they did not know
the site of negation!"[34] According to Moses de León, there is glory in
nothingness. *Ayin* is revealed as the only name appropriate to the divine
essence.

The new positive sense of *ayin* derives, in part, from the eleventh-
century poet Solomon ibn Gabirol. In his masterpiece, *Keter Malkhut*, in
a stanza dealing with divine wisdom, we read, "To draw the flow of the
yesh [something] from the *ayin*, as the light emerging from the eye is
drawn forth. . . . He called to the *ayin* and it was cleft, to the *yesh* and it
was infixed."[35] The abstract terms "*ayin*" and "*yesh*" are here animated
mythically, but Gabirol was a philosopher as well as a poet, and *ayin* may
allude to formless matter or to the realm of essence prior to existence.
Shlomo Pines has suggested that Gabirol based his description of this
primal ontological event on a passage from Avicenna, "Praise be to God,
who cleaved the darkness of nothingness [or privation] with the light of
existence." Gabirol's cryptic and pregnant words in *Keter Malkhut* seem
to endow *ayin* with a new dimension of meaning: ontological essence.[36]
Since we know that the kabbalists were indebted to Gabirol for a number
of images and terms, it is not surprising that the mystical career of *ayin* is
linked to his poetry.

Another poet, who lived some fifteen hundred years before Gabirol,
provided the kabbalists with a precious prooftext for their reevaluation of
nothingness. In order to bolster the new theory, the kabbalists were fond
of intentionally misreading various scriptural verses in which the word
"*ayin*" appears. In biblical Hebrew, *ayin* can mean where as well as
nothing. The poet who composed the twenty-eighth chapter of the book
of Job poses a rhetorical question (28:12): "Where [*me-ayin*] is wisdom to
be found?" The kabbalists of the thirteenth century transform this question
into a mystical formula, "Divine wisdom comes into being out of nothingness." Asher ben David writes, "The inner power is called *ayin* because
neither thought nor reflection grasps it. Concerning this, Job said, 'Wisdom comes into being out of *ayin*.' " As Bahya ben Asher puts it, the verse
should be understood "not as a question but as an announcement."[37]
Refracted through a mystical lens, Job's question yields its own startling
answer. In the words of Joseph Gikatilla, "The depth of primordial
being . . . is called Boundless. It is also called *ayin* because of its concealment from all creatures above and below. . . . If one asks, 'What is
it?,' the answer is, *Ayin*, that is, no one can understand anything about
it. . . . It is negated of every conception."[38]

AYIN AND THE SEFIROT

As we have noted, the kabbalists adopted Maimonides' negative approach to the description of the essence of God. They parted company with him, however, in their discussion of divine attributes. Maimonides, subjugating biblical thought to Greek thought, denied the existence of real, unequivocal attributes. The kabbalists sensed that the philosophical unmoved mover was incompatible with the traditional Jewish view of God as a living, responsive being. Despite their appropriation of theological negation, certain kabbalists criticize the philosophers on just this point, "Their wisdom is based solely on negation. . . . All their words are intended to negate the divine designations; they keep on negating and negating." The poet Meshullam Da Piera complains that "those who deny the proper attributes of God speak out until faith has been drained."[39]

The kabbalists insisted on an entire array of positive, vibrant attributes: the ten *sefirot*. The *sefirot* are stages of divine being and aspects of divine personality. Prior to the emanation of the *sefirot,* God is unmanifest, referred to simply as *ein sof,* Infinite (literally, there is no end). The *sefirot* reveal what can be conveyed of the divine nature. By advocating this system of mystical attributes, the kabbalists sought to counter extreme intellectualism and preserve the fabric of faith. It is insufficient, they claimed, to believe in the denuded infinity of God. Such an abstract theology endangers the daily regimen of holiness. Isaac of Akko dreams that he sees a "curse against the rebels who believe only in *ein sof* . . . and neither pray nor bless, for they say, 'What need does He have for our prayers? What benefit can He derive from our blessings?' " Isaac castigates "The foolish philosophers . . . ignorant of the ten *sefirot,* the name of the Holy One, Blessed be He. Their faith is deficient and wrong, for they disdain prayer and blessings and are frivolous toward the *mizvot.*"[40] The *sefirot* are like a body for the infinite divine soul; they provide a name for the nameless and an address for prayer. Certain philosophers had charged that the kabbalists' descriptions of the *sefirot* were corporeal or heretical. Shem Tov ibn Gaon retorts, "This is the principle upon which all depends: what the philosophers think is the site of rebellion is really the site of faith."[41] The *sefirot* are referred to as *raza di-meheimanuta* (the mystery of faith.)

From above to below, the *sefirot* enact the drama of emanation, the transition from *ein sof* to creation. From below to above, they are a ladder of ascent back to the One. *Keter 'elyon* (highest crown) is the first *sefirah,* coeternal with *ein sof.* It is this *sefirah* that the kabbalists identify as *ayin.*

The other *sefirot* portray God in personal, anthropomorphic terms; they represent, among other things, divine wisdom, understanding, love, judgment, compasssion, and dominion. The highest *sefirah*, however, is characterized by undifferentiation and impersonality. It verges on *ein sof*, and some kabbalists do not distinguish between them.

The designation of the first *sefirah* as *ayin* may date from the twelfth century, though it does not appear in the earliest kabbalistic text, *Sefer ha-Bahir*. It was conveyed by the Gerona kabbalists in the thirteenth century and accepted on their authority and the authority of their teacher, Isaac the Blind, "the father of Kabbalah."[42] Moses de León offers an explanation of the symbolism and then draws an analogy between divine and human ineffability:

> *Keter 'elyon* . . . is called the pure ether that cannot be grasped.[43] It is the totality of all existence, and all have wearied in their search for it. . . . The belt of every wise person is burst by it, for it is the secret of the Cause of Causes and brings all into being. . . . God, may He be blessed, is the annihilation of all thoughts; no thought can contain Him. Since no one can contain Him [with] anything in the world, He is called *ayin*. This is the secret of what is said: "Wisdom comes into being out of *ayin*."
>
> Anything sealed and concealed, totally unknown to anyone, is called *ayin*, meaning that no one knows anything about it. Similarly . . . no one knows anything at all about the human soul; she stands in the status of nothingness, as it is said [Eccles. 3:19]: "The advantage of the human over the beast is *ayin*"! By means of this soul, the human being obtains an advantage over all other creatures and the glory of that which is called *ayin*.[44]

Certain kabbalists maintained that the first *sefirah* is symbolized by *alef*, the first letter of the Hebrew alphabet, but de León objects: *ayin* cannot be represented by even a single letter.[45] Gikatilla, de León's friend and colleague, suggests that among the letters of the divine name *YHVH* only the tip of the *yod*, the smallest letter of the alphabet, alludes to *keter*. The highest *sefirah* "has no specific letter of its own, for there is no one who can estimate, imagine or draw it, even by the shape indicating a letter." The name that God gives Himself, "I am" ("*Eheyeh*," Exod. 3:14), signifies that "His existence is not conceived by anyone other than Him. . . . 'I alone know my existence.' "[46] *Keter* is so transcendent that, according to one view, it does not stoop to know the other layers of divinity, the nine lower *sefirot*. "Because of the nature of His concealment, *keter 'elyon* does not recognize the other levels."[47] On their part, the *sefirot* cannot comprehend *ein sof*, the infinite nature of God. Even *ayin,* which is coeternal with *ein sof,* has only a vague knowledge of It. In the words of the Zohar:

> *Ein sof* does not abide being known. . . .
> All these lights and sparks [*sefirot*] are dependent on It
> but cannot comprehend.
> The only one who knows, yet without knowing,
> is the highest desire, concealed of all concealed, *ayin.*
> And when the highest point and the world-that-is-coming
>   [the second and third *sefirot*] ascend,
> they know only the aroma,
> as one inhaling an aroma is sweetened.[48]

AYIN AND *YESH*

The deepest mystery of the sefirotic process and of the entire chain of being lies in the transition from *ayin* to *yesh* (from nothing to something.) Like the Christian and Islamic Neoplatonists, the kabbalists, too, reinterpreted *ex nihilo* as emanation from the hidden essence of God. Ezra of Gerona, paraphrasing Maimonides, cites Plato against the literal meaning of *ex nihilo:*

> Plato . . . says that it is absurd to think that the Creator should produce something out of nothing; rather there is preexistent matter, which is like clay to the potter or iron to the blacksmith, who form it as they please. So the Creator, may He be blessed, forms from matter heaven and earth and sometimes something different. The fact that He does not create something out of nothing does not indicate any deficiency on His part, just as it does not indicate any deficiency that He does not produce what is logically absurd, e.g., creating a square the diagonal of which is equal to its length or combining two contraries at the same instant. Just as this does not imply any deficiency in His power, so there is no deficiency if He does not emanate something from nothing, but rather from something.[49]

Unlike Maimonides, who rejected Plato's theory of primordial matter, Ezra manages to harmonize this too with emanation. He insists that the roots of the revealed *sefirot* are preexistent; in the process of emanation, they simply emerge from their primordiality. "The essences were in existence; the emanation was innovated."[50] For the kabbalists, there *is* a "something" that emerges from "nothing," but the nothing is brimming with overwhelming divine reality; it is *mahut,* the "whatness," the quiddity of God.[51] The something is not a physical object but rather the first ray of divine wisdom, which, as Job indicates, emerges from *ayin*. It is the primordial point that marks the beginning of the unfolding of God. In the lyrical words of the Zohar:

> The flow broke through and did not break through its aura.
> It was not known at all
> until, under the impact of breaking through,
> one high and hidden point shone.
> Beyond that point, nothing is known.
> So it is called Beginning.[52]

The opening words of Genesis, "In the beginning," allude to this first point, which is the second *sefirah*, that is, *hokhmah* (divine wisdom). Though second, it "appears to be the first" and is called *beginning* because the first *sefirah*, that is, *ayin*, is unknowable and uncountable. In the words of Moses de León, the point is "the beginning of existence":

> The beginning of existence is the secret of the concealed point and is called . . . primordial wisdom. It is the mystery of the conceptual point . . . the beginning of all the hidden things [the *sefirot*]; from there they spread out and emanate according to their species. . . . From a single point you can draw forth the emanation of all things. You should understand that when that which is hidden and concealed arouses itself to existence, it produces at first something the size of the point of a needle; afterwards, it produces everything from there. . . . Contemplate this: When the emanation was emanated out of *ayin* . . . all the levels [the *sefirot*] were dependent on thought. . . . That which . . . rests in thought is called *hokhman* [wisdom]. It has been said, "What is *hokhmah*? *Hakkeh mah*." This means that since . . . you will never attain it, *hakkeh*, "wait," for *mah*, "what" will come and be. This is the primordial wisdom emerging out of *ayin*.[53]

Whereas *ayin* cannot be symbolized by any letter, the primordial point of wisdom is identified with *yod*, "the letter that is smallest among all the letters." *Ayin* is "the ether that cannot be grasped," whereas this conceptual point is "the ether that can be grasped." It is "the beginning of all beginnings," the potentiality of all things.[54] The transition from nothingness to something, from *ayin* to *yesh*, is the decisive act of creation, the real context of Genesis. Azriel of Gerona, the first kabbalist to speak at length about *ayin*, describes the relatedness of these two opposite states:

> If one asks you, "How did He bring forth something from nothing? Is there not a great difference between something and nothing?!" Answer him . . . "The something is in the nothing in the mode of nothing, and the nothing is in the something in the mode of something."[55] Therefore they have said [*Sefer Yezirah* 2:6]: "He made His nothing into His something" and not "He made something from nothing," to indicate that the *ayin* is the

yesh and the *yesh* is the *ayin*. . . . And the node of *yesh* as it begins to emerge from *ayin* into existence is called faith. . . . For the term "faith" applies neither to the visible, comprehensible *yesh,* nor to *ayin,* invisible and incomprehensible, but rather to the nexus of *ayin* and *yesh.*[56]

The wording of *Sefer Yezirah* could mean, "He made [relative] non-being [i.e., prime matter] into being" or "He made nothing into something." But Azriel insists that the transformation takes place within God: divine wisdom emerges out of divine nothingness.[57] Creation originates in this nothingness, which is the medium of every transformation.

At times, Azriel employs the term "*efes,*" which also means "nothing," rather than *ayin,* as when he speaks of the three principles of being: matter, form, and *efes.*[58] In Hebrew philosophical terminology, *efes* represents the Aristotelian concept of *steresis* (privation).[59] For Aristotle, no thing comes into being simply from nonbeing. Change involves a substrate (matter) acquiring a form that it did not previously possess. Unrealized forms lie hidden in every thing, and each succeeding form realizes part of what matter can become. To have one form is *ipso facto* to be deprived of the opposite form. The substrate neither comes into being nor passes away; it is always in existence and is free of nonbeing. Privation refers to nonbeing in the sense of the absence of a particular form, the absence of a potentiality.[60] One may say that a thing comes into being from its privation, but not from naked privation, only from privation in a substrate. A new thing comes into being from that which it is potentially but not actually.

Azriel transforms privation into a mystical category. A hundred years earlier, the philosopher Avraham bar Hiyya had written, "When it arose in the pure [divine] thought to actualize [form and matter], He removed *efes* from them and attached form to matter."[61] Here it is already difficult to recognize Aristotelian privation. For Azriel *efes* represents the entirety of potential forms that can inhere in matter, each one "invisible until its moment of innovation." New forms emerge as a pool spreads out from a spring.[62] Reading his sources through the eyes of a Neoplatonic mystic, Azriel misunderstood them creatively. On the one hand, as in the actual Aristotelian theory, the transformation of matter is traced back to the privation of the particular new form. On the other hand, change is linked with the concept of mystical nothingness out of which all creation emerges. As matter adopts new forms, it passes through the Divine Nothing; thus, the world is constantly renewed. An explicit formulation appears in the teaching of Joseph ben Shalom Ashkenazi (early fourteenth century), who speaks of the "stripping away of form and its privation, resulting from the power of *ayin*." "Being constructs, while *ayin*, which is privation, destroys."[63] In every change of form, in each gap of existence, the abyss of nothingness is crossed and becomes visible for a fleeting moment.

THE RETURN TO *AYIN*

Contemplation enables one to uncover this depth of being by retracing the individual words of prayer. Azriel counsels, "You should know that one who prays must push aside every hindrance and obstruction and restore each word to its nothingness [*afisato*]. This is the meaning of *efes*." A true prayer is one in which "we have directed the words to the nothingness of the word [*efes davar*]."[64] Though humans "walk in the multiplicity" of the material world, "one who ascends from the form of forms to the root of roots must gather the multiplicity . . . for the root extends through every form that arises from it at any time. When the forms are destroyed, the root is not destroyed."[65]

At the deepest levels of divinity, all opposites and distinctions vanish, overwhelmed by oneness. Azriel describes this undifferentiated state in language influenced by John Scotus or other Neoplatonists who speak of *indistinctio* and *indifferentia*. Scotus had written that God "is the circuit of all things that have or do not have being . . . and that seem contrary or opposite to Him. . . . He gathers and composes them all with an ineffably beautiful harmony into a single concord."[66] Azriel speaks of "the complete undifferentiation [*hashva'ah gemurah*] in the perfect changeless oneness." *Ein sof* "is undifferentiated by anything [*shaveh la-kol*], and everything unites in its undifferentiation [*hashva'ato*] . . . for all is undifferentiated [*shaveh*] in it."[67] Paraphasing another Neoplatonic formula, Azriel insists that it is not enough to believe that "God is more than all and that there is nothing outside of Him." If one does not also believe that "He is *shaveh la-kol* . . . one detracts from God's power . . . by not acknowledging this essential point: that He is both openly and secretly undifferentiated by *ayin* or *yesh* without distinction. He is in a state of simplicity and total undifferentiation, that is, oneness."[68] The Infinite is neither this nor that, "neither *yesh* nor *ayin*."[69]

The mystic must assimilate to the divine undifferentiation (*hashva'ah*) and manifest complete equanimity (*hishtavvut*). According to a tradition cited by Isaac of Akko, indifference to praise or blame is a prerequisite for "linking your thought" with God. Here the kabbalists drew upon Bahya ibn Paquda and Sufi teaching, transforming the Cynic and Stoic moral ideals of *ataraxia* and *apatheia* into mystical goals.[70]

While God's undifferentiation is reflected in human equanimity, the divine incomprehensibility is mirrored by a contemplative "unknowing." David ben Judah he-Hasid describes this as "forgetting":

> The Cause of Causes . . . is a place to which forgetting and oblivion pertain. . . . Why? Because concerning all the levels and sources [the *sefirot*], one can search out their reality from the depth of supernal wisdom. From there it is possible to understand one thing from another. However, concerning the Cause of Causes, there is no aspect anywhere to search or probe; nothing can be known of It, for It is hidden and concealed in the mystery of absolute nothingness [*ha-ayin ve-ha-efes*]. Therefore forgetting pertains to the comprehension of this place. So open your eyes and see this great, awesome secret. Happy is one whose eyes shine from this secret, in this world and the world that is coming![71]

The *sefirot* are stages of contemplative ascent; each one serves as an object and focus of mystical search. In tracing the reality of each *sefirah*, the mystic uncovers layers of being within himself and throughout the cosmos. This is the knowledge that the kabbalist strives for, supernal wisdom. However, there is a higher level, a deeeper realm, beyond this step-by-step approach. At the ultimate stage the kabbalist no longer differentiates one thing from another. Conceptual thought, with all its distinctions and connections, dissolves. Ezra and Azriel of Gerona call the highest *sefirah* "the annihilation of thought" ("*afisat ha-mahshavah*"):

> The ancient *hasidim* elevated their thought to its source. They would recite the *mizvot* and the *devarim*,[72] and through this recitation and the cleaving of [their] thought [to the divine], the *devarim* were blessed and increased, receiving an influx of emanation from the annihilation of thought. This can be compared to one who opens a pool of water, which then spreads in all directions. Thought . . . rises to contemplate its own innerness until its power of comprehension is annihilated.[73]

> Here, the mystic cannot grasp for knowledge, rather, he imbibes from the source to which he is joined. In the words of Isaac the Blind, "The inner, subtle essences can be contemplated only by sucking. . . . not by knowing."[74]

Ayin cannot be known. If one searches too eagerly and pursues it, he will be overtaken by it, sucked in by the vortex of nothingness. Ezra of Gerona warns:

> Thought cannot ascend higher than its source [the *sefirah* of wisdom]. Whoever dares to contemplate that to which thought cannot extend or ascend will suffer one of two consequences: either he will confuse his mind and destroy

his body or, because of his mental obsession to grasp what he cannot, his soul will ascend and be severed [from the body] and return to her root.[75]

Here, the return to the source is viewed as a danger and a negative experience, though Ezra's colleague, Azriel, is aware of a positive return, characteristic of Neoplatonic mysticism. He explains that when the priest offers a sacrifice, his soul ascends "and returns to her root, whence she was taken."[76] Similarly, Isaac of Akko notes that "*ein sof* . . . surrounds everything, and this [rational] soul will cleave to *ein sof*, becoming total and universal. Having been individual, imprisoned in her palace, she will become universal, in accord with her original nature."[77]

Devequt (cleaving to God) was the primary goal in early Kabbalah. Isaac the Blind is reported to have said, "The essence of the service of the enlightened and of those who contemplate His name is 'Cleave to Him' [Deut. 13:5]."[78] Isaac of Akko balances the positive and negative aspects of the experience of return. He describes *devequt* as "pouring a jug of water into a flowing spring, so that all becomes one," yet he warns his reader not to sink in the ocean of the highest *sefirah*, "The endeavour should be to contemplate but to escape drowning. . . . Your soul shall indeed see the divine light and cleave to it while dwelling in her palace."[79] A Hasidic mystic combines the motifs of the root and the ocean, "The branch returns to its root and is unified with it. The root is *ein sof*; thus the branch too is *ein sof*, for its [independent] existence is annihilated, like a single drop that falls into the ocean. . . . It is impossible to recognize it as a separate entity."[80]

In Kabbalah the theme of returning pertains not only to the individual mystic, but to the entire realm of the *sefirot*, in accord with the Neoplatonic principle that spiritual entities tend to ascend to their source. As we have noted, the essences of the *sefirot* exist primordially,[81] and many kabbalists would agree with Moses de León, "From her [*keter*] they [the *sefirot*] emerged; to her they will return."[82] At the culmination of cosmic history, all things return to God. Moses Nahmanides describes the great Jubilee, "when the Will reverses itself, restoring all things to their original essence, as someone drawing in his breath . . . [upon which they] will return to . . . absolute nothingness [*ha-afisah ha-muhletet*]."[83] David ben Judah he-Hasid concurs, *keter* "absorbs and swallows all the levels [*sefirot*] and everything that exists in the year of . . . the great Jubilee."[84]

For various thirteenth-century kabbalists the return is an immediate goal of prayer and meditation. In a text that appears to stem from Gerona, we hear about "those who contemplate and unify the great Name, stirring the fire on the altar of their hearts. By means of [the mystic's] pure thought, all the *sefirot* are unified and linked to one another until they are drawn to the source of the endlessly sublime flame."[85] In a commentary on the *Shema,* we read: "One should intend, as it were, to cause all of them [the lower nine *sefirot*] to enter *keter,* whence they emanated."[86]

Ezra of Gerona teaches that the *sefirot* were uprooted from their hidden preexistence and transplanted into the present pattern of emanation.[87] They strive to return, but the human task, according to him, is to counteract this upward tendency so as to ensure the continued flow of blessing toward the lower worlds. "Their desire and intention is to ascend and cleave to the place from which they suck. Therefore our sages established the [prayers of] blessing, sanctification and union in order to emanate and draw forth the source of life to the other *sefirot.*"[88]

Not only does contemplative prayer maintain the orientation of the *sefirot* toward the world, but righteous action does so, too. Human evil contributes to their return and removal. In this context, Ezra cites Isaiah 57:1, "Because of evil, the *zaddiq* is taken away."[89] The *zaddiq* (righteous one) is understood as referring to the ninth *sefirah,* which includes the emanation of all the lower *sefirot.*

The notion that human beings play a vital role in the functioning of the divine world is characteristic of Kabbalah. Joseph Gikatilla is one of many who promote such mystical activism:

> The attribute of . . . *zaddiq* looks out and gazes at humanity. When he sees that humans are engaged in Torah and *mizvot,* that they want to purify themselves and act accordingly, then *zaddiq* expands and widens and is filled with all kinds of flowing emanation from above, to pour out on [*malkhut,* the last *sefirah*]. . . . Thus the entire world is blessed by means of those righteous individuals. . . . If, God forbid, humans defile themselves and remove themselves from Torah and *mizvot,* perpetrating evil, injustice and violence, then *zaddiq* . . . gathers and contracts itself and ascends higher and higher. Then all the channels and flows are interrupted, and [*malkhut*] is left as a dry and empty land, lacking all good. This is the secret meaning of "Because of evil, the *zaddiq* is taken away." . . . One who understands this secret will understand the great power of a human being to build and destroy. Now come and see the great power of the righteous who maintain Torah and *mizvot:* they are able to join all the *sefirot.*[90]

The continuity of emanation is dependent on human righteousness. Several kabbalists advance a precise theory of correspondence between individual *mizvot,* which perfect the human body, and the *sefirot,* the divine "limbs." Joseph of Hamadan speaks of "limb strengthening limb" (*ever mahaziq ever*), "which means that when one's limbs are complete, and one maintains all the limbs of the Torah, namely, the 613 *mizvot,* one thereby maintains all the limbs of the chariot [the *sefirot*] and strengthens them."[91] In *Sefer ha-Yihud,* written toward the end of the thirteenth century in Joseph's circle, the limb imagery appears in the context of the return to nothingness:

> When a human being below blemishes one of his limbs [by not performing a specific *mizvah*] . . . it is as if he cuts the corresponding limb [*sefirah*] above. The meaning of this cutting is that the supernal limb is cut, contracted and gathered into the depths of being, called *ayin.* It is as if that limb is missing above. When the form of a human being is perfect below, it causes perfection above. In the same manner, the impurity of a limb below causes its paradigm above to be gathered into the depths of nothingness [*'imqei ha-ayin*], thereby blemishing the supernal form, as it is written: "Because of evil, the *zaddiq* is taken away," literally![92]

The correlation between human sin and the negative aspect of the return is formulated concisely by David ben Abraham ha-Lavan: "One who sins returns the attributes to *ayin,* to the primordial world, to their original state of being, and they no longer emanate goodness down to the lower world."[93] For this kabbalist the depths of nothingness are a danger lurking behind the return. "If, God forbid, she [the universal soul] were to return to the depths of nothingness, to her original world, the powers [of all human souls] would be rendered void."[94] In the aftermath of the cosmic return, the infinite nature of God would be all that is, as it originally was, "The cause that has no cause actualizes *yesh* from *ayin* and acts through the word. If all the powers were to return to *ayin,* then the Primordial One, the Cause of all, would stand in Its unity in the depths of nothingness, in undifferentiated oneness, blessed be He and blessed be His name."[95]

Typically, the Jewish mystic cannot resist appending a personal formula to the divine, even when his object of contemplation is undifferentiated oneness concealed in the depths of *ayin.* The kabbalist does not merely acknowledge the divine mystification, he implores God to emerge and manifest. "Out of the depths I call you, *YHVH.*" Mystically understood, this verse from Psalms (130:1) describes a human cry not *from* one's own state of despair but *to* the divine depths in which God lies hiding, from which the mystic calls God forth.[96] This is not to deny the reality of human suffering. On the contrary, adversity leads one to appreciate the resources of *ayin,* "Human beings must quickly grasp this *sefirah* to secure healing for every trouble and malady, as it is written [Ps.121:1]: 'I lift up my eyes to the mountains; my help comes from *ayin.*' "[97]

AYIN IN HASIDISM

In eighteenth-century Hasidism the kabbalistic material is recast and psychologized; now the experimental aspect of *ayin* becomes prominent. The emphasis is no longer on the *sefirot,* the inner workings of divinity, but on how to perceive the world mystically and how to transform the ego. Dov Baer, the Maggid (Preacher) of Mezritch, encourages his followers to permute *aniy* (I) into *ayin,* to dissolve the separate ego in nothingness.[98] As we will see, this is not a destructive but a dialectical and ultimately creative process.

The kabbalists refer occasionally to "the annihilation of thought" and a state of "forgetting" that overwhelm the mystic as he or she approaches *ayin.* The Maggid elaborates, describing how one arrives at the gate of *ayin* and enters.[99] *Ayin* is no longer simply a theological concept; the theosophical processes have become psychological reality:

> One must think of oneself as *ayin* and forget oneself totally. . . . Then one can transcend time, rising to the world of thought, where all is equal: life and death, ocean and dry land. . . . Such is not the case when one is attached to the material nature of this world. . . . If one thinks of oneself as something [*yesh*] . . . then God cannot clothe Himself in him, for He is infinite, and no vessel can contain Him, unless one thinks of oneself as *ayin.*[100]

We must shed the illusion that we are separate from God. There is, of course, a danger that the breakthrough to *ayin* will generate megalomania. Perhaps for just this reason, the Maggid emphasizes the link between *ayin* and humility. On the one hand, nothingness has an ethical and interpersonal dimension: it is a prerequisite for intimacy, "One cannot bind himself to his fellow human being unless he makes himself small and considers himself as *ayin* compared to his fellow."[101] Moreover, there is a progression from awe to humility and finally to *ayin.* To defend an independent sense of self is a sign of false pride; the most profound humility is the consciousness of *ayin.*

> The essence of the worship of God and of all the *mizvot* is to attain the state of humility, namely, . . . to understand that all one's physical and mental powers and one's essential being are dependent on the divine elements within. One is simply a channel for the divine attributes. One attains such humility through the awe of God's vastness, through realizing that "there is no place empty of Him" [*Tiqqunei Zohar* 57]. Then one comes to the state of *ayin,* which is the state of humility. . . . One has no independent self and is contained, as it were, in the Creator, blessed be He. . . . This is the

meaning of the verse [Exod.3:6]: "Moses hid his face, for he was in awe. . . ." Through his experience of awe, Moses attained the hiding of his face, that is, he perceived no independent self. Everything was part of divinity![102]

Moses surpassed Abraham, who, in saying, "I am dust and ashes [Gen.18:27]," still claimed a certain degree of existence. By posing the question: "What are we? [Exod.16:7]," Moses demonstrated that "he did not consider himself to be even dust!"[103]

The kabbalists had taught that *ayin* is the only name appropriate for God. For the Maggid *ayin* is the only state of mind appropriate for one who seeks to become a divine vessel. In "the annihilation of the intellect" distinctions vanish: "all is equal."[104] The mystic empties himself and makes room for an infusion of divine wisdom from beyond the normal borders of consciousness, "One must leave intellect and mind to reach the fence of nothingness. Afterwards, 'wisdom comes into being out of nothingness.'"[105]

The historical exodus from Egypt is interpreted as a paradigm of the liberation of consciousness from narrowness, "This is the meaning of the redemption from Egypt [*mizrayim*]. As long as our intellect is concerned with our selves, situated within the gate of being, it is contracted and narrow [*mezarim*], but when we come to the root it expands."[106] Normally, God is contracted in human thought; we think divine thought but in a constricted mode. The annihilation of thought, of the thinking subject, liberates the divine element that thinks within and leads it to its source. New letters from the Divine Mind then flow into the human mind and again contract, becoming defined in and by the human intellect. The immersion in nothingness does not induce a blank stare; it engenders new mental life through a rhythm of annihilation and thinking. "One [should] turn away from that [prior] object [of thought] totally to the place called nothingness, and then a new topic comes to mind. Thus transformation comes about only by passing through nothingness." In the words of the Maggid's disciple, Levi Yitzhak of Berditchev, "When one attains the level of . . . gazing at *ayin*, one's intellect is annihilated. . . . Afterwards, when one returns to the intellect, it is filled with emanation."[107]

The creative pool of nothingness is described as the "preconscious" ("*qadmut ha-sekhel*"), that which precedes, surpasses, and inspires both language and thought. "Thought requires the preconscious, which rouses thought to think. This preconscious cannot be grasped. . . . Thought is contained in letters, which are vessels, while the preconscious is beyond the letters, beyond the capacity of the vessels. This is the meaning of: 'Wisdom comes into being out of nothingness.' "[108]

The goal of contemplation is to pass beyond discursive thought, and this goal could easily conflict with the traditional Jewish value of Torah study. The relative neglect of book learning in early Hasidism may be due, in part, to just such a conflict, though social factors contributed a great deal. The annihilation of self would seem to be incompatible also with teaching Torah, but here the Maggid offers advice, "I will teach you the best way to say Torah: not sensing oneself at all, only as an ear listening to how the world of speech [*shekhinah*] speaks through him. One is not himself the speaker. As soon as one begins to hear his own words, he should stop." The student of the Maggid who cites this teaching adds a reminiscence:

> Several times when he opened his mouth to speak words of Torah, it seemed to everyone as if he were not in this world at all. The *shekhinah* was speaking out of his throat! I saw this with my own eyes. Sometimes, even in the middle of a subject or the middle of a word, he would pause and linger for a while. This all shows that one who is enlightened has to wait for knowledge; then speech comes forth conveying that knowledge.[109]

We encounter here the phenomenon of automatic speech, of the mystic serving as a mouthpiece for *shekhinah*, the divine presence. Another witness reports:

> I have seen great *zaddiqim* who were joining themselves to the higher worlds and were stripped of bodily garments—and the *shekhinah* rested upon them and spoke out of their throats. Their mouths spoke prophecies and told of the future. Afterwards those *zaddiqim* themselves did not know what they had said because they had been joined to the higher worlds and the *shekhinah* had been speaking out of their throats.[110]

Such a theory has social consequences; the preacher should not fear criticism because, like a prophet, he is transmitting God's word:

> "Proclaim with full throat, do not hold back; like a *shofar* [ram's horn] raise your voice!" [Isa.58:1] . . . One who preaches for the sake of heaven must consider that the intellect and the sermon are not his; rather he is as dead as a trampled corpse, and all is from God, may His name be blessed. Therefore one should not hold back the moral message nor fear anyone, for he is really like a *shofar* that lets the sound in and lets it out. . . . God is putting into his mind the words and the moral message that he is delivering to the congregation; so each word should feel like burning fire and he should feel compelled

to let them all out. Otherwise, he is like a prophet who suppresses his prophecy.[111]

By dissolving the separate sense of self, *ayin* reveals the divine source of both speech and thought: "Arriving at the gate of *ayin*, one forgets his existence altogether. . . . All his speech is a vessel for the supernal word, as it were, namely, for the combinations of the supernal letters. The word emanates from the higher worlds and [words] are cast into his mouth";[112] "When one is *ayin*, his thought is the world of thought [the *sefirah* of *binah*] and his speech is the world of speech [*shekhinah*]. . . . When one arrives at *ayin*, he comprehends that 'wisdom comes into being out of *ayin*' and that the worlds of thought and speech speak through him";[113] "One is simply like a *shofar*, emitting whatever sound is blown into it. If the blower were to remove himself, the *shofar* would produce no sound; so, when God is absent, one cannot speak or think."[114]

Hasidic prayer provides a context for such an experience. The mystic's only active role is the decision to pray and the effort to maintain the clarity essential for conveying divine energy:

> The one in awe merely activates the will, for he wills to pray, but the praise is not his. . . . One who merits this level is nothing but a channel through whom are conducted words from on high. This person merely opens his mouth. . . . The essential condition for prayer is that one be clean from all dross, so that the voice from above not be corporealized in his voice. Everyone can merit this level. . . . Their voice is the voice of the *shekhinah*, as it were; they are simply vessels.[115]

In such a state the subject and the object of prayer are one and the same. One "worships God with God." God becomes like a high priest, serving Himself through human prayer.[116]In proclaiming the oneness of God ("Hear O Israel, YHVH our God, YHVH is one [Deut.6:4])," the *hasid* "should intend that there is nothing in the world but the Holy One, blessed be He. . . . You should consider yourself to be absolute nothingness. Your essence is only the soul within, part of God above. Thus only God is! This is the meaning of 'one.' "[117]

Self-consciousness during prayer, even the thought of one's own devotion, dilutes the experience, "The body should be God's house, for one should pray with all his strength until he is stripped of corporeality and forgets his self; everything is the vitality of God. All of one's thoughts should be focused on Him, and one should not be the least bit aware of the intense devotion of his prayer, for if he is, he is aware of his self."[118]

The contemplative union attained by the mystic is fragile and could be shattered even by the multiplicity of letters on the page of the prayerbook.

Initially, the sight of the letters may enhance the experience of prayer, "but when one is cleaving to the upper world, it is better to close one's eyes, so that the sight will not undo his communion." According to one student of the Maggid, at the climax of contemplation, one sees all the words of prayer merging into a single point.[119]

Ideally, such unitive consciousness extends beyond prayer. For the mystic who is aware of the pervasive immanence of God all activity is divine activity, "Whatever one does, God is doing it."[120] Such selfless action reunites the physical world with its divine source. "When the *zaddiq* has the attribute of surrender, then the divine portion within him performs the action. Thus everything is from God: decree and revocation. The *zaddiq* is simply the throne and the palace for His name. Since God clothes His presence and portion in the *zaddiq*, the *zaddiq* can act and bind the worlds to their root."[121]

In the mystic's gaze the world no longer appears as essentially distinct from God, "If we perceive the world as existing [independently], that is merely an illusion." In the Habad school of Hasidism, acosmism becomes a fundamental teaching: "This is the foundation of the entire Torah: that *yesh* [the apparent somethingness of the world] be annihilated into *ayin*.";[122] "The purpose of the creation of the worlds from *ayin* to *yesh* was that they be transformed from *yesh* to *ayin*."[123] This transformation is realized through contemplative action:

> It is stated in the Gemara [*Ketubbot* 5a]: "The deeds of the righteous are greater than the creation of heaven and earth." This means that the creation of heaven and earth was *yesh me-ayin* [something from nothing], while the righteous transform *yesh* back into *ayin*. In everything they do, even physical acts such as eating, they raise the holy sparks, from the food or any other object. They thus tranform *yesh* into *ayin*. As our rabbis have said [*Ta'anit* 25a]: "The latter miracle is greater than the former!"[124]

The mystical perspective is neither nihilistic nor anarchic. Matter is not destroyed or negated but rather enlivened and revitalized. The awareness that divine energy underlies material existence increases the flow from the source (*ayin*) to its manifestation (*yesh*):

> When one gazes at an object, he brings blessing to it. For when one contemplates that object, he knows that it is . . . really absolutely nothing without divinity permeating it. . . . By means of this contemplation, one draws greater vitality to that object from divinity, from the source of life, since he binds that thing to absolute *ayin*, from which all beings have been hewn from *ayin* to *yesh*. . . . On the other hand . . . if one looks at that object . . . and makes it into a separate thing . . . by his look that thing is cut off from its divine root and vitality.

God is really the only "thing," the only existent. "Apart from Him, all are considered nothing and chaos." The world, though, is allowed to enjoy the illusion of separate existence so that it not lie utterly passive in the pool of *ayin:*

> If the material world were constantly attached to the Creator without any forgetting, the creatures' existence would be nullified, [since] they would be attached to the root, to *ayin.* Thus they would do nothing, considering themselves to be *ayin.* So there had to be a breaking [of the vessels], which brought about forgetting the root. Everyone could then lift his hand and act. Afterwards, through Torah and prayer, they attach themselves to the root, to *ayin . . .* and thereby raise the sparks of the material world . . . bringing pleasure to God. Such pleasure is greater than constant pleasure, as when a father who has not seen his son for a long time is reunited with him: the father is more overjoyed than if the son had been with him always. The son too, having not seen his father for a long time, has greater desire and yearns all the more to be together with his father.[125]

In Lurianic Kabbalah the image of the breaking of the vessels [*shevirat ha-kelim*] pertains to a flaw in the flow of emanation in the upper worlds; here the Maggid psychologizes it to explain the gap that allows for the human sense of self. This interpretive strategy is typical of the Maggid, "I teach the world to understand that all the things described in the book *Ez Hayyim* pertain also to this world and to the human being."[126] The breaking functions in ways similar to *zimzum,* the divine "contraction" that enables the world to occupy space and time. "Without *zimzum,* all would be the simple oneness of the Infinite. It is a great act of grace . . . that God contracts His *shekhinah* and radiates His light to the worlds according to the power of the recipients. . . . Otherwise, the existence of the worlds would be nullified by the brilliance of the light and they would turn into *ayin.*"[127]

Mystics are acutely aware of the gap that allows for separate existence. They know that attachment to the self, to one's own will, prevents a bridging of that gap and blocks the path of return. The mere assertion of human will is incompatible with *ayin,* which "does not desire anything."[128] Yet by following the lead of the soul, says the Maggid, one can enter the gate of nothingness. "How can a human being be in the state of *ayin?* If one does only that which pertains to the soul, one is in *ayin,* for the soul is something no one comprehends." The soul shares in the incomprehensibility of *ayin,* "that which thought cannot grasp." As we heard from Moses de León, the soul "stands in the status of nothingness."[129]

World, mind and self dissolve momentarily in *ayin* and then reemerge.

Every object, every thought is revealed as an epiphany of *ayin*. Yet *ayin* is not the goal in itself; it is the moment of transformation from being through nonbeing to new being. The Maggid conveys this thought with the image of the seed that disintegrates before sprouting. Annihilation is a natural process engendering new life, "When one sows a single seed, it cannot sprout and produce many seeds until its existence is nullified. Then it is raised to its root and can receive more than a single dimension of its existence. There in its root the seed itself becomes the source of many seeds."[130]

Ayin is the root of all things, and "when one brings anything to its root, one can transform it." "First [each thing] must arrive at the level of *ayin*; only then can it become something else." Nothingness embraces all potentiality. The Maggid identifies *ayin* with divine wisdom, which is also *hyle* (primordial matter) capable of assuming any form. *Ayin* "strips off one form and puts on another"; "Transformation is possible only through . . . *ayin*."[131]

Every birth must navigate the depths of *ayin*, as when a chick emerges from an egg: for a moment "it is neither chick nor egg."[132] Human rebirth is also engendered in *ayin*, "When one brings oneself to one's root, namely, to *ayin* . . . one's attributes, such as love and awe, can be transformed and focused solely on the divine." As long as the ego refuses to acknowledge its source, to participate in the divine, it is mistaking its part for the all and laying false claim to that which cannot be grasped. In the words of Menahem Mendel of Kotsk, "The I is a thief in hiding."[133] When this apparently separate self is ayinized, the effect is not total extinction but the emergence of a new form, a more perfectly human image of the divine. Only when "one's existence is nullified . . . is one called 'human.' "[134]

Ayin is a window on the oneness that underlies and undermines the manifold appearance of the world. The ten thousand things are not as independent or fragmented as they seem. There is an invisible matrix, a swirl that generates and recycles being. One who ventures into this depth must be prepared to surrender what he knows and is, what he knew and was. The ego cannot abide *ayin*; you cannot wallow in nothingness. In *ayin*, for an eternal moment, boundaries disappear. *Ayin*'s "no" clears everything away, making room for a new "yes," a new *yesh*.

We have seen how negative theology culminates in *ayin*, dissolving familiar and confining images of God. *Ayin* succeeds in "laying bare the white" of God.[135] This "*Nichts* of the Jews," writes the metaphysical poet Henry Vaughan, exposes "the naked divinity without a cover."[136] One can extend the *via negationis* further and strip even nothingness of its conceptual abstractness. David ben Judah he-Hasid reduces the abstract noun to the simplest negation possible, calling God "No."[137] But *ayin* conveys more than a curt no. It implies the God beyond God, the power that is closer and further than what we call "God." *Ayin* symbolizes the fullness of being that transcends being itself, "the mysterious palace of *ayin*, in which everything dwells."[138] The appearance of things belies their origin, when all was "undifferentiated in the depths of *ayin* . . . like ink concealed in the inkwell, which becomes visible only through the power of the writer who draws it forth with his pen and draws the writing as he wishes."[139] The reality that animates and surpasses all things cannot be captured or named, but by invoking *ayin* the mystic is able to allude to the infinite, to *alef* the ineffable.

NOTES

1. See Steven T. Katz, "Language, Epistemology and Mysticism," in *Mysticism and Philosophical Analysis,* ed. Steven T. Katz (New York: Oxford University Press, 1978), pp. 51–54.

2. See David ben Abraham ha-Lavan's *Masoret ha-Berit,* ed. Gershom Scholem, *Qovez 'al Yad* 1 (o.s. 11) (1936): 31. On Gregory Palamas and Eckhart, see Vladimir Lossky, *The Mystical Theology of the Eastern Church* (London: Clarke, 1957), p. 37; and Gershom Scholem, "Schöpfung aus Nichts und Selbstverschränkung Gottes," In *Über einige Grundbegriffe des Judentums,* ed. Gershom Scholem (Frankfurt: Suhrkamp Verlag, 1970), p. 74.

3. Philo, *Deter.* 160; cf. David Winston, *Philo of Alexandria* (Ramsey, N.J.: Paulist Press, 1981), pp. 132–33.

4. Philo, *Somn.* 1:60.

5. See Winston, "Philo's Doctrine of Free Will," in *Two Treatises of Philo of Alexandria,* ed. David Winston and John Dillon (Chico, Cal.: Scholars Press, 1983), pp. 186–89.

6. Philo, *Heres* 24–30.

7. *The Gospel of Truth,* in James M. Robinson, ed., *The Nag Hammadi Library in English* (San Francisco: Harper & Row, 1981), p. 38; and Hans Jonas, *The Gnostic Religion* (Boston: Beacon Press, 1963), p. 287.

8. Hippolytus, *Refutatio omnium haeresium* 7:20; see John Whittaker, "Basilides on the Ineffability of God," *Harvard Theological Review* 62 (1969), 367–71. Cf. Augustine, *Christian Doctrine* 1:6: "God should not be said to be ineffable, for when this is said something is said. . . . That is not ineffable which can be called ineffable."

9. Hippolytus, *Refutatio omnium haeresium* 7:26; *Allogenes,* in Robinson *Nag Hammadi Library,* pp. 450–51.

10. Hippolytus, *Refutatio omnium haeresium* 7:21–22; see Harry A. Wolf-

son, *The Philosophy of the Church Fathers* (Cambridge: Harvard University Press, 1956), 1:551.

11. See Aristotle, *Metaphysics* 11:6:1062b; David Winston, "The Book of Wisdom's Theory of Cosmogony," *History of Religion* 11 (1971), 185–202; Jonathan A. Goldstein, "The Origins of the Doctrine of Creation *Ex Nihilo*," *Journal of Jewish Studies* 35 (1984), 127–35; and the exchange between Winston and Goldstein in *JJS* 37 (1986), 88–89; 38 (1987), 187–94; Gerhard May, *Schöpfung aus dem Nichts* (Berlin: Walter de Gruyter, 1978).

12. Augustine,*Confessions* 11:7; Theophilus, *To Autolycus* 2:4. See Robert M. Grant, *Miracle and Natural Law in Graeco-Roman and Early Christian Thought* (Amsterdam: North-Holland, 1952), pp. 135–52.

13. Maimonides, *The Guide of the Perplexed* 2:25.

14. See *Bereshit Rabba* 1:9. Jonathan A. Goldstein has claimed that in this Midrash Rabban Gamaliel II is attacking the theory of creation from primordial matter and defending creation ex *nihilo;* see his article and the exchange with David Winston referred to earlier, n. 11. Cf. Alexander Altmann, *Studies in Religious Philosophy and Mysticism* (Ithaca, N.Y.: Cornell University Press, 1969), pp. 128–29.

15. *Sefer Yezirah* 2:6. See Yehuda Liebes, "*Sefer Yezirah ezel R. Shelomoh ibn Gabirol u-ferush ha-shir Ahavtikh,*" in *Re'shit ha-Mistiqah ha-Yehudit be-Eiropa,* ed. Joseph Dan, *Mehqerei Yerushalayim be-Mahshevet Yisra'el* 6:3–4 (1987): 80–82.

16. Aristotle, *Physics* 1:9:192a.

17. Maimonides, *Guide of the Perplexed* 2:25; Joseph Albo, *Sefer ha-Iqqarim* 1:2. The phrase *yesh me-ayin* appears for the first time at the end of the eleventh century in the anonymous Hebrew paraphrase of Saadia Gaon's *Kitab al-Amanat wa'l-I'tiqadat;* see Ronald C. Kiener, in *AJS Review* 11 (1986): 10–12.

18. See Plotinus, *Enneads* 5:3:14; 5:5:13; 6:7:41; 6:9:3–4.

19. Ibid., 4:8:1; 6:7:36; 6:9:4.

20. Ibid., 6:9:11. Gregory of Nyssa writes (*Life of Moses* 2:165): "Every concept that comes from some comprehensible image by an approximate understanding and by guessing at the divine nature constitutes an idol of God and does not proclaim God." Cf. Eckhart, "On Detachment": "Detach yourselves from the image, and unite yourselves to the formless being." Cf. the advice of the ninth-century Zen patriarch I-Hsüan in the *Rinzairoku*: "If you meet the Buddha, kill him!"

21. Plotinus, *Enneads* 6:9:10–11; cf. 6:8:11: "To see the divine as something external is to be outside of it; to become it is to be most truly in beauty." Cf. Eckhart's report of his mystical journey (C. F. Kelley, *Meister Eckhart on Divine Knowledge* [New Haven, Conn: Yale University Press, 1977], p. vii): "There God-as-other disappears."

22. Augustine, *Confessions* 13:33.

23. Pseudo-Dionysius, *The Divine Names* 1:1; cf. 4:3.

24. Idem, *Mystical Theology* 1:1.

25. John Scotus, *Periphyseon* 634d, 680d–681a; see Donald F. Duclow,

"Divine Nothingness and Self-Creation in John Scotus Eriugena," *Journal of Religion* 57 (1977), 110.

26. John Scotus, *Periphyseon* 678c–d, 681a.

27. Scholem, "Schöpfung aus Nichts," pp. 70–71.

28. Maimonides, *Guide of the Perplexed* 1:57. This sense of ambiguity originates in Alexander of Aphrodisias's commentaries on Aristotle; see Harry A. Wolfson, *Studies in the History of Philosophy and Religion,* ed. Isadore Twersky and George H. Williams (Cambridge: Harvard University Press, 1973), 1:143–69, 455–77.

29. Aquinas, *Summa theologiae* 1:13:2; cf. *Contra gentiles* 1:33; Gersonides, *Milhamot Adonai* 3:3; see Wolfson, *Studies in the History of Philosophy* 1:142; 2:195–246.

30. Maimonides, *Guide of the Perplexed* 1:58–59.

31. On silence, cf. the Hermetic prayer quoted earlier, at n. 7, wherein God is called: "ineffable, inexpressible, nameable by silence." Eckhart writes (Josef Quint, ed., *Meister Eckhart: deutsche Predigen und Traktate* [Munich: Carl Hanser, 1965], p. 353): "The most beautiful thing that one can express about God is found in the fact that, out of the wisdom of inner treasures, one is able to keep silent about God."

32. Azriel of Gerona, *Perush 'Eser Sefirot,* in Meir ibn Gabbai, *Derekh Emunah* (Warsaw: n.p., 1890), p. 2b: "*Ein hassagateinu ki im 'al derekh lo*"; cf. Joseph Dan and Ronald C. Kiener, eds. and trans., *The Early Kabbalah* (Mahwah, N.J.: Paulist Press, 1986), p. 90. In another text, Azriel writes similarly: "*Yada'ti ki ein hassagato ki im 'al derekh lo, ke-lomar ayin va-afisah, she-ein lo heqer* (ed. Gershom Scholem, *Madda'ei ha-Yahadut* 2 [1927]: 231). The divine incomprehensibility leads one kabbalist to call God simply "No" (*lo*); see David ben Judah he-Hasid, *The Book of Mirrors: Sefer Mar'ot ha-Zove'ot,* ed. Daniel C. Matt (Chico, Cal: Scholars Press, 1982), p. 261.

33. Shem Tov ibn Gaon, "Treatise on the 10 Sefirot," ed. Gershom Scholem, in *Qiryat Sefer* 8 (1931–1932): 400–401.

34. Joseph Gikatilla, *Sha'arei Zedeq* (ed. Efraim Gottleieb, *Mehqarim be-Sifrut ha-Qubbalah,* ed. Joseph Hacker [Tel Aviv: Tel Aviv University, 1976]), p. 140.

36. Liebes, "*Sefer Yezirah ezel R. Shelomoh ibn Gabirol,*" p. 82. We cannot rule out the possibility that Gabirol is simply giving poetic expression to the literal sense of *yesh me-ayin;* see Pines, "Ve-Qara el ha-Ayin ve-Nivqa'," p. 347, n. 32. Even if this were the case, the kabbalists could easily have read a more positive, substantive meaning into Gabirol's depiction of *ayin.*

37. Bahya ben Asher on Gen. 1:2; cf. his comment on Deut. 10:20; and Jacob ben Sheshet, *Meshiv Devarim Nekhohim,* ed. Georges Vajda (Jerusalem: Israel Academy of Sciences and Humanities, 1968), p. 153. For Asher ben David's statement, see Efraim Gottlieb, *Ha-Qabbalah be-Khitevei Rabbenu Bahya ben Asher* (Jerusalem: Kiryath Sepher, 1970), p. 84. For other early versions of the mystical interpretation of Job 28:12, see Ezra of Gerona's letter edited by Gershom Scholem in *Sefer Bialik,* ed. Jacob Fichman (Tel Aviv: Omanut, 1934), p. 156, where Ezra cites the authority of Isaac the Blind; Ezra's *Commentary on the Song*

of Songs, in *Kitevei Ramban*, ed. Hayyim D. Chavel (Jerusalem: Mosad ha-Rav Kook, 1964), 2:483; Nahmanides toward the end of his commentary on Job 28. Nahmanides cites both the literal and mystical interpretations of the verse but expresses a reservation concerning the latter: "This is their way [of interpreting] those verses. While the words themselves are most praiseworthy, we do not know whether the context bears such an interpretation. If it is an authentic tradition, we shall accept it [*ve-im qabblah hi' neqabbel*]." Nahmanides had learned this interpretation from his colleagues but did not receive it from his teacher, Judah ben Yaqar. Isaac the Blind's letter to Nahmanides, in which he accuses his former student Ezra of disclosing kabbalistic traditions, might be one reason for Nahmanides' hesitation; see Scholem in *Sefer Bialik*, pp. 143–46; Moshe Idel, "We Have No Kabbalistic Tradition on This," in *Rabbi Moses Nahmanides (Ramban): Explorations in His Religious and Literary Virtuosity*, ed. Isadore Twersky (Cambridge: Harvard University Press, 1983), pp. 52–73, esp. pp. 57–58. In his commentary on the first verse of Genesis, Nahmanides mingles the exoteric and esoteric meanings of ex *nihilo*.

38. Joseph Gikatilla, *Sha'arei Orah* (Warsaw: Orgel brand 1883), pp. 44a–b. In *Sha'arei Zedeq* (ed. Gottlieb, *Mehqarim*, p. 140), Gikatilla says simply: "All her answers are *ayin*." Azriel of Gerona in his *Perush ha-Aggadot* (ed. Isaiah Tishby, 2d ed. [Jerusalem: Magnes, 1983], p. 103) writes: "There, questioner and questioned stand still." Cf. Moses de León, *Sheqel ha-Qodesh*, ed. A. W. Greenup (London: n.p.t, 1911), p. 7; idem, *Sod 'Eser Sefirot Belimah*, ed. Scholem, *Qovez 'al Yad*, n.s. 8 (1975), p. 374; and Shim'on Labi, *Ketem Paz* (Jerusalem: Ahavat Shalom 1981), 1:91a: "Concerning everything that cannot be grasped, its question is its answer."

39. See Daniel Matt, "The Mystic and the *Mizwot*," in *Jewish Spirituality: From the Bible through the Middle Ages*, ed. Arthur Green (New York: Crossroads Press, 1986), p. 396.

40. Isaac of Akko, *Ozar Hayyim*, cited by Amos Goldreich in his edition of Isaac's *Me'irat Einayim* (Jerusalem: Hebrew University, 1981), pp. 411, 414; see Matt, "Mystic and the *Mizwot*," p. 374; cf. *Tiqqunei Zohar* 70, p. 131b; Gershom Scholem, *Kabbalah* (Jerusalem: Keter, 1974), p. 90.

41. Shem Tov ibn Gaon, "Treatise on the 10 Sefirot," p. 401. On the juxtaposition of rebellion and faith, cf. the Hebrew translation of Judah ha-Levi, *Kuzari* 1:77; Azriel of Gerona, *Perush 'Eser Sefirot*, p. 2b; Dan and Kiener, *The Early Kabbalah*, p. 90; Azriel of Gerona, *Derekh ha-Emunah ve-Derekh ha-Kefirah*, ed. Scholem, "*Seridim Hadashim mi-Kitevei R. Azri'el mi-Gerona*," in *Sefer Zikkaron le-Asher Gulak ve-li-Shemu'el Klein*, ed. Simhah Assaf and Gershom Scholem (Jerusalem: Hebrew University, 1942), pp. 207, 211; Ezra of Gerona, in Azriel, *Perush ha-Aggadot*, p. 41, variants to lines 9–11.

42. A cryptic remark on *ayin* is attributed to twelfth-century Abraham ben Isaac of Narbonne, who was the teacher and then father-in-law of Abraham ben David of Posquieres and the grandfather of Isaac the Blind. This remark is cited by Shem Tov ibn Gaon in his *Baddei ha-Aron*; see Gershom Scholem, *Ursprung und Anfänge der Kabbala* (Berlin: Walter de Gruyter, 1962), p. 178. Issac the Blind is called *avi ha-qabbalah* by Bahya ben Asher in his commentary to Gen. 32:10.

43. Cf. *Sefer Yezirah* 2:6, cited earlier, at n. 15; Azriel, of Gerona, *Perush ha-Aggadot*, p. 107; Zohar 3:2a; David ben Judah he-Hasid, *Book of Mirrors*, introduction, p. 25, n. 183.

44. Moses de León, *Sheqel ha-Qodesh*, pp. 23–24; cf. idem, *Sod 'Eser Sefirot Belimah*, p. 374. Azriel of Gerona, in *Perush ha-Aggadot*, p. 107, also cites the verse from Ecclesiastes but does not mention the human soul; cf. Jacob ben Sheshet, *Ha-Emunah ve-ha-Bittahon*, chap. 12, in Cheval, *Kitevei Ramban* 2:385; Hanokh Zundel, *'Anaf Yosef* on *Tanhuma, Emor,* 15. (For this last reference I thank Dr. Ze'ev Gries.) John Scotus taught that the human intellect, "while it bursts out into various forms comprehensible to the senses, does not abandon the always incomprehensible condition of its nature" (*Periphyseon* 633c). Human self-ignorance is a sign of the *imago Dei:* "If in any way it could understand what it is, it would necessarily deviate from the likeness of its Creator" (*Periphyseon* 585b–c).

45. Moses de León, *Sheqel ha-Qodesh*, p. 111.

46. Gikatilla, *Sha'arei Orah*, pp. 44a–b; cf. Zohar 3:65a–b. On the tip of the *yod* cf. Talmud, *Menahot* 29a, 34a in a halakhic context.

47. David ben Judah he-Hasid, *Book of Mirrors*, p. 279.

48. Zohar 3:26b; see Daniel Matt, *Zohar: The Book of Enlightenment* (Ramsey, N.J.: Paulist Press, 1983) pp. 147, 267–68. The Gnostics taught that the aeons (except for *nous*) are ignorant of the hidden God; see *The Gospel of Truth*, in *Nag Hammadi Library*, p. 40. On knowledge as aroma cf. *Shir ha-Shirim Rabbah* 1:20.

49. Ezra of Gerona, *Commentary on the Song of Songs*, in Cheval, *Kitevei Ramban* 2:494; cf. Ezra's letter in *Sefer Bialik*, pp. 157–58; Azriel of Gerona, *Perush ha-Aggadot*, pp. 110–11; Altmann, *Studies in Religious Philosophy*, pp. 136–39; Gottlieb, *Mehqarim*, pp. 82–83. Ezra draws on Maimonides, *Guide of the Perplexed* 2:13, 26.

50. Ezra of Gerona's letter in Scholem, *Sefer Bialik*, p. 158; cf. his *Commentary on the Song of Songs*, in Cheval *Kitevei Ramban* 2:494 (to be corrected according to Gottlieb, *Mehqarim*, p. 531); Azriel of Gerona, *Perush 'Eser Sefirot*, p. 3a–b; Dan and Kiener, *The Early Kabbalah*, p. 94; Shem Tov ibn Gaon, "Treatise on the 10 Sefirot,": 538; idem, *Qiryat Sefer* 9 (1932–1933): 126; Joseph ben Shalom Ashkenazi, *Perush Qabbali li-Vere'shit Rabbah*, ed. Moshe Hallamish (Jerusalem: Magnes Press, 1985), pp. 77; 209, n. 5; Idel, "*Ha-Sefirot she-me-'al ha-Sefirot*," *Tarbiz* 51 (1982): 241–43. "Essences" ("*havayot*") is modeled on Arabic "*huwiyyah*," Greek "*ousia*," or Latin "*essentiae*."

51. On *keter* as *mahut* see Azriel of Gerona, ed. Scholem, *Madda'ei ha-Yahadut* 2 (1927): 231. In *Sha'arei Zedeg* (ed. Gottlieb, *Mehqarim*), pp. 140–42, Gikatilla contrasts the mystical and literal interpretations of *yesh me-ayin*.

52. Zohar 1:15a; see the full passage and commentary in Daniel Matt, *Zohar: The Book of Enlightenment*, public pp. 49–50, 207–10. Cf. Gabirol's image of the cleaving of *ayin*, cited earlier, at n. 35. The same image was applied by thirteenth-century mystics of the *Iyyun* circle to the primordial ether (*avir qadmon*). In this Zohar passage the aura (or ether [*avira*]), symbolizing *ayin*, is broken through. Cf.

cited earlier, at nn. 15, and 43 see Scholem, *Ursprung und Anfänge der Kabbala,* pp. 292–93, 301–303.

53. Moses de León, *Sheqel ha-Qodesh,* pp. 25–26. On the primordial point see Gershom Scholem, *Major Trends in Jewish Mysticism,* (New York: Schocken, 1961), pp. 173, 218; idem, an: in *Tarbiz* 2 (1931): 195, 206–207. The Pythagorean Philolaus of Croton (fifth century BCE) suggested that the point is the "first principle leading to magnitude." On *hakkeh mah* see Asher ben David's wording cited by Tishby in Azriel of Gerona, *Perush ha-Aggadot,* p. 84, n. 4; Cf. Moses de León, *Sod 'Eser Sefirot Belimah,* p. 375. Asher ben David is also the source for the statement that wisdom "appears to be the first *sefirah*"; see Gottlieb, *Ha-Qabbalah be-Khitevei Rabbenu Bahya ben Asher,* p. 83; cf. Joseph ben Shalom Ashkenazi, *Commentary on Sefer Yezirah* (printed under the name of the Rabad), *Sefer Yezirah* (Jerusalem: Lewin-Epstein, 1965), 1:5.

54. See Moses de León, *Sheqel ha-Qodesh,* pp. 110–11; Jacob ben Sheshet, *Meshiv Devarim Nekhohim,* p. 113; cf. Azriel of Gerona, *Perush ha-Aggadot,* p. 84: "*Koah mah she-efshar li-heyot,*" and Tishby's n. 4 (p. 84) on the kabbalistic reinterpretation of *hyle.* On the ether cf. cited earlier, n. 52.

55. Cf. the anonymous Neoplatonic *Liber de causis,* chap. 11: "The effect is in the cause after the mode of the cause, and the cause is in the effect after the mode of the effect" (*The Book of Causes* [*Liber de causis*], trans. Dennis J. Brand [Milwaukee, Wis.: Marquette University Press, 1984], p. 30). This thesis concerning the "first things" is applied by Azriel to being and nothingness. On Azriel's probable knowledge of *Liber de causis,* see Scholem, *Ursprung und Anfänge der Kabbala,* p. 375.

56. Azriel of Gerona, *Derekh ha-Emunah ve-Derekh ha-Kefirah,* ed. Scholem, "*Seridim Hadashim,*" p. 207. Cf. Liebes, "*Sefer Yezirah ezel R. Shelomoh ibn Gabirol,*" p. 83.

57. Cf. Eckhart's experiential description of nothingness as the source of God (cited by Bernard McGinn, "The God Beyond God: Theology and Mysticism in the Thought of Meister Eckhart," *Journal of Religion* 61 [1981]: 10): "When the soul comes into the One, entering into pure loss of self, it finds God as in nothingness. It seemed to a man that he had a dream, a waking dream, that he became pregnant with nothingness as a woman with child. In this nothingness God was born. He was the fruit of nothingness; God was born in nothingness."

58. Azriel of Gerona, *Sod ha-Tefillah,* ed. Scholem, "*Seridim Hadashim,*" p. 215.

59. See, e.g., Judah al-Harizi's Hebrew translation of Maimonides' *Guide of the Perplexed* 1:17: "*ha-efes ha-mugbal.*" Samuel ibn Tibbon renders Maimonides' Arabic *'adam (steresis)* with the Hebrew *he'der.*

60. See Aristotle, *Physics* 1:9:192a: "Matter accidentally is not, while privation in its own nature is not; . . . matter is nearly, in a sense, *is* substance, while privation in no sense is." On *steresis* see W. D. Ross, *Aristotle* (London: Methuen, 1964), pp. 63–66; W. K. C. Guthrie, *A History of Greek Philosophy,* vol. 6 (Cambridge: Cambridge University Press, 1981), pp. 119–24.

61. Abraham bar Hiyya, *Megillat ha-Megalleh,* ed. Adolf Posnanski (Berlin:

Mekize Nirdamim, 1924), p. 5; see Scholem, *Ursprung und Anfänge der Kabbala,* p. 372, n. 120.

62. Azriel of Gerona, *Sod ha-Tefillah,* ed. Scholem, "Seridim Hadashim," p. 215.

63. Joseph ben Shalom Ashkenazi, *Commentary on Sefer Yezirah,* introduction, p. 3a; idem, *Perush Qabbali li-Vere'shit Rabbah,* p. 32; cf. Scholem, *Major Trends in Jewish Mysticism,* p. 217.

64. Azriel of Gerona, *Sod ha-Tefillah,* ed. Scholem, "Seridim Hadashim," p. 215; idem, *Commentary on the Prayers,* in Scholem, "The Concept of *Kavvanah* in the Early Kabbalah," in *Studies in Jewish Thought,* ed. Alfred Jospe (Detroit Mich: Wayne State University Press, 1981), p. 167.

65. Azriel of Gerona, *Sod ha-Tefillah,* ed. Scholem, "Seridim Hadashim," p. 216; cf. idem, *Perush ha-Aggadot,* pp. 82–83, where Azriel cites the identical teaching in the name of Plato. Plotinus (*Enneads* 4:3:32) notes that "the higher soul . . . gathers multiplicity into one. . . . In this way it will not be [clogged] with multiplicity but light and alone by itself."

66. John Scotus, *Periphyseon* 517b–c. Cf. Meister Eckhart (cited in McGinn, "The God beyond God," p. 7): "God is something indistinct, distinguished by His indistinction."

67. Azriel of Gerona, *Perush 'Eser Sefirot,* p. 2b; Dan and Kiener, *The Early Kabbalah,* p. 90; idem, *Commentary on Sefer Yezirah* (printed under the name of Nahmanides) 1:7; see the list of passages assembled by strame Tishby, *Hiqrei Qabbalah u-Sheluhoteha* (Jerusalem: Magnes, 1982), pp. 18, 22–23. John Scotus is apparently the source for both Azriel and Nicholas of Cusa (1401–1464), who developed the notion of *coincidentia oppositorum.* Johannes Reuchlin, in *De arte cabalistica,* connects Azriel's and Nicholas's terminologies; see Scholem, *Ursprung und Anfänge der Kabbala,* p.389. Amos Goldreich has raised the possibility of an Iśma'ili source for Azriel's terminology; see Goldreich's *"Mi-Mishnat Hug ha-'Iyyun: 'Od 'al ha-Meqorot ha-Efshariyyim shel 'Ha Ahdut ha-Shavah,' "* in *Re'shit ha-Mistiqah ha-Yehudit be-Eiropa,* ed. Josefsh Dan, pp. 141–56. Cf. the wording of Shem Tov ibn Gaon, "Treatise on the 10 sefirot, p." 541): "the undifferentiated oneness that has neither front nor back and in which no opposites can be imagined."

68. Azriel of Gerona, *Derekh ha-Emunah ve-Derekh ha-Kefirah,* ed. Scholem, "Seridim Hadashim," pp. 208–9. Azriel's wording, "more than all" (*yater 'al ha-kol*), reflects Scotus's Latin *superesse* and the earlier Greek *hyperousia;* cf. cited earlier nn. 18 and 23. In *Sefer ha-'Iyyun,* whose author(s) were apparently influenced by Azriel, we hear of "the unfathomable and infinite light that is concealed in the excess [*tosefet*] of the hidden darkness." *Tosefet* may be another Hebrew version of *superesse;* see Scholem, "Colours and Their Symbolism in Jewish Tradition and Mysticism," *Diogenes* 108 (1979): 103. For other parallels between Scotus and Azriel see Gabrielle Sed-Rajna, "L' Influence de Jean Scot sur la doctrine du kabbaliste Azriel de Gérone," in *Jean Scot Érigène et l'histoire de la philosophie* (Paris: Editions du Centre National, 1977), pp. 453–63. For evidence that certain early kabbalists knew Latin, see Scholem "Seridim Hadashim," p.

218, where Asher ben David recounts a dream in which he heard a Latin interpretation of a divine name.

69. On the phrase "neither *yesh* nor *ayin*," see Gottlieb, *Ha-Qabbalah be-Khitevei Rabbenu Bahya ben Asher*, p. 229. Cf. Pseudo-Dionysius, *Mystical Theology*, 5: "It is . . . not something among what is not, not something among what is." Cf., ibid., 1:1: "In the earnest exercise of mystical contemplation, abandon . . . all nonbeings and all beings; thus you will unknowingly be elevated, as far as possible, to the unity of that beyond being and knowledge." Cf. idem, *Divine Names* 5:8: "For it is not this but not that." The *Brhadaranyaka Upanishad* (4:5:15) states that the only suitable description of the Absolute is *neti neti* ("not this, not this").

70. See Isaac of Akko, *Me'irat Einayim*, p. 218; Idel, "*Hitbodedut* as Concentration in Ecstatic Kabbalah," in *Jewish Spirituality*, ed. Arthur Green, pp. 414–15; Moshe Idel, "*Hitbodedut* qua Concentration in Ecstatic Kabbalah," in *Da'at* 14 (1985): 47–49, 76; Scholem, *Major Trends*, pp. 96–97; R. J. Zwi Werblowsky, *Joseph Karo: Lawyer and Mystic* (Philadephia: Jewish Publication Society, 1977), pp. 161–62; Obadyah Maimonides, *The Treatise of the Pool*, ed. Paul Fenton (London: Octagon Press, 1981), introduction, pp. 63–64.

71. David ben Judah he-Hasid, *Book of Mirrors*, p. 227; see my introduction, pp. Various mystics describe an experience of forgetting. Plotinus states (*Enneads* 4:3:32): "The higher soul ought to be happy to forget what it has received from the worse soul. . . . The more it presses on towards the heights, the more it will forget." The ninth-century Sufi Abu Yazid al-Bistami, who develops the notion of *fana* (passing away) reports: "When He brought me to the brink of divine unity, I divorced myself and betook myself to my Lord, calling upon Him to help me. 'Master,' I cried 'I beseech Thee as one to whom nothing else remains.' When He recognized the sincerity of my prayer and how I had despaired of myself, the first token that came to me proving that He had answered this prayer was that He caused me to forget myself utterly and to forget all creatures and dominions" (cited by Arthur J. Arberry, *Revelation and Reason in Islam* [London: Allen & Unwin, 1957], p. 96). The anonymous author of *The Cloud of Unknowing* writes (chap. 5): "You must fashion a cloud of forgetting beneath you, between you and every created thing. . . . Abandon them all beneath the cloud of forgetting." Saint John of the Cross counsels (*Collected Works*, tr. Kieran Kavanaugh and Otilio Rodriguez [Washington: Institute of Carmelite Studies, 1973], p. 675): "Forgetful of all, abide in recollection with your Spouse." In a Hasidic text edited in the circle of the Maggid of Mezritch (*Shemu'ah Tovah* [Warsaw: 1938], p. 71b, cited by Rivka Schatz Uffenheimer, *Ha-Hasidut ke-Mistiqah* [Jerusalem: Magnes Press, 1968], p. 99) we read: "Arriving at the gate of *ayin*, one forgets his existence altogether."

72. Here *devarim* may refer to the words of prayer or the *sefirot*; see Scholem, *Ursprung und Anfänge der Kabbala*, p. 268; Azriel, *Perush ha-Aggadot*, ed. Tishby, p. 40, n. 11. The word may also be vocalized *dibberim*, referring to the Ten Commandments; see Idel, *Kabbalah: New Perspectives* (New Haven Conn.: Yale University Press, 1988), p. 46.

73. Azriel of Gerona, *Perush ha-Aggadot,* pp. 40, 116. Cf. Ezra of Gerona, *Commentary on the Song of Songs,* in *Kitevei Ramban* 2:494, 526; Ezra's letter, ed. Scholem, *Sefer Bialik,* p. 160; Moses de León, *Shushan 'Edut,* ed. Scholem, *Qovez 'al Yad,* n.s. 8 (1975), p. 334; Menahem Recanati, *Perush 'al ha-Torah* (Jerusalem: Monzon, 1961), p. 51b; idem, *Sefer Ta'amei ha-Mizvot,* ed. Simhah Lieberman (London: Lieberman, 1962), p. 13c; and cited earlier, at n. 44: " . . . the annihilation of all thoughts." On the *hasidim,* cf. Mishnah, *Berakhot* 5:1.

74. Isaac the Blind, *Commentary on Sefer Yezirah,* ed. Scholem, *Ha-Qab-balah be-Provans* (Jerusalem: Akademon, 1970), appendix, p. 1 and cf. pp. 9, 13; Scholem, *Ursprung und Anfänge der Kabbala,* pp. 246–47. On the image of sucking, cf. *Sefer ha-Bahir,* ed. Reuven Margaliot (Jerusalem: Mosad ha-Rav Kook, 1978), par. 177; Ezra of Gerona, *Commentary on the Song of Songs,* in *Kitevei Ramban* 2:485–86, 504–505; Azriel of Gerona, *Perush ha-Aggadot,* pp. 82 (and Tishby's n. 7), 110; Jacob ben Sheshet, *Meshiv Devarim Nekhohim,* p. 113; *Zohar* 1:35a, 84b, 183a; and 3:166b. Cf. the comment of Isaac of Akko (ed. Scholem, *Qiryat Sefer* 31 [1956]: 383): "No creature can understand them [the hidden paths of wisdom] except through contemplative thought, not through knowing, through the effort of study, but rather through contemplation."

75. Ezra of Gerona, in Azriel of Gerona, *Perush ha-Aggadot,* p. 39 and variants. Cf. Azriel's note of caution on p. 104: "One should not probe that which thought cannot grasp [*mah sheein ha-mahshavah masseget*]." This last phrase is a designation for *keter,* though it is applied to *ein sof* by Isaac the Blind; see his *Commentary on Sefer Yezirah,* p. 1; Scholem, *Ursprung und Anfänge der Kab-bala,* pp. 238–39; and the passages cited by Tishby, *Perush ha-Aggadot,* p. 104, n. 6; cf. nn. 15, 37, 43 cited earlier; Moses de León, *Shushan 'Edut,* p. 347; idem, *Sod 'Eser Sefirot Belimah,* p. 371; idem, *Sheqel ha-Qodesh,* p. 4; Recanati, *Perush 'al ha-Torah,* pp. 37d–38a.

76. Azriel of Gerona, *Commentary on the Sacrifices,* MS Oxford, Christ Church, 198, fol. 12b; see Idel, *Kabbalah,* p. 52.

77. Isaac of Akko, *Ozar Hayyim,* MS Moscow-Günzberg 775, fol. 112a; see Gottlieb, *Mehqarim,* pp. 237–38; Idel, *Kabbalah,* pp. 47–48.

78. Isaac the Blind is cited by Ezra of Gerona, *Commentary on the Song of Songs,* in *Kitevei Ramban* 2:522; cf. Azriel of Gerona, *Perush ha-Aggadot,* p. 16; Matt, "The Mystic and the *Mizwot,*" pp. 399–400; Idel, *Kabbalah: New Perspec-tives,* pp. 35–58.

79. Isaac of Akko, *Ozar Hayyim,* MS Moscow-Günzberg 775, fols. 111a, 161b; see Gottlieb, *Mehqarim,* p. 237; Idel, *Kabbalah,* p. 67; cf. idem, in *Da'at* 14 (1985):50.

80. Yehiel Mikhel of Zloczew, *Mayim Rabbim* (Warsaw: A. Schriftgiessen, 1899), p. 15a. Cf. *Katha Upanishad* 4:15: "As pure water poured into pure becomes like unto it, so does the soul of the discerning sage become [like unto Brahman]." As Idel notes (*Kabbalah* pp. 67–70), Sufi and Christian mystics em-ploy the image as well.

81. Cited earlier, at n. 50.

82. Moses de León, *Sheqel ha-Qodesh*, p. 6.

83. Moses Nahmanides, *Commentary on Sefer Yezirah*, ed. Gershom Scholem, *Qiryat Sefer* 6 (1929–1930): 401–2, and n. 5; cf. Gershom Scholem, *Ursprung und Anfänge der Kabbala*, p. 397. This represents a kabbalistic version of the Christian doctrine of *apokatastasis;* cf. the Neoplatonic formula: *restitutio omnium rerum ad integrum;* and John Scotus, *Periphyseon* 696b.

84. David ben Judah he-Hasid, *Book of Mirrors*, p. 224; introduction, p. 33. The image of being swallowed is also applied, both positively and negatively, to mystical experience; see David's interpretation of Num. 4:20 in Book of *Mirrors*, p. 119; and Isaac of Akko's interpretation of the same verse, cited by Gottlieb, *Mehqarim*, p. 237; cf. Isaac's *Me'irat Einayim*, p. 189; Moses de León, *Sheqel ha-Qodesh*, p. 4; Idel, *Kabbalah*, pp. 70–73; Jonas, *Gnostic Religion*, p. 182. Saint John of the Cross, in *The Dark Night* 2:6, alludes to Jonah's terrible experience in the belly of the great fish. Shneur Zalman of Lyady writes (*Seder ha-Tefillah* [Warsaw: n.p., 1866], 1:26a): "This is the true *devequt:* becoming one substance with God, in whom one is swallowed."

85. See Scholem, "The Concept of *Kavvanah* in the Early Kabbalah," pp. 168; 178, n. 38; Idel, *Kabbalah*, pp. 53–54; Meir ibn Gabbai, *'Avodat ha-Qodesh*, 2:6, p. 29a; cf. Isaac the Blind, *Commentary on Sefer Yezirah*, p. 6.

86. See Idel, "*Ha-Sefirot she-me-'al ha-Sefirot*," p. 280.

87. Ezra of Gerona, *Commentary on the Song of Songs*, in *Kitevei Ramban* 2:504. Ezra offers a mystical interpretation of a passage in *Bereshit Rabba* 15:1 concerning the trees of the Garden of Eden: "The Holy One, Blessed be He, uprooted them and transplanted them in the Garden of Eden." Nahmanides objects to this Midrash in his commentary on Gen. 2:8; cf. Zohar 1:35b, 37a; 2:177a; Moses de León, *Maskiyyot Kesef*, cited by Scholem, in *Tarbiz* 3 (1931): 54; Joseph ben Shalom Ashkenazi, *Perush Qabbali li-Vere'shit Rabbah*, pp. 208–209; Recanati, *Perush 'al ha-Torah*, p. 9d; Idel, *Kabbalah*, pp. 181–82; Labi, *Ketem Paz*, pp. 3a, 76d, 87a, 109a–b, 111a. For the references to *Ketem Paz* I am grateful to Boaz Hus, Hebrew University, Jerusalem.

88. Ezra of Gerona, *Commentary on the Song of Songs*, in *Kitevei Ramban* 2:486; see Idel, *Kabbalah*, p. 182. Cf., though, Ezra's description of prayer in 2:494: "The entire structure [of the seven lower *sefirot*] will cleave to, unite with, and ascend to *ein sof.*"

89. Ezra of Gerona, *Commentary on the Song of Songs*, in *Kitevei Ramban* 2:504.

90. Gikatilla, *Sha'arei Orah*, p. 19a–b.

91. See Matt, "The Mystic and the *Mizwot*," pp. 392; 402, n. 56; Idel, *Kabbalah*, p. 185.

92. *Sefer ha-Yihud*, MS Milano-Ambrosiana 62, fol. 112b; cf. Recanati, *Commentary on the Torah*, p. 51b; Moshe Idel, "Ferush Eser Sefirot," in *Alei Sefer* 6–7 (1979): 82-84; idem, *Kabbalah*, pp. 184–85.

93. David ben Abraham ha-Lavan, *Masoret ha-Berit*, p. 39; cf. David's comment on *ayin* and *yesh*, cited earlier, at n. 2.

94. David ben Abraham ha-Lavan, *Masoret ha-Berit*, p. 38.

95. Ibid., p. 31. Cf. Gabbai, *Derekh Emunah,* p. 16c: "Everything was hidden and concealed in the depths of nothingness." Labi refers to *'imqei ha-ayin* frequently in his *Ketem Paz,* often in connection with the mystical interpretation of *Bereshit Rabba* 15:1 or the notion of "undifferentiated oneness"; see n. 87 cited earlier; and *Ketem Paz* 1:4a, 27c, 45d, 49b, 72c, 86b, 91b, 92c–d, 138d, 261b, 262c. In Kabbalistic literature *keter* is often referred to as depth (*'omeq*).

96. See Zohar 2:63b; 3:69b–70a; Gikatilla, *Sha'arei Orah,* pp. 37b–38a, 95a–b. On the conflict between the biblical conception of a personal God and the impersonal Neoplatonic conception, see Scholem, "Das Ringen zwischen dem biblischen Gott und dem Gott Plotins in der alten Kabbala," *Über einige Grundbegriffe des Judentums,* pp. 9–52. The Zohar (1:72b; 3:288b) enjoys confusing the Jewish Father in Heaven with the Aristotelian Prime Mover: it plays with the divine names *Sibbeta de-Sibbatin* (The Cause of Causes) and *Saba de-Sabin* (The Old Man of Old Men).

97. Gikatilla, *Sha'arei Orah,* pp. 102b-103a. Here again, the literal meaning of *ayin* (where) is exchanged for mystical nothingness; cf. at n. 36, cited earlier, concerning Job 28:12: "Wisdom comes into being out of *ayin.*" Cf. the teaching of the Hasidic rabbi Hayyim Haika of Amdur (*Hayyim va-Hesed* [Jerusalem: n. p., 1953], p. 47): "God cannot come to my help unless I bind myself to *ayin.* This is the meaning of 'My help comes from *ayin.'*" Cf. Jaläl al-Dīn Rūmi, *Mathnawi* 6:822: "The whole world has taken the wrong way, for they fear nonexistence, while it is their refuge."

98. See Gershom Scholem, *The Messianic Idea in Judaism* (New York: Schocken Books, 1971), p. 214. On the kabbalistic roots of this play on words, see Gikatilla, *Sha'arei Orah,* p. 103a; *Sefer ha-Peli'ah* (Jerusalem: n.p., 1976), p. 14b–c, where *aniy* is a symbol of *shekhinah.*

99. Dov Baer, *Maggid Devarav le-Ya'agov,* ed. Rivka Schatz Uffenheimer (Jerusalem: Magnes Press, 1976), pp. 91, 94. Cf. Uffenheimer, *Ha-Hasidut ke-Mistiqah,* pp. 99, 101; and end of n. 71, cited earlier.

100. Dov Baer, *Maggid Devarav le-Ya'aqov,* p. 186.

101. Ibid., p. 230; see Ze'ev Gries, "Mi-Mitos le-Etos," in *Ummah ve-Toledoteha,* ed. Menachem Stern and Shmuel Ettinger (Jerusalem: Merkaz Zalman Shazar, 1983–1984), 2:139–41; cf. Joseph Weiss, "Rabbi Abraham Kalisker's Concept of Communion with God and Men," *JJS* 6 (1955): 88–90. Weiss draws too sharp a distinction between ethical and mystical *ayin.*

102. Issachar Ber of Zlotshov, *Mevasser Zedek* (Berditchev, U.S.S.R: n.p., 1817), p. 9a–b; see Schatz, *Hasidut,* p. 114; cf. Baer, *Maggid Devarav le-Ya'aqov,* pp. 197–98. Cf. John of the Cross, *The Ascent of Mount Carmel* 2:7: "When one is brought to nothing [*nada*], the highest degree of humility, the spiritual union between one's soul and God will be effected." Cf. Abraham Abulafia (cited by Idel, "*Hitboded*" p. 48): "One who knows the truth of reality will be more humble and lowly in spirit than his fellow." *Keter* is called *'anavah* (humility) in an early kabbalistic text; see Scholem, "Index to Commentary on the Ten Sefirot" *Qiryat Sefer 10* (1933–34): 507. Cf. Talmud, *Sotah* 21b: Rabbi Yohanan said, "The words of Torah become real only for one who makes himself as one who is not, as it is written: 'Wisdom comes into being out of *ayin.'*"

103. Hayyim Haika, *Hayyim va-Hesed* (Warsaw: n.p., 1891), p. 17b–c; cf. Baer, *Maggid Devarav le-Ya'aqov*, p. 229; Philo, *Heres* 24–29.

104. Hayyim Haika of Amdur, a student of the Maggid, describes the attachment to divine will as *afisat ha-sekhel* the annihilation of the intellect); see his *Hayyim va-Hesed*, p. 26c; cf. Schatz, *Hasidut*, p. 24; Joseph Weiss, *Studies in Eastern European Jewish Mysticism*, ed. David Goldstein (Oxford: Oxford University Press, 1985), pp. 152–53.

105. *Shemu'ah Tovah*, p. 49b; see Schatz, *Hasidut*, p. 101; idem, "Contemplative Prayer in Hasidism," in *Studies in Mysticism and Religion Presented to Gershom G. Scholem*, ed. Ephraim E. Urbach et al. (Jerusalem: Magnes Press, 1967), p. 217.

106. *Shemu'ah Tovah*, p. 70b; see Schatz, *Hasidut*, p. 101; idem, "Contemplative Prayer," pp. 216–17.

107. Baer, *Maggid Devarav le-Ya'aqov*, p. 224; Levi Yitzhak, *Qedushat Levi*, p. 71d; see Schatz, *Hasidut*, pp. 122–23.

108. Dov Baer, *Or ha-Emet*, ed. Levi Yitzhak of Berditchev (Bnei Brak, Isr.: Yahadut, 1967), p. 15a. On *qadmut ha-sekhel*, see Gershom Scholem, *Devarim be-Go* (Tel Aviv: Am Oved, 1976), 2:351–60; Siegmund Hurwitz, "Psychological Aspects in Early Hasidic Literature," in *Timeless Documents of the Soul*, ed. James Hillman (Evanston, Ill.: Northwestern University Press, 1968), pp. 151–239.

109. Ze'ev Wolf of Zhitomir, *Or ha-Me'ir* (New York: n.p., 1954), p. 95c; see Schatz, *Hasidut*, p. 120. On the *shekhinah* speaking out of one's throat cf. Zohar 1:267a; 3:219a, 306b (all in Ra'aya Meheimna).

110. Kalonymous Kalman, *Ma'or va-Shemesh* (New York: n.p., 1958), p. 51a; see Schatz, *Hasidut*, pp. 118–19.

111. Benjamin ben Aaron of Zalozce, *Torei Zahav* (Mohilev, U.S.S.R.: n.p., 1816), p. 56d; see Schatz, *Hasidut*, pp. 117–18; cf. Weiss, "*Via Passiva* in Early Hasidism," *JJS* 11 (1960): 140–45. According to Mishnah, *Sanhedrin* 11:5, a prophet is forbidden to suppress his prophecy. The liberating effects of self-annihilation can be compared to the freedom expressed by the author of the Zohar who surrenders his identity and adopts the pseudonyms of Shim'on bar Yohai and his circle; cf. Matt, *Zohar: The Book of Enlightenment*, pp. 27–30.

112. *Shemu'ah Tovah*, p. 71b; see Schatz, *Hasidut*, p. 99; idem, "Contemplative Prayer," p. 214.

113. Baer, *Maggid Devarav le-Ya'aqov*, p. 273.

114. Baer, *Or ha-Emet*, p. 3c; see Schatz, *Hasidut*, pp. 111–12.

115. Uziel Meizlish, *Tif'eret 'Uzzi'el* (Tel Aviv: n.p., 1962), p. 53b–c; see Schatz, *Hasidut*, pp. 119–20.

116. Avraham Hayyim of Zlotshov, *Orah la-Hayyim* (Jerusalem: n.p., 1960), p. 280a; see Schatz, *Hasidut*, p. 119. The Sufi mystic Ibn al-Farid writes in his *Ta'iyya*, verse 153 (cited by Schimmel, *Mystical Dimensions* p. 154): "Both of us are a single worshiper, who, in respect to the united state, bows himself to his own essence in every act of bowing."

117. *Liqqutei Yeqarim* (Lemberg [nowloov], Pol.: 1865), p. 12b; see Schatz, *Hasidut*, pp. 27–28.

118. Baer, *Or ha-Emet*, p. 4c; see Schatz, *Hasidut*, p. 103; idem, "Contemplative Prayer," p. 218.

119. *Liqqutei Yeqarim*, p. 1c; Asher Zevi, *Ma'ayan ha-Hokhmah* (Koretz, U.S.S.R.; n.p. 1816), p. 43d; see Schatz. *Hasidut*, pp. 97, 108; idem, "Contemplative Prayer," pp. 211, 224.

120. Baer, *Maggid Devarav le-Ya'aqov*, p. 12

121. Reuven ha-Levi Horowitz, *Duda'im ba-Sadeh* (Isr.: n. p. 1944), p. 9b; see Schatz, *Hasidut*, p. 121.

122. *Boneh Yerushalayim* (Jerusalem: 1926), p. 54; Shneur Zalman of Lyady, *Torah Or* (Vilna: 1899), p. 11a. On the Hasidic concept of *bittul-ha-yesh* (the nullification of *yesh*) see Rahel Elior, " *'Iyyunim be-Mahshevet Habad*," *Daat* 16 (1986): 157–66; idem, *Torat ha-Elohut be-Dor ha-Sheni shel Hasidut Habad* (Jerusalem: Magnes, 1982), pp. 178–243; "Habad: The Contemplative Ascent to God," in *Jewish Spirituality: From the Sixteenth-Century Revival to the Present*, ed. Arthur Green (New York: Crossroads Press, 1987), pp. 181–98; Yoram Yakovson, "*Torat ha-Beri'ah shel R. Shne'ur Zalman mi-Ladi*," *Eshel Beer-Sheva* 1 (1976): 345–50. Cf. Eckhart's view (cited by McGinn, "God Beyond God," p. 11): "Let us eternally sink down into this Unity from something to nothing."

123. Zalman, *Torah Or*, p. 22b.

124. Baer, *Maggid Devarav le-Ya'aqov*, p. 24.

125. Ibid., pp. 124–27; see Schatz, *Hasidut*, p. 61; cf. Haika, *Hayyim va-Hesed*, p. 58d.

126. Baer, *Or ha-Emet*, p. 36c–d. *Sefer Ez Hayyim* ('The Book of the Tree of Life'), compiled by Hayyim Vital, is the major text of Lurianic Kabbalah.

127. Baer, *Maggid Devarav le-Ya'aqov*, pp. 196, 296; cf. pp. 138, 144, 196, 227. On the Hasidic understanding of *zimzum* see Yakovson, *Torat ha-Beri'ah shel R. Shne'ur Zalman mi-Ladi*, pp. 314–31; Elior, *Torat ha-Elohut be-Dor ha-Sheni shel Hasidut Habad*, pp. 61–77; cf. Scholem, "Schöpfung aus Nichts," pp. 84–88.

128. Baer, *Maggid Devarav le-Ya'aqov*, pp. 94, 230, and cf. p. 125: "The breaking [of the vessels] came about because everyone said, 'I will reign,' " Plotinus (*Enneads* 5:1:1) sees self-assertion and the wish to belong to oneself as causing the soul's ignorance of its divine source. Azriel of Gerona identifies Adam's sin as his assertion of will, which split him off from the divine; see Isaiah Tishby, *Mishnat ha-Zohar* 2:291; Bezalel Safran, "Rabbi Azriel and Nahmanides: Two views of the Fall of Man," in *Rabbi Moses Nahmanides (Ramban)*, ed. Twersky, pp. 76–77. Cf. Weiss, *Studies in Eastern European Jewish Mysticism*, pp. 142–54; and Mishnah, *Avot* 2:4: "Nullify your will in the face of His will."

129. The Maggid's statement is recorded in Baer, *Or ha-Emet* (Brooklyn, N. Y.: 1960), p. 45b; see Schatz, *Hasidut*, pp. 101–2. For Moses de León's remark and the similar view of John Scotus see n. 44, cited earlier. On the phrase "that which thought cannot grasp" see n. 75, cited earlier.

130. Baer, *Maggid Devarav le-Ya'aqov*, p. 209; cf. pp. 134, 199, 210. This image is widespread. Cf. John 12:24: "Unless a grain of wheat falls into the earth and dies, it remains alone; but if it dies, it bears much fruit." Cf. 1 Cor. 15:36:

"What you sow does not come to life unless it dies." Cf. Plotinus, *Enneads* 4:8:6; and Koran 6:95: "God is the one who splits the grain of corn and the date-stone. He brings forth the living from the dead." Cf. Judah ha-Levi, *Kuzari* 4:23; and the Sabbatian tract cited by Scholem, *Mehqarim u-Meqorot le-Toledot ha-Shabbeta'ut ve-Gilguleha* (Jerusalem: Mosad Bialik, 1982), p. 43: "Belonging to these sects are those who believe that [with the advent of the Messiah] the Torah has been nullified and that in the future it will exist without *mizvot*. They claim that the nullification of the Torah is its fulfillment, and they illustrate this by the image of a grain of wheat that rots in the earth." Abraham Isaac Kook writes (*Orot ha-Qodesh* 1:152): "This rotting of the seed is analogous to what the divine light does in planting anew the vineyard in Israel, in which the old values are forced to be renewed by the insolence that comes in the footsteps of the Messiah." See Dov Sadan, "Hittah she-Niqberah," *Divrei ha-Agademiyah ha-Le'umit ha-Yisre'elit le-Madda'im* 1:9 (1966): 1-21; Gries, "Mi-Mitos le-Etos," p. 140.

131. Baer, *Maggid Devarav le-Ya'aqov*, pp. 49, 91, 134. On *hyle* cf. n. 54, cited earlier. Joseph ben Shalom Ashkenazi (cited earlier at n. 63) speaks of the "stripping away of form and its privation, resulting from the power of *ayin*."

132. Baer, *Maggid Devarav le-Ya'aqov*, pp. 83-84; see Schatz, *Hasidut*, p. 100; idem, "Contemplative Prayer," p. 215.

133. See P. Z. Gliksman, *Der Kotzker Rebbe* (Warsaw: 1938), p. 32; Schatz, *Hasidut*, p. 67.

134. Baer, *Maggid Devarav le-Ya'aqov*, pp. 39, 134; cf. pp. 253-54; Scholem, *The Messianic Idea in Judaism*, pp. 226-27. Cf. the explanation of *fana* by the tenth-century Sufi Abu Nasr al-Sarraj in *Kitab al-Luma* (cited by Reynold A. Nicholson, "The Goal of Muhammadan Mysticism," *Journal of the Royal Asiatic Society* [1913]: 60): "Humanity does not depart from the human being any more than blackness departs from that which is black or whiteness from that which is white, but the inborn qualities of humanity are changed and transmuted by the all-powerful radiance that is shed upon them from the divine realities."

135. The phrase, "laying bare the white [of God]' appears in Gen. 30:37 and is applied to *keter* in early Kabbalah; see the passages cited by Scholem in *Qiryat Sefer* 10 (1933–1934): 505–5; cf. Shem Tov ibn Gaon, *Migdal 'Oz* on Maimonides, *Mishneh Torah, Hilkhot Teshuvah* 5:5.

136. Scholem, "Schöpfung aus Nichts," p. 84.

137. Hebrew, *lo*; see n. 31, cited earlier.

138. Joseph Taitazak, cited by Scholem, *Sefunot* 11 (1967-1978): 82.

139. Labi, *Ketem Paz*, pp. 92d–93a.

Part II
THE PHILOSOPHICAL INVESTIGATION

Contemporary Epistemology and the Study of Mysticism

DONALD ROTHBERG

> A man saw Mulla Nasrudin searching for something on the ground.
> "What have you lost, Mulla?" he asked.
> "My key," said the Mulla.
> So the man went down on his knees, too, and they both looked for it.
> After a time, the other man asked: "Where exactly did you drop it?"
> "In my own house."
> "Then why are you looking here?"
> "There is more light here than inside my own house."
>
> traditional Middle Eastern story

What epistemologies and methodologies help us to understand the phenomena of mysticism?[1] How do these epistemologies and methodologies clarify some aspects of these phenomena while obscuring or occluding other aspects? When we investigate mystical traditions, how and where do we look? Do we look only where we think there is more light to see? In this essay I would like to help open up these questions more by focusing especially on the limits of one influential contemporary approach, which emphasizes study of the *contexts* of mysticism—the core texts, practices, social relations, and historical traditions out of which a given form of mysticism develops—and the way that mystical experience is, at least in part, *constructed* on the basis of a particular background context. Such an approach has been recently developed in two collections of essays edited by Steven T. Katz.[2] I will, following others in this volume, identify this approach as constructivism (although it is important to note that there are other contemporary variants of constructivism with differing assumptions).[3]

I will argue that such an emphasis on context and the construction of experience (in the form taken by Katz and his colleagues) is problematic in two main ways. First, such constructivism is not, as its advocates claim, somehow a "neutral" and unproblematic guide to achieving "objective"

163

results in the study of religion. Rather, this approach, like any other, both reveals and conceals. While Katz and others help to bring more attention to the specifics of mystical traditions, they implicitly prejudge, on a priori epistemological grounds and against their pretended neutrality, that some interpretations of mysticism (and implicitly the claims of some spiritual traditions) are invalid. Second, constructivists do not and could not adequately account for two modes of mystical experience, the first of which (identified in the present volume as the experience of pure consciousness) shows no apparent contextual trace and the second of which involves a progressive deconstruction of the structures of ordinary experience.

In part, constructivist accounts manifest these problems because the emphasis on context is, ironically, not taken seriously enough. There is not an adequate inquiry into *our* historical context, that of the contemporary investigation of mysticism in modern and post-modern secular society. To make such an inquiry leads, in part, to considering the contemporary epistemological situation (and arguably crisis) and the extent to which the present epistemological alternatives, the Katzian constructivist approach among them, do or do not permit making sense of mysticism.

In the first section of this essay, I will identify the main intentions and claims of this constructivist perspective, particularly as developed by Katz and his colleagues. In the next section, I will give a fuller treatment of the philosophical setting in which this kind of position has developed, examining more carefully the epistemological background for contemporary constructivism. In the third section, I will develop my critical arguments concerning the ways in which constructivists (a) implicitly prejudge as invalid some mystical claims, (b) do not adequately account for the ways in which there is deconstruction of experiential structures, and (c) remain incapable of thematizing modes of knowledge rooted in such deconstruction. These reflections suggest the need for alternative epistemologies capable of retaining the virtues of constructivist approaches while overcoming the identified weaknesses.

THE CONSTRUCTIVIST APPROACH TO THE STUDY OF MYSTICISM: INTENTIONS AND CLAIMS

Before identifying the main tenets of the constructivist approach, it is helpful to refer to the two major philosophical questions that have dominated discussions of mysticism since William James: (1) Is there a core mystical experience, a universal experience common to humans across cultures and traditions? (2) Do mystical experiences give veridical insights into certain aspects of reality and into reality as a whole such that mystical claims should be accepted?[4] In large part such philosophical issues are related, respectively, to two major contemporary cultural concerns.[5] The first is the ecumenical interest in interreligious dialogue in an increasingly global context and the question of whether there are what we might call "spiritual universals" and marked similarities between traditions. The second is the major contemporary interest in traditional as well as secular forms of spirituality (especially mystical spirituality) as a major part of a response to contemporary cultural problems, on individual, social, and ecological levels. This second interest commonly leads philosophically to the attempt to show how mystical and spiritual claims might be recognized as valid in contemporary terms. Sometimes this attempt is made through current models and theories, despite the fact that such models and theories generally take as their point of departure criticisms of religious claims as irrational, superstitious, and oppressive.

Indeed, the two issues and the corresponding concerns are, in the contemporary secular context, closely related. Those philosophers such as C. D. Broad and Huston Smith who identify a common mystical core, often use this supposed unanimity of mystical experiences as a key premise in arguments for the validity of mystical claims.[6] Likewise, many secular critics of the validity of mysticism such as Freud also start from a perception of cross-cultural religious commonality, but they take this rather as a sign of a general structure of human illusion (where not pathology) occurring at a stage of human development outgrown with the rise of rationality and science.[7]

The constructivist position rests on the claims that these two basic questions about mysticism, despite their contemporary cultural allure, are pseudoquestions often rooted in epistemological confusions and, hence, are not promising guides to inquiry. I would like to clarify this position by unpacking two basic constructivist arguments countering the arguments of the advocates of perennial philosophy (whom I will call perennialists) and other philosophers (particularly Walter Stace) on the questions of a common mystical core and validity.[8] These arguments have been most prominently developed by Steven Katz in his essay "Language, Epistemology, and Mysticism"—and by several of those contributing to Katz's volumes—as well as by Wayne Proudfoot in his *Religious Experience*.[9]

On the first question of whether there is a common mystical core experience, many respond affirmatively and identify an experience of something like pure consciousness or undifferentiated unity. For W. T. Stace this "undifferentiated unity is the essence of . . . mystical experience."[10] Huston Smith, a perennialist, likewise holds, that in such an experience, the traditions converge indistinguishably.[11]

Steven Katz argues that these philosophers, often out of their overzealous attempt to respond to the two basic cultural concerns I mentioned, have commonly made two related errors in their attempts to show a mystical core (as well as in arguing for the validity of mystical claims). First, they have not recognized the basic epistemological insight that experience always comes, as it were, through a series of cultural and personal filters, that all experience is necessarily mediated and (at least in part) constructed from within a tradition. (Recognition of the full implications of this insight prevents acceptance of the claims of perennialists and Stace concerning both the issue of a common core and that of validity.) Nor, second, have those claiming a common mystical core given enough attention to the details of the differences among various mystical traditions. At best, Katz holds, any comparative work in mysticism must follow much more careful study of specific traditions within their full contexts, with clear awareness of the differences among traditions, not to mention differences within traditions. Correction of these errors leads to a new kind of program of study of mystical traditions, one that is more adequate to the actual data. Such study must be neutral and scientific; it must be neither dogmatic nor prejudiced toward findings of mystical sameness:

> Our primary aim has been to mark out a new way of approaching the data. . . . [W]e do not hold one mystical tradition to be superior or "normative." . . . Nor have we any particular dogmatic position to defend in this discussion. Our sole concern has been to try and see, recognizing the contextuality of our own understanding, what *the mystical evidence* will allow in the way of legitimate philosophical reflection. . . . [O]ur account neither (a) overlooks any evidence, nor (b) has any need to simplify the available evidence to make it fit into comparative or comparable categories, nor (c) does it begin with *a priori* assumptions about the nature of ultimate reality.

Although Katz brings in the practical and doctrinal details of several mystical traditions in order to support his arguments, his primary thrust is actually heavily epistemological. In response to the question of a common core to mysticism, Katz argues—largely on epistemological grounds—that there is not and could not be such a common core(!). His epistemology is simple and straightforward (although extremely undeveloped and lacks reference to a fuller philosophical articulation of such an epistemology).[13] All experience (and hence all knowing) is mediated by cultural factors such that experience and knowing always show contextual traces and never somehow escape from such influences: "There are NO pure (i.e., unmediated) experiences."[14] All experience, we might say, occurs within the context of a tradition, a form of life, a cultural situation, a set of social and historical relations. As such, every moment of experience is influenced in an extremely complex way and is, at least in part, constructed, by the elements that determine its context: guiding ideological, perceptual, emotional, somatic assumptions and structures; core ideas and texts of the tradition; social, economic, and political relations; activities and practices of the community; the individual's memories, preoccupations, and plans, and so on.

At this point the reader may expect a sophisticated philosophical argument on behalf of such an epistemological claim. But there is virtually none.[15] Katz and his colleagues seem to take this claim about mediation, along with the examination of mystical texts, as a basis for their series of critical claims. There can not possibly be, Katz argues, the kind of pure consciousness or awareness free of all mediations that many students of mysticism see as the (cross-cultural) essence of mystical experience because all experience *is* mediated (!). The differences between traditions, hence, remain real in all experiences, even mystical ones. Mystical experience is, no matter how profound, always the mediated experience from within a particular tradition or context. In this, it does not differ from ordinary experience. The experience of *Brahman* for Katz and others is always a Hindu experience, the experience of *nirvāṇa* always Buddhist, and both are fundamentally different from the Christian experience of God or the Jewish kabbalist's experience of the higher levels of reality (the *sefiroth*).[16] Robert Gimello, a contributor to both of Katz's volumes, presents a more extreme version of the thesis about mediation, namely, "Buddhist mystical experiences . . . are in no sense the same as the Christian mystic's experience of the Trinity, Christ, or the Godhead; nor the same as the Jewish mystic's experience of *En-sof;* nor even the same as the Vedantist's experience of the identity of *ātman* and *brahman.*"[17] There may well be, the constructivists argue, certain similarities among these experiences, but there is not a sameness of identical unmediated experiences freed of any and all cultural content. Indeed, the data of mysticism suggest that pluralist conclusions are more appropriate; there are most likely a set of radically different forms of mysticism.

Katz argues that mystical texts, which for him supply the fundamental data in the study of mysticism, bear out these conclusions, for they show us different core concepts of the sacred, different ontologies, different mystical states, and different normative models of the kind of person a mystic aims to become.[18] Furthermore, we have no reason to think that these forms of mediation are merely found in the interpretations of texts or reports and that they are not given within the experiences themselves. Rather, we must think that conceptual activities such as discrimination and integration are part and parcel of mystical experiences; they make them what they are and give such experiences meaning.[19] Experience, as it were, never outruns conceptualization and tradition to reach some common nonlinguistic mystical realm of pure consciousness. Cultural mediation and construction of experience furnish both the conditions of a mystical experience and the milieu in which it occurs and has meaning. It is as if such cultural mediation is the very air in which the mystic must always breathe.

If this is the case, then there follows a crucial corollary to the claim about mediation—mystical traditions can also not be interpreted as somehow leading the practitioner from the conditioned to the unconditioned. Such traditions are much more forms of reconditioning than of deconditioning.[20] Katz and his colleagues give no indication of accepting that mystical traditions might guide a lessening of conditioning or a freeing from context in general. The perennial dream of some kind of ultimate freedom from all human conditioning is an illusion that is seen through with the aid of epistemological insight. All experience, all understanding, all wisdom, is ultimately a product of the elements of the contexts out of which they develop. However, this argument, which is not adequately developed by Katz and his colleagues and which concerns (I believe) a very important issue, seems wrong (I will argue) in one important way. Many mystical traditions involve the deconstruction of many—where not all—of the structures of ordinary experience and social context and, hence, can arguably be seen as leading to less conditioned knowledge.[21]

When we move from this first question of a common core to the consideration of the second question of the validity of the claims of mystical traditions, we also find that the epistemological claim about the construction of experience guides the constructivist response, a response that again differs strongly from the responses of many of the prominent philosophers of mysticism since William James. For instance, many nonconstructivist philosophers of religion respond to this question of validity by arguing that the fact that a certain subject undergoes a mystical experience is in itself a justification of mystical claims; no further argument is necessary. Such an argument has been made in several ways. For instance, C. D. Broad argues if there is unanimity of claims about a given subject and no reason to think that there is a collective delusion, then it is rational to accept those claims. Such a situation holds, Broad maintains, in the case of mysticism; there is a "common nucleus" of claims and no reason to think that mystics are uniformly deluded.[22] James claims that mystical experience both is (as "a matter of psychological fact") and should be authoritative for the individual, although not necessarily for the outside observer, even if mystical experience does suggest other modes of knowledge and truth.[23] For mystical experiences are, like ordinary perceptions, "face to face presentations of what seems immediately to exist" and, hence, provide evidence no different from that given by the senses in ordinary "rational" belief.[24]

On this question of the validity of mystical claims, the constructivist counterargument is again primarily epistemological and rooted in the denial of the possibility of unmediated experience. Katz, although (surprisingly) not justifying his claims, suggests the contours of the argument; my reconstruction of the argument, however, largely depends on Proudfoot.[25] Katz first claims that there can be no public and independent grounds for accepting mystical claims.[26] Nor, second, can mystical experiences serve as "evidence" for accepting the validity of mystical claims.[27] This is not to rule out the possibility that mystical claims may be valid or to suggest that such claims are meaningless, as logical positivists like Ayer hold.[28] Mystical claims may, indeed, be valid, but there is no philosophically adequate way to demonstrate that they are or are not. Katz claims:

> [N]o veridical propositions can be generated on the basis of mystical experience. As a consequence it appears certain that mystical experience is not and logically cannot be the grounds for *any* final assertions about the nature or truth of any religious or philosophical position nor, more particularly, for any specific dogmatic or theological belief. . . . [Furthermore,] no philosophical argument is capable of proving the veracity of mystical experience.[29]

As in many contemporary discussions in the philosophy of religion, we are apparently left in an agnostic position, with no strong arguments that can be summoned either for or against many of the most basic mystical claims. (As I will show in the third section, "The Question of Validity and the Forms of Mystical Knowledge," however, such apparent agnosticism and neutrality betrays, on analysis, an implicit rejection of many of the core claims of mystical traditions.)

Proudfoot further clarifies the argument. Suggesting that mystical experience cannot furnish an independent ground for mystical claims, he gives as a primary reason the fact that such experience is, in part, "constructed."[30] He develops his arguments through a critique of William James's assertion that the subject of mystical states usually does and should accept mystical claims. Proudfoot, who elsewhere accepts the claim that mystical experience is necessarily mediated,[31] asserts that the occurrence of mystical experience does not provide evidence for belief, either for the subject or for the outside observer. He suggests that James's argument presumes an analogy between the immediacy of mystical experience and the immediacy of sense experience; both represent, for James, givens that the subject cannot rightfully reject.

But, Proudfoot maintains, James's analogy between mystical and sense experience does not, on analysis, hold. Mystical experience involves a substantial conceptual molding in a way that sense perception does not. Hence, mystical experience, in that it is significantly mediated, does not *necessarily* ground mystical claims since the very experience can only occur when the core beliefs of a given tradition have already been assumed prior to the experience; accepting such claims, in part, makes possible the experience. These claims or beliefs may lead the subject to judge that a given experience has provided insight into "objective" reality rather than simply being a "subjective" artifact of certain practices or merely subjective states. Hence, the very description of the experience as mystical or religious (or even as meaningful) carries conceptual and explanatory corollaries rather than simply being a report of a a kind of "pure experience." In this way the presence of such conceptual and explanatory dimensions within mystical experience also prevents the outside observer from accepting mystical experience as conclusive "evidence" for mystical claims. Mystical experience is necessarily too "mediated" by the concepts of a given tradition to function as an independent ground for accepting mystical claims. The experiences, in effect, presume the validity of the claims, both in order to occur at all and in order to be coherently recognized after they have occurred.

In these two arguments concerning both a common core and validity, constructivists emphasize the inescapability of context and the mediated nature of all experiences. The implication of these arguments is that an approach resting on such an understanding of context might give us a more "objective" way to understand mysticism. Freed from epistemological error and enthusiasm, we might attend much more fully to the details of mystical traditions, particularly to texts, getting on with the tasks of explanation and understanding. The root of this project is an epistemology based on claims about the mediated nature of experience, an epistemology that tends to be pluralist and apparently agnostic on the fundamental questions of religion.

Not surprisingly, the resultant methodology seems quite close to the prevailing academic modes of the study of religion as well as close to the dominant epistemology of our time (as I will show). But is such an epistemology itself somehow "neutral" or does it, too, come from a given context along with certain aims, projects, and assumptions that influence its usefulness as a tool for understanding mysticism?

CONSTRUCTIVISM IN CONTEXT

We might take such a basic epistemological claim about the necessary mediation of all experience as unproblematical and commonsensical until we recall that it has been precisely the aim and claim of many of the most prominent philosophical and mystical projects in the dominant world traditions of the last twenty-five hundred years to come to a *direct* knowledge of what is ultimately real. Western philosophers prior to Kant, to be sure, generally do not understand such direct knowledge through a metaphor like that of mediation, in which direct knowledge is understood as dependent on the elimination of all that stands between knower and known.[32] Plato, for instance, using metaphors of knowledge as the result of an ascent and knoweldge as the result of a journey (e.g., out of the cave), sees this direct knowledge in more ontological terms, as the certain knowledge of "higher" realities.[33] Descartes, using the metaphor of knowledge (particularly scientific knowledge) as requiring a firm foundation, understands this direct and certain knowledge as the quality of thinking purified from its connection with the body, summarized in the *cogito*. Locke, using the metaphor of knowledge as a representation of reality, proclaims that "[o]ur knowledge, therefore, is real only so far as there is a conformity between our ideas and the reality of things."[34] Among the philosophers taken as central by the tradition prior to Kant, there thus seems to be a consensus that direct knowledge of reality is possible, that there are not problems caused either by the limitations of human capabilities or cultural differences.[35]

In many mystical traditions, there is also commonly a claim that the knowledge sought is a direct knowledge of reality. In such traditions, although there are a great variety of metaphors used, metaphors resembling that of mediation are quite common; something stands between our ordinary consciousness (or knowledge) and reality. In many of the traditions emanating from India, for instance, we find the claim that our ordinary awareness and knowledge do not bring us knowledge of what is most real. Rather, we ordinarily exist within the realm of *māyā*, blocked from the truth by our desires, the presence of which prevents direct knowledge of the real. The Upanisadic traditions counsel meditation on *Brahman*, bringing "cessation from every illusion" and "a falling off of all fetters."[36] The dramatic message of the Buddha is that it is possible to "wake up" and no longer cognize reality inaccurately as if in a dream, but rather come to see things "as they really are" (*yathābhūtam*).

In Western mystical traditions, there are similar metaphors showing both the problems of ordinary cognition and the possibilities of direct knowledge. Meister Eckhart points to the ways that knowledge of our own nature is obscured; "A man has many skins in himself, covering the depths of his heart. Man knows so many things, but he does not know himself. Why, thirty or forty skins or hides, just like an ox's or bear's, so thick and hard, cover the soul."[37] Traditionally ascribed to Muhammad is the invocation "O Lord, show me all things as they truly are."[38] Elsewhere in the Islamic tradition, a Sufi mystic describes the "seventy thousand veils" separating Allah, the One Reality, from the ordinary world.[39] I mention these examples from philosophical and mystical traditions to show the historical prominence of claims to direct knowledge, claims which have often been presented through metaphors similar to that of knowledge as the result of eliminating mediations through the appropriate spiritual development.

However, in the recent history of Western thought, these claims to direct knowledge, both from the classical philosophical and the mystical traditions, have been criticized and rejected. It is with the work of Kant that the traditional Western philosophical model shifts in a momentous way. In his Copernican Revolution, the knower and the known are now seen as fundamentally interconnected in the knowledge of phenomena, that is, in the system of appearances in the everyday world. There is no direct, unmediated knowledge of reality; all knowledge and all human experience are structured by human categories and the forms of human sensibility, that is, time and space. The main historical claims to direct mystical or metaphysical insight into reality have no means of justification. Such claims, therefore, can never become accepted as a genuine part of human knowledge.[40]

Despite the radical shift from the classical model, the possibility of valid knowledge is saved. Kant assumes that the mediating categories and the framework of space and time within which they are employed represent universal human ways of structuring experience. The fact of mediation renders impossible the project of knowing reality as it "truly" is, but not the project of gaining or at least moving toward universally valid knowledge.

We might construe much of the cutting edge of Western epistemology since Kant (and the growing crisis of philosophy as a discipline) as the discovery and articulation of further kinds of mediation between knower and known.[41] In time, even Kant's categories have been argued to be mediated in more ways than he believed, namely, that they are nonuniversal and dependent on a particular way of structuring experience within modern Western culture. Accompanying such findings of newly identified forms of mediation has been a search for epistemological alternatives to the classical model (and often more sophisticated restatements of this model).[42]

Many, from Vico and Hegel up to contemporary investigators of narrative, have identified *history* as a core form of mediation; knowledge is situated both in a given sociohistorical context and within a general story or narrative. Others, from Marx to Foucault and contemporary feminists, have specified the extent to which embeddedness in *economic and political relations* structures knowledge. In the twentieth century, awareness of language has become paramount, and many, such as Hans-Georg Gadamer and Jacques Derrida, following Heidegger, have denied the very possibility of ever transcending the particulars of one's *linguistic tradition* to reach some reality independent of language and tradition. Gadamer claims, "Language is the fundamental mode of operation of our being-in-the-world and the all-embracing form of the constitution of the world. . . . Being that can be understood is language."[43] All knowledge is mediated by a particular set of concepts and metaphysical assumptions, which can never be disengaged from the "object," from "reality."

Other philosophers have insisted on the necessary mediation of those individual dimensions (particularly *emotions, passions, and the body*) supposedly transcended in the kind of "pure reason" cultivated in the more "rationalist" approaches to Western philosophy. Writers inspired especially by phenomenology, body-oriented therapies, and the great advances in scientific knowledge of human physiology have insisted on the role of the body in knowledge; others have linked emotions to cognitive projects.[44] Psychotherapeutic investigations, furthermore, have suggested the presence in human knowledge of unconscious mediations: libidinal drives, unresolved conflicts and traumas, deeply rooted potentialities toward creativity and self-actualization.

Common, epistemologically, to these historical, political, economic, sociological, and psychological identifications of mediations has been a critique of the traditional model and an insistence on the ineliminability of mediation. At times, this has issued in variants of relativism and despair about the possibility of valid knowledge; at other times, the presence of mediations has not posed an insurmountable problem or an end to the quest for knowledge.[45] In other words, for many there might be a third option between the kind of absolute knowledge promised by the classical model of direct knowledge and the apparent nihilism and extreme relativism sometimes associated with the rejection of this model.[46] Much of contemporary epistemology is now exploring this option.[47]

It is not surprising that the classical claims concerning direct knowledge—associated with the traditional models in philosophy and mysticism—have been sharply criticized as epistemologically naive. Such criticism has contributed significantly to the powerful series of modern and postmodern critiques of the knowledge-claims of classical metaphysical and religious traditions.[48] Where such classical claims are not simply superstitious, dogmatic, self-contradictory, or flatly oppressive (so these critiques go), analysis discloses the mediated quality of what is purported to be some sort of unmediated revelation or gnosis. Scholars studying mystical traditions, for example, identify the mediations of historical milieu, social and political relations, philosophical or religious tradition, and individual history.

Katz's central emphasis on mediation, then, locates him squarely in post-Kantian epistemology, announcing agreement with perhaps the founding assumption of contemporary epistemology. No wonder, therefore, that he and some of his coauthors take the thesis on mediation as a fundamental starting point. Katz speaks of it as "the single epistemological assumption that has exercised my thinking and which has forced me to undertake the present investigation."[49] Penner writes that his basic assumption is "that there are no direct experiences of the world."[50] Proudfoot holds that "one can say there is no uninterpreted experience," and he extends this thesis to warn against purportedly neutral and noninterpretive descriptions that actually carry interpretive and explanatory commitments.[51]

To assess the epistemological adequacy of constructivism as a guide to the study of mysticism, however, we need to know more than the thesis about mediation. For that thesis, after all, is shared generally by most of the major streams of post-Kantian thinking and is developed in a great variety of ways. How is this epistemological starting point developed by constructivists like Katz? Unfortunately, we learn very little more about Katz's epistemology. This is a great problem. What kinds of mediation are central? How do they operate exactly? Are all elements and all concepts of the background context involved at once in the social construction of experience? Is there a way of minimizing mediations? What, in light of the critique of the traditional epistemological ideal, is the goal of knowledge? Can the traditional epistemological ideal be reconceptualized as a regulative ideal to which we may approach more closely, even if we cannot possibly realize the ideal? Or must alternative epistemologies be articulated? Can we and should we avoid forms of extreme relativism or nihilism? Can we and should we avoid forms of extreme idealism, in which reality is understood as totally constituted or constructed? Is there a shared cognitive unity in a pluralist world of many ways of structuring reality? Are there any human universals? These questions are central to contemporary epistemology, the contours of which are determined by responses to such questions.

There is unfortunately no indication (on my reading) of the full-blooded epistemology upon which the constructivism of Katz and his coauthors rests. Thus, I will present what seems to me to be the two main kinds of knowledge—naturalistic and interpretive—recognized in contemporary epistemology. Any constructivist approaches seemingly would rely on an epistemology thematizing either or both of these forms of knowledge.[52] Following such a brief discussion, we can then proceed to ask about the adequacy of the Katzian thesis, in general, and about the adequacy of these forms of knowledge, in particular, for understanding mystical traditions.

In the last twenty-five years, there has been, in the Anglo-American philosophical world, a considerable epistemological shift. In the terms of the historical account just given, we might understand this shift as an increasing recognition of the mediated quality of knowledge that has resulted in serious criticisms of those recent versions of empiricism and rationalism that have maintained versions, even in the twentieth century, of the traditional model of knowledge as a direct cognition of reality as it is. Initially, the impetus to this shift came from work in the history and philosophy of natural science (N. R. Hanson, Michael Polanyi, Thomas Kuhn, Paul K. Feyerabend, etc.) critical or empiricism, showing that observations are theory-laden and that there are apparently no independent criteria either for verifying theories or for choosing between radically different theories.[53] The resulting inquiries led to increased openness to the work of many who had, since Kant, investigated the different ways in which knowledge is mediated, whose voices had often been ignored in the empiricist-dominated Anglo-American tradition. Connected with this change has been a growing receptivity to interpretive epistemologies in the human sciences, where there were, from the beginning, many articulate opponents of empiricism, such as Wilhelm Dilthey and Max Weber.[54]

Contemporary epistemology generally recognizes two main interrelated forms of knowledge: (1) naturalistic and (2) interpretive. (Some, of course, maintain the priority or even the exclusivity of one of the two forms.[55]) Although there is not a clear consensus about the nature of naturalistic explanation, on the one hand, or interpretive understanding, on the other, there are some general starting points for further discussion.

Naturalistic inquiry aims at empirical *explanation*, conceived of as the development of theories that identify lawful or lawlike regularities and causal connections between variables. The most prominent model of such explanation given in recent philosophy of science has been what is often called the covering law model (sometimes called the model of deductive-nomological explanation).[56] Although this model may not accomodate all forms of explanation and although there are many complications of, and some problems with, the model, it seems useful for articulating, at least in a preliminary way, what it is to "explain" a phenomenon.[57]

According to this model, the statement (or statements) of causal regularity is one of the premises in a deductive argument. (e.g., "If an object is lead carbonate and combines with sulfur to form lead sulfide, then it will turn black"). (A deductive argument is an argument in which the conclusion follows necessarily from the premises.) The conclusion of the argument is the statement (or statements) describing what is to be explained (e.g., "Why did the walls of a room painted in white blacken?"). The other premise states that the conditions specified in the statement of a causal regularity were present (e.g., "The paint contained lead carbonate and sulfur was contained in the gas used for lighting the room").[58]

Those giving recent accounts of naturalistic inquiry accepting the broad outlines of the covering law model frequently give up earlier claims about there being some direct relation between naturalistic theories and "reality," and they point out the mediated and pragmatic qualities of such theories. W. V. Quine, for instance, argues that empirical knowledge involves a necessary ontological indeterminacy (what we take to be "real" is dependent on our conceptual needs and conceptual system, which is one of many possible systems), an underdetermination of theory by observation (many possible theories follow from a given set of observations), and an indeterminacy of translation from one system of theories to another (since, to a certain extent, each system is an autonomous construction rather than a set of statements each matching some real "state of affairs").[59]

Despite such an emphasis on the complexly mediated nature of our knowledge, there remains the possibility of empirical theories rooted in systematic observation and description of the relevant phenomena, identifying causal regularities and making predictions where possible. A naturalistic approach to mystical experiences might look for explanations of why such experiences occurred, why certain accounts of the experiences were given, how the experiences are related to beliefs, what the results of these experiences were, and so on. Such an account would likely make use of interpretive understanding of mystics' texts and of religious doctrines and practices, but it would not limit the account to what might be accepted by the religious subjects.[60]

Interpretive inquiry aims, it is commonly held, at the *understanding* of meanings, whether subjective or intersubjective.[61] The goal is to understand the meaning of an individual's action (e.g., "What did that mean to her?" or "What did that mean in that specific context?"); the often only implicit rules of a group or society (e.g., "What implicit and explicit rules do we follow in social interaction as students, as co-workers, or as husband and wife?"); and the implicit or explicit meanings of texts and other expressions of human creative activities. Meanings are, of course, at times elusive, and it is difficult to specify what is involved in the understanding of meaning. However, from Wilhelm Dilthey and Max Weber to the contemporary work of Hans-Georg Gadamer, Karl-Otto Apel, Jürgen Habermas, and Charles Taylor, the argument has been that such meanings cannot be reduced to the identification of causal connections and require accounts making use of intentional language rather than simply neutral descriptive language.[62] Charles Taylor makes this point while analyzing the institution of voting. This institution does not simply involve marking and counting papers (or pulling a lever and reading a machine). Rather, such actions can only be fully understood by appealing to intentional descriptions that have to do with meanings.[63] A similar argument is also behind justification of the participant–observer method (e.g., in cultural anthropology, where there is a need to study the foreign culture from within in order to understand the local meanings of actions, rituals, and beliefs even if the anthropologist may later develop explanations at odds with the local interpretation). The general claim is that understanding meanings is a primary aim in the social sciences, one that cannot be attained without a different model of knowledge than that connected with the covering law model.

Among theorists of interpretive inquiry, there are major differences between what we might broadly call contextualists (or cultural relativists) and universalists. The former insist that there are no fixed meanings or rules "out there" in the world or embedded "in here" in the subject. Their approaches include: Ludwig Wittgenstein's emphasis on language games and on the claim that there is no neutral epistemological vantage point; Peter Winch's focus on local standards of meaning and rationality; Hans-Georg Gadamer's theory of hermeneutical dialogue; Richard Rorty's talk of edifying conversation among different traditions following the overturning of the classical epistemological project; and Jacques Derrida's attempt to deconstruct and decenter the philosophical enterprise.[64] Their work tends to underscore the pluralistic, relativistic, and constructed nature of knowledge.

The universalists, on the other hand, believe it possible to identify human universals that function as the implicit meanings or rules behind language, human communication, and human development (cognitive, moral, or spiritual). Their work includes: Noam Chomsky's theory of language, Jürgen Habermas's models of universal pragmatics and the development of communicative competence, and the developmental theories of Jean Piaget, Lawrence Kohlberg, and Ken Wilber.[65] Although most of these universalists criticize the classical epistemological model and agree that knowledge and experience are to a significant extent culturally mediated or constructed, they emphasize the limits to the constructivist model and the extent to which there may be both "surface" (constructed) as well as "deep" cognitive, moral, and spiritual structures. It is the deep structures that are universal, nonrelative, and not arbitrarily constructed. Hence, constructivist themes, even if limited, appear across the board in both naturalistic and interpretive accounts and in both more relativist and more universalist varieties of interpretive theory.

Katz's constructivist approach to mystical traditions seems to come closest to a combination of naturalism and especially to what I have called contextualist interpretive theory. His starting point, like that of such interpretive theory, is a serious skepticism toward the possibility of experiential meanings not being culturally mediated: there are no meanings "out there" and no experiences without the influence of concepts and the many dimensions of a given tradition. The task of interpretive theory, for Katz, is to be faithful to the specific details of traditions, to understand local language games and the meanings of specific texts and actions within the given traditions as well as disclosing causal regularities. The point of departure is the avoidance of the major interpretive mistake of the past (identified, for instance, in the works of Wittgenstein, Gadamer, Rorty, and Derrida), the mistake of imposing culturally local grids on the phenomena while proclaiming such grids universal.

To investigate the adequacy of the constructivist approach for the study of mysticism, then, we would have to treat not only the particular, rather undeveloped epistemology given by Katz, but also consider naturalistic and interpretive forms of constructivism. And in examining interpretive theory, we would have to remember that Katz's version of the interpretive form of constructivism (which I have here called contextualist) may be vulnerable both from within such an epistemology (from a more universalist perspective pointing to the limits of constructivism) and from without.

THE LIMITS OF CONSTRUCTIVIST EPISTEMOLOGIES

My aim in this more critical section is to examine the adequacy of Katzian constructivism as a guide to understanding mysticism. I will reflect on how Katz's general thesis about mediation and on how the accounts of the nature of naturalistic and interpretive knowledge on which this thesis is based do and do not help us to respond to the two fundamental questions concerning mysticism: a common core and validity.

There are three main ways in which the Katzians' constructivist thesis about mediation is, I believe, questionable. First, constructivists are led to prejudge as invalid the claims of many mystical traditions (to offer a kind of unmediated knowledge) on the basis of the generally uncritically accepted contemporary epistemological tenets about mediation. Second, they are inclined to ignore considerable evidence from mystical traditions that suggest there are at least two basic ways in which the thesis about mediation must be seriously qualified. On the one hand, a fundamental class of mystical experiences does not show evidence of mediation. On the other hand, many mystical traditions can be read as offering paths of deconstruction or deconditioning of the fundamental forms by which experience and knowledge are mediated or constructed. Third, constructivists systematically rule out the possibility that mystical claims might involve forms of knowing (hence *valid* knowing and knowledge) other than the naturalistic or interpretive forms of knowledge. But arguably both unmediated experience and the paths of deconstructing the ordinary structures of experience can be reconstructed as involving distinct forms of knowing. I will now address these three problems with Katzian constructivism. The general problem with Katzian constructivism is not the presence of insights into the extent to which experience is constructed, but the way in which such insights have been turned into a fixed assumption that obscures some of the phenomena of mysticism.

Constructivist Prejudices in the Study of Mysticism

Katz, we might remember, asserts that the thesis that there is no unmediated experience is the starting point for a nondogmatic treatment of mystical traditions. This is highly problematic for several reasons. We can recall the argument, presented in the "Introduction" to this volume, that an apparently unmediated experience of pure consciousness is central to several mystical traditions. If that argument is correct—and if I have been correct in suggesting that we find, as hallmarks of many classical philosophical and mystical traditions, something like a claim to direct knowledge and (often) metaphors suggesting something like an overcoming of mediation—then it is surely quite remarkable that the thesis about all experience and knowledge being mediated be taken as *the* core assumption in the study of mysticism. For to assert such a thesis is implicitly to announce the rejection of one core claim of many mystical traditions. It is to imply that the underlying epistemologies of many mystical traditions are at best naive and at worst simply wrong.

But if this is the implication of Katz's starting point, then Kantian and post-Kantian epistemologies are not somehow neutral and nondogmatic tools with which to understand ancient traditions. Katz's use of these tools may thus be viewed as, in part, an imposition of recent Western cultural assumptions upon those of other cultures and other epochs, violating Katz's own stricture to respect the inherent differences contained within each tradition.

Examining how Katz's approach would have us respond to the two philosophical questions (about a universal mystical experience and about the validity of mystical claims) shows the extent to which this approach is *not* neutral—prejudging some issues, obscuring others. To be sure, Katz claims, at least on the surface, that he does not want to rule out the possibility of a common mystical core, leaving it open to adequate consideration of the relevant material [66]. However, we are led to rule out the interpretations of an experience of pure consciousness or the unconditioned as the core mystical experience primarily for a priori epistemological reasons. Moreover, we are also led to reject any interpretations *from within mystical traditions* of something like such a pure consciousness, again presumably on a priori epistemological grounds developed within recent Western philosophy rather than from within mystical traditions.

Do we find that the *Yoga Sūtra* speaks of the possibility of realizing a pure consciousness separated from all impurities? We must conclude, then, that there is an epistemological mistake.[67] Do we find that Buddhist texts speak of wisdom as a way of experiencing untainted by conceptualization? We must conclude, then, that the Buddhists were not aware of their own way of structuring even enlightened experience.[68] Do we find a Neoplatonic report of the experience of the undifferentiated One?[69] Look for hidden mediations!

Katz has, in effect, institutionalized a "hermeneutics of suspicion" toward those mystical traditions not sharing his epistemology.[70] Whenever we find claims that seem to suggest experiences of overcoming mediation, whether involving cognition of a kind of undifferentiated unity or a direct knowing of the multiplicity of things—whether of what is taken to be eternal or of what is temporal—we raise our eyebrows and look for mediations.

Now, of course, Katz may be right that there cannot be unmediated experience and knowledge. To the extent that mystical traditions make claims for unmediated experience and knowledge they may be epistemologically naive, bound by a lack of philosophical sophistication. The task of the first part of this volume has been to argue that there are good reasons to think that these traditions, at least on this point, are not so naive. The aim of my argument here is not to resolve the question but rather to open it up more by showing that it is implicitly and prematurely closed by Katz's work.

Katz prejudges in a similar manner the question of validity, rejecting implicitly the epistemological frameworks in which many mystical claims find meaning, without making it clear how mystical claims might possibly be valid. How might the claims associated with mystical experiences be accepted, if at all, from a constructivist perspective, in view of Katz's assertions that there are no unmediated experiences and that mystical traditions do not represent paths of deconditioning? There seem to be only two possible ways to accept mystical claims, given that, for Katz, mystical experiences do not provide the evidence for mystical or other religious claims and given that there are no independent grounds for the verification of mystical claims. The first way (not articulated explicitly by Katz) seems to be to justify these claims as implicit naturalistic or interpretive claims.[71] The second way is apparently to not take such claims as cognitive and to accept them on other grounds (e.g., faith) from within a tradition. This is implicitly to reaffirm the contemporary split between rationality and religion. To live with such a split is precisely the modern dilemma, but accepting such a dilemma as final presupposes (wrongly I believe) that there is not a third alternative.[72] This third alternative— implicitly prohibited by Katzian constructivism—would be to support assertions of the validity of certain mystical claims that cannot be totally translated into naturalistic or interpretive claims within epistemological frameworks in which the elimination of mediations is thematized.

The point here is that it follows from Katz's arguments that there are no contemporary secular ways of understanding the core mystical claims about unmediated experience as valid. If mystical epistemologies that involve claims to unmediated knowledge or pure consciousness are rejected, then the primary classical way of understanding mysticism as valid is also rejected. Again, Katz may be right, but he is surely not being neutral.

Katz's thesis about mediation furnishes a neutral and nondogmatic starting point only if we accept certain contemporary epistemologies fully, including their rejections—explicit and implicit—of metaphysical and mystical traditions. In this sense contemporary epistemology can be seen as neutral in the study of mystical traditions, but only in the very abbreviated way in which it is neutral toward different kinds of fundamentally devalued traditions. We may study Buddhist or Islamic or Christian mystical texts and practices perhaps with no particular preference toward one or the other. But if we accept Katz's strictures, there is at least implicitly a preference for contemporary epistemologies. To study mystical traditions in this way is to study many of them as devalued, on fundamental issues as deluded.

Perhaps the ideal of neutral, nondogmatic study of a pervasive human illusion. Perhaps we all must study others and come to knowledge (as Gadamer would say) only on the basis of particular prejudgments or prejudices (*Vorurteilen*), which open up the world for us.[73] There is much in Katz's constructivism and pluralism that suggests that we should be epistemologically honest and admit that we are necessarily in such a predicament. Hence, there is an unresolved incoherence in affirming both such a constructivism *and* the more universalist claim to neutrality, lack of dogmatism, and some kind of objectivity (which presumably would be the basis for the academic study of mysticism). On the basis of Katz's epistemology, it is not clear how this could happen. Without a more sophisticated epistemology, Katz's epistemology flounders in the *aporia* created by affirming that all viewpoints are situated and mediated while implicitly affirming that his own approach is an exception. To put this another way, the claims to neutrality and nondogmatism are (properly) claims to a certain kind of objectivity, claims to be able to suspend or go beyond at least some of the limits of one's own original personal and cultural constructions. But these claims are incoherent without some account of how they are possible, given constructivist emphases.[74]

We should be very clear, however, that all of my comments here are only preparatory. Katz and contemporary constructivists may, indeed, be in possession of epistemological truth. Mystics who assert that they have gone beyond conceptual constructs may not know what they are talking about. I have tried to show that Katz's epistemological assumptions decide the question prior to deeper examination of mystical traditions and, thus, offer a questionable point of view from which to study mystical traditions.[75] As I will suggest, we might actually preserve some post-Kantian insights into the extent of the mediation or construction of experience and knowledge without Katz's epistemology, thus remaining more open to the insights of mystical traditions.

Unmediated Experience and the Deconstruction of Experience in Mystical Traditions

Is there a reading of the evidence from mystical traditions rendering, at least, plausible countertheses to Katz's thesis that all experience is mediated? There are, I find, at least two kinds of possible countertheses possible on alternative readings of mystical traditions. The first—supported by the analysis of the reports of many mystics that show no clear signs of mediation—is that some experiences are not mediated, are not constructions rooted in religious traditions. The second—suggested by the practices of many mystics—is that there is an important class of spiritual practices designed to recognize, work with, and overcome in significant ways the mediated or constructed quality of human experience. The experiences of mystics seems to suggest that these practices are effective. Hence, in a very significant way, many forms of mysticism do not represent—against the claims of Katz and others—simply forms of reconditioning; arguably, they involve substantial deconditioning.

On the first point—that some experiences are not constructed—it is clear that many mystics claim that they experience a transcendence of the various ordinary forms of mediation. Phenomenologically, this experience is described positively as one of pure consciousness or undifferentiated unity, and it is described more negatively as an experience of the unconditioned. One main task of the present work is to argue that humans can at times be wakeful but in a way devoid of content and intentionality and that this way of experiencing is central to many mystical traditions. I will not add to the array of evidence and argument mustered by others, especially in the first part of this book. Instead, I will concentrate on a second way in which the Katzian thesis might be challenged, a way which complements the argument that it is plausible to suppose that humans experience something like pure consciousness.

The second point—that some traditions attempt to overcome constructive activity—develops a counterthesis to a less obvious argument that follows from Katz's main thesis about mediation: that there can be no transcendence of mediation in a supposed experience of pure consciousness. For Katz and the constructivists, there can also be no development *toward* such a goal in the sense of a kind of progressive deconditioning of

experience. The experience of mystics remains, for the Katzian constructivist fundamentally mediated and not, on this score, distinct from ordinary, premystical experience. Katz is quite clear on this point in speaking
of yoga, "Properly understood, yoga, for example, is *not* an *un*conditioning or *de*conditioning of consciousness, but rather it is a *re*conditioning of
consciousness, i.e. a substituting of one form of conditioned and/or contextual consciousness for another, albeit a new, unusual, and perhaps
altogether more interesting form of conditioned-contextual consciousness."[76]

Alternative readings of many mystical traditions—including, incidentally, the yogic traditions summarized in the *Yoga Sūtra,* which are supported by considerable study of the psychology of mystical practices—
suggest a different conclusion, the possibility of which is excluded by
Katz's epistemology. Rather than offering simply a reconditioned form
of experience, many mystical traditions can be read as offering paths of
deconditioning. In what follows I want to argue briefly for the cogency of
this reading; a fuller account would be crucial but is beyond the scope
of this essay.[77]

For instance, Robert Forman, in the "Introduction" to this volume, has
proposed a model of mystical development (in many traditions) as involving the "forgetting" (Meister Eckhart's term) of the major cognitive and
affective structures of experience; Forman's model is based especially on
consideration of several mystical approaches, including those of Eckhart,
Zen, and Theravāda Buddhism. In this process of "forgetting," there is an
intentional dropping of desires, ideas, conceptual forms (including those
of one's tradition), sensations, imagery, and so on. The end of this process
is a contentless mystical experience in which the constructs of the tradition are transcended. Such a model makes sense of much of the
physiological data concerning some mystical paths, particularly those
emphasizing meditation, and develops some of the implications of Arthur
Deikman's well-known model of mystical paths as involving the "deautomatization" of psychological structures.[78]

Daniel Brown—in a major comparative study of the *Yoga Sūtra,* of the
Theravāda Buddhist approaches to meditation systematized in Buddhaghosa's *Visuddhimagga (Path of Purification),* and in the Mahāyāna
Buddhist tradition of one of the major Tibetan *Mahāmudrā* texts—has
given a subtle, extended development of the thesis that many mystical
paths are essentially paths of deconditioning. He understands the unifying
features of the traditions he studies as organized around a common process in which the ordinary mediating structures of experience are deconstructed:

This underlying path is best conceptualized as a systematic *deconstruction* of the structures of ordinary waking consciousness. . . . the paths of meditation in every tradition entail progressive *deconstruction* of each of these structures of ordinary waking consciousness: attitudes and behavioral schemes (stage I); thinking (stage II); gross perception (stage III); self-system (stage IV); time-space matrix (stage V). As a result of dismantling the coordinates of ordinary perception, the meditator gains access to a non-ordinary, or extraordinary, structure of consciousness which does not operate by ordinary psychophysical laws. Deconstruction of even this deep structure results in enlightenment (stage VI).[79]

Brown's study thus supports in some ways the conclusions of the other authors of the present volume, but it also suggests the extent to which a constructivism less dogmatic than that of Katz and his colleagues may still be appropriate. Brown does hold that both theoretical and practical investigation of these three traditions leads to an understanding of the initial enlightenment experience (what he calls basis-enlightenment) as a transcendence of all constructed states of consciousness. This is the state of cessation (*vinivṛtti* in the *Yoga Sūtra* and *nirodha* in the *Path of Purification*), a state of "vast awareness" in which "the association between event and awareness is permanently severed."[80] Such a state seems identical to that described in the first part of this volume.

However, Brown holds that a kind of constructivist analysis makes considerable sense of the extent to which the different philosophical perspectives guiding the three traditions examined continue to structure experience up to the first moment of enlightenment and in succeeding moments of enlightenment. Even as the main structures of consciousness are deconstructed, that is, as the main structures of mediation are transcended, the resulting experiences occur in ways patterned by the particular traditions. Brown argues that his findings help us to respond to the question of a common mystical core experience:

The conclusions set forth here are nearly the opposite of that of the stereotyped notion of the perennial philosophy according to which many spiritual paths are said to lead to the same end. According to the careful comparison of the traditions we have to conclude the following: *there is only one path, but it has several outcomes.* There are several kinds of enlightenment, although all free awareness from psychological structure and alleviate suffering. . . . The beginner rigorously studies the basic philosophical tenets of the tradition until these "influence" the perspective adopted during *samadhi*. There can be no escape from such influence except in the basic moment of enlightenment, i.e., so long as awareness is not permanently freed from psychological structure.[81]

Strictly speaking, Brown is not totally accurate concerning his own findings when he claims that there are actually several distinct outcomes of the mystical paths he has considered. For he has maintained, at least in terms of the traditions he has studied, that there is one identical outcome on all, the initial basis-enlightenment experience, phenomenologically the same as what has been identified herein as pure consciousness. He does, however, go on to distinguish several aspects of enlightenment, showing that this experience of pure consciousness does not exhaust the understanding of the final outcome of these mystical paths, a point on which Forman concurs. Brown thus gives more specificity to the question of the constructed or mediated nature of mystical experiences and practices.[82]

From the work cited (as well as similar work on this question), there are four main conclusions we might draw at this point that primarily have to do with the question of the commonalities and differences of mystical traditions. (I will reflect on the second question—that of validity—in the next subsection of my discussion.) First, there seem to be "enlightenment" experiences in which the ordinarily constructed or mediated quality of experience is fully transcended. These experiences, if we can still use the term "experience"[83], are a main goal in many, but not all, spiritual traditions.

Second, the path toward spiritual goals involves, in many traditions, a process of progressive deconstruction of the structures of experience. In such a process there is deconstruction both of the structures by which ordinary experience is constructed or mediated as well as of the structures of spiritually guided experience short of initial enlightenment (following Brown's terminology).

Third, there have been many different ways developed to facilitate such paths. To put it somewhat paradoxically, each path of deconstruction or deconditioning is itself constructed or conditioned in a certain way. Katz and his colleagues are, thus, correct to suggest that the experiences of mystics are almost always, in part, constructed or mediated, but arguably thay are wrong in not seeing that there are experiences in which all or certain forms of construction and mediation are not present. Furthermore, they are unable to identify the deconstructive or deconditioning project of many mystical approaches, in large part because this makes no sense for them epistemologically.

Fourth, it is important to limit the claims involved in these conclusions. Forman and Brown, in emphasizing the way that deconditioning occurs in some mystical traditions, do not make the claim that pure consciousness is *the* universal goal of all mystical paths (although Brown's analysis would support the claim that pure consciousness is a universal goal). Forman acknowledges that some traditions do not utilize forgetting techniques; furthermore, different traditions may develop and actualize such methods more or less effectively. Brown does make universalist claims about the stages of spiritual development, although not the kind of claims made by most perennialists. He does claim that some kind of progressive deconstruction of ordinary mediations is a universal pattern in spiritual development.

Brown's conclusions, however, seem overly ambitious, on the basis of the evidence and argumentation in his essay and in the related essays with which it was published. Arguably, the three traditions that Brown studies give too restricted a base of study from which to make universalist claims about the deep structure behind meditative traditions. We would need to see parallel studies of those traditions in which some distinction between the mystic and God often persists (particularly Jewish, Christian, and *bhakti* Hindu mystical traditions).[84]

Thus, the work I have considered does lead to questioning and limiting the kind of constructivism evident in the two Katz volumes. It offers, arguably, a more adequate reading of those mystical traditions that involve progressive forgetting or deconditioning and that lead to experiences of pure consciousness. This reading places us, on the question of a common mystical core, somewhere between the position that all mystical traditions aim for and attain the same goal and the Katzian constructivist position. In the last critical subsection on the limits of constructivism, I would like to examine the question of the validity of mystical claims in the light of the discussion thus far.

The Question of Validity and the Forms of Mystical Knowledge

One of the implicit assumptions of many constructivists (as well as most philosophers rooted in contemporary epistemology) is that mystical claims need to be reinterpreted as naturalistic and interpretive claims in order to be regarded even as potentially valid cognitive claims. (To recapitulate, naturalistic claims give, generally speaking, explanations of causal regularities; interpretive claims concern the understanding of the meanings of texts, actions, social practices, etc.) I will argue here that this assumption precludes taking seriously other forms of knowledge that can be reconstructed from mystical traditions.

Proudfoot, for example, believes that naturalistic and interpretive studies are perfectly adequate in order to understand mystical traditions and that mystics, where they would claim knowledge, must operate in the context of these kinds of inquiries. He takes the constructivist argument that concepts are at least partly constitutive of mystical experience to be the basis for asserting that mystical experiences in themselves offer no conclusive evidence for mystical claims, that is, for knowledge.[85] Knowledge for Proudfoot presumably is provided only by naturalistic explanation and interpretive understanding.[86] Mystics, too, must justify their claims—just as must the theorist of mysticism—on the basis of evidence and argumentation rather than on the basis of the supposed authority of certain experiences. Both are, as it were for Proudfoot, at least implicitly in the same boat.

Both mystic and naturalist, for example, attempt explanations: "Those who identify their experiences in religious terms are seeking the best explanations for what is happening to them. The analyst should work to understand these explanations and discover why they are adopted."[87] The inquiry of the analyst of mysticism also leads to explanation. For Proudfoot, this process involves first an identifying description of an experience or even followed by an explanation of why that experience or event was taken to be religious. In general this will be a "historical or cultural explanation"[88]. Such an explanation might make use of the full resources of empirical studies whether from human physiology and psychology, political and economic history, or the life histories of mystics. Proudfoot claims that this naturalistic approach is a perfectly appropriate way to investigate mystical claims *and* that it is not somehow illicitly "reductionistic," that is, that there is nothing about mystical experience that makes this mode of inquiry inappropriate.

For constructivists the mystic also has no privileged position in relation to the project of the *interpretation* of mystical experience; both mystic and interpreter must follow the same guidelines. The aim of the interpreter is to come to an "understanding" (*Verstehen*) of the "meaning" of the core mystical texts or practices (to the extent that they are accessible). Such a project is no different in principle that other attempts at understanding in the social or human sciences, the methodology of which is reconstructed in hermeneutic theory. There is no special inaccessible understanding which is only the possession of the mystic. Proudfoot comments:

> There is no reason, in principle, to despair about the possibility of understanding the experience of persons and communities that are historically and culturally remote from the interpreter. The difficulty is not posed by an unbridgeable gap between an experience that can only be known by acquaintance and the concepts in which that experience is expressed. *Because the concepts and beliefs are constitutive of the experience,* careful study of

the concepts available in a particular culture, the rules that govern them, and the practices that are informed by them will provide access to the variety of experiences available to persons in that culture. Though it may be difficult to reconstruct, the evidence required for understanding the experience is public evidence about linguistic forms and practices.[89]

Like Proudfoot, many of the contributors to Katz's volumes, including Katz, Peter Moore, and Hans Penner, also suggest that the only data for the interpreter is public data, particularly that offered by accounts given in texts.[90] Reliance on such public data is then presumably adequate to be able to come to an understanding of mysticism.

Arguably, however, such a naturalistic and interpretive approach to mysticism, aiming at empirical explanation and understanding of meanings (and reflecting directly the accepted kinds of knowledge in contemporary espistemology), again excludes, in a systematic and a priori manner, the possibility that important kinds of mystical claims might be accepted as valid. The root problem is that mystical claims seem to involve forms of knowledge different from the forms explicated through the accounts of naturalistic and interpretive knowledge.

Certainly, many claims associated with mystical traditions are essentially naturalistic or interpretive in nature. Furthermore, many mystical claims not resolvable through contemporary naturalistic or interpretive inquiry may still receive support or criticism on the basis of such inquiry. As I have suggested in my discussion of mystical deconstructive paths, I do not mean at all to exclude mystical traditions from contemporary inquiry and scrutiny, as do some authors when they argue that mystical traditions are somehow not at all commensurable with empirical theories.[91]

Many claims in mystical traditions, for instance, are essentially psychological; it is no coincidence that one of the most promising contemporary approaches to mysticism occurs in (transpersonal) psychology.[92] For instance, much of Buddhism has to do with psychological generalizations, which might easily be investigated, at least partly, through conventional empirical inquiry—generalizations about the relationship between compulsive grasping and suffering, about the nature of the process of construction of the concept of self, about ways of developing a more expansive sense of self.[93] It seems accurate to understand such generalizations, if supported empirically, as contributions to naturalistic theories, for instance, to cognitive or developmental psychology.[94] Similarly, there is commonly a vital interpretive dimension in mystical traditions, for traditions require clarity about how to interpret canonical texts, actions, and histories. To the extent that mystical traditions are pursuing naturalistic and interpretive tasks, the contemporary naturalist or interpreter is, indeed, on the same level as the mystic. The modern psychologist may discuss the mechanisms of attachment or the nature of the concept of self with the Buddhist meditator; the contemporary interpreter may have a kind of dialogue with a fourteenth-century mystic about the life of Jesus. Whether naturalistic and interpretive knowledge are the only forms of knowledge that mystics attempt is, however, problematic.

There remain two particular kinds of mystical claims that seem to be involved with different goals, different processes of inquiry, and different forms of knowledge than the naturalistic or interpretive. These two kinds of claims are related to the two ways in which there seems, on the reading presented in the last subsection, to be an overcoming of mediation and of the constructed nature of experience. The first is the kind of claim associated with the experience of pure consciousness. The second is the kind of claim associated with experiencing the world in a way progressively freed from the ordinary constructions of consciousness.

The claim about pure consciousness appears to be a claim to knowledge; most commentators on mysticism, from William James to the present, have identified claims to the noetic quality of the experience as central to mysticism.[95] Yet it is a claim to a special kind of knowledge radically different in nature from naturalistic or interpretive knowledge. These latter two types of knowledge are structured, according to the standard accounts, by conceptual distinctions and notions of knower and known absent in the apparently nondualistic and nonconceptual experience of pure consciousness. There is neither the naturalistic assumption of a researcher (as part of a community of inquiry) investigating the lawlike relationships among abstracted variables of an objectified process, nor the interpretive assumption of a kind of dialogue with a symbolically and intentionally patterned text or action. Rather, the presuppositions of these forms of knowledge are no longer present.

Whether there are experiences of pure consciousness is an open question, answered affirmatively by the contributors to this volume. Whether such an experience, if it does occur, should be identified as offering a distinct form of knowledge is another (also controversial) question, generally answered affirmatively by mystical traditions. If it can be argued that such an experience is also a distinct kind of knowing, with differing presuppositions than those of the standard forms of knowledge, then the naturalistic and interpretive study of such a mystical experience could never be fully adequate. This is analogous to the way in which naturalistic inquiry, as presently understood, can arguably never adequately treat questions of (interpretive) meaning.

My argument is twofold. First, it is at least plausible that pure consciousness is also a distinct way of knowing, although adequate support of this claim is beyond the aims of this essay. Suffice it here to say that many mystical traditions make such a claim, explicitly using concepts of "knowledge" even when the experience is, in a sense, contentless. The question obviously hinges on what we mean by knowledge and whether we should take certain forms of knowledge (such as naturalistic or interpretive) as paradigmatic. In many mystical (and philosophical) traditions, arguably, the experience of pure consciousness may be taken as paradigmatic knowledge. My second, related point is my main one here. It is to argue that constructivists exclude the possibility of this way of knowing on a priori epistemological grounds.[96] The Katzian thesis about mediation and the construction of experience implies at once both the denial of the possibility of pure consciousness and the denial of the distinctiveness of any mystical form of knowledge based on this experience.

We can make this point in another way by showing that no naturalistic or interpretive versions of mystical claims could establish the kind of knowledge connected with the experience of pure consciousness.[97] Suppose that there were somehow an identifiable brain state correlated with the report of the experience of pure consciousnes or Christian mystical union. Let us also suppose that somehow this showed no signs normally correlated with conceptual activity or even that such mystics appear close to a state of clinical death along several parameters. We might have a presumption that something unusual was happening, but why need we conclude that there is a somehow a tremendously deepened insight into "reality"? At best, such data might make plausible certain mystical claims, but such claims would have to be redeemed on another level and could not be verified naturalistically.

Similarly, it is clear that work on mystical traditions in the phenomenology of religion (i.e., from the perspective of an interpretive discipline investigating the "meaning" of mystical experiences through the reconstruction of accounts) admittedly does not and could not lead to resolving the question of the validity of these experiences.[98] There is, at least in most interpretive theory, a distinction between meaning and validity.[99] The task of interpretive theory is merely to identify the meanings involved in a text, action, or social practice. Its task is not to settle questions of validity.[100]

How might claims about pure consciousness be redeemed, if not naturalistically or interpretively? At this point, we enter into a thicket of issues, which I will not attempt to disentangle here. Are such claims verified finally only by mystical experiences themselves, as many mystical traditions suggest?[101] Are mystical experiences in a way self-verifying? Katz and Proudfoot's objections to such a response are based on their rejection of the possibility and actuality of the experience of pure consciousness. So, if their rejection is invalid, their objections are left without support.

In addition to being incapable of dealing adequately with claims related to pure consciousness, naturalistic and interpretive forms of knowledge also seem inappropriate tools with which to attempt to understand in a full may mystical claims about the deconstruction of experience. Rather, such claims arguably point to the possibility of reconstructing new, distinct forms of knowing and knowledge. Although it is also an open question whether this process of deconstruction involves something meriting the name of "knowledge," many mystical traditions have distinguished what are claimed to be ways of knowing (short of the experience of pure consciousness) differentiated from more ordinary kinds of knowledge. (Many Western philosophers, most recently Heidegger, in his discussion of "meditative thinking" (*"besinnliches Denken"*) have also argued for other modes of knowing.[102]) Contemplative traditions, both East and West, offer ways of knowing oneself and the world that, following Forman and Brown, seem to involve the deconstruction of core structures present in naturalistic or interpretive knowledge. For instance, in the meditative traditions studied by Brown, there is typically, in concentrative training, a suspension of processes of categorization of phenomena. At a later stage, there is a decentering of experience as the ordinary observer, the self, collapses. At a still later point, the meditator no longer experiences phenomena through the categories of time and space.

In this process there remains awareness and cognition. But such forms of knowledge, which I will here generally (and somewhat arbitrarily) label "meditative," are radically different than the naturalistic and interpretive. They seem, again following Forman and Brown, to involve a suspension of many modes of language and categorization, although this is not to say that all forms of mediation or conceptualization are transcended.[103] Rather, such deconstruction occurs in what we might call a constructed or mediated manner. Still, the way of knowing does not primarily issue in linguistically mediated forms, that is, explanations and interpretations. Knowledge is here essentially a "way of being," a mode of experience in which categorization is drastically reduced and not active, and in which the knower might, in the rare moments of speech, make statements about the inadequacy of language of even the ineffability of the experience. Processes of abstraction and objectification of phenomena, which make possible naturalistic knowledge, are greatly reduced.

In later stages of the process, there is a progressive decentering of experience and overcoming of the division between knower and known.

Without these structures, it seems impossible to imagine naturalistic or interpretive knowledge as we know them, although there still remain what we might call naturalistic or interpretive elements. Finally, with the transcendence of the categories of time and space, the deconstruction of the presuppositions of naturalistic and interpretive knowledge is completed.

The problem with the constructivist account of mysticism as construed by Katz is again that such distinct forms of knowledge are not deemed possible; they are excluded as potentially valid. For Katz and others any purported meditative or contemplative knowledge is taken to be fundamentally mediated or constructed and, hence, implicitly reducible to naturalistic or interpretive knowledge. But this argument neglects the extent to which there is progressive deconstruction of the core categories of experience and the extent to which there seems phenomenologically to be distinct forms of knowledge related to the process of deconstruction.

Again, we can suggest how any possible naturalistic or interpretive accounts of this deconstructive process would not capture the nature of the knowledge involved; no naturalistic or interpretive reworkings of mystical claims could be equated with the kinds of knowledge found in deconstructive mystical paths. Suppose, for instance, that we conduct physiological studies of Hindu yogins and find that records of their brain waves at times indicate no reception of sensory stimuli or that experienced Zen meditators do not habituate to constant stimuli like normal subjects?[104] Such naturalistic knowledge might be very helpful in developing an empirical theory of what occurs in the deconstruction of ordinary consciousness, but it would lack the interpretive meaning of such a deconstructive process. It could also not establish that there is another major form of meditative knowledge in which there is a kind of valid knowledge; at best, it might make such a contention plausible. Similarly, no interpretive studies in the phenomenology of religion could establish the validity of meditative knowledge, for the same reasons given in the case of pure consciousness. In fact, Katzian constructivist epistemology, even if directing the most penetrating naturalistic and interpretive studies, still rules out the possibility of the validity of the other forms of knowledge we have mentioned here.

CONCLUSIONS

At least four conclusions follow from our discussion. The first, ironical in a critique of constructivism, is that the background epistemological context of *any* study of mystical traditions must be clearly identified. There is a close connection between epistemological assumptions, how and where one looks, and what one finds or does not find, as the motto to this essay reminds us. The work of Katz and his colleagues is lacking by not adequately situating itself historically in terms of epistemological issues, by not adequately clarifying the constructivist espistemology, and by not adequately justifying such an epistemology (or, at least, stating dependence on others who have made this attempt). We have seen that these problems are especially pressing in the study of mysticism owing to the particular historical origins of modern epistemology, especially the way that it has been founded on the ruins of metaphysical and religious epistemologies.

Emphasis on the historical background of constructivist epistemology helps us to clarify a second conclusion, namely that Katzian constructivism is inadequate to deal with the whole spectrum of mystical experience. Constructivists prejudge, on a priori epistemological grounds, that certain mystical modes of experience and knowledge are both impossible and invalid. This is a problem in two main ways: first, we find claims to these modes of experience and knowledge from within many mystical traditions; second, it is possible to give at least plausible contemporary reconstructions—not, to be sure, on the basis of Katzian constructivist epistemology—that make sense and suggest the possible validity of these modes.

My arguments, of course, are naturalistic and interpretive and have operated in naturalistic and interpretive territory. I have not been arguing that there is a fundamental incommensurability between naturalistic and interpretive knowledge, on the one hand, and the two forms of "mystical" knowledge, on the other, an incommensurability in which one simply has to choose (in some way) between rival kinds of standards of knowledge. We do not have to *become* mystics in order to come to the conclusions of this essay, but we do, I believe, have to *be open* to the claims of mystics. The incommensurability arises, rather, from the perspective of Katzian constructivism in which the possibility of these two forms of mystical knowledge are excluded. My arguments and evidence, furthermore, have been marshaled according to the *conventional* notions of the naturalistic and interpretive tasks. These arguments suggest, I believe, that there are superior naturalistic and interpretive treatments of the data of mysticism not constrained by the Katzian epistemology.

The main point has been that constructivist epistemology as construed by Katz and others should *not* be taken as the necessary background for such tasks, that such epistemology itself is problematical. In fact, it is precisely the study of mysticism that shows not only the limits of constructivism, but also the limits of naturalistic and interpretive forms of knowledge, and that leads to articulating epistemologies that can deal with the full range of mystical experience. The study of mysticism, thus, has important implications for contemporary epistemology in general.

Third, I have also identified plausible reconstructions of two basic aspects of the mystical life: the experience of pure consciousness, on the one hand, and the paths of the deconstruction of ordinary experiential structures, on the other. I have not myself, in this essay, argued in depth for why we should accept such reconstructions, although the authors in the present volume have made such an argument for the experience of pure consciousness. My intent rather has been to open up the question of the adequacy of such reconstructions more and to show how the question cannot arise in a (Katzian) constructivist framework; thus, my first two conclusions hold independently of the results of inquiring into the question.

However, such reconstructions, if supported by evidence and argument, offer important ways to address the questions of a common mystical core and validity, although, again, I have at best only suggested the lines any arguments might follow. For instance, the experience of pure consciousness may well be common to many (although certainly not all) traditions, although such an experience does not appear to be the end goal of all traditions in which it appears. Perhaps more significant to the discussion may be the hypothesis that many mystical traditions offer paths of deconstruction, often leading to the experience of pure consciousness (as well as other mystical phenomena). If this hypothesis is supported, it would help make sense both of important commonalities of mystical traditions while recognizing vital differences. The hypothesis would also be useful in suggesting a distinct mode (or modes) of knowledge, although considerable work would be required to show why this mode should be identified as yielding knowledge and in what sense there can be validity.

Examining such paths of deconstruction may be a very important way to examine mystical traditions, and one potentially more fruitful than concentrating on extremely rare experiences about which there is often little to say. Such deconstructive paths are certainly far more accessible to study, both from psychological and textual points of view, than is the experience of pure consciousness. Furthermore, this investigation may be a way to connect the study of mysticism with a host of other cultural phenomena in which there appear to be other modes of experience or knowing in which certain common presuppositions are suspended or transcended, for example, aesthetic experience, communion with the natural world, aspects of intimate interpersonal relations, nonordinary states of consciousness and so on. If carried out, such investigations might shift considerably the assumptions of contemporary epistemology. Such an epistemological shift might involve retention of many constructivist emphases on context without the extreme relativism often accompanying constructivism as well as without the dogmatism criticized in this essay.

My fourth and final conclusion is that these questions need considerable further *open* study, taking these first three conclusions as a point of departure. Such study requires: (1) remaining open to the possibility of the validity of the core insights of classical mystical traditions; (2) acknowledging the importance of differences between traditions, studying the basic texts and traditions carefully; (3) considering the lack of full articulation by traditional epistemologies of the different forms of mediation and incorporating many of the insights of contemporary epistemology; and yet (4) attempting to develop a contemporary framework in which mystical claims can be understood as valid.

At the present moment, there is, to my knowledge, no current project that adequately meets all of these criteria. However, there is ongoing inquiry in at least five major areas, the first three more based in major historical traditions and the last two more based in contemporary issues and thinking. These different general projects, furthermore, may not be so much competing to give the "correct" epistemology as rather complementary:[105]

1. There are contemporary reconstructions and (to some extent) reworkings of mystical approaches from within the major religions and esoteric traditions. In some cases, these inquiries are energized through a connection to ongoing life practice in active spiritual communities.

2. There might also be a reworking from within the framework of Western mystically inclined philosophical traditions, rooted in the work of Plato, Plotinus, Spinoza, Hegel, and so on.[106]

3. Such an approach is often especially close to another major alternative— the development of a more sophisticated version of the perennial philosophy—able to meet the Katzian objections.[107]

Perhaps more promising for those rooted in contemporary epistemology are two approaches coming out of recent work in philosophy and psychology, that are able to integrate empirical studies and contemporary epistemology more fluidly than classically rooted theories.

4. We could point first to work appropriating mystical traditions in the light of contemporary philosophical and cultural issues, particularly emerging from the work of Continental philosophy: Georg Hegel, Friedrich Nietzsche, Martin Heidegger, Maurice Merleau-Ponty, and Jacques Derrida, to name the most prominent influences.[108]

5. From a more psychological perspective, especially promising is the approach generally now identified as transpersonal psychology, or more generally as transpersonal theory.[109]

Out of the combined work in all of these areas might come a deeper understanding of mysticism. With such an understanding, there might also be a fuller response to the more practical concerns of how to balance commonalities and differences among human spiritual traditions and how to interpret, in the postmodern situation, such traditions as contributing to the resolution of contemporary cultural problems. In such a context, many of these more theoretical questions appear charged with practical urgency.

NOTES

1. There is certainly a problem in using the term "mysticism," a problem both with the popular connotations of the term and with many of the various typologies designed to distinguish different kinds of mystical experience. I will be following the general characterization of mysticism given by Robert K. C. Forman in his "Introduction" to the present volume. For a critique of the concept of mysticism from something like the constructivist position I discuss in this essay, see Hans Penner, "The Mystical Illusion," in Steven Katz, ed., *Mysticism and Religious Traditions* (New York: Oxford University Press, 1983), pp. 89–116.

2. Steven Katz, ed., *Mysticism and Philosophical Analysis* (New York: Oxford University Press, 1978); Katz, *Mysticism and Religious Traditions*.

3. Generally, the term "constructivism" may be used to refer to the emphasis in post-Kantian epistemology on the extent to which the background of knowledge must be considered at least, as partially constitutive of experience and knowledge. This is not to suggest that there is unanimity about the nature or meaning of such construction or that all constructivists reach the same conclusions regarding mystical traditions as do Katz and others. Nor would many post-Kantian epistemologists use a term like constructivism, with its idealist overtones. Katz and his colleagues do not explicitly identify their approach as constructivist, although Katz, for instance, speaks of the "constructive conditions of consciousness," the "intentionality" of experience, and the "creation" of experience, and Robert Gimello holds that "mystical experience is simply the psychosomatic enhancement of religious beliefs and values or of beliefs and values of other kinds which are held 'religiously.'" See Katz, "Language, Epistemology, and Mysticism," in Katz, *Mysticism and Philosophical Analysis*, pp. 62–65; Katz, "The 'Conservative' Character of Mystical Experience," in Katz, *Mysticism and Religious Traditions*, p. 51; Robert Gimello, "Mysticism in Its Contexts," in Katz, *Mysticism and Religious Traditions*, p. 85.

The term is also used widely in congnitive psychology. For a recent statement of "radical constructionism," see Ernst von Glaserfeld, "An Introduction to Radical Constructivism," in Paul Watzlawick, ed., *The Invented Reality: How Do We Know What We Believe We Know? (Contributions to Constructivism)* (New York: Norton, 1984), pp. 17–40. For an attempt to give a biological basis for constructivist epistemology, see Francisco Varela, *Principles of Biological Autonomy* (New York: North-Holland, 1979).

4. The fullest treatment of these issues can be found in W. T. Stace, *Mysticism and Philosophy* (London: Macmillan, 1960; rpt. Atlantic Highlands, N. J.: Humanities Press, 1978). The work of Katz and his colleagues is to a large extent a critique of Stace. William Wainwright has given the most recent comprehensive study of philosophical issues concerning mysticism, in his *Mysticism: A Study of Its Nature, Congnitive Value, and Moral Implications* (Madison: University of Wisconsin Press, 1981).

5. Katz notes the same major motivations in looking into questions of mysticism. See his "Editor's Introduction" to *Mysticism and Philosophical Analysis,* p. 1.

6. See C. D. Broad, *Religion, Philosophy and Psychical Research* (London: Routledge and Kegan Paul, 1953), "Arguments for the Existence of God," pp. 175–201, especially pp. 191ff.; Huston Smith, *Forgotten Truth: The Primordial Tradition* (New York: Harper Row, 1976).

7. Freud's arguments are found most clearly in *The Future of an Illusion* (Garden City, N.Y.: Doubleday, 1964).

8. Katz is not particularly precise about the claims of the representatives of perennial philosophy; his attacks are mostly against the claims of Walter Stace. Prominent perennialists and representative writings include: Frithjof Schuon, *The Transcendent Unity of Religions,* trans. Peter Townsend (Wheaton, Ill.: Theosophical Publishing House, 1984, rev. ed.); Réné Guénon, *The Multiple States of Being* (Burdett, N.Y.: Larson, 1984); H. Smith, *Forgotten Truth;* Ken Wilber, *The Atman Project* (Wheaton, Ill.: Theosophical Publishing House, 1980); Seyyed Hossein Nasr, *Knowledge and the Sacred* (New York: Crossroads Press, 1981). For a short summary of basic perennialist claims, see Huston Smith, "Is There a Perennial Philosophy?" *Journal of the American Academy of Religion* 55 (Fall 1987): 553–66, particularly pp. 560ff.

9. Wayne Proudfoot, *Religious Experience* (Berkeley: University of California Press, 1985). See, especially, the chapter on "Mysticism," pp. 119–54.

10. Stace, *Mysticism and Philosophy,* p. 87. Stace limits his claim to what he calls "introvertive" mysticism.

11. H. Smith, "Is There a Perennial Philosophy?" p. 564. Smith correlates this kind of experience with the negative or apophatic aspect of the metaphysical idea of the unbounded and undifferentiated Absolute or Infinite.

12. See Katz, "Language, Epistemology, and Mysticism," pp. 65–66.

13. See also Katz's summary of his position in "'Conservative' Character," pp. 4–5.

14. Katz, "Language, Epistemology, and Mysticism," p. 26.

15. Ibid., pp. 30, 62–65; here Katz does give some brief general discussions.

16. Ibid., pp. 34–46. Katz writes (p. 62), "The Buddhist experience of *nirvāṇa*, the Jewish of *devekuth*, and the Christian of *unio mystica*, the Sufi of *fana*, the Taoist of *Tao* are the *result*, at least in part, of specific conceptual influences, i.e. the 'starting problems' of each doctrinal, theological system." Presumably, then, the basis for the differences between mystical experiences is the differing and ineliminable conceptual traditions in which they are embedded as well as the "starting problem" of each tradition.

17. Gimello, "Mysticism in Its Contexts," p. 63.

18. Katz, "'Conservative' Character," pp. 43–51.

19. Katz, "Language, Epistemology, and Mysticism," pp. 59–60.

20. Ibid., pp. 57–58.

21. See subsection entitled "Unmediated Experience and the Deconstruction of Experience in Mystical Traditions" in this essay.

22. Broad, *Religion, Philosophy and Psychical Research*, pp. 191ff. Broad mentions the "common nucleus" on p. 193.

23. William James, *The Varieties of Religious Experience* (New York: Longmans, Green and Co., 1902; rpt. Modern Library, 1982), pp. 413–20. The quote is from p. 414.

24. Ibid., p. 415.

25. Katz, "Language, Epistemology, and Mysticism," pp. 22–23. For Proudfoot's development of this argument, see *Religious Experience*, pp. 151–54.

26. As I will explore in the section on "The Limits of Constructivist Epistemologies" in this essay III, there are actually a variety of *types* of mystical claims possible, that Katz does not adequately distinguish. To the extent that mystical claims aim at explanation or interpretive understanding there might be some public grounds (in the contemporary secular sense) for accepting or rejecting mystical claims.

27. Katz, "Language, Epistemology, and Mysticism," p. 22.

28. "But the mystic, so far from producing propositions which are empirically verified, is unable to produce any intelligible propositions at all." A. J. Ayer, *Language, Truth and Logic* (London: Gollancz, 1946, 2d ed.), p. 118.

29. Katz, "Language, Epistemology, and Mysticism," p. 22.

30. Proudfoot does not give, on my reading, a reconstruction of the argument that there can be no independent grounds for accepting mystical claims. The implication of his remarks is that to the extent that mystical claims invoke explanatory or interpretive goals, they can be examined and supported or undermined. See the subsection entitled "The Question of Validity and the Forms of Mystical Knowledge" in this essay.

31. Proudfoot writes in *Religious Experience* (p. 121), "The terms in which the subject understands what is happening to him are constitutive of the experience; consequently those in different traditions have different experiences."

32. The very metaphor of mediation that Katz uses implicitly reminds us of such a model; that which *mediates* functions as a *go-between* for two otherwise independent entities. The metaphor seems to leave open the possibility of over-

coming the need for mediation. Arguably, however, the metaphor loses its coherence if one gives up the traditional model of potentially independent knower and known, for there is then no independent knower and known there to be mediated. Mediation, to continue the metaphor, is all there is, but then it really is not mediation. We might be reminded here of Nietzsche's insight that, with the end of the real world, there is also no (merely) apparent world. See his "How the 'True World' Finally Became a Fable," in *Twilight of the Idols,* in *The Portable Nietzsche,* trans. and ed. Walter Kaufmann (New York: Viking, 1954), pp. 485–86.

For a very interesting account of ten basic metaphors used in spiritual traditions, see Ralph Metzner, *Opening to Inner Light: The Transformation of Human Nature and Consciousness* (Los Angeles: J. P. Tarcher, 1986). Metzner treats the following metaphors of transformation: from dreaming to being awake, from illusion to reality, from captivity to liberation, through purification by fire, from darkness to light, from fragmentation to wholeness, as a journey to places of vision and power, as a return to the source, as a death and rebirth experience, and as an unfolding of the tree of our life.

33. Plato claims that "dialectic . . . attempts to apprehend methodically, with regard to each, what each really is" (*Republic,* 533b). The translation is by G.M.A. Grube (Indianapolis, Ind.: Hackett, 1974).

34. John Locke, *An Essay Concerning Human Understanding,* 2 vols., ed. John Yolton (London: Dent, 1961), vol. 2, p. 167 (Bk IV, chap. IV, 3).

35. Aristotle gives this basic assumption of the unproblematic nature of language and human differences in this way, "Spoken words are the symbols of experiences in the soul, written words the symbols of spoken words. As all men have not the same script, so not all have the same speech sounds, but the experiences, which these primarily symbolize, are the same for all, and so are the things of which our experiences are the likenesses" (*On interpretation,* 16ᵃ4ff.). Quoted in G.R.G. Mure, *Aristotle* (New York: Oxford University Press, 1964), p. 178.

36. *The Thirteen Principal Upaniṣads,* trans. Robert Ernest Hume (New York: Oxford University Press, 1931, 2d rev. ed.), p. 396 (Śvetāśvatara Upaniṣad, I, 10–11).

37. Quoted in Aldous Huxley, *The Perennial Philosophy* (New York: Harper & Row, 1945), p. 162.

38. Quoted in Javad Nurbakhsh, *Traditions of the Prophet: Ahadith* (New York: Khaniqahi-Nimatullahi Publications, 1981), p. 32. (I thank Alan Godlas for this and the reference in n. 39.)

39. "Verily, there exist seventy thousand veils of light and darkness before God," Ibid., p. 56.

40. Kant's epistemology, to be sure, is often murky when probed. On the very murky problem of the nature of Kant's "thing-in-itself," see George Schrader, "The Thing in Itself in Kantian Philosophy," in Robert Paul Wolff, ed., *Kant: A Collection of Critical Essays* (Garden City, N.Y.: Doubleday, 1967), pp. 172–88.

41. It is interesting to note that Hegel criticizes the assumptions informing this

metaphor right at the beginning of the *Phenomenology of Spirit,* the entrance to his "system," to Hegel's (immediately post-Kantian) attempt to redeem the claim to direct knowledge of reality. In the "Introduction" to the *Phenomenology,* he implicitly attacks Kant's claim that knowledge is inherently mediated, by questioning the related metaphors of *knowledge as an instrument* and *knowledge as a medium* between the knower and what is to be known. With both of these metaphors, Hegel charges, there is an assumption that "between knowledge and the Absolute there lies a boundary which completely cuts off the one from the other," an assumption that Hegel attacks as incoherent and fearful. See G. W. F. Hegel, *Phenomenology of Mind,* trans. J. B. Baillie (New York: Harper & Row, 1931), pp. 131ff.

42. Of course, this is the story many of us tell now, a story which directs our reading of the last two centuries. In actuality, most active philosophers until very recently followed the traditional model of direct knowledge in different ways. For a similar narrative account of the epistemological shift, see Charles Taylor, "Overcoming Epistemology," in Kenneth Baynes, James Bohman, and Thomas McCarthy, eds., *After Philosophy: End or Transformation?* (Cambridge: MIT Press, 1987), pp. 464–88.

43. See Hans-Georg Gadamer, *Philosophical Hermeneutics,* trans. and ed. David Linge (Berkeley: University of California Press, 1976), pp. 3, 31. Gadamer also tells us that we never reach the fullness of being in language: "*Bewusstsein* is inescapably more *being* than consciousness and being is never fully manifest" (ibid., p. 38).

Mark Taylor, in "Deconstruction: What's the Difference?" *Soundings* 66 (1983): 387–403, summarizes the deconstructionist position of Derrida in this way:

> Consciousness, therefore, deals *only* with signs and never reaches the thing itself. More precisely, the thing itself is not an independent entity (be it "real" or "ideal") to which all signs refer, but is itself a sign. . . . In the absence of any primal signified which can serve as a secure anchor, signifiers float freely within a field of signification that appears to be endless. . . . There is no logos to be revealed, no secret to be uncovered, no truth to be discovered" (pp. 397, 400).

44. See, for instance, David Michael Levin, *The Body's Recollection of Being: Phenomenological Psychology and the Deconstruction of Nihilism* (London: Routledge & Kegan Paul, 1985); Don Johnson, *Body* (Boston: Beacon Press, 1983); Sam Keen, *The Passionate Life: Stages of Loving* (San Francisco: Harper & Row, 1983); Robert Solomon, *The Passions: The Myth and Nature of Human Emotion* (Garden City, N.Y.: Doubleday, 1976).

45. Some feminist epistemologists (e.g., Evelyn Fox Keller and Sandra Harding) recognize fully the mediations involved in knowledge may indicate an epistemological goal complementary to the goal of attempting to eliminate them. Such a former goal may be rooted in a metaphor of knowledge as relationship and communion rather than a metaphor of knowledge as distanced seeing. See Evelyn

Fox Keller, "Dynamic Objectivity: Love, Power, and Knowledge," in her *Reflections on Gender and Science* (New Haven, Conn.: Yale University Press, 1985), pp. 115–26; Sandra Harding, "Conclusion: Epistemological Questions, in Sandra Harding, ed., *Feminism and Methodology: Social Science Issues* (Bloomington: Indiana University Press, 1987), pp. 181–90.

46. Nietzsche sees the eclipse of the classical epistemological model as necessarily ushering in a period of nihilism. Nihilism is what happens when a core unifying cultural ideal is devalued. See Nietzsche, *The Will to Power,* trans. Walter Kaufmann and R. J. Hollingdale, ed. Kaufmann (New York: Random House, 1967), pp. 3ff. Nietzsche writes, "What does nihilism mean? *That the highest values devaluate themselves*" (p. 9).

47. For a good overview of the contemporary epistemological predicament in terms of developing such a middle way, see Richard Bernstein, *Beyond Objectivism and Relativism: Science, Hermeneutics, and Praxis* (Philadelphia: University of Pennsylvania Press, 1983). For key articles by many of the philosophers articulating the main contemporary alternatives, see Baynes, Bohman, and McCarthy, eds., *After Philosophy.*

48. For an account of the main modern and postmodern philosophical critiques of classical religious traditions, particularly of those traditions rooted in the model of a hierarchical ontology, see my "Philosophical Foundations of Transpersonal Psychology: An Introduction to Some Basic Issues," in *Journal of Transpersonal Psychology* 18 (1986): 1–34.

49. Katz, "Language, Epistemology, and Mysticism," p. 26. This emphasis is surely more than what he later calls, in " 'Conservative' Character" (p. 4), a working hypothesis.

50. Penner, "Mystical Illusion," p. 89.

51. The quote is from Proudfoot, *Religious Experience,* p. 45.

52. Proudfoot, for example, who is in many ways very much of a constructivist, recognizes both kinds of knowledge, although his primary focus seems naturalistic; he is especially interested in framing explanatory hypotheses.

53. For an account of the implications of this work for the study of religion, see Ian Barbour, *Myths, Models, and Paradigms: A Comparative Study in Science and Religion* (New York: Harper & Row, 1974).

54. On these developments, see Donald Polkinghorne, *Methodology for the Human Sciences* (Albany: SUNY Press, 1983).

55. For a recent monograph on the philosophy of the social sciences identifying these two main types of knowledge, see David Braybrooke, *Philosophy of Social Science* (Englewood Cliffs, N.J.: Prentice-Hall, 1987). The distinction is somewhat standard. For another version, see Jürgen Habermas, *Knowledge and Human Interests,* trans. Jeremy Shapiro (Boston: Beacon Press, 1971).

Perhaps the main alternative epistemology not clearly included in the standard account is that of a critical social theory in which the aim is a kind of knowledge that liberates, on both social and individual levels. See Braybrooke, *Philosophy of Social Science,* pp. 68–91; David Held, *Introduction to Critical Theory: Horkheimer to Habermas* (Berkeley: University of California Press, 1980); and Brian Fay,

Critical Social Science (Ithaca, N.Y.: Cornell University Press, 1987). In some recent critical theory, such as that of Habermas, there is no longer a claim to a third distinct form of knowledge. See Habermas, *The Theory of Communicative Action,* 2 vols., trans. Thomas McCarthy (Boston: Beacon Press, 1984–87), vol. 1: *Reason and the Rationalization of Society* (1984).

56. See Carl Hempel, *Philosophy of Natural Science* (Englewood Cliffs, N.J.: Prentice-Hall, 1966). For the application of this model to the social sciences, see Braybrooke, *Philosophy of Social Science,* pp. 20–46; and Polkinghorne, *Methodology for the Human Sciences,* pp. 71–91.

57. For a summary of some of the main problems of the covering law model with regard to the social sciences, see Polkinghorne, *Methodology,* pp. 93–133.

58. The example is quoted in Polkinghorne, *Methodology,* 74–75. The model can be schematized as follows:

Premise 1	$L_1, L_2, L_3 \quad . \quad . \quad . \quad L_m$	(laws or lawlike statements)
Premise 2	$C_1, C_2, C_3 \quad . \quad . \quad . \quad C_n$	(circumstances, causes, conditions)
	———————	
Conclusion	E	(statement or statements describing the phenomenon to be explained)

The schema is from Carl Hempel, "The Logic of Functional Analysis," in his *Aspects of Scientific Explanation* (New York: Free Press, 1965), pp. 297–330.

59. See W. V. O. Quine, *Word and Object* (Cambridge: MIT. Press, 1960); *Ontological Relativity and Other Essays* (New York: Columbia University Press, 1969). For a good general account of Quine's work, see George Romanos, *Quine and Analytic Philosophy* (Cambridge: MIT Press, 1983).

60. See Proudfoot, *Religious Experience,* pp. 190–227. He criticizes what he calls "protective" strategies attempting to insulate religious traditions against naturalistic inquiry by attacking any attempt at explanation of religious experiences as "reductive." Proudfoot (ibid., p. 226) suggests the kind of explanation appropriate for religious experience: "What must be explained is why they understood what happened to them or what they witnessed in religious terms. This requires a mapping of the concepts and beliefs that were available to them, the commitments they brought to the experience, and the contextual conditions that might have supported their identification of their experiences in religious terms."

61. For a good collection of many of the main writings on interpretive understanding, see Fred Dallmayr and Thomas McCarthy, eds., *Understanding and Social Inquiry* (Notre Dame, Ind.: University of Notre Dame Press, 1977). A good summary of these views can be found in Polkinghorne, *Methodology,* pp. 20–57, 201–40.

62. Rather, it is usually held that causal analysis is dependent on interpretive operations for the very meaning of the key terms. For development of this argument, see Karl-Otto Apel, "The A Priori of Communication and the Foundation of

the Humanities," in Dallmayr and McCarthy, *Understanding and Social Inquiry*, pp. 292–315.

63. See Charles Taylor, "Interpretation and the Sciences of Man," in Dallmayr and McCarthy, eds., *Understanding and Social Inquiry*, p. 118.

64. Ludwig Wittgenstein, *Philosophical Investigations*, trans. G. E. M. Anscombe (New York: Macmillan, 1953); Peter Winch, *The Idea of a Social Science* (London: Routledge & Kegan Paul, 1958); Peter Winch, "Understanding a Primitive Society," in Bryan Wilson, ed., *Rationality* (New York: Harper & Row, 1970), pp. 78–111; Hans-Georg Gadamer, *Truth and Method* (New York: Seabury Press, 1975); Richard Rorty, *Philosophy and the Mirror of Nature* (Princeton, N.J.: Princeton University Press, 1979); Christopher Norris, *Derrida* (Cambridge: Harvard University Press, 1987).

65. Noam Chomsky, *Aspects of the Theory of Syntax* (Cambridge: MIT Press, 1965); Jürgen Habermas, "What Is Universal Pragmatics?" in his *Communication and the Evolution of Society*, trans. Thomas McCarthy (Boston: Beacon Press, 1979); Jean Piaget, *The Essential Piaget*, eds. Howard Gruber and J. Vonèche (New York: Basic Books, 1977); Lawrence Kohlberg, *Essays on Moral Development*; vol. 1, *The Philosophy of Moral Development* (San Francisco: Harper & Row, 1981); Ken Wilber, *The Atman Project*. Whether these latter theories are a part of interpretive theory is controversial. They are empirically based reconstructions of underlying rules or competences. Some would locate these reconstructions as part of empirical theory; others would distinguish them from both empirical and interpretive findings.

66. Katz, "Language, Epistemology, and Mysticism," pp. 65–66.

67. We find in the *Yoga Sūtra* (II, 20): "The seer is consciousness only." See the *Yoga Sūtra*, trans. Rama Prasada, in Sarvepalli Radhakrishnan and Charles Moore, eds., *A Sourcebook in Indian Philosophy* (Princeton, N.J.: Princeton University Press, 1957), p. 465. We find in Katz's "Language, Epistemology, and Mysticism" (p. 57) the assertion that yoga "properly understood" does not lead to an "unconditioned" form of consciousness but only another, even if interesting, form of "conditioned-contextual consciousness."

68. We find in the *Ashtasahasrika* (VII, 177), "Where there is no perception, appellation, conception or conventional expression, there one speaks of 'perfect wisdom.' " In Edward Conze et al., eds., *Buddhist Texts Through the Ages* (New York: Harper & Row, 1954), p. 150. However, Robert Gimello, from the perspective of his Buddhist studies, argues, "[I]t is difficult to imagine that the intellect is entirely absent from the mystic's transport" and that mystical experience is "simply the psychosomatic enhancement of religious beliefs and values." The first quote is from Gimello, "Mysticism and Meditation," in Katz, *Mysticism and Philosophical Analysis*, p. 176; the second is from "Mysticism in Its Contexts," in Katz, *Mysticism and Religious Traditions*, p. 85. For further discussion of the issue, see Robert K. C. Forman, "Paramartha and Modern Constructivism: Epistemological Monomorphism vs. Duomorphism," *Philosophy East and West* (forthcoming).

69. Plotinus writes (*Enneads* VI, 9, [9], 11), "The vision [of the One], in any

case, did not imply duality; the man who saw was identical with what he saw. Hence he did not 'see' it but rather was 'oned' with it. . . . In that state he had attained unity, nothing within him or without effecting diversity. When he had made his ascent, there was within him no disturbance, no anger, emotion, desire, reason, or thought." See *The Essential Plotinus,* trans. Elmer O'Brien (Indianapolis, Ind.: Hackett, 1981, 2d ed.), p. 87.

70. The phrase, "hermeneutics of suspicion," is from Paul Ricoeur. See his *Freud and Philosophy: An Essay on Interpretation,* trans. Denis Savage (New Haven, Conn.: Yale University Press, 1970), pp. 32–36.

71. Presumably Katz, when he denies the possibility of giving independent grounds to support mystical claims, is refering to *certain kinds* of mystical claims about (something like) unmediated experience. See n. 26, cited earlier.

72. I discuss alternative models in the subsection entitled "The Question of Validity and the Forms of Mystical Knowledge."

73. Cf. Gadamer, *Truth and Method,* pp. 235 ff.

74. Of course, this problem of the nature of "truth" or standards in a seemingly pluralist and constructivist model emerges as well in much more sophisticated interpretive theories such as those of Gadamer or Rorty. See David Ingram, "Hermeneutics and Truth," in Robert Hollinger, ed., *Hermeneutics and Praxis* (Notre Dame, Ind.: University of Notre Dame Press, 1985), pp. 32–53; Kenneth Gallagher, "Rorty on Objectivity, Truth, and Social Consensus," *International Philosophical Quarterly* 24 (1984): 111–24; Donald Rothberg, "Gadamer, Rorty, Hermeneutics, and Truth: A Response to Warnke," *Inquiry* 29 (1986): 355–61.

75. Jürgen Habermas does make a sustained attempt to argue that the modern way of understanding the world *is* a proper starting point for study. For Habermas, what most clearly characterizes this modern way of understanding is the differentiation of three worlds (external, social, and subjective) which have been mixed in religious and metaphysical worldviews. For Habermas, the modern worldview *does* represent a universal framework which requires the devaluing of religious and metaphysical frameworks. He might thus argue that because the contemporary rational framework is a developmental achievement it is, in a sense, neutral. Katz, of course, is not a universalist like Habermas, but Katz as well would have to make the argument that his epistemological insights, although devaluing classical traditions, can be understood as neutral in some way. Pluralists and relativists have a harder time, however, making such arguments. For Habermas's account, see especially *Theory of Communicative Action, vol. 1.* I have criticized this argument, especially in the context of mystical traditions, in "Rationality and Religion in Habermas' Recent Work: Some Remarks on the Relation Between Critical Theory and the Phenomenology of Religion," *Philosophy and Social Criticism* 11 (1986): 221–43.

76. Katz, "Language, Epistemology, and Mysticism," p. 57.

77. In what follows I will understand deconstruction as an activity in which the ordinary structures are suspended. This is a simplification. There seems to be another type of deconstruction in which the constructions of experience are recognized as such, even if they still remains operative. (E.g., this distinction

parallels the two main types of Buddhist meditation, concentrative, and insight.) Such a reflective rather than active deconstruction still seems an important type of knowledge.

78. See Arthur Deikman, "Deautomatization and the Mystic Experience," in Richard Woods, O. P., ed., *Understanding Mysticism* (Garden City, N.Y.: Doubleday, Image Books 1980), pp. 240–69.

79. Daniel Brown, "The Stages of Meditation in Cross-cultural Perspective," in Ken Wilber, Jack Engler, and Daniel Brown, *Transformations of Consciousness: Conventional and Contemplative Perspectives on Development* (Boston: Shambhala, 1986), pp. 263–64. [Emphasis added.]

80. Ibid., p. 262.

81. Ibid., pp. 266–67.[Emphasis in original.]

82. The work of Stanislav Grof—a psychiatrist who has investigated transpersonal experiences perhaps more than any researcher in our century (although not directly examining representatives of classical mystical traditions)—provides some further support for the claim that many spiritual traditions involve, in part, the deconstruction of the mediations of ordinary experience. From his observations of "non ordinary" states of consciousness, occurring through therapeutic techniques and in psychedelic sessions, Grof has noted that there are a very wide range of phenomena in which the usual boundaries of the structures of "ordinary" consciousness (time, space, patterns of thinking and sensory perception, sense of self, etc.) are extended or transcended. Such transpersonal experiences, he finds, can be classified into three large groupings: the first involves experiential extension within space–time and the ordinary physical reality; the second involves an experiential extension beyond the usual sense of reality and space–time to encounter the "spiritual" realities identified in many shamanic and mystical traditions; and the third involves unusual links between consciousness and matter (supernormal physical feats, healing, "siddhis," etc.). Grof would certainly agree that access to such experiences is contextually mediated and that hearing reports of such experiences does not in itself require us to accept any associated claims. Nonetheless, his work does give very rich evidence of the centrality of the deconstruction of ordinary states of consciousness in experiences that are phenomenologically very close to the range of experiences described in many mystical traditions. To take Grof's work, however, as support for my general claim about deconstruction would require further justification of the relevance of such research for claims about classical mystical traditions, both in terms of phenomenological similarity and in terms of the veridicality of the experiences he discusses.

Grof's main works include: *Realms of the Human Unconscious: Observations from LSD Research* (New York: Dutton, 1976); *Beyond the Brain: Birth, Death and Transcendence in Psychotherapy* (Albany: SUNY Press, 1985); and *The Adventure of Self-discovery: Dimensions of Consciousness and New Perspectives in Psychotherapy and Inner Exploration* (Albany: SUNY Press, 1988). His classificatory schema and description of transpersonal experiences can be found in *The Adventure of Self-discovery*, pp. 37–150. He discusses some of the philosophical implications of transpersonal experiences at length in *Beyond the Brain,* chap. 1 and, more briefly, in *The Adventure of Self-discovery,* pp. 160–64.

83. We might be reminded that in Hegel's more theoretical account of the coming to "absolute knowledge" in his *Phenomenology of Spirit,* he claims that "experience," which is defined by a relationship of subject and object, is transcended, and is no longer an appropriate term to use. See also Martin Heidegger, *Hegel's Concept of Experience* trans. J. Genn Gray and Fred Wieck (New York: Harper & Row, 1970), and Stephen Bernhardt's contribution to the present volume, "Are Pure Consciousness Events Unmediated?"

84. The other studies in the volume that Brown has coedited, *Transformations of Consciousness,* do not adequately examine this issue. The one explicit text on Eastern Orthodox Christian traditions ("Developmental Stages in Eastern Orthodox Christianity," by John Chirban, pp. 285–314) does not go into enough detail for us to know how these stages parallel the very clearly differentiated stages identified by Brown. We also do not have a clear sense of whether "union" involves "pure consciousness." Ken Wilber's theory of stages—presented in "The Spectrum of Development" (pp. 65–105) in Wilber, Engler, and Brown, *Transformations of Consciousness,* and in "A Mandalic Map of Consciousness" (pp. 83–100) in Wilber's *Eye to Eye: The Quest for the new Paradigm* (Garden City, N.Y.: Doubleday, 1983)—has very few references to non-Asian traditions.

In addition to having more evidence for universalist claims, we would also need considerable philosophical work weaving together responses to the many questions that exist about such claims, questions coming both from Katz and his colleagues as well as from those reflecting on the universalist claims of writers such as Piaget, Kohlberg, and Habermas concerning cognitive, moral, and communicative development. For an analysis of some of the philosophical problems of such developmental theories, see Owen Flanagan, *The Science of the Mind* (Cambridge: MIT Press, 1984), pp. 119–72.

85. Proudfoot, *Religious Experience,* pp. 151–54.

86. Proudfoot's work follows the standard distinction between explanation and (interpretive) understanding, although he, differing from standard usage somewhat, regards both explanation and understanding as forms of interpretation. See *Religious Experience,* pp. 69–74.

87. Ibid., p. 227.

88. Ibid., p. 223.

89. Ibid., p. 219 [Emphasis added.]

90. See Peter Moore, "Mystical Experience, Mystical Doctrine, Mystical Technique," in Katz, *Mysticism and Philosophical Analysis,* p. 101; Katz, " 'Conservative' Character," pp. 4–5; Penner, "Mystical Illusion," p. 91 ("We must remember that all we have for understanding mysticism is language, not experience.")

91. See, for instance, D. Z. Phillips, *Religion Without Explanation* (Oxford: Basil Blackwell, 1977). Such a view is one of the main targets of Proudfoot's work. See *Religious Experience,* pp. 190ff. Ian Barbour has given a clear account of how

there are commensurable cognitive projects in both science and religion. See, for example, his *Myths, Models, and Paradigms*.

92. For an introduction to the field, see Roger Walsh and Frances Vaughan, eds., *Beyond Ego: Transpersonal Dimensions in Psychology* (Los Angeles: J. P. Tarcher, 1980).

93. Hence, it is not surprising to see a considerable and fruitful dialogue occurring between Buddhist and contemporary Western psychological approaches, especially in the realm of psychotherapy. See, for example, Nathan Katz, ed., *Buddhist and Western Psychology* (Boulder, Colo.: Prajna Press, 1983).

94. Is Buddhist meditation in a certain sense a naturalistic methodology by which to access data? We might understand Buddhist psychology (the *Abhidharma*) as involving a general process of making observations, gathering evidence, and formulating models and theories. However, there are also substantial differences with the standard account of naturalistic inquiry. Buddhist psychology is highly pragmatic; the aim is not theory building per se but liberation. Hence, such inquiry is, we might say, more like critical social science, in that the inquiry is linked intimately to values and norms. Second, much of the data involve reports from nonordinary states of consciousness not accessible to all investigators. Third, such psychology is heavily descriptive or phenomenological, although there is an explanatory component.

95. William Wainwright, in his account of monistic mystical experience, differs on this point. He regards such a contentless experience as noncognitive, as more like the noncognitive experience of pain or a stomachache than like the (for him) paradigmatic cognitive act of sense-perception. See *Mysticism,* pp. 117ff.

However regarding senseperception as paradigmatic for knowledge is highly questionable and seems, as in the work of Katz and others, to determine in advance their findings on the basis of epistemological assumptions. Why should sense perception be taken as paradigmatic? Such an assumption is problematic, even apart from matters of studying mysticism, as any number of rationalists (such as Plato, Descartes, Hegel, or Husserl) might tell us.

96. Wainwright also excludes the possibility of pure consciousness as a way of knowing on (empiricist) epistemological grounds; senseperception is the paradigm of knowledge.

97. Katz also makes this point (while of course not seeing it as a problem) when he claims that there can be neither independent, public grounds for justifying mystical claims nor that mystical experiences can justify any claims. See Katz, "Language, Epistemology, and Mysticism," p. 22.

An inability to distinguish adequately the different kinds of knowledge used in mystical traditions has sometimes led to the confusion of attempting to justify mystical claims through psychology or physics by using the standard conception of naturalistic inquiry.

98. For reasons of space I will not go into the question of whether interpretive understanding can penetrate the "meaning" of mystical experience. We have seen that many interpreters, like Proudfoot (*Religious Experience*, p. 219, cited earlier in n. 89), do not see a problem here. There are resources in the arguments

I have developed in this section for challenging this assertion.

99. This separation between meaning and validity has its philosophical roots in the phenomenological notion of bracketing or suspending questions of the "reality" and "validity" of (here, religious) experience.

100. Some, such as Habermas, challenge this distinction, holding that there cannot really be understanding without resolving the question of validity. See his *Theory of Communicative Action*, vol. 1, pp. 102–20.

101. We might think of the Buddha counseling his followers, in the *Kālāma Sutta*, not to accept particular views simply on the basis of tradition, scripture, or spiritual social authority, but rather to investigate the validity of the views for oneself. See *Kālāma Sutta*, trans. Soma Thera (Kandy, Sri Lanka: Buddhist Publication Society, 1959).

102. See Martin Heidegger, *Discourse on Thinking*, trans. J. M. Anderson and E. Hans Freind (New York: Harper & Row, 1966), pp. 46ff. Heidegger claims that meditative thinking involves a direct experience of Being, and transcendence of the subject-predicate structure. He contrasts such thinking with calculative thinking, which concerns 'beings' and makes use of representations (*Vorstellungen*) and the laws of logic, and which most closely conforms to what we have called naturalistic knowledge. See also John Caputo, *The Mystical Element in Heidegger's Thought* (Athens: Ohio University Press, 1978); and Graham Parkes, ed., *Heidegger and Asian Thought* (Honolulu: University Press of Hawaii, 1987).

103. Examining which categories are suspended and which remain in particular mystical paths is an important area for research.

104. See B. K. Anand, G. S. Chhina, and Baldev Singh, "Some Aspects of Electroencephalographic Studies in Yogis," and Akira Kasamutsu and Tomio Hirai, "An Electroencephalographic Study on the Zen Meditation," both in Charles Tart, ed., *Altered States of Consciousness* (Garden City, N. Y.: Doubleday, 1969), pp. 515–18 and 501–14, respectively.

105. Study of different mystical traditions and approaches to mysticism may, in fact, help illuminate one of the main questions in contemporary epistemology—the meaning of theoretical pluralism.

106. See, for instance, the work of John Findlay, for example, *The Discipline of the Cave* (London: Allen & Unwin, 1966); *The Transcendence of the Cave* (London: Allen & Unwin, 1967); and James Cutsinger, *The Form of Transformed Vision: Coleridge and the Knowledge of God* (Macon, Ga.: Mercer, 1987).

107. See H. Smith's rejoinder to Katz, "Is There a Perennial Philosophy?"; Sheldon Isenberg and Gene Thursby, "A Perennial Philosophy Perspective on Richard Rorty's Neo-Pragmatism" *International Journal for Philosophy of Religion* 17 (1985): 41–65.

108. See, for example, Keiji Nishitani, *Religion and Nothingness*, trans. Jan Van Bragt (Berkeley: University of California Press, 1981); Masao Abe, *Zen and Western Thought*, ed. William LaFleur (Honolulu: University Press of Hawaii, 1985); David Michael Levin, *The Opening of Vision: Nihilism and the Postmodern Situation* (New York: Routledge & Kegan Paul, 1988).

109. The main theorists in transpersonal psychology are Stanislav Grof and

Ken Wilber. For Grof's main works, see n. 82, cited earlier. Representative of Wilber's writings are: *The Spectrum of Consciousness* (Wheaton, Il.: Theosophical Publishing House, 1977); *The Atman Project* and *Eye to Eye*. See also Wilber et al., *Transformations of Consciousness* and Michael Washburn, *The Ego and the Dynamic Ground: A Transpersonal Theory of Human Development* (Albany: SUNY Press, 1988).

Mysticism and Its Contexts

PHILIP ALMOND

[C]an we, as is so commonly assumed, come to understand mysticism aright if we pluck it out of its socio-historical parameters and separate it from its philosophical-theological environment, thus treating it as a pure, nonrelational, unmediated sort of human experience? Or, in contradistinction to this currently dominant interpretation, is it necessary in order to understand mysticism to ground the mystic in his polyform context so that one comes to realize what may well be the *necessary* connection between the mystic's way and his goal, the mystic's problematic and the mystic's solution to this problematic; the mystic's intentions and the mystic's actual experiences?

KATZ, *Mysticism and Religious Traditions*

In 1983 Steven Katz thusly characterized the methodological dilemma which has come to dominate discussion of mysticism and mystical experience since the publication of his edited collection entitled *Mystical Experience and Philosophical Analysis* in 1978.[1] My overall aim in this essay is to demonstrate that the philosophical analysis of mysticism is not compelled to adopt either of these apparently mutually exclusive positions and that it is possible, perhaps even necessary, to formulate a methodology which coherently steers between the Scylla of mystical essentialism, on the one hand, and the Charybdis of mystical relativism, on the other. In particular I will argue that the recognition of the context-dependent nature of all mystical experience is neither incompatible with experiential novelty nor with the occurrence of what Ninian Smart labels the experience of consciousness-purity.[2]

Although there are some ambiguities in Katz's position, his methodological stance may be summarized as follows:

1. There are no unmediated experiences; and therefore
2. the content of mystical experience is determined by the religious tradition in which it occurs; consequently,
3. there are as many different types of mystical experience as there are religious traditions in which they occur.

The position adopted by Katz is not an original one. I find it, as early as 1909, clearly expressed in Rufus M. Jones's *Studies in Mystical Religion,* "There are no experiences of any sort which are independent of pre-formed expectations or unaffected by the prevailing beliefs of the time. . . . Mystical experiences will be, perforce, saturated with the dominant ideas of the group to which the mystic belongs, and they will reflect the expectations of that group and that period."[3] In the writings of Mircea Eliade, it is intimated, too, of H. P. Owen, and informs Bruce Garside's theory of mysticism.[4] Moreover, the role that prior belief, concepts, and so on, play in the structuring of religious experience in general had been common place well before the arrival of Katz's theory.

However that may be, the dominant *episteme* for the study of mysticism for the greater part of this century had been an essentialist one. That is to say, the study of mystical texts proceeded on the presupposition that they all, to a greater or lesser extent, were the varied expressions of an identical experience or of so many varied expressions of a limited number of experiences. In addition, they were motivated by a quest for religious truth and proceeded on the assumption that religious experience, or more particularly mystical experience, provided the crucial point of connection between religious propositions and the transcendent referent to which they variously pointed and which they more or less adequately expressed. It was then in the quest for the essence of mysticism (i.e., that essential experience(s) that remained when the postexperiential layers of interpretation were progressively removed) that the study of mysticism was grounded. And the heterogeneous analyses of Sarvepalli Radhakrishnan, Evelyn Underhill, Rudolf Otto, W. T. Stace, and R. C. Zaehner, were the result of it.[5]

In part, these studies were vitiated methodologically by their inability conceptually to bridge the gap between mystical texts and the mystical experiences of which they were putatively expressions. But more important, they were vitiated by what amounts to a contemporary paradigm shift in epistemology toward the view that there are no human experiences except through the sociolinguistic relations which mediate them.[6] It was as a result of this paradigm shift that earlier studies of mystical experience—to the extent that they viewed mystical experiences outside of the sociolinguistic context that informed them—appeared epistemologically unsophisticated.

Katz's theory has had its pervasive influence and its persuasive power because it adopted an *episteme*—which was and is becoming progressively culturally dominant—to overcome the conceptual impasse caused by the essentialists' inability cogently to bridge the gap between postexperiential mystical discourses and the experience(s) from which they supposedly arose.

Katz's model of the relationship between mystical experience and its interpretation is epistemologically a more subtle one than that of the essentialists. Most significantly, it enables us to take more cogently into account the plurality of mystical utterances. As noted earlier, it entails that there are a wide variety of phenomenologically discrete mystical experiences which are due to the cultural and conceptual settings in which they originate. Thus, in interpreting mystical texts, we can avoid the problems of having to accommodate very different interpretations to an identical experience as their core. Katz's theory gives us theoretical grounds for proceeding on the assumption that there may be a correspondence between a mystical experience that is shaped by a particular context and a retrospective interpretation that reflects the same context and, consequently, that reflects the mystical experience also.

However, although more subtle than its essentialist counterpart, it remains somewhat conceptually opaque. Primarily, this is the result of an absence of what is intended by context. The overall thrust of Katz's model is that there is a *necessary* connection between context and experience: "The significance of these theoretical and methodological considerations," he writes, "is that they *entail* that the forms of consciousness which the mystic brings to an experience set structured and limiting parameters on what the experience will be, i.e., on what will be experienced, and rule out in advance what is 'inexperienceable' in the particular, given, concrete context."[7] I want to argue that this claim, if true, is only so in a trivial sense.

In the passage quoted, Katz seems to suggest that the relationship between a mystical experience and the context out of which it arises is a logically necessary one, that the mystic *cannot but* experience in contextually determined ways. While one can agree with Katz that there is a strong *contingent* correlation between a mystical experience and its context, he has not given us any reasons that the connection is a necessary one. Consequently, he has failed to show how the mystical experience is *constituted* by the religious traditions out of which it arose.

Indeed, it is difficult to see how he could do so. As William Wainwright remarks, "The gastronomic experiences of Eskimos, Parisians and Vietnamese are quite different. There is a strong correlation between these experiences and their cultures. Nevertheless, it would be absurd to suppose that the connection was anything but contingent, and that a person from a different culture could not have the gastronomic experiences of an Eskimo."[8] So also with mystical experience: there is no logically compelling reason why a Christian could not have the experience of a Hindu, though one recognises that there are persuasive contingent grounds for this not often being the case.

To be sure, mystical experience may have, and often does have, a conservative ambience. By virtue of the fact that the mystic's context may be incorporated into his experience, he may experientially reaffirm or "verify" the tradition in which he is involved. The influential effect of the pre-experiential context is also reinforced by the role, on the mystic way, of the spiritual guide. The function of the teacher is, in part, psychological for he or she prevents the student from straying into dangerous psychological states. But just as significant is the teacher's sociological function. The teacher guides the student into experiences that reinforce the tradition, for he or she represents (in some cases is) the religious authority.

But all this does not entail that the mystic cannot experientially go beyond the confines of his religious tradition. It is simply a matter of historical fact that mystical experiences (religious experiences in general, for that matter) lead to the creative transformation of religious traditions. As Gershom Scholem points out, the kabbalist Isaac Luria "fully accepted the established religious authority, which indeed he undertook to reinforce by enhancing its stature and giving it deeper meaning." He continues, "the ideas he employed in this seemingly conservative task were utterly new and seem doubly daring in their conservative context."[9] Katz himself recognizes the hermeneutic artifices necessary to bring radical experiences into line with incompatible traditional texts:

> [T]he presupposition on which the mystical use of allegory and symbolic modes of exegesis depends is that the canonical books of one's tradition do in fact possess the *truth and authority* claimed for them. In the absence of this presupposition one need not bother with allegory or other hermeneutical aids, the text could be dispensed with altogether in favour of the new "higher" mystical truths vouchsafed to the mystics through their experience. But, in fact, there is no displacement of scripture; there is only "re-interpretation." Through this "re-interpretation" the extant spiritual classics *are shown to teach the very doctrines revealed anew to the mystic*.[10]

Through a radical hermeneutic, novel experiences take on a conservative ambience through the creative transformation of traditional repositories of religious truth and authority. In sum, this implies that (at least in some cases) mystical experiences can go beyond the structured and limiting parameters of the particular religious traditions which form them.

It can, of course, be argued that what appear to be exceptions to the constitutive nature of the pre-experiential context are not so at all, for the reason that, although they are not constituted by the received tradition, they are nonetheless constituted by another tradition. This is the move employed by Katz to explain the fact that there is a tension between mystical experiences of union between God and the soul, and mystical experience of the unity of God and the soul. Katz continues:

> It should also be noted that even the absorptive, non-absorptive dichotomy at work in Christian mysticism which might appear to contradict the contextual rootedness of mystical experience in fact supports it. The unitive Christian mystics are invariably those such as Eckhart, Tauler, and Suso, who have been schooled on Plotinus, Dionysius the Areopagite, and Augustine, i.e., the strong Neoplatonic current in Christian intellectual history.[11]

This kind of tactic renders the quest to find examples of experiences which are at odds with their apparent context a nugatory one; and it gives Katz's theory a flavor of unfalsifiability. In short, experiential novelty is ruled out *a priori*. Explanations of the sort cited by Katz herein secure the theoretical consistency of his account. Unfortunately, in so securing it, the theory appears epistemologically trivial. For, although the necessary connection between context and experience has been maintained, the meaning of the former has become so inclusive as to be, to all intents and purposes, indefinable. In the final analysis, therefore, while it is trivially true that the experience of a Christian mystic is formed by his cultural context, it is clearly not true that the experience of a Christian mystic is formed *solely* by a Christian context.

Moreover, the fact that Neoplatonism has played a role not only in the forming of Christian, but also in Judaic and Islamic mystical experiences is itself a strong argument against the implicit assumption in Katz's theory that the various mystical experiences of, say, Judaism, Islam, and Christianity are conceptually incommensurable. On the contrary, by virtue of the role that Neoplatonism plays in all the mystical traditions of these three traditions, there is a comparability between them. And this comparability is not merely at the level of mystical discourse but, if we follow Katz, at the level of experience, too. Put quite simply, there are not merely Christian and Islamic experiences, but Christian–Neoplatonic and Islamic–Neoplatonic mystical experiences which are commensurable by virtue of their shared Neoplatonic context.

The basic epistemological assertion which underlies Katz's claim that the content of mystical experiences is determined by its context is that there are no unmediated experiences. It is not obviously clear what Katz intends by this statement. No argument for it is offered and no clear explanation of it is given. In *Mysticism and Philosophical Analysis,* we are told that it means "*all* experience is processed through, organized by and makes itself available to us in extremely complex ways." And the same explanation is given *verbatim* with no further elaboration some five years later.[12] As such, it is uncontroversial.

But it is clear that, for Katz, this statement entails that there cannot be what Ninian Smart calls "consciousness-purity," what I have called elsewhere "contentless experience" or what Robert Forman calls a pure consciousness event.[13] In so doing Katz hopes to rule out the logical possibility of the occurrence of mystical experiences which, by virtue of their contentlessness, transcend the cultural contexts that produced them and which are, as a result, identical irrespective of the contexts in which they occur.

At the current stage of the debate, Katz has yet to offer any epistemological argument of a sufficiently general kind to compel assent to his claims that there cannot be pure experiences. He has merely asserted that all experience is *by definition* mediated, and he has attempted to persuade us to accept this with all the rhetorical power at his disposal. But until he provides us with a sufficiently elaborate epistemology to justify his claim, there is no logical compulsion for us to accept this epistemological premiss.

It is important to recognize that the decision not to accept Katz's claim that there cannot be pure consciousness events in the absence of any argument to that effect does not imply rejecting the notion that mystical experiences are intimately related to the contexts in which they occur. In the first place, insofar as we are talking of contentful mystical experiences, it is to be expected that there will be a strong correlation between experience and context. In the second place, it is clear that some religious and philosophical contexts are more conducive to the attainment of contentless experiences than others. That is to say, the contentless experience is more probably to be attained in the context of a set of doctrines which, say, are not grounded in the assumption of an essential discontinuity between God and the world, the transcendent and the mundane. Theravāda Buddhism is more conducive to consciousness—purity than is Evangelical Protestantism. Thus, it is possible to hold without inconsistency that all contentful mystical experiences are context-related and that contentless mystical experiences, although arising out of appropriate contexts, are qua contentless context-free.

I have maintained elsewhere that an appropriate methodology for the study of mystical experience needs to take into account not only the possibility of a variety of contentful mystical experiences which are context-related, but also the possibility that it is of the very nature of the practices and techniques associated with the "inward way" to conduce (though not necessarily) toward the attainment of contentless states of consciousness.[14] Although the analyses of mystical experience by Ninian Smart have tended to have proceeded on the methodological assumption of the unity of mystical experience,[15] he has more recently endorsed a position identical with the above:

> Though it is quite obvious that there are different varieties of mystical experience, and though it is quite obvious that interpretation gets, so to speak, built into experiences—thus making experiences of the same type different in particular ways—it does not follow that there does not exist a type to be identified cross-culturally as "consciousness-purity" or as "mystical". Such a view has the merit of making sense both of the facts the perennialists point to and of the undoubted differences of exposition, flavour, and significance as between the various traditions.[16]

Granting that there are no logical problems in admitting the possibility of pure consciousness events, there are, to be sure, hermeneutical difficulties in establishing their occurrence from the analysis of mystical texts. Whether we adopt Katz's model or the model I have proposed, we are still faced with the necessity of establishing the nature of any particular mystic's experiences by examining the retrospective interpretations of those experiences. Whatever one's theoretical position might be, common hermeneutical problems abound, and all textual analyses are corrigible. However, I would want to argue that the most appropriate methodology to adopt is one which enables us to take most seriously the only data we have, that is, the mystic's reports. Moreover, I remain still convinced that there are some mystical reports which are most appropriately to be construed as interpretations of pure consciousness events. Consequently I am reluctant to endorse any a priori theory of the nature of mystical experience which may impose unjustified theoretical restrictions on the hermeneutic task.

One must admit that Katz is right to point out that all mystical language is grounded in specific syntactical and semantic structures and that, therefore, the meaning of any one particular mystical term is only to be discerned in the totality of mystical discourses of which it is a part. But different mystical discourses are not totally incommensurable anymore than are different languages. And it is clearly not absurd to argue, as I have suggested above, that mystical discourses can be compared.

Moreover, even if *descriptions* of mystical experiences from different religious traditions were incommensurable, it would still be possible to argue that they were derived from phenomenologically identical pure consciousness events. For the contentless experience is, by its formless nature, compatible with a number of incompatible or incommensurable doctrinal systems, and herein lies its appeal for those who would argue for the unity of all religions on the basis of it.

If the arguments above are cogent, then there is nothing impossible in principle (however, difficult in practice) in determining from mystical interpretations the nature of the experiences on which they were based, irrespective of whether the experiences are contentful or contentless. And there is no conceptual absurdity in arguing that the analysis of mystical texts could demonstrate both that there are contentless experiences and that they can occur within a number of different religious contexts.

All this suggests the need for a more complex theory of mystical experience than that suggested either by Katz or the essentialists. In the analysis of mystical discourse, we need to recognize that contexts may shape the nature of the experience by being incorporated into it. But also, because mystical experience may transcend its apparent context, we have to recognize that mystical experience may be decisive in the formulation of new, or the revision of existing, religious traditions, and this, whether it be content-filled or contentless.

NOTES

1. S. Katz, ed., *Mysticism and Philosophical Analysis*, (London: Sheldon Press, 1978).

2. N. Smart, "The Purification of Consciousness and the Negative Path," in Katz, ed., *Mysticism and Religious Traditions* (Oxford University Press, 1983), pp. 117–29.

3. R. M. Jones, *Studies in Mystical Religion* (London: Macmillan, 1909), p. xxxiv.

4. See, e.g., M. Eliade, *The Two and the One* (London: Harvihill, 1965), H. P. Owen, "Christian Mysticism," *Religious Studies* 7 (1971), 31–42, B. Garside, "Language and the Interpretation of Mystical Experience," *International Journal for the Philosophy of Religion* 3 (1972), 93–102, and P. C. Almond, "On the Varieties of Mystical Experience," *Sophia* 18 (1979), 1–9.

5. P. C. Almond, *Mystical Experience and Religious Doctrine* (Berlin: Mouton, 1982).

6. See, e.g., H. H. Penner, "The Mystical Illusion," in Katz, *Mysticism and Religious Traditions*, p. 89.

7. Katz, *Mysticism and Religious Traditions*, p. 5, [Emphasis added.]

8. W. J. Wainwright, *Mysticism: A study of Its Nature, Cognitive Value, and Moral Implications* (Madison: University of Wisconsin Press, 1981), pp. 20–21.

9. G. Scholem, *On the Kabbalah and Its Symbolism* (New York: Schocken, 1965), p. 21.

10. Katz, *Mysticism and Religious Traditions*, p. 30. [Emphasis added.]

11. Katz, *Mystical Experience*, p. 42.

12. Ibid., p. 26; Katz, *Mysticism and Religious Traditions,* p. 4.

13. See Almond, *Mystical Experience,* and Robert K. C. Forman, "Pure Consciousness Events and Mysticism," *Sophia* 25 (1986), 49.

14. See Almond, *Mystical Experience,* pp. 157–80.

15. See, especially, N. Smart, "Interpretation and Mystical Experience," *Religious Studies* 1 (1965), 75–87.

16. Smart, "Purification," p. 125.

Are Pure Consciousness
Events Unmediated?

STEPHEN BERNHARDT

During the summer of 1986 Steven Bernhardt was killed in an automobile accident. The present paper was submitted and accepted at that time, although it was overlong and in a fairly rough form. In order to include it in the present collection, and to ensure that Bernhardt's contribution did not go unacknowledged, I have substantially revised his paper. While clarifying and condensing, I have tried to remain as close to the spirit and letter of the original as possible. It is my fond hope that the author would approve of the paper as it now appears.—Ed.

The experience of pure consciousness can be characterized as follows: The subject is awake, conscious, but without an object or content of consciousness—no thoughts, emotions, sensations, or awareness of any external phenomena. Nothing. During the event the subject is not even aware "Oh, I am experiencing *X*" or "I am having an extraordinary experience." Yet the subject is not asleep and may afterwards also report confidently that he or she was not asleep. Because one of the problems with the experience of pure consciousness is that it differs so radically from other types of experience, we may not want to call it an *experience*. With Forman, I will henceforward refer to it as the pure consciousness event.[1] Whether it deserves the name "experience" is a question to which I will return later.

It is not part of my object to prove that the pure consciousness event is veridical: based on evidence put forward in Part I of this volume, I will assume that this event occurs. Rather, I want to discuss what seem to me to be the key philosophical issues raised by this phenomenon. In the first section of this essay I will argue that we can reconcile the nonintentionality, which the mystics indicate to be a characteristic of this state, with the intentionality of some descriptions of this state. In the second section I will argue that this state may be phenomenally identical, even though the supposed objects of the experiences may differ. In the third section I will expand on this to consider the problem of the universality of mystical experiences. In the fourth section I will address the objections which contemporary students of mysticism, specifically those in accord with Steven Katz (the so-called constructivists), would be likely to bring against my position. Here, the essay takes a polemical turn, arguing that pure consciousness events are counterexamples to Katz's claims (1) that pure consciousness does not exist, (2) that there are no universal mystical experiences, and (3) that there are no unmediated experiences. In the final section I will briefly consider whether pure consciousness should be understood as an experience.

RECONCILING THE NON-INTENTIONALITY OF THE PURE CONSCIOUSNESS EVENT WITH THE INTENTIONALITY OF SOME DESCRIPTIONS

During the pure consciousness event the subject is awake, conscious, but without an object or content of consciousness. Yet sometimes mystics say that there is a very definite content or object with which the mystic comes into relation during the experience in question. In the Yoga system described by Christopher Chappel in this volume, it is Purusha, or the absolute self (as opposed to the empirical self), that is realized during the experience of Kaivalya.[2] For the experiences, described by Charles Alexander and others, that result from the practice of the transcendental meditation (TM) technique, it is the Self that is equated with the Absolute or Being—that substance which in its various permutations and combinations gives rise to the subjective and objective worlds—which the mind "reaches" during the experience of transcendental consciousness.[3] And in the writings of Eckhart it is the "Godhead" with which one merges during the experience of *gezucket*.[4] This divergence presents two problems.

First, to identify these experiences as pure consciousness events seems to contradict the claims of the mystics who have them.[5] The authors in this volume have claimed that there is no object or content of consciousness during the event, whereas these mystics' language would imply that their experiences are without a doubt the experience "of" some definite *X*.

I do not propose to determine whether or not any individual scholar(s) has accurately represented his or her primary figures. What I do hope to do is to show how it may be that such a discrepancy as this could plausibly and rightly be said to exist. That is, I hope to show how a mystic may use intentional language to express a nonintentional event.

Here is my proposed solution: it may be that the experience said to be "of *X*" *just is* a contentless, objectless pure consciousness event. That is, with reference to what it is like to have an experience (while it occurs), an experience may be a contentless alert consciousness, whereas with reference to how it is analytically understood, it may be presented as an occasion wherein an *X* is encountered. For Eckhart, for example, the experience of the One is not something which one gets *after* the elimination of all "creatures" and all diversity from the soul. Rather, the undifferentiated state of the soul *just is* the experience of the One. This is what Eckhart means when he says that "when the soul is unified and there enters into total self-abnegation, then she finds God"[6] or "where creature stops, there God begins to be."[7]

Generally, intentional experience talk (*A* encounters *X*) implies that a conscious subject is aware of something distinguished from his or her own consciousness. Yet here there is, *per hypotheosi*, no such match. It seems to me that to make sense of this divergence we need only believe that the mystic is using that intentional language in a novel or askew sense. We need only not read an experiential intentionality off a grammatical one.

This is not an implausible way of reading mystical texts. Mystics are renowned for asserting that the ordinary relations of experience do not hold for mystical experiences. Franklin Merrell Wolff, for example, a twentieth-century mystic, describes his relation with the one as a "knowledge through identity."[8] In this epistemological structure, the ordinary (intentional) relations of subject and object which characterize all other knowledge states do not obtain. Maharishi Mahesh Yogi echoes this notion when he says that the mind knows the Absolute "by being it."[9] For Eckhart one comes to know the Godhead by finding It at the ground of one's own soul. None of these relations are intentional in structure, yet all are described with intentional grammar.

An Eckhart or a Franklin Merrell Wolff, for obvious reasons, are driven to use intentional language. Largely because it was developed in a world in which subject/object relations obtain, it is the language they inherited. In addition an Eckhart is religiously driven to conceive of any mystical state(s) as in some sense connected with God. That is, given his conceptual framework, there may be perfectly plausible reasons (other than that the experience is "of" some *X*) to analytically associate a pure consciousness event with the Godhead.

In other words, to make sense of the claimed distinction between intentional language and nonintentional experiences all we need to maintain about the language used by mystics is that the ordinary intentional experiential implications cannot be assumed to hold for this bit of intentional grammar.

What the mystic needs is a language for experience which carries no dualistic implications. Much of their language may be seen (as I have just noted) as an attempt to develop or push toward such a syntax. Expressions like "merges with," "is engulfed by," "like a drop becoming the ocean," and so on, may be thus construed.

HOW THE EXPERIENTIAL EVENTS CAN BE PHENOMENALLY IDENTICAL WHILE THE SUPPOSED "OBJECTS" OF THE EXPERIENCE ARE DIVERSE

A second problem arises from the divergence between intentional language and nonintentional experiences. If experiences of Purusha, Maharishi's Absolute, or Eckhart's Godhead may all be described as instances of pure consciousness events—vis-à-vis what it is like to have the experience (hereafter simply "vis-à-vis phenomenal properties")—and if scholars are not mistaken when they say that the experience of Purusha, the Absolute, or the One are states of consciousness without content, then it follows that vis-à-vis their phenomenal properties these experiences are identical. However, this is not to say (what would be absurd) that the experiences are numerically identical. Any two pure consciousness events are had by definite persons at certain times and places; the mystics' bodies and positions and conditions differ; they got into their respective states in a certain way; and so on. All these militate for a numerical nonidentity. Therefore, when I say that the experience of Purusha, the Absolute, and the One are identical, it is a form of type identity that I affirm. I mean that the experiences are identical vis-à-vis their phenomenal properties. From now on I will say simply that they are "phenomenally identical."

The problem raised is this: the identification of the experiences of the One, Purusha, and the Absolute affirmed herein might seem to imply that my position presupposes or entails the identification of Patañjali's Purusha, Maharishi's Absolute, and Eckhart's Godhead. After all, if the event described in each system is described as an experience of some X, how could the experiential event in these cases be identical if that X is different in each case?

Again, I do not propose to determine whether or not any particular set of mystics is, indeed, describing pure consciousness events. My attempt here is to show what must be the case if two mystics can be said to have phenomenally identical experiences.

Here is my proposed solution: two pure consciousness events may be identical insofar as *what it is like* during those experiential are identical.

To explain, let me distinguish between an objective and a subjective sense of "what is experienced" as inspired by the work of Thomas Nagel.[10] In the objective sense of the phrase, a bat and a human being each experience the same thing when a insect is two feet in front of their noses. "What is experienced" in both cases is an insect. However, in the subjective sense of the phrase, what is experienced is quite different. For what it is like to sense an insect by means of sonar must be quite different from what it is like to sense one by vision. Here there are *two distinct subjective experiences*—a human's and a bat's—of a single object of experience. In the case of the pure consciousness event, the reverse is true: there is a *single subjective experience* which the mystics claim to be the experience of *quite different objects*.

Another example of the difference between the objective and subjective senses of "what is experienced" is a mirage. This is more symmetrical with the pure consciousness case. When a man dying of thirst in a desert hallucinates an oasis in the distance, what it is like for him to "see" that oasis is (at least with respect to what it is like *visually*) much the same as what it is like to really see an oasis. If it were not, we would not call it an hallucination of an oasis and not something else. For the very reason we call it a mirage *of X* is that what it is like to have it is much the same (we might even say exactly the same) as what it is like to have a veridical experience of *X*. However, it is not veridical: in the objective sense of "what is experienced," there is a difference between his oasis and ours. The point is that "what is experienced" in the subjective sense can be identical, whereas "what is experienced" in the objective sense differs. Claims of objective identity or divergence are not enough to guarantee subjective identity or divergence.

Turning now to mystical texts, after careful textual analysis, we may determine that no characteristics are apparent to the subject while the mystical event is taking place. If this is true of events reported in two texts, then there are no differences on the basis of which we can differentiate the subjective sense of what it is like to experience the one mystical event (say of Purusha) from another (say of the Godhead). If any two texts describe contentless events, then we might reasonably conclude that what is experienced in each case is phenomenally the same. Under these circumstances the differences between the supposed "objects" of these experiences is immaterial to the phenomenal identity of the subjective sense of the experiences themselves.

In conclusion if we maintain that there may be a difference between the subjective and objective senses of what is experienced and if this applies to mystical experiences, then we may conclude that two mystical experiences may be alike despite differences in purported "objects." If two mystical experiences are both determined to be instances of pure consciousness events, then there would be nothing on whose basis we should phenomenally distinguish them. We could, therefore, assert them to be phenomenally identical.

Two caveats: such expressions as "phenomenal properties," "'what it is like' to have an experience," and "'what is experienced' in the subjective sense"—and the distinctions of which they are a part—are not intended to resurrect some form of the myth of the given or a sense-data theory. On the contrary my distinction slices up experience at quite different angles. The phenomenal properties of an experience are that set of properties the conjunction of which specify what it is like to have that experience. These may include, but are not limited to, sensory properties and ordinary-object concepts. Others of these properties might require a talented poet to portray. Furthermore, when I speak of a subjective sense of "what is experienced" I do not mean that what we *really* experience, that is, what we are *immediately* aware of, is phenomenal properties. For, to say that we can specify what it is like to have an experience is to say nothing about what is "really" or "immediately" experienced.

IS THE PURE CONSCIOUSNESS EVENT UNIVERSAL?

Contemporary students of mysticism who are sensitive to the doctrinal differences in the system under consideration will, no doubt, balk at the conclusion that the experiences of Kaivalya, transcendental consciousness, and Eckhart's *gezucken* may be identical in any interesting sense. For the central theme of most of the philosophical work done on mysticism in the last decade has been an emphasis on the culturally relative nature of mystical experiences. The recent fashion[11] has been to call into question the old standards in the study of mysticism—Evelyn Underhill, Rudolf Otto, W. T. Stace, R. C. Zaehner, and William James[12]—with their espousals of universal characteristics or typologies for mysticism, which assume that mysticism in its essentials is basically the same everywhere. But as the pendulum swings, I believe there is a tendency to commit the converse error, namely, to conclude that mystical experiences are everywhere different. The pure consciousness event, I will argue now, is the most likely available candidate for the title of "universal mystical experience."

The engine which drives the contemporary reaction against claims of a universal experience is the epistemological doctrine that all of our experiences are mediated by conceptual or cognitive elements of some kind and that these mediating factors are, at least in part, cultural acquisitions which, in part, restrict the occurrence of certain experiences to certain definite cultural contexts. In his recent "Language, Epistemology and Mysticism," Steven Katz—perhaps the most outspoken opponent of these views—states the first part of the doctrine:

> To get a clearer conception of what this paper is after when it speaks of the issue of "Why mystical experiences are the experiences they are," let me state the single epistemological assumption that has exercised my thinking and which has forced me to undertake the present investigation: *There are NO pure (i.e., unmediated) experiences.* Neither mystical experience nor more ordinary forms of experience give any indication, or any grounds for believing, that they are unmediated. That is to say, *all* experience is processed through, organized by, and makes itself available to us in extremely complex epistemological ways. The notion of unmediated experience seems, if not self-contradictory, at best empty.[13]

The remainder of Katz's paper argues: first, that the forms of consciousness (the mediating elements), which the mystic brings to experience and which, in part, create it are ideologically and culturally grounded; and, second, that "this process of differentiation of mystical experience into the patterns and symbols of established religious communities is experiential and not only takes place in the postexperiential process of reporting and interpreting the experience itself, but is also at work before, during, and after the experience."[14]

Though Katz makes perfunctory bows to the possibility of mystical experiences which are the same across different cultures or different ideological and theological traditions,[15] his general position comes out somewhat as follows: wherever there is a difference in the conceptual scheme which the mystic brings into his experience, the mystical experience will be different. I will call this Katz's thesis of radical pluralism. The related methodological directive is that understanding mysticism is as much a matter of understanding the conceptual schemes which in large part shape mystical experiences as it is a matter of examining any postexperiential reports. Katz, thus, believes that he has an answer for both to the question of why mystical experiences are the experiences that they are and of how we can determine why they are what they are. The experiences are what they are because the mystic's conceptual scheme (ideological, theological, cultural) mediates and informs them. And we can determine why the experiences are what they are by discerning the relevant context of conditioning.[16]

My claim that mystics of quite diverse mystical traditions place different interpretations on experiences which are phenomenally identical (the pure consciousness event) would not fare well on Katz's account, for it flies in the face of his claims that all experiences are interpreted. On this view, we do not have raw experiences and interpret them later. Rather, we as it were experience our interpretations; to experience is (at least in part) to interpret. Yet I am claiming that the pure consciousness event is in some sense uninterpreted.

I will grant for the sake of the argument, and because I think it is reasonable, that some epistemological doctrine (such as Katz's) holds for ordinary (nonmystical) experiences. However, just as Katz argues against proving "in essentially circular fashion" by a priori assumptions that all mystical experiences are the same or similar,[17] I would argue against *dis*proving the possibility of an unmediated experience in like fashion.

How does Katz disprove the possibility of unmediated experiences? This comes up in his disproof of pure consciousness. His first remarks suggest that he does not acknowledge the existence of a state of pure consciousness for empirical reasons: "there is no substantive evidence to suggest that there is any pure consciousness *per se* achieved by these various, common mystical practices, e.g., fasting yoga and the like."[18] What "substantive evidence" does he examine and debunk? In the passage which follows this remark, he contents himself with noting that the way and the "goal" are understood by the various yogic systems differently.[19] While his insights are interesting, why should such differences necessarily imply that the adepts of these various schools are having different *experiences* during what they each call *samādhi?* The only way we can make the leap from doctrinal differences to experiential differences is by making two assumptions: (1) whenever a mystic seeks his mystical experience in the context of a tradition of belief, his experience must be mediated by that belief system, and (2) wherever there are doctrinal differences there must necessarily be differences in the experiences themselves. But these two assumptions are just Katz's claims: the mediation claim and the thesis of radical pluralism! I need hardly observe that this is a form of arguing "in essentially circular fashion" on the basis of a priori assumptions.

The question about pure consciousness, then, comes down to the question, Are there any counterexamples to his central thesis that all mystical experiences are contextually mediated?[20] Instead of addressing the issues, Katz simply begs it by assuming the very thesis in question to illustrate his point. The obvious possible counterinstance, pure consciousness, has been excluded outright on a priori principles. This is ironic when viewed against the last passage of his essay in which he summarizes what he sees as the advantages of his contextual approach:

> A strong supporting element in favor of our pluralistic account is found in the fact that our position is able to accomodate *all* the evidence which is accounted for by non-pluralistic accounts without being reductionistic, i.e., it is able to do more justice to the specificity of the evidence and its inherent distinctions and disjunctions than can the alternative approaches. That is to say, our account neither (a) overlooks any evidence, nor (b) has any need to simplify the available evidence to fit into comparative or comparable categories.[21]

On the contrary Katz *does* overlook the kind of evidence offered in Part I of this volume and *is* reductionistic. He maintains that mystical experience is epistemologically identical to ordinary experience in that it is mediated by elements picked up from the context in which the experience occurs. This approach must force mystical experience into the same general category—mediated experience—that all (most?) other experiences fall into. He has ignored the radical disjunction which some mystics claim to hold between ordinary experience and the pure consciousness event, thereby reducing in effect mystical experiences to ordinary ones.

Katz must also argue that certain mystical texts are mistaken about the phenomenal characteristics of mystical events. He holds that differences of doctrines necessarily imply differences of experience. If this is true, then two mystics—say Patañjali and Farrow's female subject—must have had different experiences during their respective events. This implies that there were differences in phenomenal content between these two. Yet Patañjali says that *asamprajñatā samādhi* is a state of mind without any fluctuations of consciousness; and Farrow's subject reports that it was as if her mind were "wiped clean." The only way that Katz's claim can be maintained for these two is to claim that both authors are *mistaken* and that there was some distinguishable content on whose basis differences could be maintained.[22] This is a form of arguing against the text.

Is the pure consciousness event a universal mystical experience? As I read the evidence in Part I of this volume, I would answer, yes, but with clarifications: that is by a "universal" mystical experience I do not mean that every mystic has undergone such or even that some mystics in each of the major traditions of mysticism has. It is doubtful that *any* kind of mystical experience can fulfill this requirement. By "universal" I mean the lesser claim that this phenomenon occurs in a variety of different religious and mystical traditions, traditions which in other respects (and even in respect of how they interpret the pure consciousness event itself) diverge radically. Finally it is only with respect to the phenomenal properties of experiences (during the event) that the pure consciousness event is universal.

IS THE PURE CONSCIOUSNESS EVENT MEDIATED?

In the foregoing I have considered the question of identity with reference to mystical experiences themselves. Now I want to consider the question of the identity between mystical experiences and other types of (ordinary) experiences. This is in amplification of my remark that Katz has reduced mystical experiences to ordinary ones.

I will grant for the sake of the argument that most or even all nonmystical experiences are mediated. The question I want to consider is this: Has it been shown that mystical experiences are mediated in the same or in a similar sense?

This is a very difficult question to answer, in part, because of the fuzziness and ambiguity with which "mediated" has been used. I believe that Katz uses the term with two general senses. First, there is a causal or extrinsic notion. In this sense our experiences are mediated in that we are led to them or seek them, allow certain of them and disallow certain others—and all of this on the basis of the influence of the particular sociocultural, theological, linguistic, or historical context in which we find ourselves. This is the notion Katz has in mind when he makes such remarks as:

> The experience that the mystic or yoga [sic] has is the experience he seeks as a consequence of the shared beliefs he holds through his metaphysical doctrinal commitments.[23]

> The preconditioning of the Buddhist consciousness is very different from that of the Jewish and this difference generates the radically different mystical experience which the Buddhist aims at and reaches.[24]

> What I wish to show is only that there is a clear causal connection between the religious and social structure one brings to experience and the nature of one's actual religious experience.[25]

> The Buddhist experience of *nirvāṇa*, the Jewish of *devekuth*, and the Christian of *uniomystica*, the Sufi of *fana*, the Taoist of *Tao* are the result, at least in part, of specific conceptual influences, i.e., the "starting problems" of each doctrinal, theological system.[26]

Thus, certain "shared beliefs," "preconditioning," religious and social structure, and "specific conceptual influences" are mediators of mystical experiences in the sense that they cause or make possible certain experiences and disallow others. Whether these various constructive mediators are, in fact, the same thing and what the "clear causal connection" is in each case between the mediator and that which is mediated is left unclear. What Katz means by his "single epistemological assumption" that there are no unmediated experiences is, at best, vague. Hence the foundation of Katz's enterprise is somewhat soft.

The second general sense of mediation in Katz's discussion does not make things firmer. It is more epistemological and intrinsic in flavor. In this sense, experiences are mediated in that what the mystic experiences, the actual subjective content of the experience—either in its form or matter (in a roughly Kantian sense)—involves, is constituted by, or is contributed from the "conceptual scheme," belief system, and so on, which the mystic brings to the experience. It is this which Katz communicates when he says such things as:

> The experience itself as well as the form in which it is reported is shaped by concepts which the mystic brings to, and which shape, his experience.[27]

> This process of differentiation of mystical experience into the patterns and symbols of established religious communities is experiential . . . it is at work before, during and after the experience.[28]

> The creative role of the self in his experience is not analogous to the passive role of the tape-recorder or camera. Even in mystical experience, there seems to be epistemological activity of the sort we know as discrimination and integration, and, in certain cases at least, of further mental activities such as relating the present experience to past and future experience, as well as traditional theological claims and metaphysics.[29]

Again, Katz mentions a diverse group of elements which all are supposed to be mediators of mystical experiences: "concepts," "patterns and symbols," and "memory, apprehension, expectation, language, accumulation of prior experiences." The activity of mediating, too, is given various names: "shaping, "process of differentiation," "discrimination and integration and . . . relating the present experience to past and future experience." One wonders how all of these elements and processes fit together, or even if they do. Again, the lack of a full-blooded and carefully thought out epistemology is felt.

Though I cannot flesh out Katz's epistemology, the following may clarify what he has in mind:

> 1. The difference between these two senses of mediation is akin to the difference between the efficient cause and the formal or material cause of an event (in the Aristotlean sense). The causal or extrinsic sense of mediation is an efficient cause; the epistemological mediation is either the formal or material cause of the event.

2. Katz may intend something like an analogy with games. Games, like experiences, can be said to be mediated in two different senses. First, a game is mediated by a certain social context which makes it possible for the game to be played. Second, a game is mediated by a referee and a set of rules which structure and define the activities within the game. Here, too, the distinct senses of cause can been seen. To determine the cause of my playing basketball I will give different answers to the question, "Why is this game played?" I could answer (a) "for fun diversion, exercise, and so on." or (b) "to win the highest score by making the greatest number of goals according to the rules." The first cause mediates the game extrinsically and is related to the efficient cause of the event that is the playing of the game. The second cause mediates the game intrinsically and is its formal cause.

Returning to the pure consciousness event, I think we can now give a more precise answer to the question whether it is mediated. In the first sense of mediation, extrinsic or efficient cause, there is no doubt that the pure consciousness event is sought as a result of certain conditions. The experience of the pure consciousness event is typically (though not necessarily)[30] sought and obtained in an external set of circumstances which make the event possible and important. Katz is on this interpretation correct when he says:

> It is in appearance only that such activities as yoga produce the desired state of "pure" consciousness. Properly understood, yoga, for example, is *not* an *un*conditioning or *de*conditioning of consciousness, but rather it is a *re*conditioning of consciousness, i.e., a substituting of one form of conditioned and/or contextual consciousness for another, albeit a new, unusual and perhaps altogether more interesting form of conditioned-contextual consciousness.[31]

Clearly, the pure consciousness event is mediated in the sense that it occurs typically in a certain context, as an effect of the influence of that context.

But this does not imply that it is mediated in the second or epistemologically heavy intrinsic sense in which Katz also intimates it is. This is the sense which is critical to his thesis as a whole, especially his radical pluralism. What I have in mind and what I think Katz has in mind when he speaks about the use of concepts during experiences is that all experiences involve recognition of something, even if it is only an unidentified something, and that this involves concept use, memory, comparison, and so on, "This much is certain: the mystical experience must be mediated by the kinds of beings that we are. And the kinds of beings that we are requires that experience be not only instantaneous and discontinuous, but that it also involves memory, apprehension, expectation, language, accumulation of prior experience, concepts, and expectations, with each experience being built on the back of all these elements and being shaped anew by each fresh experience."[32] All experience is the experience of *something,* perceived as an instance of some concept or set of concepts. This philosophical idea finds its first clear formulation in Kant's *Critique of Pure Reason,* "Now all experience does contain in addition to the intuitions of the senses through which something is given, a concept of an object as being thereby given, that is to say, as appearing."[33]

Does the pure consciousness event involve concepts in this Kantian sense? No, not if the reports of the mystics are correct. For, on their account the mystic is not aware *of* anything during the event. This is no something, no instance of a concept, of which the mystic is aware.

In other words, it is hard to see how one could say that the pure consciousness event is mediated, if by that it is meant that *during the event* the mystic is employing concepts; differentiating his awareness according to religious patterns and symbols; drawing upon memory, apprehension, expectation, language or the accumulation of prior experience; or discriminating and integrating. Without the encounter with any object, intention, or thing, it just does not seem that there is sufficient complexity during the pure consciousness event to say that any such conceptually constructive elements are involved.

IS THE PURE CONSCIOUSNESS EVENT AN EXPERIENCE?

When we ask this question we are dealing with a term with a whole range of uses, some of which do and some of which do not imply intentionality. Some do not even imply consciousness: "Chicago experienced its coldest winter in recorded history this year" or "Most adults are experienced sleepers." No doubt, most of us would find no difficulty in accepting that the pure consciousness event is an experience is some such broad sense. No one would feel uncomfortable if someone said, after having been through a pure consciousness event, "I just had a most extraordinary experience!" Nor would most of us feel uncomfortable with a physiologist saying, "These are the typical physiological correlates of her pure consciousness experiences which preceded her button pushes."

However, among our uses of the term "experience" there is a narrower, more philosophical use. It is that experiences are one and all experiences *of* something. This meaning is of a piece with Husserl's claim that intentionality is a "peculiarity distinctive of experiences,"[34] "the unique peculiarity of experiences."[35] Experiences in this sense are ordinarily mediated by concepts, are contextual, and so on. If by "experience" we mean something in this sense, then we might want to deny that the pure consciousness event is an experience. For as I understand this phenomenon, it is a state of consciousness which is nonintentional and not mediated by concepts. It is a state in which consciousness, though not extinguished, stands in conscious relation to nothing; consciousness is by and in itself.

Yet, paradoxically, this is the one factor which might encourage us to call this event an experience in the narrow philosophical sense. For vis-à-vis experiential characteristics, it has in common with intentional experiences just that the mystic is conscious. Being conscious may serve as a plausible determinative sign of what we should regard as an experience.

It seems to me that rather than denying "experiencehood" of this event, we would be wiser to expand our philosophical notion of "experience" to include any and all events had by conscious beings. Along these lines we should also expand our definition of other mind-terms. Brentano's famous definition of the mental seems too narrow, "Every mental phenomenon is characterized by what the scholastics of the Middle Ages called the intentional (and also mental) inexistence . . . of an object . . . and what we would call, although in not entirely unambiguous terms, the reference to a content, a direction upon an object."[36] It is too limiting to claim that everything mental is intentional. For if we say nothing else, simply by virtue of the subject's being conscious, we want to say that this state is *mental*. What the pure consciousness event suggests is that there is no simple nontrivial characterization of the "mental" on whose basis we can rule out the possibility of certain events.[37] On the other hand, this does not mean that based solely hereon, we can identify an alternative characterization of "the mental," as, for example, equivalent to "conscious." Such a definition would exclude unconscious beliefs, for example, which we would want to call mental. Hence, the pure consciousness event stands as evidence not for the building of a new theory, but for the abandonment of an old one.[38]

Similarly, certain definitions of consciousness begin to seem too narrow. Sartre and Husserl claimed that "all consciousness is consciousness *of* something."[39] This cannot be maintained, for if the mystic is anything during this state, she or he is conscious. At best, this phenomenon must disabuse us of certain proposals, for example, this claim concerning the intentionality of all consciousness. I would suggest that, again, there is no single, nontrivial definition of consciousness;[40] instead the term "consciousness" has a range of uses with family resemblances, not all of which necessarily carry an intentional implication.

We would be wise to let the full range of phenomena dictate the meanings of our terms "consciousness," the "mental," and "experience."

NOTES

1. Robert K. C. Forman, "Mysticism and Pure Consciousness Events", *Sophia* 25, no. 1, (April 1986), pp. 49–58.

2. Christopher Chappel, "The unseen seer and the Field: Consciousness in Sāṃkhya and Yoga," in the present volume.

3. Charles Alexander et al., "Pure Consciousness During Transcendental Meditation: Phychophysiological Correlates and Subjective Experiences," unpublished paper. See also Maharishi Mahesh Yogi, *On the Bhagavad Gita* (Baltimore, md.: Penguin, 1967), pp. 144, 344, 393–94, and 423 for his claim that transcendental consciousness is an experience of consciousness of the Self and Absolute or Being. Idem, *Science of Being and Art of Living* (Livingston Manor, N.Y.: MIU Press, 1966) for his claim that the Absolute Being is the "stuff" of creation, pp. 25–44, especially pp. 27–29). On pp. 50–56 he explains how it is possible to contact and experience being.

4. See Robert K. C. Forman, "Eckhart, *Gezücken* and the Ground of the Soul," in the present volume.

5. I am taking a certain liberty in calling Maharishi or the practitioners of his system "mystics," since Maharishi repudiates such a label for himself or for anyone who practices the TM program. He claims that the practice of the TM technique and the state of transcendental consciousness are, far from being strange or impractical, very natural and highly practical (meaning that they make one more effective in daily life). My use of the term however does not carry with it the connotations or value judgments which Maharishi seems to associate with it, but rather refers only to the kind of person who has or has had certain types of experiences.

6. *Meister Eckhart: Sermons and Tractates,* trans. M. O'C. Walshe, (London: Watkins, 1979–1981), vol. 1, p. 157.

7. Ibid., vol. I, p. 118.

8. Franklin Merrell Wolff, *Pathways Through to Self* (New York: Warner Book, 1973).

9. Maharishi Mahesh Yogi, "Mechanics of Gaining Knowledge of an Object," (Fairfield, Iowa: MIU Film and Tape Library; recorded August 1971, Amherst, Mass.).

10. Thomas Nagel, "What Is It Like to Be a Bat?" *Philosophical Review* 82 (October 1974), pp. 435–50.

11. See Stephen Katz, ed., *Mysticism and Philosophical Analysis* (New York: Oxford University Press, 1978), especially the articles by Katz, Streng, Gimello, Keller, and Moore. See also Stephen Katz, ed., *Mysticism and Religious Tradi-*

tions, (New York: Oxford University Press, 1983), especially the articles by Katz, Penner, and Gimello.

12. Evelyn Underhill, *Mysticism* (New York: Dutton, 1911); Rudolf Otto, *Mysticism East and West* trans. Bertha Bracey and Richerda Payne (New York: Macmillan, 1932, repr. 1960); W. T. Stace *Mysticism and Philosophy,* (London: Macmillan, 1960; rpt. Atlantic Highlands, N.J.: Humanities Press, 1978); R. C. Zaehner, *Mysticism Sacred and Profane* (Oxford: 1961); William James, *The Varieties of Religious Experience* (1902).

13. Steven Katz, "Language, Epistemology, and Mysticism," pp. 25–26. [Emphasis in original.]

14. Ibid., p. 27.

15. Ibid., p. 65.

16. Katz does mention that the "object" of experience influences the content of experience. But no sooner does he mention it than he takes it away by saying that the mystic "only knows things as they 'appear' to him" (Ibid., p. 64.) Thus, the object is constituted at least in part by the cultural context.

17. Ibid., p. 65.

18. Ibid., p. 57.

19. Ibid., pp. 57–58.

20. This is clear from the discussion preceding his remarks on pure consciousness, ibid., pp. 56–57.

21. Ibid., p. 66.

22. J. T. Farrow and J. R. Hebert, "Breath Suspension During the Transcendental Meditation Technique," *Psychosomatic Medicine* 44 (1982), 133–153. See Anthony N. Perovich, Jr.'s article "Does the Philosophy of Mysticism Rest on a Mistake?", in the present volume.

23. Katz, "Language, Epistemology, and Mysticism, " p. 58.

24. Ibid., p. 36.

25. Ibid., p. 40.

26. Ibid., p. 62.

27. Ibid., p. 26.

28. Ibid., p. 27.

29. Ibid., p. 60.

30. See William McCready and Andrew Greely, "Are We a Nation of Mystics?" *New York Times Magazine,* 26 Jan. 1975, pp. 12–25.

31. Katz, "Language, Epistemology, and Mysticism." p. 57.

32. Ibid., p. 59.

33. Immanuel Kant, *Critique of Pure Reason,* trans. N. K. Smith (New York: St. Martin's Press, 1965), A93–B126.

34. Edmund Husserl, *Ideas,* trans. W. R. Boyce Gibson (New York: Humanities Press, 1931), p. 241.

35. Ibid., p. 242.

36. Franz Brentano, *Psychologie vom Empirischen Standpunkt,* trans. D. B. Terrell, vol. I, bk. II, chap. 1, "The Distinction Between Mental and Physical

Phenomena" (Leipzig, E. Ger.: 1874). From R. Chisholm, *Realism and the Background of Phenomenology*, trans. D. B. Terrell (Atascadero, Ca: n.p. 1960), p. 50.

37. Paul J. Griffiths "Pure Consciousness and Indian Buddhism," in the present volume, argues from Yogacarin thinkers that the pure consciousness event cannot be mental. I believe that his characterization of the mental is oversimple and excludes the evidence of the pure consciousness event. He would do well to include the evidence of this phenomenon as he developed a new definition of the mental.—Ed.

38. Other philosophers, like Richard Rorty (*Philosophy and the Mirror of Nature* [Princeton, N.J.: Princeton University Press, 1979], pp. 17–32), have argued that Brentano's difficulties in accommodating sensations, pleasure, pain, and so on, as "mental" militate for the surrender of his thesis. If we agree, then the pure consciousness event is further evidence for this claim.

39. Jean Paul Sartre, *The Transcendence of the Ego*, trans. Williams and Kirkpatrick (New York: Farar, Straus and Giroux, 1937), p. 44. Sartre is quoting Husserl's *Ideas*, secs. 36, 84.

40. If there is no single exemplar of "consciousness," then, the reader might ask: Why should I call this event "the *pure* consciousness event"? My use of the word "pure" is not intended to indicate a judgment concerning the word "consciousness." I call it "pure" because it is a state of consciousness in which what is denoted by the term "consciousness" in one of its many senses stands by itself without relation to anything.

Does the Philosophy of Mysticism Rest on a Mistake?

ANTHONY N. PEROVICH, JR.

Although Immanuel Kant was unremittingly hostile in his attitude toward the claims of mystics to have experience of the divine already in this life, a great many philosphers of mysticism have subsequently been attracted to the epistemological scheme of the Critical Philosophy, at least in its general outlines. Kant denied the possibility of genuine mystical experience (as opposed to merely mislabeled feelings of illumination) because such experience would require the possession in our present state of cognitive faculties for which no provision was, or seemingly could be, made in his epistemology. Yet numerous philosophers who wittingly or unwittingly have taken their lead from him have assumed that his general approach marks the most natural starting point for the analysis of all sorts of experience, including all those types typically referred to as mystical. The claim for which I will argue is that in the sphere of the epistemological understanding of mysticism (as in so many others) Kant is far more penetrating than the Kantians. In fact, we will see that the Kantian analysis of mystical experience (unlike Kant's own) is based on a mistake, a paralogism as it were, whose identification, nevertheless, offers some useful insight into the way the study of mystical experience ought to be pursued.

I

The fundamental tenet of Kant's epistemology is that the knower plays an active role in the production of experience. Not only the incoming content of intuition, but also the organizing form of the subject's conceptual scheme contributes to the ultimate experiential result. The forms of sensibility, space and time, have neither the function nor the significance for the Kantians that they do for Kant and will, consequently, be ignored in the discussion. On this view, no experiences are simply given, but rather are always mediated through the organizing structures that knowers bring with them.

This general framework is shared by many students of mystical experience. Some explicitly acknowledge their indebtedness to Kant. Bruce Garside, recognizing that "it is necessary to have some general model of experience in order to discuss mystical experience in particular," offers the following sketch and comment, "The main premise of the model is that experience is a product of the interaction of the organism and the environment, involving both external stimuli and interpretive structures of the perceiver. . . . Philosophically the model is of Kantian inspiration, experience being the product of the synthesis of percepts and the a priori structures of the understanding."[1]

In other authors, while Kant is not explicitly mentioned, the echo of Kantian sentiments is unmistakeable. Compare H. P. Owen's opening remarks, ("A question that then arises is how mystical experiences are related to beliefs concerning God or the Absolute. There are two possible answers: first, that mystical experiences generate beliefs and, secondly, that antecedently held beliefs shape the character of mystical experiences. My contention is this essay is that with regard to Christian mysticism the second answer is the right one. Christian forms of mystical experience are shaped by antecedently held beliefs."[2]) with Kant's remarks in the "Transition to the Transcendental Deduction of the Categories" regarding the function that pure concepts of the understanding (categories) have in making objects of experience possible:

> There are only two possible ways in which synthetic representations and their objects can establish connection, obtain necessary relation to one another, and, as it were, meet one another. Either the object alone must make the representation possible, or the representation alone must make the object possible.

> The objective validity of the categories as a priori concepts rests, therefore, on the fact that, so far as the form of thought is concerned, through them alone does experience become possible. They relate of necessity and a priori

to objects of experience, for the reason that only by means of them can any object whatsoever of experience be thought.[3]

When patterns of thinking resemble one another to this extent, references become superfluous.

Although the writings referred to that adopt a Kantian epistemology for the study of mystical experience are all relatively recent, it would be an error to assume that this approach is at all new; on the contrary, it merely reproduces a point of view already made familiar by earlier students of mysticism. Early in the century, Rufus Jones insisted:

> The most refined mysticism, the most exalted spiritual experience is *partly* a product of the social and intellectual environment in which the personal life of the mystic has formed and nurtured. There are no experiences of any sort which are independent of preformed expectations or unaffected by the prevailing beliefs of the time. . . . Mystical experiences will be, perforce, saturated with the dominant ideas of the group to which the mystic belongs, and they will reflect the expectations of that group and that period.[4]

Only a few years later W. R. Inge was to accompany his claim, "It is difficult to describe the generic type of ecstasy, especially in what may be called its lower forms, since its manifestations are determined partly by the nature of the means employed and partly by the mental state and character of the experimenter" with a longish list whose point is that the Persian mystic, the Roman Catholic ecstatic, the Neoplatonist, the *yogi*, and so on, each has the mystical experience associated with, and expected by, his or her own tradition.[5] Recent articles have expanded and embellished this list; whether they are able to supplement it with cogent philosophical argument is the issue with which we are here concerned.

For argument is what many of these recent writers are about. They are to be distinguished from Jones and Inge not by their epistemological presuppositions, but by their polemical purpose. The thesis that they oppose claims that mystical experiences wherever they are encountered—no matter how varied the cultures, periods, and traditions may be within which they are situated—are phenomenologically identical (or reduce themselves to a small number of types). This thesis is attibuted to a number of writers,[6] although W. T. Stace's doctrine of the "universal core" is perhaps the favorite source.[7]

The method of attack consists in declaring one's allegiance to the Kantian epistemology sketched earlier, affirming that the intellectual and practical context of each religious tradition performs the function of Kant's categories in shaping the religious experience of the adherents of that tradition and pointing out that these claims are incompatible with the

view that the experience of mystics from different traditions can be phenomenologically identical. As Garside succinctly states, "If experience is
the product of stimuli and conceptual framework as suggested . . . , then
people of different cultures and different religious traditions would necessarily have different religious experiences."[8] This argument is often con-
joined with an account of the reports by mystics from one or more
traditions, along with the suggestion that the clearly tradition-specific
character of these reports offers empirical evidence in support of the
conclusions already deduced on philosophical grounds.[9]

Although no one would doubt that the latter empirical studies form the
fundamental basis for assessing the resemblances and differences among
the experiences described in testimonies within the various religious
traditions, it is only on the assumption of the formative influence of
tradition on experience that these reports, employing the language suited
to their religious contexts, can be taken as evidence of the variety of
mystical experience without further ado. Hence, it is the philosophical
side of the attack on which the rejection of the thesis of the universal core
here depends. I am concerned to show that this "Kantian" approach,
when applied to matters mystical, is unsatisfactory. In the three sections
that follow I shall argue (1) that Kantian epistemology seems singularly
inapposite when applied to certain sorts of mystical experience; (2) that,
ironically, Kant was himself no "Kantian"[10] in this area; and (3) that
Kant's own position reveals the mistake on which the "Kantian" philosophy of mysticism rests and helps us to orient ourselves toward more
promising paths in this area of study.

II

Fundamental to Kantian epistemology is the distinction between form and
content.[11] Roughly speaking, passively received intuition offers (according to Kant) the content for which our conceptual scheme provides the
organizational form. Both of these components are necessary conditions
for experience, as Kant puts it in a famous passage, "Thoughts without
content are empty, intuitions without concepts are blind."[12] And both
components, or something like them, are recognized by the "Kantians"
as necessary for mystical experience; indeed, it is the interaction between
these two that provides the theoretical foundation for current philosophical interpretations. Katz states the dual commitment nicely, "Above all,
the interpenetration of the mystical event and the religious tradition out of
which the mystic grows has emerged as a central concern requiring new
and innovative study."[13] Thus, I will proceed to consider how this form/

content distinction might be applied to mystical experience; the result will be that at least *some* sorts of mystical experience are resistant to this treatment, suggesting that the approach rests on a mistake.

For Kant, the categories provide the form of experience, and so it seems initially plausible to interpret the "Kantians" as maintaining that the religious tradition via concepts, beliefs, practices, and so on, contributes the form for the structuring of the mystical "given." Such a position is certainly suggested by passages in Katz's writing:

> All "givens" are also the product of the processes of "choosing," "shaping," and "receiving." That is, the "given" is appropriated through acts which shape it into forms which we can make intelligible to ourselves given our conceptual constitution, and which structure it in order to respond to the specific contextual needs and mechanisms of consciousness of the receiver. . . . This means that the mystic *even* in his state of reconditioned consciousness is also a shaper of his experience; that he is not a *tabula rasa* on which the "ultimate" or the "given" simply impinges itself—whatever ultimate he happens to be seeking and happens to find."[14]

Now the function of a conceptual scheme, viewed as making a formal contribution, is to produce objective unities (objects of experience) which are absent from the formless given. This function is accomplished in one of two ways, depending on how one views what is to be formed or shaped.

For a philosopher like Kant, we are given a manifold of intuition, and the categories—those concepts that bring objective unity to the manifold—provide the forms for its synthesis: this is one way in which the conceptual context may intelligibly shape experience. It is easy to imagine (although Kant does not himself recognize this possibility) how different conceptual schemes could form experience differently by uniting the manifold in different ways.

On the other hand, some writers start not from a manifold but from an undivided whole; the task of concepts, then, is not to unify, but to cut up this continuum. And again, this slicing can be done in different ways. Thus Whorf claims that "each language performs this artificial chopping up of the continous spread and flow of existence in a different way"[15] and Quine has described in numerous writings the potential for conceiving in terms of rabbit parts or rabbit stages rather than in terms of rabbits.[16]

While both of these accounts make the claims of experience being shaped by a conceptual framework intelligible, they both seem poorly suited to elucidate the genesis of some sorts of mystical experience. For consideration, I would like to add to the examples from Part I of this volume the description left by Plotinus of the One with which the mystic unites: it is formless and precedent to all being, not in space or time, without multiplicity and without difference.[17] It simply cannot be represented as the product of formal conceptual shaping: no combination of a manifold with produce a result that lacks all multiplicity and no delimitation of a continuous whole produces a result that is formless and without distinction.

The trouble here is clear enough. To understand "shaping" in terms of imposing a conceptual form on a given content does not transform that content except to add connections or divisions that are not present in the content itself: the manifold may be synthesized, but the result is still a synthesized *manifold*; the "spread and flow of existence" may have its continuity interrupted by conceptual slicings, but such interruptions *introduce* difference, multiplicity, and form rather than do away with them. It is implausible to regard the Neoplatonic experience of the One, formless and without multiplicity, as the result of slicing a whole or unifying a manifold. Hence, there are some mystical experiences, at least, for which the claim that the mystic's conceptual scheme shapes his or her experience—if understood formally—is implausible.

This result suggests that the formal interpretation of the "shaping" metaphor, despite the philosophical history of that reading and its obvious sanction in at least some of the statements of the authors considered, is not intended by the "Kantians" at all; perhaps the metaphor should be explicated by reference to content rather than to form. In that case we should say that concepts shape experience in the sense that the conceptual structures with which the intellectual context of our tradition provides us produce certain expectations in us as to what our experience should be like, these expectations then color our experience so as to be satisfied by it. There is evidence that this is the interpretation some of the authors under consideration intend. Robert Gimello, for example, objects to a merely formalist understanding of the way in which conceptual schemes are involved in the constitution of mystical experience:

> All mystical experiences, like all experiences generally, have specific structures, and these are neither fortuitous nor *sui generis*. Rather they are given to the experiences, at their very inceptions, by concepts, beliefs, values, and expectations already operative in the mystics' minds. Nor are these structures of meaning mere "forms" which the discrete "content" of mysticism may happen to take. They are more immanent than that. They are of the essence of mystical experience. They engender it. They inform its very identity.[18]

The attempt to locate the conceptual contribution of the tradition in the content rather than the form represents the suicide of the Kantian epistemological model, however. To whatever extent the intellectual structure of the religious tradition is depicted as the source of experiential content, to that degree the notion of an independent "given" that requires shaping and structuring (in different ways by different conceptual frameworks) is rendered vacuous. Once the "given" evaporates from one's account, a Kantian theory of knowledge is no longer appropriate: if there is nothing to be mediated, then there is no point in insisting on the mediated character of all experience. One does not require the intricacies of Kantian epistemology (or even "Kantian" epistemology) to represent mystical experience as fabrication. And to whatever extent one seeks to supplement such content generated by the mystic's tradition with an independent content for which that tradition now acts as a form, to that degree the difficulties already mentioned arise once more.

The fact is that beyond these problematic explanations of the application of Kantian epistemology to mystical experience, the position under discussion has little to fall back on beyond unexplicated metaphors of "shaping" and the like. This is enough to suggest that there is something fundamentally misguided with the employment of "Kantian" ideas in this sphere. It will help to bring this error to light by showing that Kant himself avoided "Kantianism" in this area, and why he did so.

III

Kant had a lifelong distaste for, and distrust of, what he called *Schwärmerei*, which he defines as follows, "The persuasion that we can distinguish the effects of grace from those of nature (virtue) or can actually produce the former within ourselves, is *fanaticism* [*Schwärmerei*]; for we cannot, by any token, recognize a supersensible object in experience, still less can we exert an influence upon it to draw it down to us."[19] Kant sometimes characterizes *Schwärmerei* more particularly; a philosophical form of it supposes that it is possible for us to be in communion with God and immediately to intuit the divine Ideas.[20] This latter he describes as mystical intuition. Mysticism, in Kant's view, loses itself in raving [*schwärmt*], leading to the feeling of "flowing into and being swallowed up in the abyss of the divinity."[21] This represents the death of reason.

Kant's grounds for adopting a negative attitude toward mysticism are complex and concern us here in only one respect. He insists that the claims of the mystics are false, that mystical "inner illuminations" are merely "pretended,"[22] because mystical cognition presupposes a faculty which we in fact lack: "for this feeling of the immediate presence of the

Supreme Being . . . would constitute a receptivity for an intuition for which there is no sensory provision in man's nature."[23]

It is interesting to note that Kant is not utterly opposed to faculties of mystical intuition, only to claims that we can employ them in the present life. He holds that after death we might know in just the way the mystics describe is possible, but we can have no certainty in the matter.[24] The mystics' error seems to lie, for Kant, not so much in their description of what is known and how it is known as in their claim to such knowledge in the present: "The mystics should have postponed it [mystical intuition] until the future life alone."[25]

We are able, therefore, to distinguish Kant's view from that of the "Kantians." According to Kant, mystical knowledge is to be distinguished from ordinary empirical knowledge not only by its object, but also by its epistemological structure: mystical knowledge consists in a communion with God and a sharing in the divine self-knowledge of His Ideas. Such intellectual intuition may be possible for us in the future, but it demands a cognitive faculty different from those employed in empirical knowledge and so, Kant believes, is not available in this life. The "Kantians," on the other hand, make no distinction between the conditions of mystical cognition and the conditions of ordinary cognition. In doing so, they not only depart from Kant's own view but also, I believe, err in doing so. It is to a detailed discussion of what is wrong with this "Kantian" position that I now turn.

IV

Our discussion of "Kantian" epistemology has enabled us to distinguish it clearly from Kant's own view of mystical cognition. This does not of itself show the former position to be incorrect. What might be said in its favor? Foremost is, I believe, the conviction of the universal validity for human experience of the general Kantian epistemological model. Thus, we have seen Garside take as obvious the need for a "*general* model of experience"[26] and then proceed to offer a "Kantian" epistemology as providing what is required. Gill insists that "The contextual and relational character of human existence so shapes the nature of meaning and under-standing that it seems impossible to do without the notion of mediation *at the heart of one's epistemology*."[27] Once the universal validity of the model is accepted, its application to mystical experience is a straightfor-ward matter. As Katz writes, "This 'mediated' aspect of *all* our experience seems an inescapable feature of *any* epistemological inquiry, including the inquiry into mysticism."[28] Or recall Gimello's statement that *"All mystical experiences, like all experiences generally,* have specific structures . . . given to the experiences, at their very inceptions, by concepts, beliefs, values, and expectations already operative in the mystics' minds."[29] Now this uncritical assumption of the universal validity for human experience in general of an epistemology developed along Kantian lines could certainly be regarded as question begging. But the point on which I want to insist here is that this assumption, at least when read in the way most likely to make it true, is too weak, too limited to support the "Kantian" argument. Even after granting this presupposition, certain features frequently encountered among mystical reports will still call into question the appropriateness of the "Kantian" analysis.

The "Kantian" argument for the application of its epistemological assumptions to the particular case of mystical experiences can be stated as follows:

> (1) All human experience is "Kantian" in structure.
>
> (2) All mystical experience is human experience. Therefore, all mystical experience is "Kantian" in structure.

The first premise expresses the claim of universal validity, the claim that all human experience is appropriately analyzed along "Kantian" lines. Now this may seem not only question begging, but a dubious claim as well: unless one is willing to accept more of the details of Kant's position than most philosophers are today willing to do, it cannot be established a priori. Consequently, it must be an empirical claim, which then must be put to the test *by* each new type of human experience analyzed, not imported into the analysis from without. Even if we leave to one side, however, the objections which naturally arise in regard to (1), it still seems to me that the conclusion does not follow. For the argument commits the fallacy of four terms: if accepting the truth of (1), we interpret "human experience" in such a way as to make the argument valid, premise (2) is false; if we interpret it in such a way as to make both premises (1) and (2) true, the argument becomes invalid. If this is correct, we have here a paralogism (of rather the same character as Kant identified in his famous chapter in the "Transcendental Dialectic").

"Human experience" can mean either experience that employs characteristically human faculties (e.g., for Kant, sensibility and understanding) that interact in a characteristically human way (e.g., for Kant, sensibility providing intuitive content, the understanding providing conceptual form) or experience that simply is had by humans. I maintain that although only the first interpretation will make the major premise true, there is evidence present in numerous reports by mystics that only the second and not the first interpretation will make the minor premise true. The evidence that I have in mind, of course, is that recorded in claims of ecstasy.

Kant himself understood the key issue here. Mystical experience for him was not ordinary human experience in the sense of employing characteristically human faculties in a characteristically human way. Rather, it involved the abandonment of our human, discursive intellect and a communion with God in which we shared in His faculty of intellectual intuition. This doctrine of leaving behind one's ordinary human faculties and assuming a new, nonhuman epistemic status is not, of course, peculiar to Kant; rather, he merely echoes a note frequently sounded by the mystics themselves. Kant's idea of replacing our discursive, human intellect with one of an intuitive, nonhuman sort reproduces very nicely claims made by Richard of St. Victor in *The Mystical Ark,* "In like manner, human understanding increases from the greatness of its enlarging so that it is no longer itself [not that it is not understanding, but that it is no longer *human*] when in a marvelous manner and by an incomprehensible change it is made more than human, and 'beholding the glory of the Lord it is transformed into the same image from splendor to splendor, as by the spirit of the Lord'" (2 Cor. 3:18).[30]

In urging Timothy to approach God "with your understanding laid aside,"[31] the Pseudo-Dionysius sounds the same basic theme, "Here, renouncing all that the mind may conceive, wrapped entirely in the intangible and the invisible, he belongs completely to him who is beyond everything. Here, *being neither oneself nor someone else,* one is supremely united by a completely unknowing inactivity of all knowledge, and knows *beyond the mind* by knowing nothing."[32] The claim that mystical cognition is nonhuman (in the first sense of "human experience") recurs again and again throughout the mystical literature. Deirdre Green puts the point quite well in connection with the doctrine of St. John of the Cross: in the later stages of the mystical path "we must learn to detach ourselves even from communications to the higher faculties, memory, will, and understanding or intellect. This is so because no natural human power or faculty, for St. John, can be a means of union with the Divine; reliance on any of these faculties will obscure the vision beyond."[33] So, at least some sorts of mystical experiences are human experience only insofar as human beings have them, in the sense that they subsequently recount them in the first person (often, admittedly, with some qualifications even here). But they are not human experiences which seem to employ typically human faculties in typically human ways. Consequently, no *presuppositions* about the mediated, shaped, conceptualized character of "human experience" (in the first sense) are relevant to the sorts of "nonhuman experience" being reported by such mystics. "Kantian" epistemological assumptions may extend as far as the "human experience" (in the first sense) that they characterize, but the experience being reported by many mystics demands a suspension of our assumptions not only of a uniformity in the *experience* had by humans, but also of a uniform *epistemological apparatus* for handling that experience. Once such epistemological preconceptions are abandoned, we will be far readier to begin the unbiased appraisal of the evidence for which the "Kantians" call.[34]

If its epistemological assumptions are found to be inappropriate and inapplicable, the polemical thrust of the "Kantian" position is blunted, for one will no longer be able to guarantee on philosophical grounds that the variety encountered in the reports of the mystics bespeaks a comparable variety in their experience. The point may be put this way: if one may hold a "Kantian" epistemology fixed or constant, then on the basis of variety in religious traditions and mystical reports, one can "solve for" the phenomenological character of mystical experience and deduce its variety. The factor, on the contrary, to which I am drawing attention is the repeated insistence by the mystics themselves that epistemology cannot remain constant when dealing with the mystical life and that by making the epistemology as well as the phenomenological character of the experience variables in our philosophical investigations, we make "solving for" the latter variable a much less straightforward affair. Thus, while I have not shown (and do not believe) that "all mysticism is one," I do believe that I have shown a basic flaw vitiating much recent philosophy of mysticism, namely, the unquestioned belief in the correctness of a uniform ("Kantian") epistemology for handling all experience, which, in turn, is based on the fallacious belief (fallacious, at least, in the minds of those whose experience we are trying to understand) that all experience had by humans both involves and is epistemologically limited to the complement of epistemic factors that are encountered in typically human (or perhaps one should simply say *human*) experience.

The fact that many mystics *report* that their experiences not only are extraordinary in content, but also demand extraordinary epistemological treatment does not itself *establish* either that the content is veridical or that their epistemological description is accurate. Consequently, it does not immediately follow from the fact that mystics claim that their experiencings do not involve the operations of the discursive intellect that the activity of conceptual structuring does not, in fact, occur. It may be the case that the epistemology involved really *is* "Kantian," although the mystics reporting are too unsophisticated philosophically to grasp the fact. Of course, this would be a peculiar objection for any "Kantian" to make who puts as much emphasis on the need for faithfulness to the mystical sources as does, for example, Katz, "It must constantly be borne in mind that however we might view the nature of mysticism and mystical experience, the only evidence we have, if we are not mystics ourselves, and even mystics do not have a privileged position here, is the account given by mystics of their experience."[35] Surely this respect must extend to accounts of the experience of the known. If one must not, as the "Kantians" insist, roughly force texts to conform to preestablished ideas of experiential uniformity, neither must one force them to conform to pre-established ideas of epistemological uniformity.

Something more, however, remains to be said in favor of the mystic claim that the faculties (i.e., the epistemologically relevant factors) involved in mystical experience are not the ordinary ones involved in (typically) human experience. The philosophical complexity of the current debate rests on two features of the reports given to us by the mystics in the accounts of their experiences. First, the mystics of different traditions employ incompatible concepts in their various descriptions, and we have at present no criteria for distinguishing which of these concepts are genuinely constitutive of the experiences and which are merely brought to already fully formed experiences for the purposes of identification and classification.[36] Second, owing to the relative inaccessibility of these experiences, the parties to the debate are not typically able to support their positions by appeals to knowledge by acquaintance.

Given this situation, I suggest that greater weight be ascribed to the denial of the applicability of concepts to experience than to the affirmation of their applicability, both in our attempts at phenomenological accuracy and in our philosophical efforts to construct a metaphysically satisfying account of the phenomena. The reason, at the phenomenological level, is that in an affirmation we have no way of telling whether the concept involved is constitutive or merely used to identify what is already fully constituted. On the other hand, a denial seems much likelier to refer to the constitution of the experience: a denial that a given concept applied to a particular experience, on the assumption that the concept was constitutive and, in fact, "shaped" that experience, would clearly indicate a misdescription of the experience itself. (And the suggestion that the denial is itself constitutive of experience is to misinterpret by giving a negation spurious positive content.) At the metaphysical level, supposing that we are free of any dogmatic assumptions (either religious or scientistic), the character of the experience is prima facie evidence of the character of the experienced, and we have just seen that negations are more illuminating in regard to mystical experience than are affirmations.

It is not unusual for mystics to insist on the significance of their negations in attempting to clarify the content of their experience; what I am suggesting here is that their negations regarding their experienced epistemic status are of comparable significance for the philosopher of mysticism. Just as I take negations to be especially revealing of the content of mystical experience, so I take the denial that ordinary human cognitive faculties are involved to be good evidence that any epistemological model based on the employment of those faculties is inapplicable to the case of mystical cognition. The "Kantian" is clearly one such epistemological model.

When we free ourselves of epistemological bias, we recognize that neither assumptions about the *content* of mystical experience nor assumptions about the *epistemology* of mystical knowing can be taken as constant and fixed. We have to "solve for" both simultaneously. Hence, if we find mystics denying that their ordinary cognitive faculties are at work and we then find them proceeding to apply concepts derived from their tradition to their experiences, what has been said here about the priority of the negative entitles us to regard any claims supporting the constitutive role of those concepts with a healthy skepticism.

The results achieved here are, I believe, of some help in providing further direction for the study of mysticism. They show that an important area for investigation—at least as fundamental as the investigation of either phenomenological content, or "the multiplicity of specific means which traditional sponsors of mysticism have provided for the achievement of mystical experiences,"[37] or the categories of mystical writing—[38] is the area of "mystical epistemology." Mystics and scholars have made various classifications that may prove useful,[39] but the confusion that the "Kantians" have succeeded in introducing into the study of mysticism is evidence that clarity will be achieved only with the advent of better epistemological understanding in this area.

The study of mystical epistemology may well help to illuminate or confirm claims about common types of mystical experience. Identity is most often claimed for those cognitive states in which the distinction between subject and object breaks down, in which what remains is a "pure consciousness" devoid of content. This is not only a key thesis of Part I of the present volume, but it is also one of the key points where Bréhier senses the affinity between Plotinus and Indian mysticism, the point where one encounters "an intuition which is no longer a thought . . . [but rather is] the thinking activity in itself, the subjective activity, in which every trace of an object has disappeared."[40] A more adequate understanding of the epistemological situation here than rigid adherence to the "Kantian" model allows may permit us to identify where claims of the identity of mystical experience are plausible and where they are not. Cognitive faculties being both fewer and more uniform than religious traditions, claims of a "universal core" based on a common, "self-contained" employment of the former are obviously more likely to succeed than if one makes the conceptual diversity of the different religions epistemologically central after the manner of the "Kantians."[41]

Therefore, it seems to me the recent "Kantian" philosophy of mysticism rests on a mistake, the mistake of assuming that mystical experience is narrowly "human" experience and, so, is subject to the same treatment as is "human" experience generally. But the mystics insist that their experiences result from ecstasy, that their knowledge is gained as the result of employing faculties which are not the ordinary "human" ones. At the very least, these claims translate as denials of the validity of "Kantian" epistemology in the mystical sphere. By studying their reports, we can also hope to learn something about the sort of epistemology that *is* appropriate here, given that we have once learned to avoid the pitfalls of a "Kantian" analysis of mystical experience. This last lesson—of course, the point is not without its irony—could have been easily learned from Kant himself.

NOTES

1. Bruce Garside, "Language and the Interpretation of Mystical Experience," *International Journal for Philosophy of Religion*, 3 (1972), 93–94. Other writers sharing this epistemological position who also explicitly refer to Kant are John Hick, "Mystical Experience as Cognition," in Richard Woods (ed.), *Understanding Mysticism* (Garden City, N.Y.: Doubleday, Image Books, 1980), pp. 422–37; and Steven T. Katz, "Language, Epistemology, and Mysticism," in Steven T. Katz (ed.), *Mysticism and Philosophical Analysis* (New York: Oxford University Press, 1978), pp. 22–74.

2. H. P. Owen, "Experience and Dogma in the English Mystics," in Steven T. Katz (ed.), *Mysticism and Religious Traditions* (New York: Oxford University Press, 1983), p. 148. Other writers sharing this epistemological approach who do not explicitly refer to Kant are (from the Katz collection just cited): Steven T. Katz, "The 'Conservative' Character of Mystical Experience," pp. 3–60; Robert M. Gimello, "Mysticism in Its Contexts," pp. 61–88; and John E. Smith, "William

James's Account of Mysticism: A Critical Appraisal," pp. 247–79; and From Katz, *Mysticism and Philosophical Analysis,* is Peter Moore, "Mystical Experience, Mystical Doctrine, Mystical Technique," pp. 101–31 and Robert M. Gimello, "Mysticism and Meditation," pp. 170–99; and also Jerry Gill, "Mysticism and Mediation," *Faith and Philosophy* 1 (1984), pp. 111–21.

3. Immanuel Kant, *Critique of Pure Reason,* trans. Norman Kemp Smith (London: Macmillan, 1970), pp. 125–26 (A92–93/B124–26).

4. Rufus Jones, *Studies in Mystical Religion* (New York: Russell & Russell, 1970), p. xxxiv. Jones refers back to Delacroix's *Etude d'histoire et de psychologie du mysticisme* (Paris: 1908) on this point. The *Studies* were originally published in 1909. Cf. Jones's remarks with the frequently quoted claim of Katz that "There are NO pure (i.e. unmediated) experiences" ("Language, Epistemology, and Mysticism," p. 26) or with Gimello's thesis that "Mysticism is inextricably bound up with, dependent upon, and usually subservient to the deeper beliefs and values of the traditions, cultures, and historical milieux which harbor it. As it is thus intricately and intimately related to those beliefs and values, so must it vary according to them" ("Mysticism in Its Contexts," p. 63).

5. W. R. Inge, "Ecstasy," in *Encyclopedia of Religion and Ethics,* ed. James Hastings (Edinburgh: T. & T. Clark, 1912), p. 157. In fairness to Inge it should be noted that later, in contrast to the dismissive attitude of this passage ("in every case the enhanced form of autosuggestion seems to project itself outside the personality"), he does identify some preferred (i.e., Plotinian) mystical states as sane, trustworthy, and incontrovertible (p. 159).

6. See, for example, the authors listed in nn. 3–8 in Katz, "Language, Epistemology, and Mysticism," p. 67.

7. W. T. Stace, *Mysticism and Philosophy* (London and Basingstoke: Macmillan, 1980), chap. 2, "The Problem of the Universal Core," pp. 41–133.

8. Garside, "Language," p. 99.

9. Cf. Katz's "Language, Epistemology, and Mysticism," as well as the essays already referred to in n. 2 by Katz, Gimello, and Owen in *Mysticism and Religious Traditions.*

10. In this essay I seek to distinguish between ideas that are Kantian, that is, held by Kant himself, from those that are Kantian, that is, inspired by, or comparable to, views held by Kant, though not, in fact, actually adhered to by him. J. William Forgie, in "Hyper-Kantianism in Recent Discussions of Mystical Experience," *Religious Studies* 21 (1985), 205–18, introduces the term "hyper-Kantian" for the latter notion, in order to indicate that the views of the philosophers of mysticism considered here go beyond Kant in certain respects. Though I believe Forgie misunderstands Kant in a number of ways (Kant's remarks, e.g., on affinity (A121–22) that undercut the claim "categories do not contribute to the phenomenological content of the experiences that they shape," [p. 208]; and his remarks on transcendental hypotheses [A779–80/B807–8] undercut the claim that "we do not even think . . . that the influence of the categories might be to distort the experience one would otherwise have were he face to face, so to speak, with the noumena" [p. 215]), nevertheless he is surely right in holding that the

hyper-Kantians go beyond Kant in a significant way by introducing experience-shaping beliefs that are not universal and inescapable, as are the categories. Of course, this notion of nonuniversal "category analogues" is already present in such twentieth century philosophers as Robin G. Collingwood, Ludwig Wittgenstein, Thomas Kuhn, and Paul K. Feyerabend.

11. What follows in this section is the revision of my paper, "Mysticism and the Conceptual Structure of Experience," that was given in the fall of 1985 at the annual meetings of the American Academy of Religion, Anaheim, Ca.

12. Kant, *Critique of Pure Reason*, p. 93 (A51/B75).

13. Katz, " 'Conservative' Character," p. 5.

14. Ibid., p. 59.

15. Benjamin Lee Whorf, *Language, Thought, and Reality*, ed. John B. Carroll (Cambridge: MIT Press, 1956), p. 253.

16. See Willard Van Orman Quine, *From a Logical Point of View*, 2d ed., rev. (New York: Harper & Row, 1961), p. 62, *Word and Object* (Cambridge: MIT Press, 1960), pp. 51ff.; and *Ontological Relativity and Other Essays* (New York: Columbia University Press, 1969), p. 2.

17. Plotinus, *Enneads*, trans. Stephen MacKenna, 2d ed. rev. B. S. Page (New York: Pantheon, 1953), pp. 617, 620, 622 (VI.9.iii, vi, viii).

18. Robert Gimello, "Mysticism in Its Contents," p. 62. Some of Katz's own examples suggest this interpretation as well; see "Language, Epistemology, and Mysticism," pp. 39, 58.

19. Immanuel Kant, *Religion Within the Limits of Reason Alone*, trans. with an introduction and notes by Theodore M. Greene and Hoyt H. Hudson and with an essay by John R. Silber (New York: Harper & Row, 1960), p. 162.

20. Immanuel Kant, Reflexion 6050, "Von der philosophischen Schwärmerey," in *Kants gesammelte Schriften* (Berlin and Leipzig: Walter de Gruyter, 1928), vol. 18, p. 435.

21. Immanuel Kant, "The End of All Things," in *Perpetual Peace and Other Essays on Politics, History, and Morals*, trans. Ted Humphrey (Indianapolis and Cambridge: Hackett, 1983), p. 99. Cf. Immanuel Kant, *Critique of Practical Reason and Other Writings in Moral Philosophy*, trans. Lewis White Beck (Chicago: University of Chicago Press, 1949), p. 224.

22. Kant, *Religion Within the Limits of Reason Alone*, p. 78.

23. Ibid., p. 163.

24. Immanuel Kant, *Lectures on Philosophical Theology*, trans. Allen W. Wood and Gertrude M. Clark (Ithaca and London: Cornell University Press, 1978), p. 87. Cf. *Critique of Pure Reason*, p. 618 (A778/B806).

25. Immanuel Kant, "Danziger Rationaltheologie nach Baumback," in *Kants gesammelte Schriften* (1972), vol. 28, p. 1268 (my translation).

26. Emphasis added.

27. Gill, *Mysticism and Mediation*, p. 111. [Emphasis added].

28. Katz, "Language, Epistemology, and Mysticism," p. 26. [Emphasis added.]

29. Emphasis added.

30. Richard of St. Victor, *The Twelve Patriarchs, The Mystical Ark, Book Three of the Trinity,* trans. with an introduction by Grover Zinn, Preface by Jean Châtillon (New York, Ramsey, and Toronto: Paulist Press, 1979), p. 323.

31. Pseudo-Dionysius, "The Mystical Theology" in *The Complete Works,* trans. Colm Luibheid, with prefatory matter by Paul Rorem, René Roques, Jaroslav Pelikan, Jean Leclercq, and Karlfried Fröhlich (New York and Mahwah: Paulist Press, 1987), p. 135.

32. Ibid., p. 137. [Emphasis added.]

33. Deirdre Green, "St. John of the Cross and Mystical Unknowing," *Religious Studies* 22 (1986), p. 33.

34. Katz, "Language, Epistemology, and Mysticism," pp. 25, 65–66. I have discussed this inability to make good on the "Kantian" claim to handle all the evidence in "Mysticism or Mediation: A Response to Gill," *Faith and Philosophy* 2 (1985), pp. 179–88.

35. Katz, " 'Conservative' Character," p. 5.

36. On this point, see my "Mysticism and the Philosophy of Science," *Journal of Religion* 65 (1985), pp. 73ff.; and Forgie, "Hyper-Kantianism" pp. 210ff.

37. Gimello, "Mysticism in Its Contexts," pp. 63–64.

38. Moore, "Mystical Experience, Mystical Doctrine, Mystical Technique," p. 103.

39. Classification of types of ecstasy may offer some guidelines. Arvind Sharma ("Ecstasy," in *Encyclopedia of Religion,* editor in chief Mircea Eliade (New York: Macmillan, 1987), vol. 5, pp. 11–17) distinguishes ecstasies on the basis of what the ecstatic utterances deal with; St. Thomas (*Summa theologiae,* 2a2ae, 175. 3 ad 1) makes use of the faculties involved in drawing his distinctions; Richard Rolle (*The Fire of Love,* trans. with an introduction by Clifton Wolters (Harmondsworth: Penguin, 1972), chap. 37, p. 166) distinguishes rapture in the senses from rapture out of the senses. Some have questioned whether Rolle's first sort of rapture deserves to be characterized as ecstasy. See Hope Emily Allen's introduction to her *English Writings of Richard Rolle Hermit of Hampole* (Oxford: Oxford University Press, 1931), p. xxix, n. 1.

40. See the essays by Chappel, Griffiths, and Forman in the present volume. Also Emile Bréhier, *The Philosophy of Plotinus,* trans. Joseph Thomas (Chicago: University of Chicago Press, 1958), p. 189. Cf. pp. 124, 127, 195–96. Even those who deny direct or indirect influence here acknowledge the affinity and are, thus, even more powerful witnesses for the claim of common experience. See A. Hilary Armstrong, "Plotinus and India," *Plotinian and Christian Studies* (London: Variorum Reprints, 1979), Essay 1.

41. For one sort of suggestion that cognitive similarities may explain the identity of experience in cases of pure consciousness, see Richard H. Jones, "Experience and Conceptualization in Mystical Knowledge," *Zygon* 18 (1983), p. 142. Jones distinguishes nonintentional from intentional mystical experience (he terms the former "depth-mystical experiences" and the latter, somewhat misleadingly, "nature-mystical experiences"), and he makes the sober suggestion that the former are universal, the latter "tradition-bound."

On the Possibility
of Pure Consciousness

MARK B. WOODHOUSE

Throughout recorded history and across major cultural and religious barriers many persons have claimed to have, had experiences of "pure" consciousness, that is, of a consciousness free of content and intention. Major spiritual traditions are built in significant ways around the existence of these experiences and the desirability of achieving them. Yet many philosophical and scientific traditions, especially in the West, deny not only their existence, but also their possibility. Consciousness often is *conceived* in ways that rule out the possibility of a pure state on a priori grounds. My purpose in this essay is to show that there are no logical or, to a lesser extent, phenomenological considerations that rule out the existence of pure consciousness.

Since I will be developing independent philosophical analyses, little is left for historical or textual critiques of what various thinkers have said on the subject. In general, however, opposition to the idea of pure consciousness is found in empiricism, positivism, pragmatism, process philosophy, analytic philosophy, phenomenology, functionalism, and much of current congnitive psychology. Writers otherwise as diverse as Hume, James, Skinner, Bergson, Sartre, Strawson, and Fodor are united in their

This is a substantially revised version of an article that first appeared in the *Monist* (January 1978).

opposition to some form of the idea of pure consciousness, which has few friends in mainstream philosophy and science.[1]

I propose, therefore, to examine four fundamental dogmas regarding consciousness found scattered throughout different schools of thought. Briefly, these dogmas claim that consciousness cannot be pure because (1) it *is* (either logically or contingently) identical with its contents; (2) it must always have objects; (3) it is essentially a relation between a subject and an object; and (4) it must be identifiable as belonging to some particular person. Each of these dogmas, I submit, is either mistaken or can be shown to be no more plausible than its denial.

While instances of pure consciousness in various spiritual traditions are amply referenced in Part I of this volume, I will find it useful to occasionally anchor my examination by reference to the doctrine of Brahman-Atman, as developed in Advaita Vedanta. My intent is not to defend that doctrine. Rather, it is to illustrate how an abstract philosophical discussion may find expression in a major spiritual tradition built, in part, around the experience of pure consciousness. For example, Eliot Deutsch authoritatively characterizes Atman as "that pure, undifferentiated self-shining consciousness, timeless, spaceless, and unthinkable, that is not different from Brahman and that underlies and supports the individual person."[2] If the dogmas I will examine were true, then Deutsch's characterization (not to mention those from the *Crest Jewel of Wisdom* or the *Mandukya Upanishad,* e.g.) would be incoherent. And this is but one of many spiritual traditions whose claims of fact stand in opposition to what other philosophical and scientific traditions claim is possible or intelligible. A critical defense, therefore, appears very much in order.

But a critical defense of what? Some preliminary amplification is in order. It should be stressed, for example, that the possibility of pure consciousness does not require that the thesis of intentionality (that consciousness has objects) is wrong except, perhaps, in a universal, unqualified and a priori formulation. It requires only that there are certain exceptional circumstances to which that thesis does not apply and would never have been intended to apply if its defenders had been more knowledgeable about them. Moreover, the ideal of pure consciousness does not require that we subtract from consciousness *all* mental content. It requires minimally only the existence of a domain of consciousness that is not reducible to its current contents. It is entirely possible, for example, that the mystic can access (fall into, e.g.) a pure, contentless domain while elsewhere in his mind be in a mild state of pain—a state to which the mystic is at the time of his or her transcendent rapture not attending. This seems to me a matter over which spiritual adepts reasonably might disagree. In this chapter, however, I shall defend the minimalist interpretation.

Some preliminary clarification of "consciousness" is in order. The sense of consciousness with which I will begin and subsequently develop is that of awareness per se, irrespective of the objects or contents of awareness. This is the sense normally contrasted with unconsciousness or a state of dreamless sleep. Thus, I am concerned with the fundamental sense of the term, not with other senses implied by the adjective form such as that involving discovery ("I became conscious of his misdeeds") or inhibition ("He is too self-conscious"). This meaning is fundamental because it is entailed by discovering, acting inhibited, perceiving, and so on, whereas being awake and aware entails nothing about what one is conscious of or how one is conscious of it.[3] While I have presented a synonym, this fundamental sense is at bottom simple and indefinable, and we are forced to rely, in part, on each person's intuitive understanding of what it means to be conscious.

Does this sense of "consciousness" beg the issue at the outset? I think not for several reasons. First, I have made no claims about whether awareness is pure (or purifiable). Second, I have shown how this sense of the term in fact has a fundamental use in our language on grounds independent of the issue of this volume. Third, inependent arguments which amplify this conception but do not presuppose it will be developed in each of the following sections.

I

Is consciousness either logically or contingently identical with its contents? If it is, then it can never be pure, that is, either partly or entirely without contents. Neither purported identification, however, is as evident as may first appear. In order to see why, we need to clarify the distinction between *contents* of consciousness, on the one hand, and *objects* of consciousness, on the other. Briefly, a content of consciousness is any occurrent mental state such as a thought or sensation. Contents are episodic, that is, they exhibit more or less identifiable beginnings and ends. In this respect they are contrasted with dispositions to behave in certain ways, for example, intelligence or introversion, which have a quite different logical structure. (One does not obtain intelligence one day and lose it the next!) Even though it is not a discrete element, a feeling such as depression also qualifies as a content insofar as it is experienced by some person. In summary, pain and depression may be part of my total current state of consciousness, but intelligence or quick-wittedness, which are dispositionally analyzable, cannot.

A pain is a content of consciousness insofar as it is had by some person. It is an intentional object of consciousness to the extent that it is attended to. Thus, not all content is necessarily intentional. While my toothache as a content endures for several hours, as an object it may come into and pass out of being many times during those few hours when, for example, I remain engrossed in a novel. It may or may not be an intended content. I may justifiably infer that my toothache persisted for several hours even though I was not consistently aware of it, since I know that toothaches in general may last many hours and that my present sensation, while less intense, is qualitatively similar in every other aspect to the sensation I had in the same place several hours earlier.

Now if consciousness were logically identical with its contents, then the distinction between a person's being conscious or unconscious, on the one hand, and his being conscious and enjoying his afternoon walk, on the other, would make no sense. Nor would the distinction between one person's awareness of a succession of phenomena versus that person undergoing a succession of awarenesses over the same period of time be intelligible. In general we could not distinguish between the fact that Jones is in pain and the fact that he or she is aware of that pain. These distinctions, however, do make sense and, in fact, are made. Hence, consciousness is not logically (conceptually) identical with its contents.

This conclusion is supported by a second argument. If consciousness were logically identical with its contents, then it would have to be identical with certain of its objects, namely, those mental contents attended to, since all contents are actual or potential objects. However, consciousness cannot be logically identical with its objects since to suppose this would be tantamount to collapsing the thesis of intentionality. We could talk about objects but not about consciousness of those objects. Consciousness, therefore, is not logically identical with its contents. Stated differently, if consciousness were identical with its contents and if consciousness and its objects were not identical, then we could not conceive of an intentional content—which surely we can.

This argument would also demonstrate the contingent nonidentity of consciousness and its contents—if we interpret the thesis of intentionality as expressing a contingent nonidentity of consciousness and its objects—as to whether they are material things or contents of mind. This seems a most reasonable interpretation. As Sartre states, "[T]o be conscious of something is to be confronted with a concrete and full presence which is not consciousness."[4]

An apparent way around this line of argument would be to suppose that consciousness is identical with some content (that not currently intended) and not identical with other content (that currently being intended). However, this leads to absurdities. We cannot consistently suppose that one minute my pain comprises part of the content of my consciousness and the next minute, while it still persists, albeit as intentional object, that it does not.

A final argument further addresses the presumed contingent identity of consciousness with its contents. If consciousness were contingently identical with its contents, then we should continually gain and lose it on a Humean account of mind, which separates mental content into distinct successive elements.[5] This consequence, however, is highly counterintuitive. Consciousness may be said to pass away when, for example, I go to sleep and to be regained when I awaken, but not during my waking hours when it is instead the contents of consciousness which change. An alternative is found in Bergson's account of conscious duration. Consciousness is its changing contents or states, for Bergson, with the important qualification that the contents interpenetrate and shade off into one another such that they cannot be said to stand alone as distinct elements as they do for Hume. Now while Bergson vividly describes the organic and evolutionary character of occurrent mental states—the contents of consciousness—he fails to account for the unity of the awareness of these states. As Kant and others have demonstrated, my very ability to individuate temporally this pain as coming before that feeling presupposes the numerical identity of a single enduring consciousness.[6] A unity grounded in qualitative similarity of content is not sufficient since the similar contents would fall in different worlds of experience. Thus, to collapse the distinction between consciousness and its contents, as Hume and Bergson do in different ways, is to give up the very possibility of distinguishing successive mental states and ultimately of entertaining a coherent concept of one's own experience. Since we do entertain such a concept and we do termporally individuate our experiences, it must be consciousness that links them together into *one* persisting mind.

Critics may point out that a "pure" consciousness is an impossibility since consciousness is always changing and change implies a change of some content. This would be a plausible challenge if it were independently established that consciousness is identical with its contents; a change in consciousness would then entail a change in contents. But such an identification is just the point at issue. It ought not be assumed to begin with. Since a pure consciousness (like Atman) does imply a changeless consciousness, we need to review those considerations that suggest that there is a legitimate sense in which consciousness may be changeless.

Three such considerations present themselves. The first is provided by the preceding Kantian argument that knowledge of temporal succession of one's experiences presupposes a changeless backdrop of consciousness against which "before" and "after" are rendered intelligible. A second is provided by the distinction between consciousness and its contents independently defended in this section. Any claim to be introspectively aware of a change in consciousness itself can be shown to be a claim about a change in the contents of consciousness. We will defend this claim further in the last section of this chapter. Finally, it may be urged that consciousness changes in the limited sense that it comes into and passes out of being for each of us in the course of a normal day and night. In the following section, however, we will see that there are no better reasons for supposing this to be true than for assuming that consciousness changelessly persists even through periods of dreamless sleep. There are, then, some provisional reasons for the thesis that consciousness, conceived as an underlying field of awareness, is changeless.

In *Philosophical Studies* G. E. Moore points out that consciousness is diaphanous, is not introspectable, that "blue is one object of sensation and green is another, and that consciousness, which both sensations have in common, is different from either."[7] While I am in essential agreement with Moore, I think that his way of stating the matter, nevertheless, has lent itself to the mistaken interpretation of consciousness as an aboriginal stuff attached in the form of a common introspectable property to its contents, the stuff which William James attacked in his famous essay "Does 'Consciousness' Exist?" I should like to dissociate my thesis from this interpretation, as would Moore. When we reflect on a pain qua pain and an afterimage qua afterimage, there is, of course, nothing intrinsic to the content of either to which we may attach the label "consciousness." Consciousness enters the picture, so to speak, as that for which pains and afterimages, together with their intrinsic properties, are objects. To treat consciousness as if it were a common property of its own contents is surely a category mistake.

It may be objected that the notion of a consciousness not identical with its contents is unintelligible. However, the charge of unintelligibility can be overworked for four reasons. First, for any person who correctly draws the distinction between being aware and being unconscious, some measure of intelligibility is entailed. Second, the concept with which we are concerned should not be assimilated to the truly unintelligible notion of a "bare particular." For nothing I have said entails that consciousness might be entirely contentless or propertyless. Somatic impressions and thoughts, for example, may be contents of consciousness though certainly not identical with it. And consciousness (like Atman) has, among others, the property of nonspatiality; it is not the kind of entity to which we ascribe predicates of location. To argue for the irreducibility of consciousness to its contents does not imply that it is something wholly other than, and only contingently attached to, its contents or its properties. It is simply to affirm that, within the total spectrum of consciousness, there is a domain of underlying awareness which may be experienced *as such*. Compressions (contents) within a field (consciousness) do not exhaust the field, even though they are expressions of it. Third, if the critic assumes that intelligibility can be achieved only by appealing to the contents of consciousness, then he is surely confused. For these contents are potential or actual objects for something other than themselves, that is, they are objects for consciousness. Fourth, if the charge of unintelligibility is to stick, then the earlier arguments supporting the distinction between consciousness and its contents must be shown to be either unintelligible or unsound. Barring this, we may assume a provisional intelligibility.

Of what significance is the preceding thesis for the concept of pure consciousness? The most plausible interpretation involves rejecting the assumption that only a consciousness from which all content had been subtracted might qualify as pure. On this interpretation, for example, Atman would be identified with consciousness but not with its contents or, alternatively, with the transcendent aspect of consciousness not exhausted by mental content of the sort we normally ascribe to persons. Thus, Atman keeps both its purity (emptiness of content) and its content by incorporating both within itself. This interpretation, or something close to it, seems required by the general Vedantic thesis that Atman is one, undifferentiated, and manifest in varying degrees of clarity through every level of human consciousness.[8] The consciousness involved in one's attending to his pain, for example, is not numerically other than pure consciousness identified with Brahman, although, of course, there are qualitative differences depending on one's stage of spiritual realization. The attached hypochondriac, for instance, dwells excessively on his pain, whereas the sage is largely indifferent to personal pain.

II

The thesis of intentionality—that to be conscious is to be conscious of something—has become such an article of faith that to question it is an act of intellectual heresy. Its qualified denial, however, is what the possibility of pure consciousness entails. While admitting that intentionality is a defining characteristic of our normal waking consciousness and dream states, it is absent in states of dreamless sleep and in *turiya*, a fourth state in which the absolute identity of Braham and Atman is realized—where consciousness persists without its objects.[9] We will focus on the third state of dreamless sleep, or what we normally depict as a state of unconsciousness. On the Vedantic view, what is "lost" in a state of dreamless sleep is not consciousness itself, but rather the objects of consciousness. One loses awareness of anything but does not become unaware.

Since the notion of an objectless consciousness is generally held to be an impossibility, our central purpose in this section will be to demonstrate its possibility. Moreover, I hope to show that this is not a mere possibility, but also that there are no better reasons for denying it than for affirming it.

From a logical point of view, the only way to guarantee the impossibility of an objectless consciousness is to identify consciousness with its objects. Such a move, however, would be self-defeating since then we could not even formulate the thesis of intentionality. Moreover, the supposition that consciousness is (conceptually) identical with its objects is unintelligible in view of the fact that we distinguish between *what* we are aware of and the fact *that* we are aware of it.

Second, the thesis of intentionality would not appear to be logically true, since it is advanced as a phenomenological description, as a fundamental thesis about experience. If it is not logically true, then its denial is not self-contradictory. From this it follows that an objectless consciousness is a logical possibility. However, the Vedantist could agree that it is an analytic consequence of someone's being conscious that he is aware of some object, and then respond by pointing out that this is analytically true only of waking and dreaming states since it is formulated within, and with respect to, those states. It does not entail the impossibility of an objectless consciousness in a state of dreamless sleep, any more than an analytic truth in one language necessarily corresponds to a counterpart in another language. In summary, the thesis of intentionality is a *descriptive* thesis about ordinary kinds of experience. Nowhere has it ever been argued that all possible forms of consciousness must be intentional.[10]

From a phenomenological point of view, the possibility of an objectless consciousness cannot be ruled out since "Jones was aware of (literally) nothing" and "Jones was unaware" (lacked awareness) describe identical states of Jones for Jones during his or her dreamless sleep. Moreover, from the fact that all persons who are awake are conscious of something, it does not follow that consciousness in certain other states cannot be objectless. Finally, from the fact that we cannot come across an objectless consciousness, it does not follow that it might not be objectless in certain contexts. For to make such a discovery would be to make consciousness its own object. To insist that an objectless consciousness be given as an object in experience would, thus, beg the issue when experience is defined as consciousness *of* some object.

It would appear, then, that logical or phenomenological arguments which might be urged against the possibility of an objectless consciousness and provide some rational basis for an unrestricted thesis of intentionality either beg the issue or turn on assumptions which can be rendered equally consistent with the possibility of an objectless consciousness. For example, since no person could directly experience the "losing" of consciousness, sentences such as "I lost consciousness around 10:30 A.M." can only be epistemologically grounded in an inference involving my memory of having been aware of no-thing after 10:30 A.M. (even though, of course, we do not make such inferences consciously).[11] Such sentences are equally consistent with having lost consciousness and its objects or just the objects themselves. To insist that, after all, if one has lost awareness of anything one has lost consciousness itself, is simply to beg the issue in favor of the thesis of intentionality. In sum, there appear to be no better (nonquestion-begging) reasons for denying the persistence of consciousness during dreamless sleep than for affirming it. An occasional objectless consciousness is, therefore, more than a bare logical possibility. It is also a fact amply documented in the first section of this volume.

III

A crucial issue raised by arguments of the preceding section is whether consciousness is fundamentally a relation between a subject and an object. For example, if consciousness is a relation and relations cannot exist without their terms, then an objectless consciousness is not a logical possibility. On the other hand, if an objectless consciousness is a logical possibility, then consciousness is not a relation. To avoid the specter of mutual question-begging, independent arguments should be forthcoming. Accordingly, I will provide several additional arguments for the thesis that consciousness is not a relation, a thesis also required by the doctrine of Brahman-Atman.

To begin, it is worth emphasizing that we seldom, if ever, treat consciousness as if it were a relation. For example, we speak of consciousness, on the one hand, and the objects or contents of consciousness, on the other. We speak of it as existing in its own right as a term that stands in relationships of intentionality to various objects. In a broader context, we speak of consciousness as a state in which persons may or may not be, just as we speak of pain as a state which some persons suffer. And pain is certainly not a relationship.

Second, it is sometimes argued that consciousness must be a relationship on the grounds that there can be no awareness without a subject who is aware of something. However, the persuasiveness of this argument depends on the false assumption that a critic of the relational view must argue that there can be awareness of something without its being awareness by a certain subject. The alternative for the critic is to point out that the conclusion is too strong for the premise. That is, (S_1) "Awareness of something entails awareness by a subject" is consistent with (S_2) "Consciousness stands in a relationship to a subject and his or her object." (S_2), However, is inconsistent with (S_3) "Consciousness is a relationship between a subject and an object." Therefore, (S_1) does not entail (S_3), thus, support for the relational view is accordingly lessened.

Third, the relational view gains some currency when the objects are other than oneself. It is at least suggested by sentences such as "I am aware of the scratch on the desk." However, if consciousness were an actual relationship between two things, a subject and an object, then self-awareness would be either impossible or require the adoption of a dubious ontology. For to be self-aware is to make an object of oneself, and the only actual relationship in which one stands to oneself is that of numerical identity. Yet, if consciousness is a relationship between two particulars, a subject and an object, then the subject who is aware of himself or herself must be distinct from the object of which there is awareness. It seems desirable, however, to avoid the excessive ontology of a transcendental self or ego implied by this consequence. From the preceding, it follows that either consciousness is not a relationship or self-awareness is impossible. But self-awareness is possible, therefore, consciousness is not a relationship.

Finally, consciousness is not a relationship since it is logically prior to the subject which it allegedly relates to an object. It is logically prior because self-consciousness, which is presupposed by one's knowing that he or she as subject stands in a certain relation to an object, itself presupposes being conscious, whereas being conscious does not entail being self-conscious. It is, of course, contingently true that conscious beings are occasionally self-conscious. Stated differently, the very distinction between subjects and their objects, between me and my world, is one that arises *in* consciousness.[12] Or again, myself, my relationships to the world, and the objects of my world are all actual or possible data for consciousness. In summary, if the preceding observations are correct, they entail that consciousness is, as Sartre and others have argued, *prepersonal.* And if consciousness is prepersonal, then it is not a relationship between persons and their objects.

IV

P. F. Strawson, among others, has argued that the defining feature of a set of experiences is that they are the experiences of some person.[13] Although it may be true that *if* consciousness is owned at all, it is owned necessarily, that is, logically belongs to some person or other, we need not think of it as being possessed in the first place. Rather, we may conceive of consciousness along the lines suggested above and as required by the Vedantic view of Atman (among others) as prepersonal. If so, then what is true of a "set of experiences" will not be true of consciousness per se. To establish this logical difference it will be necessary to show how the function of "my" in "my thoughts (sensations, feelings, and so on)" is not shared by the "my" in "my consciousness." Indeed, we will see that "my consciousness" does not even have a standard use with which to compare "my pain."

The logical wedge I wish to point out is this. The psychological expressions "my pain," "my depression," "my thoughts," and so on, each admit of informative predication upon which the significance of "my" is logically dependent. For example, "My pain is severe." The significance of "my" is that it individuates the possessor of the severe pain. It completes the phrase " . . . pain is severe." "My consciousness," on the other hand, does not admit of any informative predication capable of sustaining the significant inclusion of "my." How might we complete "My consciousness is . . . "? The addition of "nonspatial," for example, says nothing about my consciousness in particular, since everyone's consciousness shares this property. The inclusion of "my" adds nothing to "Consciousness is nonspatial."

Three counterexamples potentially undermine this analysis. First, one might urge equally that "My body has dimension" adds nothing to the concept of my body in particular. In response, however, it must be pointed out that my body admits of many other types of properties (e.g., color, height, etc.) which give a point to the question "Whose body is sunburned?"

A second counterexample is illustrated by "My consciousness is fading" or similar assertions implying degrees of consciousness. Surely, something informative about my consciousness in particular is being expressed here. The problem, however, is that such assertions are *not* about consciousness or awareness per se. Rather, they may be plausibly construed as circumlocutions for the facts expressed by, say, "My thoughts are becoming hazy" or "I am increasingly unable to differentiate the furniture in my room." Indeed, the latter sentences are the only way to explicate the meaning of "fading consciousness." Moreover, it is contradictory to suppose that one might be introspectively aware of fading awareness itself, that is, of something other than the furniture, thoughts, sounds, and so on, of which I am aware. Fading is with respect to the objects of consciousness, not to consciousness per se. In sum, it is the contents of consciousness which fade or change by degree, not consciousness itself.

A third counterexample is suggested by the question "Whose consciousness is focused on *X*?" for which an appropriate answer would be "Mine is" or "*Y*'s is." While such a question is a bit queer-sounding, it is perfectly intelligible. Its critical thrust, however, can be avoided; it does not logically commit us to thinking of consciousness as belonging to a certain person. For it can be rephrased as "For whom is *X* an object (of awareness)?" or more simply as "Who is aware of *X*?" And these translations leave it an open question whether the awareness invoked is someone's in particular or is conceivably a universal consciousness, numerically the same consciousness involved in "*X* is conscious," "*Y* is conscious," and so on. For what is expressly individuated in these sentences are persons, not individual consciousnesses.

We may conclude, then, that consciousness—as opposed to its contents and objects—is not the type of thing that is owned logically by each person. But what is the significance of this moderately technical foray into the domain of experiential ownership for the question of pure consciousness? For one thing, a pure consciousness (as the idea has been developed in this essay and elsewhere in this volume) is not individuatable. Widely discussed criteria of personal identity such as memories, physical appearance, and location in space under normal circumstances serve to individuate *persons*. Each person possesses such features. But since consciousness is not identical with its contents or objects which provide the stuff of personal identity, it follows that a pure consciousness (objectless, contentless, etc.) is not individuatable. Stated differently, if pure consciousness were individuatable in principle at any time, this would tend to rule out the possibility of pure consciousness on some occasions because such individuation could only be undertaken by reference to the very descriptive contents and objects which are lacking in pure consciousness. Any defender of the idea of pure consciousness needs to examine the question of whether it logically can be said to "belong" to the person who reports it. Any critic of that possibility needs to make the case for ownership of awareness per se. I hope to have shown why that case is not likely to be made.

There is an even larger implication lurking in the background. If consciousness is not logically ownable, then it is not necessarily plural, that is, there need not be an indefinitely large number of consciousness, each necessarily attached to some person. Indeed, there might well be but one universal consciousness manifesting itself through each of us in virtually infinite variety. Giving up the idea that a state of pure consciousness is logically possessed does *not* mean that someone else might possess it or that one might become confused about whose consciousness it is. It means that there may be no more than one (universal consciousness) to farm around.

Certainly, such an idea is consistent with the experience of pure consciousness. For those who report such experiences never describe consciousness identical with any empirical objects (e.g., a brain) as being located either inside or even in the vicinity of their body or, indeed, as having any *boundaries* whatsoever. A consciousness without intrinsic boundaries is a good candidate for an infinite universal consciousness. Such conclusions lend themselves to the type of cosmology developed in Advaita Vedanta where Atman, the apparently individual consciousness, appears in the context of progressive spiritual practices to be without boundaries and at its most fundamental level identical with Brahman, the infinite consciousness which is both source and sustainer of the universe.

In such a proposal consistent with the logic of introspective testimony? I submit that introspection is equally consistent with an underlying pluralism *or* a monism; it does not support the former any more than the latter. For what is given in introspection are data or objects for consciousness, namely, thoughts, emotions, sensations, and so on, not a numerically distinct consciousness. If consciousness cannot be its own object, then it cannot be given as one among several of my mental objects. It is not given as an individual or as a universal entity. The antecedent of this claim, however, requires further clarification and defense.

Can consciousness be its own object? On the one hand, such a possibility seems unintelligible. What would it be like to discriminate consciousness, to place it within the flux of one's experience in the way, say, that one might compare the severity of this morning's pain with this afternoon's pain? On the other hand, if consciousness can be its own object or datum and if to be an object is to be an object for consciousness, then such a possibility encounters the need for an infinite series of consciousnesses, the function of each of which would be to be conscious of another "lower order" consciousness. Of course, there may be awareness of internal or external activity such as deliberate motion, which we designate as "conscious" activity; one can obviously be aware of the fact that one is aware. But this does not make a datum of consciousness any more than the eye's reflection in a mirror is an instance of actually looking at itself. In self-knowledge, consciousness is never given as one among many objects.

A rebuttal to this argument is presented by Sartre.[14] He points out that there is consciousness of consciousness in the very act of its positional focus on objects other than itself. If we wish to avoid an infinite regress of consciousnesses, he argues, then we must posit an immediate, "nonpositional" relation of consciousness to itself. We may grant Sartre's claim with the rejoinder that it is only positional consciousness of (mental) objects that is at stake. In Sartrean terms, my argument depends only on the fact that there cannot be positional consciousness of consciousness—which Sartre would grant. The claim that consciousness cannot be its own object remains intact.

In summary, just as (with the early Wittgenstein) nothing in my visual field allows me to infer that its objects are seen with my eyes, nothing in my experience permits me to logically infer that its contents are objects for my consciousness rather than for a universal consciousness. The transcendental character of consciousness escapes particularization, whether depicted as the spaceless, timeless Atman of Vedanta, as the nothingness of Sartre, the void of Buddhism, or the boundless radiance of Sufism.

It should be stressed that the experience of pure consciousness per se does not entail any particular metaphysical schemes such as the monistic one just suggested. Still less does it entail the truth of any particular spiritual tradition such as Vedanta. I have offered these concluding speculations only by way of encouraging further discussion of the larger metaphysical implications of the experience of pure consciousness. My principal aim in this essay has been to show that there are no considerations of a logical or phenomenological nature that rule out the possibility of that experience.

NOTES

1. For example, see Brand Blandshard and B. F. Skinner, "The Problem of Consciousness: A Debate," *Philosophy and Phenomenological Research*, 27 (1967), and Kenneth Sayre, *Consciousness: A Philosophic Study of Minds and Machines* (New York: Random House, 1969), especially chap. 7, where it is argued that consciousness is essentially a form of information processing.

2. Eliot Deutsch, *Advaita Vedanta: A Philosophical Reconstruction* (Honolulu: East-West Center Press, 1969), p. 48.

3. A more extensive discussion of this fundamental sense of consciousness is given by C. O. Evans in *The Subject of Consciousness* (London: Allen & Unwin, 1970), sect. 2.

4. Jean-Paul Sartre, *Being and Nothingness*, trans. Hazel Barnes (New York: Philosophical Library, 1956), p. ix.

5. Hume's genetic and atomistic epistemology is well known. In *A Treatise of Human Nature*, ed. Selby-Bigge (City Oxford University Press, 1978), p. 259, he argues that "every distinct perception [content], which enters into the composition of the mind, is a distinct existence, and is different, and distinguishable, and separable from every other perception, either contemporary or successive." In so doing he raises what some have described as the problem of the gap. What connects one's changing mental contents? For Hume the answer was "nothing" except the force of habit generated by repeated qualitative similarity.

6. A defense of the transcendental unity of apperception is given by P. F. Strawson in *The Bounds of Sense* (London: Methuen, 1966), pt. III, sect. 2. Whether Kant's arguments demonstrate the identity of a persisting self is a different issue.

7. G. E. Moore, *Philosophical Studies* (New York: Macmillan, 1959), p. 17.

8. This interpretation is supported by Deutsch, *Advaita Vedanta* p. 63, and by Troy Organ in *The Self in Indian Philosophy* (The Hague: Mouton, 1964), chap. 6.

9. For textual exigesis and comment on this thesis from the *Mandukya Upanishad*, see S. Prabhavananda, *Vedic Religion and Philosophy* (Madras, India: Jupiter Press, 1957), pp. 60–65.

10. This point is developed in greater detail by Robert K. C. Forman, "Constructivism in Dogen, Yogacara Buddhism, and in Heister Bockhart" PhD. d. ss., Columbia University, 1988. See also R. L. Franklin's chapter entitled "Experience and Interpretation in Mysticism" in the present volume.

11. Advaitins argue that if consciousness were absent during a state of dreamless sleep, no subsequent memory affirmation about this period could be made. However, we do say "I remember nothing while I was asleep," hence, consciousness must persist. This argument's plausibility depends on the interpretation given to "memory affirmation." For a discussion see Deutsch, *Advaita Vedanta* p. 61.

12. This point is the familiar Kantian one. However, it is also taken by developmental psychologists as an empirical truth when the priority is temporal. Infants, for example, are conscious before they learn to distinguish between themselves and their world.

13. P. F. Strawson, *Individuals* (London: Methuen, 1959), p. 92.

14. Sartre, *Being and Nothingness*, p. liii.

Is Mystical Experience Everywhere the Same?

NORMAN PRIGGE and GARY KESSLER

The belief that mystical experience or that some especially important variety thereof is everywhere the same, regardless of the idiosyncracies of the individual mystic or of his or her cultural tradition, has been tacitly presupposed, dogmatically asserted, or explicitly argued for in much scholarly and popular literature on mysticism. All of this notwithstanding, Steven T. Katz, in a recent article entitled "Language, Epistemology, and Mysticism,"[1] has attempted to show this belief false.

This attempt came to the two of us as a direct challenge, for we had long assumed (rather uncritically it must be confessed) that the belief in question was true, even obviously so. In trying to respond to Katz's challenge, we became more aware of a defect that inheres in most of the literature on mysticism, including Katz's article. That defect consists in the lack of precise definitions of 'mystical experience' (and of such related terms as 'consciousness,' 'intentionality,' 'content of consciousness,' etc.) and of 'sameness' as applied to experiences in general and to mystical experience in particular.[2] Without adequate definitions of these terms, the belief concerning the sameness of mystical experience is not even intelligible, much less true, or for that matter false. We propose to

This is a revised version of a paper first published in *Sophia* 21 (April 1982), 39–55.

rectify this defect by providing the requisite definitions. Based on these, we will show that in one important respect mystical experience of at least one important variety is everywhere the same.

KATZ'S CHALLENGE

Because Katz's argument largely takes the form of a critique of Walter T. Stace's views on mysticism, it is appropriate that we begin with an examination of the latter. Stace recognizes at least two major types of mystical experience: the extrovertive and the introvertive. Their characteristics are identical but for one exception: the extrovertive experience is characterized by seeing all phenomenal things as one, and the world as a living presence, whereas the introvertive type is an experience of undifferentiated unity which transcends space and time. Stace believes that the introvertive experience is the highest form of the mystical experience, and he maintains that such mystical experience is everywhere the same. In order to support the latter position, he distinguishes between experience and interpretation. Thus, though Stace acknowledges the diversity in reports mystics have given, he does not account for that diversity in terms of differences among experiences. Rather, he attributes the diversity to the theologically and culturally bound interpretations of those experiences.

Although Stace acknowledges that it is often difficult to distinguish an experiential given from its interpretation, still he insists that the distinction can be made. He offers an anecdote about the American visitor in London who tried to shake hands with a waxwork policeman at the entrance of Madame Tussaud's as an example of its possibility. He writes, "If such an incident ever occurred, it must have been because the visitor had a sense experience which he first wrongly interpreted as a live policeman and later interpreted correctly as a wax figure."[3]

What Stace fails to see is that the American visitor has not had one experience with two different interpretations but that, in fact, he had two different experiences. To see a wax policeman as alive and to see a wax policeman as wax are two different experiences. Stace's failure to recognize this point is due to his particular model of experience. Stace believes that there is something given in experience which is not contaminated, so to speak, by interpretation and that it is possible, given adequate analysis, to isolate this pure given and thereby to distinguish it from its interpretation.

Katz criticizes Stace's position on the grounds that it fails to recognize the "two-directional symmetry" between experience and interpretation.[4]

Katz argues that there is no such thing as a pure experience. All experience is mediated by psychological, cultural, and conceptual factors. The context of an experience is crucial for determining the nature of that experience.

Armed with these views, Katz attacks various versions of the thesis that mystical experiences are everywhere the same. He concludes, as might be expected, that they are everywhere different because their context is everywhere different. In so concluding, it is clear that Katz is assuming a model of experience which is different from Stace's model. Katz's model pictures experience as constituted by the interactions of both content and context.[5]

Katz's radical contextualism, that is, his position that all experiences are mediated by their context, leads to the conclusion that all experiences are so unique that it is impossible to speak of various experiences being the same in this or that sense. The conclusion not only falsifies the claim that all mystical experiences are essentially the same—and this is Katz's intention—but it precludes speaking of any *kinds* of experience, for to say experiences are of the same kind is to say that they are the same in some respect taken as essential for the purposes at hand. To preclude speaking thus is clearly not Katz's intention since he speaks again and again not only of different kinds of experiences, but also of different kinds of mystical experiences. Katz does not explain why certain experiences constitute legitimate kinds, whereas mystical experiences do not. Presumably he would argue that mystical experiences do not constitute a legitimate kind because they have no necessary and sufficient characteristic or, what is the same, because 'mystical experience' has no real definition. This argument does not persuade us, however; instead it challenges us to seek such a characteristic, to articulate such a definition.

Stace's analysis, however wrong it may be, suggests a useful procedure whereby an alternative explication might be devised which does not preclude, *ab initio,* the possibility of mystical experiences being the same. Stace begins, if we can infer the process from the product, with clear-cut cases or reports of cases of actual mystical experiences. He chooses as his clear-cut cases various experiences of what he calls the unitive or introvertive variety. Keeping these in mind, he examines ordinary experience for some distinction, applicable there, which would also be applicable to the clear-cut cases of mystical experience in such a way as to illuminate the essential nature of such experience. The distinction Stace finds is (as we have seen) that between an experiential given and its interpretation. Thereupon he tries to apply this distinction to other candidates for mystical experience.

We, like Stace, will choose experiences of the unitive and introvertive variety as paradigmatic of mystical experience of a certain type. Taking our lead from Katz, we will not employ Stace's actual distinction between an experiential given and its interpretation, but we will seek others that will do the work that Stace requires but that are also compatible with Katz's contextualism. We will not try to prove that other candidates for mystical experience can be assimilated to the cases we have chosen as a clear-cut, and we will thereby escape the criticism that we should have chosen another kind of putative mystical experience as our paradigm. If it should turn out that such assimilation is impossible, at the very least we will have given the phenomenology of one important kind of experience, a phenomenology that Katz promises but does not deliver.

A DEFINITION OF 'MYSTICAL EXPERIENCE' AND OF RELATED TERMS

'Consciousness' and its variants have an everyday meaning (or ordinary usage), and it is with the latter that the process of forming a definition of the former must begin. To state of anything *X*—usually, of course, of a person but sometimes also of an animal—that *X* is conscious, is to deny that *X* is unconscious in a mode which can usually be inferred from the situation in which the statement is made or to which it refers. Thus, for example, to state that *X* is conscious where *X* has been asleep is to deny that *X* is still asleep or, what is the same, to affirm that *X* is awake; to state that *X* is conscious where *X* has been knocked out of drugged is to deny that *X* is still knocked out or drugged; to state that *X* is conscious where *X* appears to have died or to be inanimate, is to deny that *X* has died or is inanimate or, what is the same, to affirm that *X* is alive or really animate; and so forth. To state of any *X* that *X* is conscious *simpliciter,* that is, conscious independent of any situation from which the particular mode of unconsciousness to be thereby denied can be inferred, can only be—in the absence of a more technical definition of 'consciousness'—to deny that *X* is unconscious in any such mode, to deny, that is, that *X* is asleep, knocked out, drugged, dead, inanimate, and so forth.

An ascription of consciousness is, then, a denial of one or another mode of unconsciousness or of all modes together. Put otherwise, the affirmative ascription takes its meaning from the negativities negated.[6] Of course, there are borderline cases, where *X* may be dreaming or just coming to or half-dead or *X* may be a not very advanced animal, evolutionarily speaking. Such cases notwithstanding, the clear-cut cases are sufficiently numerous to permit the following ordinary language definition of 'consciousness' and its variants: an instance of "*X* is conscious" is true if and only if the corresponding instance of "*X* is not asleep, knocked out or drugged . . . " is true. Derivatively, more simply, and rather more loosely, we can say that consciousness is the absence of any modes of unconsciousness.

Many philosophers will be put off, no doubt, by the looseness, negativity, and open-endedness of this ordinary language definition. Indeed, many since Brentano and perhaps even earlier have sought a strict, affirmative, closed definition, one which captures some relatively simple essence of all consciousness. Specifically, they have sought first to reduce consciousness to consciousnesses and second to define 'a consciousness' in terms, *inter alia*, of intentionality. But before we can assess the success of these two quests, we must be clear what we mean by 'a consciousness,' or—to prevent obvious confusions with 'consciousness' (without the article)—of what will henceforth be called 'a content of consciousness.'

Let a subjective statement be defined as one that can be false only if the person making the statement is dissembling or is misusing the language. Examples of subjective statements would be, "I am in pain" and "I am perceiving what I take to be a table." These particular statements could be false only if the person making them were either dissembling about his pain or about the apparent object of his peception or if he were misusing language—for example, if by "pain" he meant "debt" or by "table" he meant "chair." It has been claimed that there are no subjective statements,[7] a claim patently belied by the above examples. It has been claimed that such statements are rare and useless.[8] This second claim is true insofar as ordinary usage is concerned. At the same time, the mere possibility of such statements, however rare their actuality, is philosophically useful minimally insofar as they provide the grammatical means of defining the notion of content of consciousness.[9]

Let a content of consciousness of a given person be defined as the truth-condition of a true subjective statement he or she could make or could have made. The pain and the perception of what is taken to be a table, which are necessary and sufficient for the truth of the aforementioned examples, respectively, are contents of consciousness of the person who could truly make or have made them. Note that contents of consciousness are not Stace's experiential givens prior to interpretation: the former, presumably unlike the latter, can be enormously complex—as is, for example, my seeming to remember what I think now that I thought then was anger caused by what I take to have been my wife—a far cry from Russell's "red-patch-here-now." Note, too, the distinction between an experiential given and its interpretation cannot be applied to contents of consciousness; on the contrary, contents of consciousness are the very gestalten that constitute consciousness from Katz's contextualist point of view. And note, finally—what must here be taken as unproblematic—that a content of consciousness may be, and usually is, the truth-condition of a merely possible rather than actual, true subjective statement.[10]

Having defined 'content of consciousness,' we can return to the matter of assessing the success of the two aforementioned quests. The first quest, the attempt to reduce consciousness to contents of consciousness, can succeed only if all instances of consciousness are instances of contents of consciousness. But it is not a priori necessary that whenever people are conscious that they have a content of consciousness, because the ordinary language definition of 'consciousness' does not require that there be a content. It is logically possible for people to be conscious (not asleeep, not knocked out, etc.) without having a content of consciousness. Further, it seems empirically false that whenever people are conscious they have a content of consciousness. It is false precisely with respect to people having introvertive unitive mystical experiences. Such experiences are sometimes referred to as experiences involving a 'pure consciousness' precisely because there is no content to these experiences. Hence, the prima facie evidence is against those who would reduce consciousness to contents of consciousness. And, hence, the burden of proof falls on those who would assert that there is always an empirical correlation between consciousness and contents of consciousness. If they are to establish their case empirically, they must do so without tautologizing the pure consciousness experience out of the realm of existence or into the realm of being-a-content-despite-all-appearances-to-the-contrary. We submit that such a proof would be not only burdensome to effect, but quite impossible.

With respect to the second quest, that of defining the notion of content of consciousness in terms of 'intentionality,' we must begin by examining the crucial notion of 'intentionality.' Let that notion be explicated thus: a content of consciousness is intentional if and only if it is a consciousness of something different from itself. Note that the "something different from itself" is usually, but not always, a spatiotemporal object (or event, or relation, etc.) of the external nonmental world. However, it can also be of (concrete but nonspatial) contents of consciousness, in which case it would be a reflective self-consciousness, or of (nonspatial, nontemporal) abstract objects.[11] This explication of intentionality cannot, however, serve as a definition of 'content of consciousness' because it would be circular (the putative *definiendum* would be employed via the expression 'a consciousness,' in the putative *definiens*). The only possible way of eliminating the circularity, namely, by defining 'a content of conscious-ness' as 'whatever is of something different from itself' would commit the fallacy of being too broad. Many types of things (e.g., photographs) are of things different from themselves but are nevertheless not contents of consciousness. Further, intentionality, far from defining content of con-sciousness, is not even a necessary condition thereof. A pain, for exam-ple, though a content of consciousness, intends no object different from itself. Thus, we cannot intelligibly use an instance of "X has a pain of. . . . " So also (though perhaps less obviously) of images of purely imagi-nary objects. For example, when a person imagines a golden mountain, there is nothing apart from the image which the image is of. The image just is the imaginary golden mountain; that there is no object of the image different from it is just what we mean by calling the object imaginary. Clearly, then, 'content of consciousness' cannot be defined in terms of 'intentionality.'

Assuming that unitive mystical experience truly is consciousness with-out content, then the following definition is in order: an instance of "X is having a unitive mystical experience" is true if and only if the corre-sponding instance of "X is conscious but has no content of conscious-ness" is true. Derivatively, more simply, and rather more loosely, we can say that unitive mystical experience is contentless consciousness, mean-ing thereby that it is a conjunction of the absence of any modes of unconsciousness with the simultaneous absence of any content of con-sciousness. This definition of unitive mystical experience as contentless consciousness is (as already noted) self-consistent; whether it is useful depends entirely on whether it really does apply to such experience. That it does will be proved by showing, in the succeeding section, that it accords with, and explains, typical characterizations of the experience, characterizations devised both by thinkers reflecting on reports of pure consciousness and by mystics reflecting on their own experience.

Before we proceed with this task, however, it should be noted that there is a second way consciousness can be contentless or (perhaps put better) a second way of describing that contentlessness. The first way, that which we have taken above, namely, that of describing the contentlessness as absolute—as such that the mystic, in recalling his experience, for exam-ple, cannot remember any content at all—is suggested not only by what mystics say, but by the kind of contemplation many practice: they system-atically blank out, often by means of intense concentration on a nondimensional point, all consciousness of external material objects, all internal sensations, all abstract thoughts, and finally all sense of will or of self, leaving only pure consciousness or, what is the same, consciousness of sheer nothingness. The second way of describing this contentlessness is as total lack of attention to whatever content is present. In such a case, one would be experiencing subliminally, as it were, such that he could, perhaps, recall contents that he was not explicitly aware of at the time but which he would have been aware of had he attended. We realize that it is extremely awkward to speak of a content of consciousness which is not conscious or not really so, for surely, regarding such contents, *esse est percipi*. Yet at the same time we realize that there are phenomena of this sort, wherein one's mind is blank, yet where one may recall explicitly contents to which one had not attended and of which, in some important sense, one was not really aware at the time. In any event, whether mystical experience is contentless in the absolute sense articulated herein; or whether it is a function of sheer nonattention, perhaps coupled with intense concentration on nothing at all; or whether it is one or the other depending on the person, time, and place—that could, it would seem, be determined empirically by asking various mystics. In any case the experiences would be the same in the sense to be articulated anon, for they would differ only with regard to after-the-fact extrinsic aspects of the experiences (e.g., the ability or inability to recall contents, etc.).

A PROOF THAT OUR DEFINITION APPLIES TO UNITIVE MYSTICAL EXPERIENCE

The unitive mystical experience is often characterized as an experience that is without object, without subject, and wholly ineffable. We propose in this section to show that the definition of unitive mystical experience as contentless consciousness accords with these three characterizations and (indeed, perhaps for the first time) explains clearly what they mean. Pure consciousness is also characterized as tranquil, intuitive, eternal, blissful, and ecstatic. We leave it to the reader to work out the manner in which our definition accords with and explains these other characterizations.

Preliminary to the discussion of the relation between our definition and the aforementioned characterizations (without object, without subject, wholly ineffable), several formulations must be set forth. These formulations are somewhat loose, but they will do nicely enough for present purposes. Let one content of consciousness be called intrinsic to another if and only if the statement of which the second content is the truth-condition logically entails the statement of which the first is the truth-condition; let all else be called extrinsic. For example, the image of whitewall tires would be intrinsic to the image of what I take to be a blue 1952 Chevrolet with whitewall tires, whereas the second image would be extrinsic to the first, since "I am imagining what I take to be a blue 1952 Chevrolet with whitewall tires" entails "I am imagining whitewall tires"—but not vice versa. Also extrinsic to the image of whitewall tires would be a simultaneous pain, a preceding anticipation, the imaginer's brain, actual whitewall tires, and so forth. Let the context of an experience be defined as the set of everything such that it is extrinsic to the experience, and either the experience is dependent on it or it is dependent on the experience.[12] 'Thing' is to include any object, event, fact, indeed, any content of consciousness and, indeed, any mystical experience.[13] One thing is dependent on another if and only if the first is such that if it did not exist or were different from what it was, then the second would not exist or would be different from what it was. For example, an image a person has is presumably dependent on the person's brain, and a subsequent memory of an image is dependent on the original image; hence, both the brain and the memory, being in addition extrinsic to the image, belong to its context.

An experience can have an object in both an ordinary and in a derivative sense. In the ordinary sense, the object of an experience is the object intended by the experience. For example, the object of a perception is the thing perceived, that of a memory is the thing remembered, and so forth. The object of an experience in this sense is (as noted earlier) usually a spatiotemporal object, though it can also be a content of consciousness or an abstract object. In any event any experience which has an object in this sense is a content of consciousness, for all intentional consciousnesses must be contents of consciousness. In the derivative sense, an experience may sometimes be said to have itself as an object. For example, an image of a golden mountain has (as we have seen) an "object," namely the golden mountain as imagined, but the image and its "object" are identical. Once again, the only kind of experience that can have an object in this sense is a content of consciousness. Since pure consciousness is contentless consciousness—since, that is, it neither is nor has a content of consciousness—it cannot have an object, either in the ordinary or in the derivative sense.

An experience can have a subject also in either an ordinary or in a derivative sense. In the ordinary sense, the subject of an experience is the person having the experience. That person is part of the context of the experience and is extrinsic to the content of the experience. In the derivative sense, the subject of the experience is the awareness of self intrinsic to the experience. That awareness can be explicit or implicit. It is explicit in the case of self-conscious or reflected experience, where one is conscious of oneself having a content of consciousness. Thus, where there is no content of consciousness or (what has been seen above to be the same) where there is no object of the experience, there can be no explicit awareness of self. In the case of ordinary unreflected experience, where awareness of self consists solely in a sense of an otherness standing over against an object intended by the experience, therein the awareness is merely implicit or prerelective (as it is sometimes called). If, of course, there is no object of the experience—if, that is, the experience is not a content of consciousness—then there can be no implicit awareness of self standing over against an object. Consequently, a unitive mystical experience, neither being nor having a content of consciousness—having no object in any sense—cannot have a subject in the derivative sense. At the same time it must, of course, have a subject in the ordinary sense. Therewith the paradox of saying of a fully embodied mystic that his mystical experience has no subject is resolved. His mystical experience has a subject in the ordinary sense, a subject, however, which is extrinsic to the experience. At the same time his experience has no subject in the derivative sense, no subject, or awareness of self, which is intrinsic to the experience.

Of course, the above analysis depends, in part, on the descriptions mystics have given. One might object, as Katz does, that trusting such accounts is problematic because many mystics also claim that their experiences are ineffable. If their experiences are ineffable, then not only is the status of their descriptions called into question, but, according to Katz, there is no possibility of comparing mystical experiences. Those who claim that mystical experiences are everywhere the same and are ineffable are caught in a contradiction. If Katz is right, however, then, as he does not seem to realize, it must be equally impossible for him to claim that such experiences are everywhere different and yet ineffable.

If we define pure consciousness as contentless consciousness, the problem of ineffability can be handled easily. One can talk about an experience either by describing what is intrinsic to it or by describing some aspect of its context. But since a unitive mystical experience neither is, nor has a content of, consciousness, no content whatsoever is intrinsic to it: in this sense it is ineffable. On the other hand, a unitive mystical experience, like any other experience, has a context, and to the extent the context can be described, to that extent the experience can be talked about. Hence, one cannot say of a unitive mystical experience what it was of, who was sensed in the experience as having it, or what simpler experiences made it up. One can say, of course, who had the experience, when and where he or she had it, and so forth, all these latter matters having to do with the context of the experience. One can also say that the experience had no object, no (sensed) subject, no simpler experiential parts, in short, that it was contentless, that nothing was intrinsic to it, and, in that sense, that nothing can be said about it. Such "descriptions" may be generalized, as herein, so as to apply to all such experiences. But these "descriptions" adhere strictly to the *via negativa:* they say what the experience is not, not what it is. Any positive description of a particular pure consciousness or of all such expriences in general will either be itself a genuine, though not readily obvious, negation—as is the case with the characterization of the unitive mystical experience as being tranquil or eternal—or else it will be an affirmation about some aspect of its con-text—as is the case with the characterization of the unitive mystical experience as bringing tranquility, or knowledge, or whatever. Therewith is resolved the paradox of saying so much about what one says one can say nothing about.

A DEFINITION OF 'SAMENESS' AS APPLIED TO EXPERIENCES IN GENERAL AND TO UNITIVE MYSTICAL EXPERIENCE IN PARTICULAR

Having defined unitive mystical experience as contentless consciousness and shown the definition accords with typical characterizations of that experience, it now remains to consider the question of sameness. Our present task is to get clear about the meaning of 'sameness' as applied to experiences in general and to the unitive mystical experience in particu-lar. Perhaps the best way of getting straight initially about what it is (or is not) for two experiences to be the same is to come to some understanding of what it is (or is not) for two experiences to be different.

There are two senses in which two experiences are necessarily differ-ent. The first is that being two, they are numerically different; they are either experiences of different people, or they are experiences of the same person at different times, or through different sense organs, or whatever. This sense is quite trivial, for difference in this sense is hardly ever what is affirmed when two things, including experiences, are said to be different and hardly ever what is denied when two things, including experiences, are said to be the same.

The second sense is that two experiences necessarily have different contexts, which is to say among other things, that some of the things, including experiences, which they are dependent on or which depend on them will be necessarily different, though the difference need not always be very great or very significant. Thus, to take an extreme case, where the difference is quite small and insignificant: a person looks at a chair and, without otherwise moving, closes his or her eyes for a brief moment, opens them, and again looks at the chair. The two visual experiences are different, not just numerically but by virtue of having (slightly) different contexts, for the later experience has as a part of its context a temporally later segment of the space–time object we call the observer's brain, a segment that the first experience does not have.

As the preceding example indicates, this second sense of difference is likewise trivial, and the reason is not hard to discern: it simply is the notion of numerical difference as applied to experiences. To say of two experiences that they are numerically distinct is to say that they are either experiences of different people, or they are experiences of the same person at different times or through different sense organs, or whatever. To say the latter is necessarily to say that they have different contexts, and vice versa. If, as is the case, the second sense of difference simply is numerical difference as applied to experience and if, as is the case, numerical difference is trivial, then so is this second sense. To be sure we often say nontrivially of two experiences (e.g., the aborigine's experience of a ballpoint pen and ours) that they are different because their contexts are different—never merely because the contexts are different, but because they are different in a very significant way. More generally, to say of two numerically distinct experiences or of their contexts that they are different is (almost) never to affirm a tautology; to say of them that they are the same is (almost) never to affirm a contradiction. Consequently, any nontrivial sense of difference (and sameness) must be sought outside the notion of numerical difference (and identity).

The foregoing affords us the means of reconstructing and simultaneously of criticizing one possible version of Katz's argument leading to the conclusion that (unitive) mystical experiences are not always the same. The argument would run thus: since all (numerically distinct) experiences necessarily have different contexts, all such experiences necessarily are different, and as with experiences in general, so then with unitive mystical experiences in particular. The criticism, of course, would run: the sense of difference employed in the argument is trivial, rendering the conclusion a tautology. If Katz would repudiate this reconstruction of his argument—which in the face of the criticism he would presumably do— he would be obliged first to explicate a notion of sameness and difference in a significant way, significant in the sense of capturing and perhaps refining our ordinary meaning when we say of two experiences that they are the same or different. Second, he would need to show that in this sense unitive mystical experiences are never the same, or anyway some-times not the same. The first of these tasks, and a *fortiori* the second, Katz does not even begin. We propose in the remainder of this essay to complete the first and to show the second futile, for as it will turn out, unitive mystical experiences, in the one most significant sense of same-ness, are everywhere the same.

Two numerically distinct experiences can be deemed the same by virtue of the similarity of that which is intrinsic to them or by virtue of the similarity of their extrinsic contexts. Thus, for example, the sameness of my experience of the table with Z's the next moment when Z assumes my point of view is not only partly dependent on, but is partly constituted by the sameness of certain qualities or aspects of the contexts of the two experiences. Nevertheless, the contexts of two experiences would never be deemed to be the same or different if the contents thereof were not thought to be the same or different. As a consequence we will concentrate here on the sameness and difference of experiences qua what is intrinsic to them, that is, qua contents of consciousness. Thus by 'qualitative sameness' we will mean the sameness of experiences thus more narrowly construed, knowing that whatever is said about their qualitative sameness and difference can be said, *mutatis mutandis,* about them construed more broadly to include their contexts.

The qualitative sameness of two numerically distinct experiences and, indeed, of any two numerically distinct things can be defined either affirmatively, in terms of the presence of similarities, or negatively, in terms of the absence of differences. More specifically with regard to the affirmative definition, to say that two numerically distinct experiences are qualitatively the same is to say that they have qualities or aspects which are the same. It is not required that they have all the same qualities or aspects. Nor need the qualities or aspects which are the same be identical in each. Thus, for example, two experiences can be said to be of the same color even when the shades in each case are not identical; indeed, complete identity is perhaps impossible. Similarity is sufficient to consti-tute sameness of quality or aspect, depending on degree of similarity and on the purposes of the person adjudging sameness. And sameness of certain qualities or aspects is sufficient to constitute sameness of experi-ences, depending on the number and importance of the similar qualities or aspects as determined by the purposes of the person adjudging same-ness.[14] Just so an image of a blue 1952 Chevrolet with whitewall tires may be deemed the same as an image of a blue 1952 Chevrolet with regular tires, provided it is the color and make of the car rather than its tires that one is focusing on. In any event absolute qualitative identity of the images is not required, nor is it perhaps even possible.

Qualitative sameness of two numerically distinct experiences can be defined negatively as well as affirmatively. The negative definition of qualitative sameness of experiences is as follows: two numerically distinct experiences are qualitatively the same if and only if they are not different. Clearly, the notion of difference of experiences must be explicated before this definition is at all illuminating. To say of two numerically distinct experiences that they are different is to say that they have qualities or aspects that are different. It is not required, nor is it possible, that they have all different qualities or aspects. Nor need the qualities or aspects which are different be radically dissimilar. Thus, for example, two experiences can be said to be of different colors even when their colors are two shades of the same generic color. Difference of certain qualities or aspects is sufficient to constitute difference between experiences, depending on the number and importance of the dissimilar qualities or aspects as determined by the purposes of the person adjudging difference. Just so an image of a blue 1952 Chevrolet with whitewall tires may be deemed different from an image of a blue 1952 Chevrolet with regular tires, provided it is the tires and not the color and make of the car that one is focusing on. In any event absolute qualitative difference of the images is not required, nor is it perhaps even possible.

Since the presence of similarity and the absence of difference are normally equivalent in meaning, it is normally a matter of indifference which definition is employed in assessing whether two numerically distinct experiences are the same. But what is normally the case is not always the case, and here it is specifically not the case with mystical experience of the pure consciousness sort. The affirmative definition of sameness is inapplicable to mystical experience insofar as the later is construed as contentless consciousness. For, it will be recalled, two numerically distinct experiences are the same—in the affirmative sense of sameness—only if they have similar qualities and aspects. But the only thing intrinsic to an experience that can have qualities and aspects is a content of cosnciousness. But since unitive mystical experiences cannot be or have a content of consciousness, there cannot obtain any similarity between them, qua contents. Hence two unitive mystical experiences cannot be deemed to be the same in the affirmative sense.

The negative definition of sameness, on the other hand, is completely applicable to unitive mystical experience. Two experiences, it will be recalled, are qualitatively the same if and only if they are not different, and they are different only if they have different qualities or aspects. But the only thing intrinsic to an experience that can have a quality or aspect is a content of consciousness. But since unitive mystical experiences cannot be or have a content of consciousness, there cannot obtain any difference between them, qua contents—and this, not because their contents are so similar, but because they have none whatsoever. And since two such experiences cannot be different, then, given the negative definition of sameness, they must be the same.

The absence of difference between two unitive mystical experiences is absolute in two senses: first, it is a priori necessary rather than contingent, for it is not that such experiences do not as a matter of fact have no differences, but that they cannot as a matter of definition; and second, it is in no way dependent on the purposes of the persons whose experiences are in question, for such purposes are germaine only to adjudging sameness and difference of contents and their qualities and aspects.

But if there can be no differences between unitive mystical experiences, and if this absence of difference is absolute in the senses specified, then these experiences must be the same, for (as has already been explicated) two things are the same if and only if they are not different; furthermore, the sameness in question must be absolute in the same senses as before, namely, that it is a priori necessary and that it is in no way dependent on the purposes of the persons whose experiences are in question, and for the same reasons as were specified above. Thus, the grounds for saying that unitive mystical experiences cannot be different are *ipso facto* grounds for saying that they must be the same, that the sameness is absolute in senses that are both possible and necessary, and that they are strong enough to satisfy the most rigorous of critics.[15]

Getting philosophically clear about the nature of mystical experience is important. But far more important than intellectual clarification is the experience itself. The mystical saints of all religions have attested to this value for transforming one's existence, and, as philosophers, we must never forget that our own tradition has taught that mystical contemplation is of greater value than rational clarification. But rational clarification can be a step along the path to the mystical. It is in this spirit that our essay is offered.

NOTES

1. Steven T. Katz, "Language, Epistemology, and Mysticism," in *Mysticism and Philosophical Analysis*, ed. Steven T. Katz (New York: Oxford University Press, 1978), pp. 22–74.

2. It would take us too far afield to document this lack, but the reader need

only peruse a typical list of definitions (e.g., Robert S. Ellwood, Jr., *Mysticism and Religion* [Englewood Cliffs, N.J.: Prentice-Hall, 1980] p. 13) in order to notice the vagueness and ambiguity of the terms used.

3. Walter T. Stace, *Mysticism and Philosophy* (London: MacMillan, 1960; repr. Atlantic Highlands, N.J.: Humanities Press, 1978), p. 31.

4. Katz, "Language, Epistemology, and Mysticism," p. 30.

5. Katz is not alone in this attempt. Bruce Garside, following what he asserts to be Kant's view of experience as a product of stimuli and conceptual framework, argues that "people of different cultures and religious traditions would necessarily have different religious experiences." See his, "Language and the Interpretation of Mystical Experiences," *International Journal for Philosophy of Religion 3* (Summer 1972), 99. Another proponent of the decisive role that context plays in human experience is Robert Gimello. He contends that "mysticism is inextricably bound up with, dependent upon, and usually subservient to the deeper beliefs and values of the traditions, cultures, and historical milieux which harbor it." See his "Mysticism in Its Contexts," in *Mysticism and Religious Traditions*, ed. Steven T. Katz. (New York: Oxford University Press 1983) p. 61.

Katz, Garside, and Gimello are but particular examples of the application of a radical, cultural relativism which characterizes much of the scholarship found in the humanities and social sciences today. We call this cultural relativism radical because it goes beyond the contention that cultural context influences human experience (Who would deny that?) to the assertion that context *determines* and, indeed, constitutes human experience. We cannot undertake a critical examination of this broader thesis here. Nevertheless, what we have to say about the possibility of the sameness of mystical experiences of a certain variety and the distinctions we will employ in the process of our analysis, may have useful implications for critically understanding some of the hidden assumptions of radical contextualism.

6. For those who eschew negative definitions, it need only be pointed out that some terms are simply negative in meaning, 'reality' and its variants follow exactly the same pattern as 'consciousness' and its variants. As J. L. Austin has shown in "Other Minds" (see pp. 54–57 of Austin's *Philosophical Papers*), to say of any *X* that *X* is real is to deny (depending on the situation) that it is not stuffed, a dummy, an hallucination, and so forth.

7. A. J. Ayer makes this claim in *Language, Truth and Logic* ([London: Gollancz, 1946, 2d ed.], see pp. 90–94).

8. This claim is to be found, in a somewhat implicit form, in J. L. Austin's "Other Minds" (see pp. 58–65 of *Philosophical Papers*).

9. Indeed, the notion of subjective statement is of considerable epistemological and metaphysical importance above and beyond its use here. Thus, from the side of epistemology, one might plausibly claim that the notion of subjective statement is necessarily central to a theory of the meaning, truth, and verification of those singular empirical statements which are not subjective and which, thus, may be called objective. More specifically, one may claim, following C. L. Lewis somewhat loosely, that singular objective empirical statements, for example,

"This is a doorknob," mean (at least in part) a conjunction of possible subjective conditionals, that is, conditionals both the antecedent and consequent of which are subjective statements, for example, "If I have the sense of reaching toward what I take to be the doorknob to touch it, then I will have the sense of touching what feels to me like a doorknob, *ceteris paribus*"—the *ceteris paribus* clause being always essential to exclude abnormal cases as when, e.g., my hand is frozen or has become paralyzed. One might claim further that the truth of singular objective empirical statements consists, ultimately, precisely in the truth of these possible subjective conditionals and that the verification of singular objective empirical statements lies ultimately in the actual verification of some subset of the conditionals in which their truth consists. We say ultimately since verification rarely needs to be pushed to the extent of verifying subjective conditionals, and is so pushed only when some reasonable challenge is forthcoming (the rareness of which accounts for the rareness of actual subjective statements). Thus, the verification of subjective conditionals is the theoretical, though rarely necessary, termination of the verification of singular objective empirical statements. Note that the aforementioned adumbrated position does not commit us to the extreme empirical position of construing singular objective empirical statements as nothing but logical constructs built from basic atomic statements, or *Protokolsaetze*, or of reducing the meaning of such statements to elements of immediate experience or of regarding the perceptual gestalten of ordinary experience as syntheses of simpler immediate sense-data. Finally, from the side of metaphysics, one might plausbily claim first that the most effective definition of the notion of content of consciousness, or (to follow more traditional parlance) of sense-datum, is to be effected in terms of the notion of subjective statement and second that the notion of sense-datum is, in turn, central to ontology—sense-data constituting a fundamental kind of reality, namely, the nonspatial, temporal realm of the phenomenal. And one can make this second claim without committing oneself to the presumably false phenomenalist position that sense-data are the (conceptually) unmediated atoms out of which material objects are built and in which they ultimately consist.

10. What is problematic about the notion of a merely possible subjective statement consists not so much in the admittedly peculiar ontological status of the merely possible, but in the phenomenological difference between a content of consciousness that would be a truth-condition of a true subjective statement that could have been uttered and a content of consciousness, similar to the first in all possible salient respects, that is the truth-condition of a true subjective statement that is, in fact, uttered (aloud or to oneself only). A moment ago, for example, I (Norman Prigge) saw what I took to be a chair (indeed, I saw a chair as well), and I could have uttered the consequently true subjective statement, "I am seeing what I take to be a chair." But if I had, as I am doing now this very moment (saying to only myself, as it happens), my consciousness would have been the same as my present experience but rather different from the original which I now recall in memory, albeit also very much the same. My present consciousness is isolated from the flow of those that preceded it, enduring, unlike the others, over a rather

longish moment, much as a stillframe from a film. In the present consciousness, I am explicitly aware of myself and as apart from the percept of the chair, whereas in the earlier percept I was, at most, implicitly aware of myself, but not as something (an ego) separate from the content of consciousness. On the other hand, the present self-conscious experience does contain within it a content of consciousness that is, so far as I can recall, qualitatively identical to the earlier content of consciousness, and this content is, just as the earlier one would have been, the truth-condition of the statement that is being made—or would have been made—by my utterance of the sentence, "I am seeing what I take to be a chair." That which is additional in the present experience, the explicit consciousness of a self apart from the content of consciousness in question, the isolation of that content vis-à-vis others, indeed, is a part of the context of the latter, but it is extrinsic to it. Thus, with respect to what is intrinsic to it, the present content of consciousness is qualitatively similar to the earlier content. Of course 'context,' 'intrinsic,' and 'extrinsic' must be defined, and will be anon. Even then, however, we will only have scratched the surface of a very complex issue.

11. Two points. First a consciousness of another consciousness is what Husserl, following Descartes, calls a *cogito* or what Sartre calls a reflective consciousness reflecting on a reflected consciousness. (Jean-Paul Sartre, *The Transcendence of the Ego*, trans. Williams and Kirkpatrick [New York: Farrat, Staus and Giroux, 1937].) Such self-consciousness, apart from possible employment in phenomenology, is thoroughly ordinary—albeit comparatively rare and frequently uncanny—in everyday experience. Second, consciousness of an abstract object is typified by the kind of philosophical reflexion that leads to the analysis and articulation of the meaning of various concepts, and it is no more problematic than is analytic philosophy itself, nominalists notwithstanding. It is not, however, that we favor an extreme realist position, for nothing that has been said here goes beyond the assertion that abstract objects exist and that they are different from spatiotemporal objects (and also different from concrete consciousness); for example, nothing that has been said here implies or should be taken to imply anything about the ultimate nature or ontological primacy of abstract objects.

12. The distinction between extrinsic context and intrinsic content makes it clear that the former can be a causal factor that determines the existence and nature of the latter. Qua effect of such a cause, the experience is construed from without. Insofar as it is construed from within, it is just that experience in and of itself and not qua effect of an extrinsic cause. It is, thus, that the question of whether drugs can cause a genuine mystical experience remains quite open: an affirmative answer would in no way make the drugs intrinsic to the experience.

13. Note that a mystical experience is a thing not by virtue of its content, content being wholly absent, but by virtue of its context. Hence, we can say that from within the mystical experience, from the point of view of content, that the experience has no object or subject, that it is of no-thing, of nothingness, or whatever. But we can simultaneously say from without the experience, from the point of view of its context, that it was X's experience, that it lasted not more than

half an hour, that during the experience *X*'s heart-rate decreased to 37 beats per minute, and so forth.

14. There is a temptation to say that experiences must be analyzable into qualities and aspects, and these into further qualities and aspects, and so on, but not *ad infinitum*, but only until one arrives at absolute simples. This temptation, and the errors which it has led to throughout the history of empiricism—from the Enlightenment through Mill to the logical positivism of Carnap, Ayer, and others—have been thoroughly diagnosed and repudiated by their once most committed victim, Ludwig Wittgenstein.

15. Philip Almond (*Mystical Experience and Religious Doctrine: An Investigation of the Study of Mysticism in World Religions* [New York: Mouton, 1982]) suggests that there is nothing logically incoherent about the notion of a contentless experience and further suggests the development of the implications of this idea for understanding how mystical experiences can be the same. He does not, however, develop this theory beyond suggesting four hypotheses for further study. We have here taken a step toward developing the theoretical foundations of such a theory.

Experience and Interpretation in Mysticism

R. L. FRANKLIN

Many among an earlier generation of scholars saw in mysticism a distinctive type of experience—a pure or contentless awareness of ultimate reality—which was often made the basis for a "perennial philosophy."[1] More recently many have distinguished several different types of mystical experience, each tending to recur across different traditions. More recently still has arisen a tendency, which I will call the "diversity view," so to emphasize the differences as to deny any common experience and hence any perennial philosophy.

The diversity view stems from an awareness, growing in many fields of thought, of how deeply our experience is mediated (i.e., organized and influenced) by our whole belief system. This is the "holism" of Quine's philosophy of science and Davidson's philosophy of language.[2] It is equally prominent in the continental hermeneutic tradition as found, for example, in Gadamer.[3] The convergence of these and other viewpoints, which are often unaware of each other, suggests that the very notion of pure experience—whether the sense-data beloved of the earlier philosophy of perception or the pure mystical experience of a perennial philosophy—is a myth. There is no such thing as sheer "experience" to be contrasted with "interpretation"; rather, all experience *is* interpreted.

The phenomenon of mediation actually applies not only to perceptual experience, but also to reflective thinking as well. I prefer to call it the *mutualism* of our mental activity, so as to emphasize that while our belief system shapes our immediate experience, in turn, experience modifies the system. However, the avoidability of mutualism varies. Sometimes, as we will see, it is only a natural temptation to conflate elements in our thinking which disciplined reasoning can distinguish. At other times it is inescapable. In particular the common distinction between fact and interpretation, though often valuable in a given context, easily hides a mutualistic interaction. Not only will our judgment of the likelihood of a purported fact depend on the rest of our belief system, but ultimately a fact is always a fact-as-conceived, that is, as interpreted. Hence, differences over interpretation may be expressed as differences about what the "facts" really are.

The question, therefore, concerns not the importance or ubiquity of mutualism, but its implications for any notion of pure mystical experience. I will argue that it does not threaten it in the way that the diversity view claims, but that the situation is more complex than some defenders of the experience have thought.

UNITY OR DIVERSITY?

The relevant debates about mysticism arise from the similarities and differences in its literature. Mysticism is as hard to define as religion; part of the problem may be that too many diverse phenomena are collected under its name. Nevertheless, a central feature of all but borderline cases is a certain turning inward, a stilling of the ordinary activity of the mind.[4] How the stilling is brought about and what happens in it varies. It may arise spontaneously; or there may be a devotional dwelling on some symbol of the divine, often with visions appropriate to that tradition; or meditative processes may aim at totally emptying the mind of all thought. But always the stillness involves deep peacefulness, joy, and absorption in the situation, and it seems like making contact with an ultimate reality. The that-with-which-contact-is-made is felt to be beyond adequate expression, though mystics struggle to suggest it. Thus, William James's classic discussion lists four common characteristics of mystical experience—ineffability, noetic quality, transiency, and passivity.[5] Ineffability indicates the inadequate expression and noetic quality the conviction that this is contact with ultimate reality. Transiency indicates his belief that such experiences could not last, and passivity that it is a stilling of the mind.

To deny these recognizable similarities would be to deny there is such a phenomenon—mysticism.[6] However, though subject to borderline cases, we can recognize mystics across religions, their writings show their religion; or else, if they have none, that they struggle to comprehend their experience in available concepts. Mystics conceive the that-with-which-contact-is-made diversely as God, Brahman, nirvāṇa, nature, or as pure consciousness without any object at all. And their notions not only are centered in their own traditions, but often seem incompatible.

The assessment of these similarities and differences revolves round these questions: (1) Is there a pure mystical experience, common to all or many traditions? That is, Do the different backgrounds mutualistically color the very experiences themselves? (2) If such experience occurs, what is its significance? The two questions mutualistically impinge on each other, but here it is possible and important to distinguish them.

THE IMPOSSIBILITY OF UNMEDIATED EXPERIENCE

I begin here with the diversity view, and for convenience I concentrate largely on Katz's forceful assertion of it.[7] Whether there is pure mystical experience looks like a factual issue, but it really concerns the interpretation of largely agreed phenomena.[8] Katz does not actually deny the points to which a perennial philosophy appeals such as James's four common characteristics or Stace's list of seven features of mysticism.[9] Rather, he argues that the mystics' "apparently similar language" masks much more important differences.[10] The debate concerns the interpretation of writings with both suggestive similarities and important differences; though different interpretations may be expressed by saying that a particular phenomenon-as-interpreted does not occur.

Katz's central argument is based on what he calls:

> [T]he single epistemological assumption that has exercised my thinking and which has forced me to undertake the present investigation: *There are NO pure (i.e., unmediated) experiences*. . . . *[A]ll* experience is processed through, organized by, and makes itself available to us in extremely complex epistemological ways. The notion of unmediated experience seems, if not self-contradictory, at best empty.[11]

This is his version of the mutualism seen in my opening remarks. It suffers, I think, by appearing to turn two-way traffic into a one-way street, that is, emphasizing how beliefs affect experience but not vice versa. But the main issue concerns its scope.

Katz uses the principle to reject pure mystical experience because it would have to be unmediated. As he writes of one of the prime techniques claimed to produce it, "Properly understood, yoga, for example, is *not* an *un*conditioning or *de*conditioning of consciousness, but rather it is a *re*conditioning of consciousness, i.e., a substituting of one form of conditioned and/or contextual consciousness for another . . . form."[12] Now the argument assumes the two alternatives are exclusive: *either* un/de/conditioning *or* re/conditioning. But why could not yoga involve both? Could there not conceivably be a practice of *reconditioning* consciousness *for the purpose of achieving a deconditioning,* that is, so as to suspend the ordinary mediated interplay between experience and belief system? This seems to be yoga's claim. It presupposes mediated consciousness as a starting point and uses it to explain and justify itself. But it adds a new aim: to still the continual activity of the mind so as to achieve a state which lies beyond it.

An objection to this claim might be based either on the stronger premise that mediation *must* hold for *all possible* experience or on the weaker one that it *does* hold for *all actual* experience. Katz certainly asserts the weaker one, but I am not sure about the stronger. For this seems incompatible with at least the most natural interpretation of his quoted remark that unmediated experience might not be "self-contradictory" (i.e., conceptually impossible?) but merely "empty" (i.e., not occurring in practice?). But whatever his view here, the problem with the weaker premiss is that we cannot show that mediation holds for *all* experience merely by showing that it holds (as it does) for all *ordinary* experience. That all ordinary experience is mediated, cannot exclude the possibility of learning to pass beyond mediation to extraordinary experience.

Hence, the argument must appeal to the stronger premises. But here it meets a basic difficulty. When our examination of some concept *C* (in this case consciousness) finds some important feature *M* (in this case mediation) in all the cases we can think of, it is tempting to build *M* into our account of *C*. If *M* really is central to all standard cases, this may be valuable and persuasive. But what if some unforeseen case *X* (e.g., some pure mystical experience) is alleged as a counterexample? It is tempting to stick by the account we have found valuable and to say that this *cannot* be a case of *C* because it lacks *M*. But insofar as the counterexamples are impressive, to rule them out in this way is merely arbitrary. The argument is valid:

$$\text{All } C \text{ are } M$$
$$X \text{ is not } M$$
$$\text{So } X \text{ is not } C$$

but the crucial premise begs the question.[13]

Since mediation is, indeed, central to ordinary consciousness, the onus of proof surely lies on those who argue we can pass beyond it. But then many mystical writings are presented as discharging the onus, and we cannot rule out a priori that they do. We must examine the claims of mystics without foreclosing the issue by purely conceptual arguments.

HOW MANY ULTIMATE ENTITIES?

Katz, however, has a second argument for the impossibility. His opponents, he says, claim "that the use of apparently similar language reflects an underlying 'core' experience."[14] This, however, is to be "misled by the surface grammar of the mystical reports they study."[15] For "language is itself contextual and words 'mean' only in contexts . . . choosing descriptions of mystical experience *out of their total context* does *not* provide grounds for their comparability but rather severs all grounds of their intelligibility for it empties [them] of definite meaning."[16] Hence, "*different* metaphysical entities can be 'described' by the same phrases if these phrases are *indefinite* enough, as are the very general descriptive phrases used in our phenomenological lists."[17]

This overstates the case. A word *may* mean the same in a new context, though it may not; and while "indefinite" phrases may describe different entities, of course, they may describe the same one. This may be a salutary warning, but it cannot, for example, decide whether the deliberately vague language I used in "Unity or Diversity" points to important common features in the experience.

The more fundamental point, however, is this. In denying any core experience, Katz repeatedly emphasizes the differences between mystics by saying they encounter different entities. Thus, he speaks of "those ultimate *objects* of concern with which mystics have had intercourse, e.g., God, Being, nirvana, etc."[18] Similarly, he says they encounter "*different* metaphysical entities"; not "dissimilar experiences of the *same* phenomenon . . . [but] different experiences of *different* phenomena."[19] Thus, he can argue as follows:

> Every system and every mystic had [sic] made claims to ultimate objectivity and to discovered [sic] Reality, but the claims are more often than not mutually incompatible. . . . It seems clear that these respective mystics do not experience the same Reality or objectivity, and therefore it is not reasonable to posit that their respective experiences of Reality or objectivity are similar.[20]

That is, since mystics "do not experience the same Reality," their experiences could not be the same.

Now these passages might be construed as moving, either from the premise that the descriptions are "incompatible" to the conclusion that the entities must be different; or, conversely, from the premise that mystics encounter "different . . . entities" to the conclusion that their experiences must differ. Either way they do not, I think, establish their conclusion. Certainly, the descriptions and experiences of mystics often differ. But to assume they are "incompatible" and are about "different entities" begs crucial questions about their relations.

To call something ultimate reality at least indicates it is the final truth about how things are, whether we acknowledge it or not.[21] In putative conflicts there are two possibilities. One is that different entities are claimed to be ultimate: as when materialists and mystics respectively present matter or some Absolute (God, Brahman, *nirvāṇa*, etc.) as ultimate reality. Since the claims are incompatible (as usually understood), at least one must be wrong. The other possibility is that different descriptions are offered of the *same* entity. Then either they can be reconciled as *complementary* (perhaps more or less illuminating or misleading) ones or, again, they are truly incompatible, so at least some must be wrong.

One objection to saying that mystics encounter different entities arises from the fact that *all* claims to ultimate reality, mystical or not, necessarily *compete for the same logical space;* for where they truly differ at least one must be wrong. In this sense no conflicting accounts can be about different *ultimate* entities, but at most about different entities each *conceived* as ultimate.

Further, there are complex problems specifically about mysticism. Take three cases: some materialists believe all mysticism is nonsense; nature mystics believe they experience the material world in a totally different and awe-inspiring way, other mystics believe they encounter some Absolute which is not material nature. The first two groups present the same material world as ultimate reality, whereas the third disagrees. Yet in many ways the second and third have stronger links than the first two. Perhaps the second and third do encounter different entities, though this assumes their prima facie conflict cannot be reconciled by appropriate redefinitions of matter and Absolute. But this does not make them less alike than they are nor make the second more like the first than it is. It only shows that the distinction between different entities and different descriptions may not always help in understanding the issues.

Finally, Katz is primarily and properly concerned with the third group, which includes virtually all the mystical religious traditions. Yet they *cannot* encounter different entities, for the nature of God, Brahman or *nirvāṇa* is not such that one of them could coexist with the others. Hence, the descriptions must apply to the same entity. Either they are complementary, as Katz simply assumes they are not or, at least, all but one of them is mistaken.

Yet if Katz has not shown either that mystics must experience different entities or that their descriptions are incompatible, neither has the contrary been shown. It is time to see what clarification has been achieved.

THE UPSHOT

Arguments for the diversity view are of two sorts: deductive ones (like those cited), that if it is true such-and-such follows; and persuasive ones, that the data suggest certain conclusions. These seem to support each other mutualistically, but for rigorous assessment, we must distinguish them.[22] We then see that Katz's deductive arguments fail to eliminate the possibility of pure mystical experience. The diversity view can, therefore, be based only on a detailed account of differences between mystics, leading to a denial of any overall similarity.

In this second task Katz and the contributors to his two volumes often make forceful criticisms of oversweeping views. Katz eruditely examines the differences between Jewish, Buddhist, Christian, and Moslem mysticism, including the variations between mystics within single traditions. He argues, "that the forms of consciousness which the mystic brings to experience set structured and limiting parameters on what the experience will be, i.e., on what will be experienced, and rule out in advance what is 'inexperienceable' in the particular given, concrete, context."[23] Though this underemphasizes how our experience can, in turn, challenge our belief system (cf. my opening remarks), the impact of beliefs on experience is undeniable. However, the material only shows there is *much* diversity in mysticism. Without the underpinning of the failed, strictly conceptual arguments, it amounts only to a warning against oversimple generalization.

I will argue that there is more unity in mystical experience than the diversity view allows, though I doubt whether we yet have an adequate account of it. However, there *are* differences within that general stilling of the mind which is characteristic of mysticism. Further (cf. the section entitled "The Impossibility of Unmediated Experience"), since all ordinary experience is mediated, an onus of proof lies on those who speak of pure mystical experience. I turn to whether this onus can be discharged.

THE ARGUMENT FOR PURE CONSCIOUSNESS

The occurrence of such experience—commonly called pure consciousness—is a central theme of this book; for convenience, I consider chiefly Forman's presentation of it in "The Construction of Mystical Experience."[24] He argues that it is found in many traditions, citing as examples "Shankara, Eckhart, and Zen adepts."[25] In opposition to Katz, Forman presents a "forgetting model," one that involves a "holding of some conceptual formula in abeyance."[26] This is a special case of the stilling of the mind found in all mysticism, namely, a complete cessation of all thought, leaving a total quietness that is conscious and alert without being conscious *of* anything.

Forman, like Katz, has both persuasive and conceptual arguments. The persuasive ones are, in effect, that much mystical literature, including the passages he quotes, fit his forgetting model very well. This is not surprising since they are what it was developed from and for. It seems that (whatever the oversimplifications of many earlier writers) mystics in many different traditions do describe or prescribe a putting aside of ordinary mediated experience to achieve a complete stilling of the mind.[27] So— the persuasive argument runs—if there are no conceptual reasons to believe it impossible, why not assume they are talking about what they have experienced?

Textual exegesis, however, is rarely conclusive. We may be unclear whether mystics are describing their own experience or prescribing what their tradition says can be achieved. Or pure consciousness might perhaps be only an "ideal type" of experience, representing a convergence sufficient to be caught by similar descriptions but never in practice totally reached. However, Forman also has a conceptual argument. This is that, despite differences in traditions, pure consciousness *could* not differ from person to person. For with a true "forgetting," we must pass beyond *everything* in ordinary experience, "[I]f a Buddhist, Hindu or African forgot every thought, sensation, emotion, etc., then no historically conditioned idea, form, category or even sensory information would remain conscious to differentiate the resultant events from one to another."[28]

The interplay of these considerations is complex. The conceptual necessity is hypothetical: *if* there is completely pure consciousness, *then* it must be the same for everyone. It cannot show there *is* any such experience; a diversity view might accept the point, but then conclude it shows there is no completely pure consciousness. Whereas in Katz there seems a confusion between conceptual arguments which fail and evidence which does not establish a sufficiently strong conclusion, by contrast, here the two sorts of considerations reinforce each other. The evidence shows a remarkable similarity in the language of mystics who knew nothing of each other; and the conceptual point shows that, if they were reaching pure consciousness, this is what we might expect. Nor, on this view, would it be surprising to find it across traditions; if such a state is possible and desirable, why should not different traditions have discovered and valued it? No doubt, attempts to understand it, either in anticipation or retrospect, would be heavily dependent on the belief system. No doubt, some mystical traditions do not seek it and, therefore, hardly experience it. But if we reject the a priori ban on unmediated experience, then the forgetting model, developed from looking at such experience, is surely the natural, if not the only possible, account of it.

Moreover, if doubt remains, we are not necessarily restricted to scholarly investigation of mystics' reports.[29] Today probably more people than ever before practice stilling the mind, whether or not they call it mysticism.[30] Hence, questions which scholars struggle to answer by interpreting texts might be clarified by *asking* reputable figures who practice "forgetting" techniques from differing traditions. In such discussion subtle similarities and differences might more easily be discovered. There are even experts in more than one tradition who might play the same role as bilingual speakers in translation. No doubt, other issues would arise, including whether we could *ever* know that two experiences were similar; but such general skeptical problems do not concern mysticism as such.[31]

THE PROBLEM OF SIGNIFICANCE

Whether pure consciousness occurs is important, but still more important is its significance. It is our whole belief system which accords or denies significance to a fact, though an obstinate fact may mutualistically require us to adjust other beliefs to it. So, we must relate the phenomenon to our other beliefs.

One issue is whether, like sense-data in classic philosophy of perception, it provides an indubitable foundation for knowledge. Thus, Gill writes, "Empiricist philosophers of the 'foundationalist' school . . . have long sought to ground experiential knowledge in some form of awareness that is epistemologically certain, such as sense-data reports. In its own way, mysticism represents a form of foundationalism in that it seeks to ground religious awareness in an incorrigible experience."[32] So, because he rejects foundationalism and assumes this to be the role of pure consciousness, Gill embraces Katz's view.

Here again, however, we easily conflate distinct considerations. Sense-data were *postulated* as intellectual constructs in epistemological theory; but the arguments in the section entitled "The Argument for Pure Consciousness" concern purported reports of actual experience rather than postulates or constructs. The case made there for pure consciousness had nothing to do with epistemological foundationalism.[33] Certainly, an adequate overall understanding, giving significance to specific elements, may show that pure consciousness has some basic epistemological role (cf. the section entitled "The Importance of Mysticism"); but it is not invented for that purpose.

Perhaps the deepest question is (cf. the section entitled "How Many Ultimate Entities") whether the admitted differences in mystical descriptions are complementary or incompatible. Here those seeking a unified picture have commonly taken as standard one type of experience and, hence, the traditions where it is found, and they have then ranked others against it as more or less adequate. Thus, we have, for example, theistic, Vedantic, and Buddhist accounts of the real significance of mysticism—all based on the principle that some animals are more equal than others. The often acid objections of diversity views show that here frequently contentious value judgments are naively presented as the only reasonable explanation of the phenomena. To suggest the difficulties I consider a generalized version of the monistic account often called a perennial philosophy.

THE SEARCH FOR A PERENNIAL PHILOSOPHY

The perennial philosophy appeals to the fact that mystical experience seems like reaching an ultimate reality which challenges us to give it due significance. It then typically focuses on pure consciousness, not only as something that occurs across traditions but as *the* centrally significant religious phenomenon. Since in pure consciousness, it claims, we are unified with ultimate reality, there is an identity between what we really are and what really exists. To say that the Atman is one with the Brahman, that both the self and the other dissolve in one *nirvāṇa* or that the soul merges ultimately with God appear as culturally conditioned variations on this theme.

Yet much within the mystical tradition resists this interpretation. Putting aside the innumerable variations on which diversity views dwell, consider only the three conceptualizations above. Though the first two speak of an ultimate merging, it is very differently conceived; and the third often refuses to do so. It rather speaks of a relationship of love which, however deep and overwhelming, requires two things to be related. Thus, while Eckhart may use phrases which could have come from Shankara, many other Christian, Jewish, and Muslim mystics will not, for to them the gulf between the soul and God remains unbridgeable.

The fact that mystical experience seems like reaching deeper reality cannot help here. For first, however great its impact and however clearly it involves pure consciousness, it can later be reinterpreted. Martin Buber experienced apparent total union, but later decided, in accordance with his deep Jewish sense of the gulf between humankind and God, that in "the honest and sober account of the responsible understanding" he must reject this interpretation.[34] Again, the response of J. Middleton Murry to an unexpected mystical experience shows how differently an agnostic can react.[35] To suggest these are misinterpretations is to offer a rival one, for the experience cannot interpret itself.

Second, (cf. the section entitled "The Upshot") the mystics' experiences are influenced by their traditions. Pure consciousness is only one form of the inward stilling, but all seem like reaching ultimate reality. Unless we ignore the complexity of the data (as diversity views allege), we must acknowledge that to give it primacy is bitterly disputed. For not only may it be seen from antimystical viewpoints as a pathological phenomenon, but even within mysticism it may seem a seductive illusion to be set firmly within its proper (i.e. theologically orthodox) context.

Nor is it that an authentic contact with reality, stemming from deepest experience, is rejected by a rigid and suspicious orthodoxy (or agnosticism); as if those without the experience are divided by ideologies, whereas mystics penetrate to a common truth. For though such rejection can occur, the situation is more complex. Mystics (as opposed to those who meet the experience unawares) are typically convinced that the framework given by their tradition is necessary to achieve and understand the experience. Surely, neither Saint Teresa nor Saint John of the Cross immersed in their Counter-Reformation Spanish Catholicism would have readily admitted the occurrence of true mystical experience among pagan non-Christians or even heretical Protestants. Shankara's attacks on Buddhism also show how mystical traditions (both here examples of the forgetting model) may bitterly clash. Typically, mystics acknowledge the validity of another tradition only if their own allows it. Their beliefs restrict not only their own experience, but also their attitude toward others' beliefs.

I do not want to belittle the perennial philosophy, but to bring out how important and how difficult is an overall understanding of mysticism. *All* views involve value judgments about significance; not only a perennial philosophy which may claim merely to outline "the facts," but also diversity views which may claim merely to challenge oversimple generalizations. For though the latter can discuss questions of detail safely and valuably without contentious presuppositions, this does not confront the basic issue. To conclude *explicitly or implicitly* that there is no unifying element, that the descriptions are incompatible rather than complementary, is also to evaluate the evidence.[36] Whatever the winner, the value judgment is the entrance money which lets us compete in the race.

THE IMPORTANCE OF MYSTICISM

If we reject the conceptual necessity of the diversity view; if we accept pure consciousness as one form of mystical experience; and if we have learned to be wary of large generalizations, What is the outcome? We need viewpoints sensitive to both the unity and the diversity. But how is this empty formula to be filled? Perhaps (cf. the section entitled "Unity or Diversity") "mysticism" covers too much, so that not only in popular contexts does it sprawl over a vast field, but even in scholarly ones we may need to forge new concepts. However, starting from where we are, if we treat mysticism as involving a stilling of the mind (thereby excluding much other religious experience), we still leave room (cf. section entitled "The Search for a Perennial Philosophy") for a standard distinction between conceiving its goal as a loving "I–Thou" relation to ultimate reality or as a total merging with it. Various other contrasts normally cluster here: theism *versus* an impersonal absolute; devotion *versus* search for self-understanding; dualism *versus* monism; the importance or unimportance of history in revelation; and so on. Though future discussion may pull the cluster apart, I take this as the strategic starting point.

Consider in this context pure consciousness. Ninian Smart has suggested that, avoiding oversimplification, it is still the central clue.[37] For, we may argue, not only does it occur across traditions, but if all mysticism involves a stilling of the mind, then is not the state of consciousness which is completely still and contentless the highest form of it? As Almond puts it, perhaps "it is of the very nature of the practices and techniques associated with the 'inward way' to conduce (though not necessarily) towards the attainment of contentless states of consciousness."[38]

I feel the attraction of this view. Yet pure consciousness surely points naturally, if not inevitably, to union rather than relation and fits the path of inward search better than that of I–Thou devotion. So, it still concludes that one animal is more equal than the others. And I still feel for those traditions which will see it as only putting a feather mattress on a Procrustean bed. I want to remain neutral here, that is why my argument is constructed to show alternatives as unproven. This is not a skeptical view that no correct answer can be found. Rather, to be frank, in my own spiritual journey I find the pull of each approach too powerful to reject, and I sense, and yearn for, a reconciliation I cannot yet conceptualize. In what is perhaps the greatest debate for the next decades or centuries of humankind, here are my own guesses.

As today we rush toward the global village, mysticism faces enormous challenge: not to survive—for (cf. the section entitled "The Argument for Pure Consciousness") the practice of mind-stilling is rapidly growing— but to find its significance for new situations while preserving its ancient treasures. The growth of communications and pluralism in our societies offers a smorgasbord of practices from many traditions, sought after by many with no grasp of their origins. So, mystical traditions face increasing and opposite pressures; to preserve their uniqueness by defining themselves against others or to enter into dialogue with them. The tension is inevitably reflected among scholars, so that here, too, we find conflicting emphases on diversity or on unity. But the issue is not just one of scholarship, in the sense of explicating how traditions understand themselves. Rather, it is about the significance of that self-understanding: whether it is to be confirmed, transformed, or rejected as irrelevant. It inherently involves value judgments, finding the right balance for assessing new considerations. So, we must distinguish our pure scholarship from our value judgments—and not imagine we can find the significance of mysticism without employing both.[39]

We may, for example, see this ever-increasing concern for the stilling of the mind as a pathetic search for security in a nuclear-threatened world, as a contempt for accurate scholarship among the ignorant, or as some other evil sign of the times—or, on the other hand, as the dawn of an age of enlightenment or the working of the spirit of God. In my own judgment, while much of it will quickly pass, it is also a great movement in the deepest forces that shape history. What I hope for is an increased understanding, both theoretical and practical, of the stilling of the mind, leading to a better grasp of our relation to ultimate reality than was previously available within any one tradition.[40] That is why studying mysticism is important.

One area for such understanding would be epistemology. I said (see the section entitled "The Problem of Significance") that though pure consciousness was not a postulate but an experience, it might have epistemological importance. In arguing against reductionist views, the new viewpoint would claim that the sense of reaching ultimate reality is veridical rather than illusory. But this sense is found in all stilling of the mind; so, we still have the problem of the specific significance of pure consciousness.

Here I hope we may increasingly find that each tradition, based on its own starting point and experience, tends to mirror coherently from its own perspective our overall explanatory theory. So, we may increasingly be able to say: "Given this starting point, mysticism will take that form here." Hence, *pace* diversity views, particular traditions would be complementary rather than incompatible: not, usually, because anything in one was "really" the same as something in another (as oversimplified accounts easily suggest) but because each as a unique, integrated, mutualistically interacting whole would fit into our overall view.[41] Yet it would also reinforce my reservations about Smart and Almond above. Certainly, as so many believe, one account might in the end be more equal than others. But I hope for a theory which, instead of taking one path as the standard for measuring others, explains at a metalevel why different ones arise; a theory which would see all forms of stilling the mind, including pure consciousness, as reflecting an as yet to be achieved conceptualization of ultimate reality.

How could this impinge on practice? I suspect it would emerge (as part of the theory itself) that we normally need a *specific* discipline to grow spiritually. For most this would come, no doubt, from our familiar tradition; we are not likely to invent something better for ourselves. If so, then the theory need be neither a threat to, nor a substitute for, particular traditions. Not a threat, for to explain is not to explain away, unless reductionist assumptions are first imported. Not a substitute, for to see why different paths work is not to advance along them. Yet to many it *would* seem a threat. For, as diversity views might legitimately emphasize, it questions something precious to the self-understanding of many traditions: their conviction that they are *the* true path to salvation. Whether this treasured belief must be abandoned seems to me one of the deepest issues in understanding mysticism.

NOTES

1. I use this phrase in the sense popularized by Aldous Huxley, *The Perennial Philosophy* (Chatto & Windus, 1950).

2. Cf. W. V. O. Quine, *Word and Object* (Cambridge, Eng.: MIT Press, 1954); D. Davidson *Inquiries into Truth and Interpretation* (Oxford: Clarendon, 1985).

3. Cf. H-G Gadamer, *Truth and Method* (Kansas City, Mo.: Sheed & Ward, 1979).

4. Two points arise here which go beyond the present discussion. First, is the stilling of the mind not only a necessary but a sufficient condition for mysticism? This would involve considering its use in relaxation therapy as well as mysticism. Second, within mysticism, some traditions distinguish between contemplation which is "acquired" (through our own efforts) or "infused" (by the grace of God). This would require much discussion. But "stilling the mind," which could cover either what we do or what happens to us, is meant to be neutral here.

5. William James, *The Varieties of Religious Experience* (Huntington, N.Y.: Fontana, 1960), pp.367–368.

6. Such writers as H. H. Penner ("The Mystical Illusion," in S. T. Katz, ed., *Mysticism and Religious Traditions* [Oxford University Press, 1983] seem almost to do so, so strongly do they emphasize the diversity. Though my position is clearly inconsistent with this, I can discuss it only implicitly.

7. S. T. Katz, "Language, Epistemology, and Mysticism," in S. T. Katz, ed. *Mysticism and Philosophical Analysis* (London: Sheldon Press, 1978) Cf. also Katz's " 'Conservative' Character" in *Mysticism and Religious Traditions* pp. 4–5.

8. This does not mean that no-one denies the validity or even the existence of mystical phenomena, but only that this is not at issue in the discussions I consider.

9. Katz, "*Language, Epistemology, and Mysticism*," pp. 49–50.

10. Ibid., pp. 47–50.

11. Ibid., p. 26. [Emphasis added.]

12. Ibid., p. 57. [Emphasis added.]

13. Similarly, we could not reject the possibility of any pure mystical experience (particularly the "pure consciousness" mentioned in section entitled "The Argument for Pure Consciousness") by appealing to the tradition of intentionality reemphasized by Brentano that consciousness must have an "object"; i.e. that we must always be conscious *of* something. For if intentionality were defined so narrowly as to exclude, for example, pure consciousness, the same objection holds as in relation to mediation. On the other hand, if it were so broadened that the object of consciousness might be *nothing,* as some mystical accounts suggest (i.e., if it conceded that being conscious of nothing need not mean not being conscious), then it fails to prove its point.

14. Katz, "Language, Epistemology, and Mysticism," p. 46.

15. Ibid.

16. Ibid., p. 47.

17. Ibid., p. 51.

18. Ibid., p. 26. [Emphasis added.]

19. Ibid., pp. 51, 52.

20. Ibid., p. 50.

21. Cf. my "The Concept of Reality" *Australian Journal of Philosophy* 64 (1986), 158–69.

22. Katz, I think, fails to do so. This leads to deep tensions, if not inconsistencies, in his position. E.g., he says (cf. section entitled "The Impossibility of Unmediated Experience") that "the notion of unmediated experience seems, if not self-contradictory, at best empty." But the former entails the latter. So a deductive argument would require "seems self-contradictory" *and therefore* "empty"; while a conclusion merely that such experience seems not to occur (that the notion "is empty"), would need to follow an exhaustive review of the evidence. See also, for example, the criticisms of P. Almond in "Mysticism and Its Contexts" in this volume.

23. Katz, "Language, Epistemology, and Mysticism," pp. 26–27.

24. R. K. C. Forman, "The Construction of Mystical Experience," *Faith and Philosophy* 3 (1988), pp. 254–267.

25. Ibid., p. 254.

26. Ibid., p. 261.

27. I must add that I am influenced here by my own practice of meditation, in which I have frequently experienced states which answer this description.

28. Forman, "The Construction of Mystical Experience," p. 264. He also draws an analogy with the well-established phenomenon of a *Ganzfeld*. This is a completely patternless visual field; a situation which may be experienced naturally, as in a blizzard, or artificially, as when two halves of a Ping-Pong ball are taped over the eyes. It leads to a complete loss of all visual experience. See pp. 261–64.

29. Katz seems to assume we are as restricted, see his *Mysticism and Religious Traditions*, p. 5.

30. I have in mind the popularity of transcendental meditation, Zen Buddhism, and other meditative practices, including their revival within the Christian churches.

31. A further possibility is systematic scientific investigation, beginnings of which have been made. Certainly such evidence as electroencephalogram recordings of brainwaves do not settle these questions, though they suggest similar patterns are found in meditative patterns across traditions. But, eventually, new light may be thrown in such ways. Cf. D. W. Orme-Johnson and J. T. Farrow *Scientific Research on the Transcendental Meditation Program* (MERU Press, 1977).

32. J. H. Gill, "Mysticism and Meditation" in *Faith and Philosophy* 1 (1984), 112–13.

33. In the section entitled "Unity and Diversity," I said only that it *seems* to

mystics that they reach ultimate reality. Claims that they actually do so must be defended against rival ones such as Freudian reductionism.

34. M. Buber *Between Man and Man* (London: Routledge & Kegan Paul, 1947), pp. 24–25.

35. See J. M. Murry's largely (and largely deservedly) forgotten book, *God* (J. Cape, 1929).

36. Katz says that he does not defend "any particular dogmatic position" (Katz, "Language, Epistemology, and Mysticism" p. 65). If "dogmatic position" means an overall viewpoint, this is, I think, inconsistent with his endorsement of the incompatibility view. However the qualifications in his penultimate paragraph leave some doubt as to how far he conflicts with my views in the final section.

37. N. Smart "The Purification of Consciousness and the Negative Path" in Katz, *"Mysticism and Religious Traditions,"* see esp. p. 125.

38. See Phillip Almond, "Mysticism and Its Contexts," in the present volume, pp. 216–217.

39. There is some parallel here to the dialectical relation of mystics to their own traditions. Just as today many who practice the stilling of the mind may claim that their experience shows what traditional formulas "really" mean, so mystics have often offered radical new interpretations while sincerely claiming not to reject but to revitalize their traditions. Nonmystical custodians of orthodoxy must decide whether this is a revitalization or a threatening heresy, and in doing so must make value judgments about overall significance.

This situation is discussed, again with erudition and frequent insight, by Katz in *Mysticism and Religious Traditions.* He stresses the conservative elements in mysticism, in opposition to the frequent claims for its radical nature. My emphasis would be rather different because I am concerned to strike a balance rather than to redress one.

40. I envisage this might draw on scientific investigation of meditative states as well as on comparative and phenomenological approaches (cf. n. 29). I can glimpse here a vast future synthesis linking the reality experienced in meditation to theories of current physics (cf. such books as Fritjof Capra's *The Tao of Physics* (Huntington, N.Y.: Fontana, 1976). For my present remarks, cf. my "Our Faith and Theirs," in *Religious Traditions* 5 (1983), 8–23.

41. We must not be absurdly optimistic. Mutualism suggests that, though the material for an overall theory must come primarily from the various traditions, the theory would indicate that particular elements in traditions were incorrect. This, of course, would be resisted; so, deep tensions would remain even as progress was made.

Contributors

Philip C. Almond is reader in and head of the Department of Studies in Religion at the University of Queensland, Australia. He is the author of: *Mystical Experience and Religious Doctrine,* (Berlin: Mouton, 1982), *Rudolf Otto,* (Chapel Hill: University of North Carolina Press, 1984), *The British Discovery of Buddhism,* (Cambridge: Cambridge University Press, 1988), *Heretic and Hero: Muhammad and the Victorians* (Wiesbaden: Harrasowitz, 1989).

Stephen Bernhardt graduated as the valedictorian of his class at Maharishi International University. At the time of his death in 1986, he was completing a doctorate in the philosophy of mysticism at the University of Chicago.

Christopher Chapple served for five years as assistant director of The Institute for Advanced Studies of World Religions at SUNY Stony Brook, and is currently associate professor of Theology at Loyola Marymount University in Los Angeles. He is the author and editor of several published works, including *Karma and Creativity* (Albany: State University of New York Press, 1986).

Robert K. C. Forman received his doctorate in religion from Columbia University. He has taught at The New School for Social Research, the Union Theological Seminary, and he is presently teaching in the department of religion at Vassar College. He has published articles on mysticism in *Faith and Philosophy, Sophia, The Journal of the American Academy of Religion, Downside Review,* among others, and is the author of *Meister Eckhart: Mystic as Theologian,* forthcoming from Amity House Press. He has practiced a neo-Advaitan form of meditation every day for twenty years.

R. L. Franklin who was born and educated in Melbourne, Australia, practiced as a lawyer until he decided that philosophy was his real love. After teaching in two Australian universities, he retired to devote more time to writing. He is now Emeritus Professor of Philosophy at the University of New England in Armidale, N.S.W.

Paul J. Griffiths is primarily interested in the history of Buddhist scholastic thought in India and in the theory and practice of cross-cultural philosophizing. He was born in England, trained in theology and Sanskrit at Oxford University, received a doctorate in Buddhist studies from the University of Wisconsin, and is currently assistant professor of Theology at the University of Notre Dame.

Gary E. Kessler received a doctorate in religious studies from Columbia University in 1970. He teaches philosophy and religious studies at California State University, Bakersfield.

Daniel C. Matt is an associate professor at the Center for Jewish Studies, Graduate Theological Union, Berkeley, California. He has written and lectured widely on Jewish mysticism and is the author of *Zohar: The Book of Enlightenment,* Classics of Western Spirituality, Paulist Press. He is currently writing a book on *ayin* and related concepts entitled *Varieties of Nothingness.*

Anthony N. Perovich, Jr. received his doctorate from the University of Chicago and teaches at Hope College in Holland, Michigan. He is the author of a number of articles dealing with the philosophy of mysticism and German idealism.

Norman Prigge received a doctorate in philosophy from the University of California, Santa Barbara, in 1974. Since 1973 he has been teaching philosophy at California State University, Bakersfield.

Donald Rothberg teaches philosophy at Kenyon College in Gambier, Ohio, having also taught at the University of Kentucky in Lexington. He has taught and written in the areas of comparative philosophy of religions, social theory, and philosophy of the human sciences, with a special interest in helping to develop and clarify forms of spirituality appropriate for our times. He has practiced Buddhist "Insight" meditation since 1976.

Mark B. Woodhouse is an associate professor of philosophy at Georgia State University, Atlanta, where he teaches courses in metaphysics, parapsychology, and Eastern thought. The author of a widely used text, *A Preface to Philosophy,* he contributes to both mainstream philosophical and leading-edge interdisciplinary journals, also serving as an editorial board member of the *Journal of Near-Death Studies.*